The AGE of NIHILISM

Christendom from the Great War to the Culture Wars

John Strickland

PARADISE AND UTOPIA

The Rise and Fall of What the West Once Was

VOLUME 4

ANCIENT FAITH PUBLISHING ✛ CHESTERTON, INDIANA

Published by:
Ancient Faith Publishing
A Division of Ancient Faith Ministries
1050 Broadway, Suite 6
Chesterton, IN 46304

Unless otherwise specified, Scripture quotations are from the New King James Version of the Bible, © 1982 by Thomas Nelson, Inc., and are used by permission.

Cover image by Olej Beksinski

ISBN: 978-1-955890-23-6

Library of Congress Control Number: 2022945497

Previous volumes of this work:
    The Age of Paradise (Ancient Faith Publishing, 2019)
    The Age of Division (Ancient Faith Publishing, 2020)
    The Age of Utopia (Ancient Faith Publishing, 2021)

For my children:
Elizabeth, Andrew, Katherine, Paul, and Gregory

Contents

By the waters of Babylon,
there we sat down and wept,
when we remembered Zion.
On the willows there
we hung up our lyres.
For there our captors
required of us songs,
and our tormentors, mirth, saying,
"Sing us one of the songs of Zion!"

How shall we sing the Lord's song
in a foreign land?
If I forget you, O Jerusalem,
let my right hand wither!
Let my tongue cleave to the roof of my mouth,
if I do not remember you,
if I do not set Jerusalem
above my highest joy!

Remember, O Lord, against the Edomites
the day of Jerusalem,
how they said, "Raze it, raze it!
Down to its foundations!"
O daughter of Babylon, you devastator!
Happy shall he be who requites you
with what you have done to us!
Happy shall he be who takes your little ones
and dashes them against the rock!

Psalm 136/137 (RSV)

Friedrich Nietzsche in Bayreuth

ONE WOULD EXPECT THE LIFE of a self-styled antichrist to be full of turbulence, but in the case of Friedrich Nietzsche it was rather boring. Apart from lightning flashes of conviction that "God is dead" and that a beastly savior called the "superman" would soon alter the culture of Christendom—thoughts inspired by brooding strolls in the Alps—there is little in his biography that can really be described as excitement.

The son of a village pastor, Nietzsche was raised for a time following his father's death by a monotonously conventional mother (along with an aged grandmother and a pair of unmarried aunts). As a young professor of philology, he was so stricken with migraines and nausea that much of his time was spent lying in the darkness of his bedchamber. At one point he took up the idea of fighting in a war, but after falling from his horse and then being stuck in a train for three days with wounded men, he abandoned it. Women did not interest him, though there was one exception: he became infatuated with a thrilling Russian freethinker named Lou Salome. She spent her life seducing great intellectuals, and her attention briefly turned toward him. One day he gathered the courage to propose marriage to her. She declined. A little later he decided to propose again, and she declined again. Nietzsche's life was thus spent alone, climbing mountains and thinking, longing for transcendence and cursing a civilization that offered him none. Externally, beyond the storms of his mind, life was never anything but dull. In fact, the only really dramatic thing Nietzsche ever did was to go insane.

Friedrich Nietzsche in the 1870s

Nietzsche's most rewarding escape from the solitude of writing came when he gained access to the inner circle of the great contemporary musician Richard Wagner. There was nothing dull about this man's life. Carried across a Napoleonic battlefield as an infant, he grew into the most precocious of romanticism's many self-taught geniuses. He considered himself a revolutionary in compositional style, and when in 1848 an actual political revolution broke out, he immediately joined in the excitement. After burning down a theater in Dresden that he considered too small for the kind of music he intended to compose, he assisted rebels in the street fighting that followed. Driven into exile, for nearly a quarter century he lived the life of an artistic vagabond—at once self-confident and estranged from society. All the while, he held court over a society of talented intellectuals who looked to the "Master" (as he preferred to be addressed) for inspiration. This he provided in abundance, holding forth on subjects ranging from music to religion to philosophy to politics. Along the way, he railed against the vulgar bourgeoisie and extolled the virtues of vegetarianism. There was no subject his brilliant and audacious genius did not address. But the center of discussion was always music—his music.

Recognizing talent (and admiration) when he saw it, the imperious Wagner invited Nietzsche to attend piano-side discussions that were more disquisitions by the Master than conversations among guests. At one point during his exile, Wagner lived in a mansion on the shores of Lake Lucerne. This is where Nietzsche first visited him and where, under Alpine peaks, he fell in love with the composer's vision of the "artwork of the future." In Nietzsche's words, Wagner was a "mystagogue for the secret doctrines of life and art."[1]

Later, Wagner moved to the Bavarian town of Bayreuth in order to build the long-desired theater worthy of his great music. There he had a new house built while he awaited the completion of the theater. As funds were slowly raised, so was the theater—though at an equally slow pace. In the meantime, Nietzsche became a regular in Wagner's drawing room and fervently participated in discussions around its piano.

---

1   Quoted in Robert W. Gutman, *Richard Wagner: The Man, His Mind and Music* (New York: Harcourt, Brace, Jovanovich, 1990), 316.

Bayreuth became, for Nietzsche no less than for Wagner, a beacon of what the West would one day become.

BY THE TIME THE MUSICALLY inclined Nietzsche met him, Wagner had produced some of the most daring and exciting compositions in history. One of these was the explosive prelude to act 3 of *Lohengrin,* a melodic adrenaline rush expressing the overpowering desire of a man for his beautiful young bride. But at the end of the prelude, the music changes tempo and transitions into something much more conventional. This was the sequence that came to be known as Wagner's "Wedding March."

Isolated from the rest of the opera, the piece would prove to be one of Wagner's most enduring works—even among those with no interest in opera (or weddings). For instance, millions in the West today would feel cheated if the "Wedding March" (otherwise known as "Here Comes the Bride") were not played when the bride makes her way down the aisle.[2] The song's absence would make the vow "I do" seem incomplete. And because of this, the composer of such a melody might be considered a champion of marriage, an anchor for one of Christendom's most important social institutions. But nothing could be further from the case. When it came to the traditional culture of the West, Wagner turned out to be a believer in nothing.

Marriage itself is an example. Serial adultery permeated Wagner's event-filled life. He abandoned his first wife, a modest former actress named Minna, following his unsuccessful experiment in revolution. Fleeing the police, he also fled her. He had in fact never been a faithful husband, and when the two later reunited he continued to conduct infidelities beneath her nose.

In the most notorious episode, he fell in love with Cosima von Bülow, the daughter of the composer Franz Liszt and the wife of a devoted friend named Hans von Bülow. The latter was a conductor, and during Wagner's time of exile when the composer could not set foot in Germany without being arrested, Hans faithfully advanced the Wagnerian cause in opera

---

2   Though they would not likely be Orthodox Christians: Orthodoxy allows for only one rite of matrimony (or "crowning"), that of the ancient Church, which has no place for secular music.

Richard Wagner in the 1870s

house after opera house. This did not prevent the Master from seducing Cosima and initiating a thinly veiled affair with her. Eventually, she bore Wagner a child while still married to Hans. Then she bore him another. And then another. Wagner saw nothing wrong in this; his creativity demanded "inspiration," and he found it in Cosima's arms. When the miserable Hans could take no more of the charade, he did what he considered the honorable thing for a man in his situation to do. This was not to challenge the rake to a duel, as many dishonored husbands of the time would have done. Instead, he valiantly surrendered his wife to the Master by granting her a divorce. Hans von Bülow remained a devoted Wagnerian for the remainder of his career. As for Minna, all of this broke her heart and she died a castaway, abandoned and forgotten.

Nietzsche found Wagner's infidelities unseemly, but the huge success of the "Wedding March" grimly impressed on him the hypocrisy of bourgeois society. That someone with Wagner's moral character could produce a monument to marital fidelity was simply absurd.

In any case, the philosopher was much more intrigued with those of Wagner's compositions that openly subverted conventional morality. These included *Tannhäuser,* which features an orgy in the opening scene and the enticements of Venus (an actual character) throughout. They also included *Tristan and Isolde,* which celebrated adultery and discredited moralism. Even bolder was *The Ring of the Nibelung,* the massive series of operas whose plot celebrates an act of adultery and "free love"—even to the point of incest.

The *Ring* contained a musical sequence known as "The Ride of the Valkyries." This would become equal in popularity to the "Wedding March." For Nietzsche, it was a mythical celebration of martial vigor, a reminder of the primitive virtues lost to the West under the civilizing influences of Christianity and humanism. Nietzsche was not a militarist, but he considered warfare necessary for the free operation of what he came to call the "will to power." Later in life, he expressed contempt for

humanity when it has forgotten how to wage war. For the present we know of no other means whereby the rough energy of the camp, the deep

14

impersonal hatred, the cold-bloodedness of murder with a good conscience, the general ardour of the system in the destruction of the enemy, the proud indifference to great losses, to one's own existence and that of one's friends, the hollow, earthquake-like convulsion of the soul, can be as forcibly and certainly communicated to enervated nations as is done by every great war. . . . Culture can by no means dispense with passions, vices, and malignities.[3]

Wagner's music, especially that contained in the *Ring*, gave expression to a new voice Nietzsche was beginning to hear within himself. He would eventually give the voice a name: Zarathustra, the terrible prophet of a new morality, which was no morality at all but a destruction of that inherited from Christianity and the secular humanism that followed it. A moral revolutionary like Wagner, Nietzsche had come to look with contempt on the bourgeois society of his time. An entirely new culture was needed—one that was vigorous, fearless, and free from the values of the past.

Bayreuth promised such a culture, and it was defined by nihilism.

THE WORD *NIHILISM* WAS COINED by Germans during the nineteenth century. Its root is *nihil,* which in Latin means "nothing." As such, nihilism has come to designate a philosophy or moral conviction that there is nothing of value in existence, that all values are empty and worthless. Human life is fundamentally meaningless.

This, in any case, is its fullest and most precise meaning. Some self-proclaimed nihilists might shy from such an extreme definition. Indeed, the movement in nineteenth-century Russia known as political nihilism did not reject the value of human life or social organization at all, just the historical forms they took under the tsarist state and the established Church. Outraged by the existing social order of Christendom, those nihilists sought to sweep it all away and establish an entirely new, post-Christian order founded on scientific standards of morality. The world had meaning for them, even

---

3   Friedrich Nietzsche, *Human, All-Too-Human: A Book for Free Spirits,* trans. Helen Zimmern (London: T. N. Foulis, 1910), 349.

Bayreuth Theater

if it must be transformed into something completely different from what it had been theretofore.

Moral and philosophical nihilists, on the other hand, claimed that there really is no ultimate meaning to human life and society, and therefore the transformation of the world, even by the standards of utopia, is ultimately pointless. For them, nothingness is absolute.

The appearance of nihilism was a turning point in the rise and fall of what the West once was. Christendom had been animated since the time of Pentecost by what can be called a "transformational imperative," a deeply embedded cultural trait that directed civilization toward a transcendent state not found in the world in its immanent or existing condition. Under the influence of traditional Christianity, this imperative was, for a millennium, directed toward the kingdom of heaven. It linked the world to the transcendent reality of paradise, revealed especially in the liturgical and sacramental life of the Church.

During the Renaissance, however, the transformational imperative was secularized. The *saeculum*—the spiritually untransformed world—offered an escape from what secular humanists considered the paralyzing pessimism of reformational Christianity. But secularism left a terrible hole in the civilization of the West. The transformational imperative no longer had a transcendent orientation. Paradise was replaced by its counterfeit, utopia, and progress became the new cultural myth. Transcendence was thus all but lost with the rise of secular humanism, despite desperate efforts by nineteenth-century romantics to restore it. In the end, it fell to the ideologies of liberalism, socialism, and nationalism—all themselves counterfeits of traditional Christianity—to reinvent transcendence. Utopian Christendom now came to look to a kingdom of posterity for its experience of harmony and fulfillment.

And it was in this new Christendom, where secular humanism had been transforming the world into utopia for four centuries, that nihilism suddenly and inevitably appeared.

NIETZSCHE WAS THE FIRST TO give nihilism a comprehensive philosophical expression. He had learned much from Wagner, perhaps too much. For despite the surging enthusiasm he felt for the Master's vision of culture, conversations at Bayreuth often disappointed and even disturbed him.

Indeed, many of Wagner's views have been proven by time to be so much heady mental junk. If one reads through the narcissistic content of the composer's innumerable articles on just about every subject under the sun, one finds in them so much of what was wrong with nineteenth-century thinking. He was not just a Renaissance Man in an age of science. He was an inveterate egoist blinded by contempt for any who failed to take up the Wagnerian cultural cause. He considered Johannes Brahms, for instance, an unskilled idiot. Convinced by modern philosophy and science that Christianity was bankrupt, he held a faddish interest in Buddhism. Though he was capable of the most convincing romantic melodies in his operas, his attitude toward the opposite sex was frequently mawkish. He was an aggressive German nationalist at a time when Otto von Bismarck's policy of "blood and iron" was despoiling Germany's neighbors and upending Europe's diplomatic balance of power. Most infamously, Wagner was an intransigent anti-Semite, detesting all Jewish influence in modern culture and being callous enough to write openly about it.

All these opinions have earned the contempt and censure of historians. Nevertheless, Wagner was Germany's greatest composer of the day, and no one could deny it. As the American Jewish conductor Leonard Bernstein would later put it, "Wagner, I hate you; but I hate you on my knees." Nietzsche himself would eventually come to hate Wagner too.

BUT IN 1876 THERE WAS much in the cult of Wagner that still fascinated the young philosopher. That year, he traveled once again to Bayreuth, where the long-awaited theater finally stood completed. Wagner was planning a grand opening marked by a festival at which the *Ring of the Nibelung* would be performed in its entirety. This had never happened before, though excerpts of the work such as "The Ride of the Valkyries" were well known and a few performances of the individual operas had been staged.

The work consisted of no fewer than four interlinked operas, to be performed in sequence over the course of successive evenings. Nothing of the sort had ever been produced in music history prior to it, though the Church had long presented liturgical narratives of the Passion and other events over the course of multiple days. Wagner, though a freethinker, would have appreciated such a comparison. For him, opera—or, as he renamed the art form, "music drama"—was to replace the outdated and culturally irrelevant liturgy of Christendom with a new ritualized piety centered on myths created by geniuses like himself.

After arriving in Bayreuth, Nietzsche paid court to the Master at his home. He then headed for the theater to observe rehearsals. There he saw something he no doubt had longed for many years to see: the dramatization of the character Siegfried, the great heroic tenor of the *Ring,* after whom one of the four operas was named. Nietzsche had long heard the composer hold forth about the hero's significance for the culture of the future. Siegfried was, significantly, nihilism personified. He was perfectly fearless, an offspring of transgression who loves without boundaries and kills without remorse. Nietzsche would later declare that Siegfried amounted to

a declaration of war on morality—he comes into this world through adultery, through incest. . . . He overthrows everything traditional, all reverence, all fear. *Whatever displeases him he stabs to death. Without the least respect, he tackles old deities.*[4]

As Nietzsche watched the character take shape at the rehearsals, he must have seen a premonition of his own nihilistic hero, Zarathustra.

At the Master's request, Nietzsche had years earlier agreed to write an essay on the cultural scene of Bayreuth. Now, to mark the year of the first Bayreuth Festival, he decided to publish it. Constituting the final part of a work entitled *Thoughts out of Season,* the essay was itself given the title "Richard Wagner in Bayreuth." An appropriate alternative title would have been "Friedrich Nietzsche in Bayreuth," for it spoke as much about the philosopher's cultural vision as about that of the composer.

Granted, at this stage in the Wagnerian philosopher's career the two were nearly one. Comparing Wagner with Alexander the Great (whose conquests had opened the way to a transformation of ancient culture), Nietzsche declared his mentor to be "one of the greatest civilising forces of his age." As with Alexander, the cultural transformation personified by Wagner could not proceed peacefully. It required violence, even destruction. In this case, it required the annihilation of the bankrupt values of utopian Christendom. "Modern culture," Nietzsche claimed, must be "stormed and conquered." And for those like him who were inspired by the fearlessly promethean figure of Siegfried, "Bayreuth is the consecration of the dawn of combat."[5]

Militantly Wagnerian, a young Friedrich Nietzsche announced the beginning of an age of nihilism.

---

4   Friedrich Nietzsche, *The Case of Wagner,* in *Basic Writings of Nietzsche*, trans. and ed. Walter Kaufmann (New York: Modern Library, 2000), 619.
5   Friedrich Nietzsche, "Richard Wagner in Bayreuth," in *Untimely Meditations,* trans. Anthony Ludovici and Adrian Collins (San Bernadino, CA: Pantianos Classics, 2017), 147–96.

PART I

The Specter of Nihilism

CHAPTER ONE

The Making of an Antichrist

Lavish praise of Wagner was typical of those drawn into the moral universe of his operas. Nietzsche regarded him as modern history's man of the hour, an Alexander the Great waging war against a decrepit order that needed to be kicked down and replaced with something totally different. Partisans in this nascent culture war—Wagnerians as they became known— hailed the German composer as the prophet not just of a new music but of a new way of life.

Nietzsche would outline this way of life in a series of exhilarating writings that read more like moral manifestos than philosophical treatises. Like the restless Siegfried, he looked upon those around him with contempt. Like Siegfried, he slew everything—every moral idea—he did not like. During the course of his career—from Wagnerian to anti-Wagnerian—he came to believe he was the "destiny" of the West. And to fulfill this destiny, he even came to believe he was an antichrist.

Nietzsche dedicated his philosophical and literary powers to unmasking Christianity in the Western forms it had assumed since the Great Division. But he did not stop there. He also unmasked what Alexander Schmemann once called its "evil stepchild," secular humanism. More than any great intellectual before or since, Nietzsche brought to the disoriented West a looming specter of nihilism.

"Whoever Fears the Tip of My Spear"

DURING THE AGE OF NIHILISM, Nietzsche became Christendom's greatest philosopher. But never was a man's philosophy so closely linked to his sense of greatness. Claiming to be the destiny of the West, he smashed to pieces almost every moral treasure in a "revaluation of all values." He did so at a time when the romantic cult of the genius was exceeding itself, advancing from indignation toward the world to utter contempt for it. Nietzsche completed the transition. He was one of modernity's first megalomaniacs.

The term *megalomania* is an archaic form of what psychologists now call *narcissism*. The disease of Narcissus, despite the allusion to an ancient myth, is a particularly modern one. It would technically be considered a personality disorder. Narcissism is a condition in which an individual cultivates a hyperexaggerated concept of self, or ego. It is true that all human beings are susceptible to egoism. What is noteworthy about megalomania is the scale of it. Such a person is maniacally preoccupied with his reputation, seeing others as either disciples or persecutors. What is more, he sees other persons as little more than the means of acquiring power and influence. The megalomaniac is compulsively drawn to attain a state of grandeur, surrounded by a network of submissive followers. Such a personality was hard to legitimate in the culture of Christendom prior to the nineteenth-century rise of romanticism, though there are examples. (One thinks especially of the chronicles of government, from Herod to Ivan the Terrible.) Traditional Christianity's commandment to love others as oneself and humanism's celebration of rational subjectivity assured this. When these values receded, however, a pathological preoccupation with the self was freed to take their place.

Egocentrism was a way of life for many in the romantic generation stretching from the French Revolution to the formation of Bismarck's German Empire. It seems to have had its origin in efforts to recover a lost experience of cosmological transcendence. Traditional Christianity had instilled in the old Christendom of the first millennium an orientation toward the kingdom of heaven, filling the world inhabited by the Church with an experience of paradise. By the nineteenth century, however, the new Christendom that dated to the Great Division of the eleventh century had been largely desecrated. Heavenly immanence had faded. Secular humanism and the deistic cosmology of the so-called Enlightenment reoriented the West toward a spiritually untransformed world. Paradise had fallen, and its counterfeit, utopia, had come to replace it. The romantics tried eagerly to restore heavenly immanence (one might say too eagerly—hence their tendency toward madness and suicide). But their idealistic approach to the world's reenchantment could never be more than a counterfeit of traditional Christianity. It was simply unconvincing. As they were living for the unstable ecstasies of artistic creativity, nature veneration, and erotic love, their efforts at transcendence proved futile.[1]

Strangely, the cult of romantic genius required adversity to function. It required a sense of persecution, even if it was largely self-generated. Gone was the paradisiacal Christendom in which the artist was expected to represent heavenly realities in his work and to embody them personally by living the ascetical life of prayer, fasting, and repentance. The utopian Christendom born of the Renaissance had transferred attention to a spiritually untransformed world, and artists now became competitors in celebrating it. But they did so in general agreement that the humanist project of cosmological reorientation, of redirecting Christendom's attention from paradise to utopia, was sound. The result was a sequence of artistic movements that all, in the end, did much to reinforce humanism. Renaissance naturalism begot mannerism; mannerism begot baroque; baroque begot rococo; rococo begot neoclassicism; neoclassicism begot romanticism. And so it went, generation after generation, from about 1450 until about 1850.

As humanism began to wane by the end of the nineteenth century, however, the role of the artist began to shift. Uncertainty and doubt about the historical direction of Christendom set in, and a kind of restless, dissatisfied innovation began to replace the comparatively serene approach of the quattrocento. Art historians note the explosion of "schools" during this period, each appearing synchronically (unlike those just mentioned, which appeared diachronically one after the other) and all scornful of tradition. In

---

1   For an account of romanticism and the problem of cosmological desecration, see volume 3 of the present work, *The Age of Utopia*, chapter 8.

this contentious atmosphere innovation was not enough. The artist found himself asserting an ingenious vision of reality at the expense of all others—against, in fact, everything that existed. Reality itself came to be defined by an act of the will.

Richard Wagner (d. 1883) breathed deeply of this toxic and yet intoxicating atmosphere. It determined the shape of his relationships. Throughout his life he exhibited remarkably little respect for others, using them as nothing more than the means of achieving grandiose creative plans. He understood the world as an arrangement of relationships centered on himself and completely at his disposal to use or abuse as he saw fit.

Like many creative artists, Wagner spent a good part of his early life in penury. It did not help that even when he landed a lucrative appointment at the court of Saxony, his contempt for the establishment compelled him to throw security to the wind when revolution broke out in 1849. He joined the revolutionaries against his royal patron. For more than a decade following this he was on the run, a hunted criminal, moving from one European town to another without any continuous source of income. In the face of this adversity, he never surrendered his vision of a series of operas that would proclaim a radically new morality grounded in power and desire. In fact, his often unbearable difficulties only strengthened his resolve.

At the same time, a creeping moral nihilism affected his relationships with acquaintances. Everyone he met was a potential donor to this cause. Everyone was expected to share in his personal creative burden. No one was exempt. He did not beg for money so much as demand it. Those who refused he treated as enemies. Those who complied he showered with praise. And those foolish enough to extend loans, he quickly forgot.

Then one day, out of the blue, he received a letter. He couldn't believe what it contained or who had sent it. It promised nearly limitless funding for his work, and it was signed on behalf of the king of Bavaria, Ludwig II. This boy king (he was then only eighteen years old) was an inept politician, and his realm would soon be swallowed up by Bismarck's united Germany. However, he was a highstrung lover of the arts. It was he who built the famous and oft-photographed castle Neuschwanstein in the Alps. Modern tourists often assume the castle to be an example of medieval architecture. It is rather an example of romanticism's restless disregard for modernity and its search for alternatives. In addition to building this and other mock castles, Ludwig was a lover of classical music. He discovered *Lohengrin* at the age of fifteen and was transported by its sensuous prelude and the memorable Wedding March. By all accounts, Ludwig struggled with homosexual desire throughout his life and may have harbored such feelings for his favorite composer when he sent the impetuous letter promising financial support. Wagner of course accepted. And for good measure, the vigorously heterosexual composer even threw in a few innuendoes and praise of the royal patron's "handsome" and "soulful" charm to keep him on the hook. The maneuver was effective. In a matter of years it was Ludwig who largely footed the costs of building Wagner's personal theater in Bayreuth.

The dawn of nihilistic Christendom was not marked by Wagner's megalomania alone, of course. His moral vacuum opened into a broader rebellion against many of the West's values. We also find in Wagner a fascination with transgression. Again, in this he was a harbinger of something new. As both traditional Christianity and secular humanism waned in influence by the end of the nineteenth century, the theme of crossing moral boundaries became more and more emphatic among members of the cultural elite. With time it would spread to popular culture.

This development is particularly noticeable in a new approach to sexual relations. The road from Bayreuth, it might be said, ultimately led to Woodstock. The journey began with Wagner. The maestro himself would have been appalled to see as far into the future as 1969, but there is a moral connection between, for instance, the enticing maidens who swim naked in the Rhine River during the opening scene of the first opera of the *Ring* and the skinny-dippers who descended into the pond waters of Bethel, New York, during the famous rock music festival a century later. Moreover, we can see a similarity of values between the bacchanalia scene from act 1 of *Tannhaüser* and the real orgies of some hippies. For the latter, "free love" in the absence of marriage was becoming the norm, and there is little the perpetually unfaithful lecher of Bayreuth would have objected to in that.

But his was not a time of public discussion of libertine sexuality. That would come later, when Christendom had acclimated itself to the specter

Richard and Cosima Wagner

of nihilism. Wagner lived under the shadow of Victoria, not Vietnam. For his generation transgression was mostly committed either in secret or in the imaginary world of artistic representation. What is remarkable is that the composer was as bold as he was, not only in placing transgression at the center of so many great operas but in living it out personally.

We have already considered his lurid infatuation with Cosima and the shabby way in which he dumped his wife Minna. Cosima, once released from her marriage to Hans von Bülow, now married Wagner. She was much more the wife he desired. Though not particularly pretty, she was the daughter of the famous composer Franz Liszt (through another adulterous affair) and possessed a refined understanding of the Master's art. According to Wagner, she now served him as a muse.

But only one of many. Having rid himself of the stultifying Minna, he was equally unfaithful to her replacement. Some of the women whose company he kept predated Cosima, such as the creative Parisienne Judith Gautier, herself a writer. It was she, thirty-two years Wagner's junior, who was honored with a seat next to him at the festive banquet marking the premiere of the *Ring* in 1876. Another paramour was the wife of a wine merchant named Jessie Lousset. She invited Wagner to stay at her home in Bordeaux, France, and, when an affair resulted, made plans to run away with the composer. But her husband learned of the matter and wrote to Wagner, threatening to shoot him. Not to be intimidated, Wagner impulsively traveled back to their town to demand Jessie's release, but by the time he arrived the couple had disappeared.

Perhaps his most famous affair is that with the lovely Mathilde Wesendonck, also married. She entered the picture after Jessie, when Wagner was still on the run from the police for his part in the revolutions of 1848. Her wealthy husband was an admirer of Wagner's music and offered the composer a cottage on his estate in which to live. It was a poor decision. In no time at all, an inevitable affair with his wife resulted. This time, however, Wagner felt he had found a true muse. He was so enthralled that he suspended work on his *Ring* to compose a separate opera based on his experience of desire for Mathilde. The result was a revolution in musical history known as *Tristan and Isolde*. The work introduced the tonality-dissolving "chromaticism" of sound that came to characterize Wagner's mature operas. The work was also morality dissolving.

Based on the medieval legend of star-crossed lovers, Wagner's rendition of *Tristan* told the story of a man who falls in love with another man's woman and cannot resist consummating the relationship with her. The act of adultery leads to the destruction of everything good, not least of which is friendship. But despite this, the love affair leads to a cathartic release from this world, bound as it is by the deathly forces of moral tradition. The most developed love scene takes place at night—in the darkness—as if to acknowledge the social transgression being committed as well as to celebrate it. In the end, Tristan dies of a wound inflicted by the sword of the offended husband's servant, and his death provokes that of Isolde through a sort of romantic, mystical sympathy. Her final song, a rousing crescendo Wagner named the "love-death" (*Liebestod*), is a celebration of self-fulfillment through moral transgression. It is a celebration of nihilism. Nietzsche considered it his favorite work.

But that was 1865. A decade and a year later, Wagner presented to the world his most ambitious work ever, the composite saga of pagan myths known as the *Ring of the Nibelung*. The four operas it contained were entitled *Das Rheingold, Die Walküre, Siegfried,* and *Götterdämmerung*. Long before J.R.R. Tolkien, Wagner brought fantasy storytelling out of the obscurity of Nordic legend and adapted it to the interests and concerns of modern Christendom.

The *Ring* is the story of power—the consuming, corrupting, and destructive desire for domination over others. It is the story of a dwarf-like creature named Alberich who craves the attention of beautiful women, but, unable to attract them, resolves instead to seize control of an object that will bring the entire world into submission beneath him. This object is a lump of gold, which he forges into a ring. But as soon as he has done so, other more powerful individuals seek to destroy him and claim the ring for themselves.

As the tragedy unfolds, the king of the gods, Wotan, intervenes. He holds within his grasp a spear, formed from the great world ash tree that predates creation. Upon the spear are engraved the runes from which he derives his power. Without the spear, he has no power. Nor can he allow the violation of any of the runes, which provide the world with a moral code, a system of moral boundaries.

One of those sacred boundaries is marriage. Wotan's wife, the goddess Fricka, is particularly concerned in Wagner's story with this law, and she harangues the king of the gods to enforce it. When Wotan allows it to be violated, she demands divine punishment. The problem is that Wotan, speaking for the composer, does not himself value marriage very highly. Having sired a demigod with another woman, he looks on his offspring as a release from the bondage of "conventional" morality.

The offspring is named Siegmund. Fired by a desire for a life that is instinctual rather than moral (this in particular caught Nietzsche's attention), Siegmund falls in love with a woman who is married. Such a scenario was, by this time, no surprise to Wagner's audiences. In this case, though, transgression reaches a new level in the composer's moral universe. The woman, named Sieglinde, turns out to be Siegmund's sister. Nothing can stop their incestuous desire for each other, though, and so they flee her husband and seek refuge away from human society in the forest (rather like Tristan and Isolde taking shelter in the darkness of night). Even so, they are pursued by the husband, who, on finding them, shatters Siegmund's sword Nothung (like Excalibur in the Arthurian legend, it actually has a name) and slays the young hero. Looking on from a distance are the gods Wotan and a daughter named Brünhilde.

All this drama, we must realize, is accompanied by some of the most brilliant and exciting music ever composed. And amidst it all, at the beginning of the final act of *Die Walküre,* the opera in which the story of the incestuous twins takes place, the most famous of all of Wagner's melodies, the "Ride of the Valkyries," is played in its fullest and most unrestrained way. The effect was then and continues to be exhilarating.

The main cause to which this glorious music is devoted is not free love, however, but power. All the characters are infected by the desire for power. From the first scene of *Das Rheingold,* in which Alberich steals the gold he will use to forge the ring of power, to the final scene of *Götterdämmerung,* in which a traitorous character named Hagen fatally plunges headlong into the Rhine to recover it, the will to domination motivates everyone.

One character symbolizes it more than any other. Siegfried is the one fig-ure whom Wagner set at the center of the complicated drama to represent the idealization of power. The spontaneous youth does not seek power so much as claim it through a series of events that serve to lift him up above all other mortals. It might be said that Siegfried was Wagner's own self-idealization. He would certainly become Nietzsche's, but that is getting ahead of our nar-rative. What can be said at this point is that in the drama of the *Ring*, Sieg-fried is a celebration of naive and unselfconscious megalomania. His ego is utterly free from moral boundaries.

In this his genealogy is significant. He is the offspring of Siegmund and Sieglinde, whose incestuous story is played out in *Die Walküre* and sets the stage for Siegfried's in the eponymous opera that follows. As such, he is the embodiment of free love. Moral nihilism is his birthright. And so it is no surprise that he shows no respect for moral custom and exhibits no fear. He actually asks at one point what fear is, so that he may understand it. But alas, he never does.

When we first meet the Wagnerian superman, one who transcends the moral limitations of humanity, he is restless. Stuck in the forest with a dwarf named Mime—the brother of Alberich—Siegfried wants to move. He wants experience. He wants adventure. The dwarf knows this and knows where it will lead. Incapable of fear, Siegfried is capable of anything else. Mime, significantly, is Wagner's personification of modern capitalism and greed, of utopian Christendom's satisfaction with material prosperity and the purely rational way of life that attains it. Mime therefore decides to use the boy as his own means toward power and wealth. He knows that the ring of power has come under the control of a dragon named Fafner. If he can fashion a sword strong enough to pierce the dragon's scales, he can ride to power on the back of the boy Siegfried, murdering him after he murders Fafner. For the countercultural Wagner, the scenario was much like that of nineteenth-century capitalists exploiting the working class to attain their wealth. What is more, in nineteenth-century Germany the Jews were fre-quently accused of such practices, and one can easily read Mime's character as one of Wagner's anti-Semitic slurs.

The problem with Mime's plan, however, is that every sword he fashions is immediately shattered by the mighty youth upon testing it. So Siegfried finally pushes the "bungler" out of the way and forges a sword himself. Here, we see again Wagner's megalomaniacal sense of mastery over even those who profess skilled leadership. As a largely self-taught composer, he had nothing but contempt for the professionally trained musicians of his day. Siegfried discovers in Mime's stash the very shards of his father's sword. Nothung, it will be recalled, had been shattered by Wotan moments before Sieglinde's vengeful husband killed Siegmund. Siegfried now reforges the heroic sword himself, to the accompaniment of some amazing music. There is a sense of destiny in it. Singing about (and to) the mighty weapon, the youth appears unstoppable.

And he is. After slaying Fafner in the second act of *Siegfried,* he finds it appropriate to slay Mime as well. Learning that a beautiful maiden lies in the midst of the forest awaiting a hero to claim her, he rushes to the spot, only to find his way barred by Wotan.

Before following him forward, however, we must pause a moment to consider other actions that have taken place in the complex narrative.

At the end of *Die Walküre,* Wotan had punished his daughter Brünhilde for ignoring the rune against adultery and incest on his spear and endeavoring to allow Siegmund to live. As punishment he stripped her of her divinity, placing her on a forest rock to await subjugation to the first man to find her. Because she is his favorite daughter, however (and here Wagner beautifully renders a father's paternal love with the orchestra's cellos), he concedes to make it so that only a great hero will find her—"one," he adds, "freer than I, the god."

Who could such a person be? One not only free from obedience

Wotan's farewell to Brünhilde

Siegfried Forges Nothung *(Arthur Rackham)*

to God, but one who surpasses God in his ability to act without moral restraint. In the emerging moral atmosphere of nihilistic Christendom, God was becoming a pathetic figure, constrained by external laws of morality and unworthy of human obedience. Such sadly was the effect of centuries of anthropological pessimism in Christendom, through which the glorious, original understanding of human life as participation in the life of God had given way to a religious system of ethical legalism and divine intimidation.

Wotan encircles the rock with a terrible magic fire, assuring that no man bound by ordinary morality will ever win Brünhilde as his bride. Having done this to the sound of the opera's famous "Magic Fire Music," Wotan then pauses before leaving to issue a final, significant challenge. Raising his spear in the air, he menacingly declares (to the sound of deep brass orchestration): "Whoever fears the tip of my spear shall never cross through the fire!"

The words are significant. With his spear upraised, Wotan symbolizes the traditional God-given morality by which members of Christendom are called to live. The German word translated as "cross through," *durchsch-reite,* might even suggest "stepping beyond" or "transgressing." Having made this imposing statement, he withdraws, and the curtain falls on one of the most stirring and memorable and beautiful scenes in all of Wagner's work.

So as we accompany Siegfried to the rock on which the slumbering Brün-hilde now lies supine, it is worth pausing to consider this previous scene and Wotan's menacing statement. Wagner, drawing on the very real dissat-isfaction of modern intellectuals with Western Christianity, is thinking here of doing much more than dismissing religion. For doing that would have been nothing new. Since the eighteenth century cultural leaders had rejected Christianity, and more recently they had rejected belief in God altogether. But the generation of atheists that made up the cultural elite during the twi-light of utopian Christendom still believed in moral absolutes. They believed a just and progressive society could be based on a rationally designed moral-ity, even if its values were not based in God. Wagner took an important step away from this belief in moral absolutes. In his personal life, as we have seen, and now in his most famous operatic composition, he suggested that moral-ity itself—represented by Wotan's spear—was set against human freedom, was an obstacle to it. The future was open to him who was fearless enough to dispense with morality. As always, Nietzsche was watching breathlessly as the spiritual drama unfolded.

And now, standing before Brünhilde's rock was Wotan, barring with his spear the man who would presume to claim her. The scene occurs during the last act of *Siegfried.* As the confrontation begins, the orchestra plays phrases of rhythmic conflict. The boy Siegfried, at first only annoyed at the obstacle before him, tells the king of the gods to step aside. When Wotan refuses, he becomes bellicose. "All my life," he declares, "an old man has stood in my way. Now I have swept him aside. If you obstinately persist in obstructing me, watch out, I say, that you don't fare like Mime!"

Wotan reacts with dismay at this and begins to reveal his identity, as if doing so would impress the fearless hero. Wotan is the guardian of the rock, he states, and he will allow no common man to pass by and claim the woman who lies there. He then adds, significantly, that "he who wins her deprives me of my power forever." Siegfried refuses to stand down and again threatens violence against the god.

Now Wotan applies his final test of the hero's fearlessness: "If you do not fear the fire, then my spear must bar your way. My hand still holds the symbol of sovereignty: This shaft once shattered the sword you bear: Once again, then, let it break on the eternal spear!"

Realizing his adversary was once responsible for the betrayal and death of his father, Siegmund, Siegfried becomes enraged and flourishes the reforged Nothung. Lunging toward Wotan, he strikes the "eternal spear" raised in opposition. The blow shatters the spear, and that which bore the divinely ordained moral law for man now lies broken at Siegfried's feet. Lightning strikes—one of only two times in the opera, indicating the composer's emphasis on the event. The king of the gods, looking utterly broken, bows down before the hero to gather up the pieces of the spear and concedes: "Forward, then. I cannot stop you." The orchestra erupts in the heroic melodies of Siegfried's victory. As he passes through the surging flames, the music shifts into the chromaticism for which the revolutionary composer is most famous, defying the tonal regulations of four centuries of Western melody and setting it on a totally new course. Approaching the maiden lying asleep on the rock, Siegfried rouses her with a kiss and lays claim to her.

In this unforgettable scene, modern Christendom's incipient nihilism had won an important victory against both paradise and utopia, though it would take a philosopher and not an opera composer to secure it. In the case of Wagner, moral absolutes had been shattered by the sword of human will.

And for the Wagnerians like Nietzsche who assembled in Bayreuth in 1876 to behold the spectacle, it may have seemed, for all intents and purposes, that the God who once defined what the West once was had died.

Unmasking Secular Humanism

DESPITE APPEARANCES, NOT ALL WAS well in the friendship between Wagner and Nietzsche as the latter departed from the inaugural Bayreuth Festival that year. Though a devoted Wagnerian, the young philosopher found the atmosphere of the festival distasteful. He was beginning to suspect that the "music of the future" being performed there was not entirely sincere.

Friedrich Nietzsche (d. 1900) was originally drawn to Wagner by the composer's efforts to create new cultural myths for the West. The image of Siegfried overthrowing the moral authority of God was chief among these, but the vision of a general "twilight of the gods" (*Götterdämmerung* in German)—fulfilled in the final scene of the last opera of the *Ring*, when Valhalla falls in fiery destruction—thrilled the young atheist. In response it was to Wagner that he had dedicated his first book. *The Birth of Tragedy from the Spirit of Music* put forward a vision of culture

Nietzsche as a youth in the military

in which instinct prevailed over ethics, or, to use the book's vocabulary, "dithyrambic madness" prevailed over critical reason. Nietzsche used the image of the pagan god Dionysus—celebrated through the ancient bacchanalia with drunkenness, lust, and violence—as a mythical foil against what he considered the paralyzing effects of Christian moralism and metaphysics. Though balanced by discretion and harmony (elements Nietzsche associated with Apollo), Dionysus was the hero of Western culture even as he was also the inspiration for its tragic tendency toward self-destruction.

Dionysian passions, Nietzsche's book claimed, are the source of the myths that inspire civilization. But with time, living myths become exchanged for an enervating religiosity rooted in tradition. As a result,

> *the mythless man remains eternally hungering amid the past, and digs and grubs for roots, though he have to dig for them even among the remotest antiquities. The terrible historical need of our unsatisfied modern cultures, the consuming desire for knowledge—what does all this point to, if not to the loss of myth, the loss of the mythical home, the mythical eternal bosom?*[2]

In his first work, then, Nietzsche compared a decadent Christendom with pagandom before the rise of Greek tragedy, presenting the myth-making figure of Dionysus as the solution for both. He believed that alongside Wagner he was contributing to a great cultural revival. Abandoning Christianity and humanism, Christendom would become a civilization with a supporting culture that directed its members toward an ecstatic though ultimately meaningless transformation of the world.

Though *Birth of Tragedy* demonstrated a brilliantly independent mind, years of intellectual conversation around Wagner's piano in Bayreuth and walking alpine slopes near Lake Lucerne had resulted in Nietzsche's intellectual subjugation to the Master. The young philosopher had even been assigned the humbling task of serving as a Wagnerian publicist. His essay "Richard Wagner in Bayreuth," as we have seen, proclaimed the composer a modern Alexander the Great, poised to launch a cultural revolution that would sweep away the rotten values and tastes of the past.

Nevertheless, Nietzsche's essay was not unambiguous in its praise. Read closely, it could be seen to contain numerous qualifications of Wagnerism and even a creeping aversion for the personality of the Master. "Deep down," one passage from the original version reads, "there surges through Wagner a mighty will with a boundless, ruthless craving for power, working its way

---

2   Friedrich Nietzsche, *The Birth of Tragedy from the Spirit of Music*, trans. Clifton P. Fadiman, in *The Philosophy of Nietzsche* (New York: Modern Library, 1954), 1078.

along paths, through caves and ravines, ever upwards to the light, with the brutality of the horned Minotaur."[3] As Joachim Köhler has put it, among "numerous bouquets of flowery oratory" delivered to Wagner's house during the Bayreuth Festival, Nietzsche with his essay thus "managed to smuggle in a funeral wreath."[4]

The philosopher was indeed increasingly dissatisfied with his relationship to the Master. Nietzsche was at this time engrossed by the image of the ancient Greek contest known as the *agon,* in which two worthy athletes struggle against one another for supremacy.[5] Like a formerly unnoticed Athenian wrestler, the young Nietzsche would topple his accomplished rival in the arena of cultural revolution. Megalomania had come to breed megalomania, and it was time for a new master to arise.

Nietzsche later claimed that at about this time he came to realize Wagner was not a cultural revolutionary after all. The coarse anti-Semitism and nationalism that permeated the atmosphere of Bayreuth were examples of this. Nietzsche despised these traits of modern German culture, and the fact that they surrounded performances of Wagner's music like a bad smell unsettled him. Most disturbing, however, was Wagner's shifting attitude toward Christianity.

The composer had long appeared to Nietzsche as a thoroughgoing atheist. He certainly acted like one. He expressed only disdain for the values Christians attached to marriage and was totally unrepentant when cheating on his successive wives. Wagner also participated in the shedding of blood during the revolutions of 1848, fleeing Germany to escape the police in the failed aftermath. Most importantly for Nietzsche, Wagner foretold the "twilight of the gods." The culture of the future, growing out of the "music of the future," was supposed to be freed of any transcendent morality. This is what Nietzsche's intellectual mentor promised.

And then came *Parsifal.* Wagner's final opera seemed to reverse or at least

---

3   Quoted in Joachim Köhler, *Nietzsche and Wagner: A Lesson in Subjugation,* trans. Ronald Taylor (New Haven, CT: Yale University Press, 1998), 121.

4   Ibid., 120.

5   Alex Ross, *Wagnerism: Art and Politics in the Shadow of Music* (New York: Farrar, Strauss and Giroux, 2020), 60.

qualify the nihilistic convictions he had always claimed to hold. Its story is based on the medieval legends of the Knights of the Holy Grail. In Wagner's telling, it features an eponymous hero who, unlike Siegfried, does not acquire power but renounces it. When seduced by the enticing Kundry with a kiss, he suddenly has an epiphany of the suffering caused by unchastity and renounces female charms. This act enables Parsifal to restore a community of knights who live under the spell of an evil magician and bring salvation to them. "Salvation to the savior!" is in fact the opera's final message. Even more remarkably, the composer used liturgical worship and eucharistic communion as the scene for some of the opera's most important action. In so doing, he appeared to endorse the culture neither of nihilistic nor even of utopian Christendom. From the heart of the West's most modern artist, the values of paradisiacal Christendom were being reborn.

The music of the massive work, which Wagner pretentiously named a "stage-consecrating festival play," was some of his best. Indeed, the composer showed no signs of creative exhaustion at the end of his amazing career. The music of *Parsifal* can be said to be the greatest of all his operas, a consistently beautiful and stirring drama of spiritual victory, from the solemn and sorrowful motifs of the prelude all the way (four hours later) to their resolution in the finale. In those last bars of music, Wagner's mastery shows itself when the earlier motifs of the prelude return, their brokenness finally "healed" by ascending phrases in the violins.

Nietzsche was stunned by the beauty of this music but disgusted by its apparent meaning. In 1876, when the project was still only an idea, he might have tolerated it. Despite the opera's narrative of salvation, he knew that Wagner was a master of music making, and the craft of music meant more to the philosopher than any other. ("Without music, life would be a mistake," he once wrote.) What he could not accept was Wagner's personal attitude toward the story's content. On one occasion, just months after the premiere of the *Ring*, Wagner confided to him that he was actually touched by the message of salvation *Parsifal* contained.

The scene of this terrible "confession" was itself dramatic. Wagner and Nietzsche found themselves once again in an exotic part of Europe, on the shores of Italy overlooking the bay of Sorrento. It was toward the end of

1876. The sun was setting into the Mediterranean Sea, and mists were rising through the cool air about them. According to Nietzsche's later account, the composer was lost in one of his typical monologues about his work. The topic was his emerging conception of *Parsifal*. Suddenly, he turned to Nietzsche and expressed a formerly undisclosed attraction toward the Christian rite of holy communion. He stated his intention of working it piously into the opera's story. With this statement, Nietzsche's respect for the Master, having endured so many years, finally collapsed. Nietzsche said nothing about his shock, but the Master perceived something was wrong. He asked, "Why are you so silent, my friend?" The philosopher said nothing in reply. He completed the walk in silence. After that, he never met with Wagner again.

Nietzsche later wrote what can be taken as a statement of why Wagner's revelation affected him so strongly:

> *It is impossible for me to recognize greatness which is not united with candor and sincerity towards one's self. The moment I make a discovery of this sort, a man's achievements count for absolutely nothing with me, as I feel that he is only playing a part and everything he does is based upon insincerity.*[6]

Nietzsche's sister, the editor of his correspondence with Wagner, explained the philosopher's turning against his master after the meeting in Sorrento. "If we ask ourselves what really took place on this last eventful evening," she observed,

> *we find that only one explanation offers itself. Two passionately cherished ideals stood opposed to one another; on the one hand, the Catholic-romantic figure of Parsifal, implying negation of life—on the other, the powerful figure of Siegfried, god-like, transfigured, and the personification of life affirmed.*[7]

---

6   *The Nietzsche-Wagner Correspondence*, ed. Elizabeth Förster-Nietzsche, trans. Caroline V. Kerr (New York: Boni and Liveright,1921), 295.

7   Ibid., 296.

It is interesting to note that for Nietzsche's sister, speaking for the philosopher himself, the affirmation of life is opposed by a "Catholic" value of its negation. Traditional Christianity, with its emphasis on man's divine participation, was emphatically affirmative about life in this world. But the pessimistic deviation from this anthropology after the Great Division had caused in modern philosophers such as Nietzsche a tragically negative misconception of Christendom's primordial values.

Nietzsche undoubtedly perceived radically opposing values in the figures of Siegfried and Parsifal. As we saw in the prologue, he identified with those of the former. However, it is hard to believe that Wagner's conception of the hero Parsifal and his all-too-brief comment about sympathy for Christianity's sacramental tradition could really have provoked a total reevaluation of the relationship by Nietzsche. As noble as his expressed standards of moral authenticity were, one senses more than just an intellectual judgment here. Nietzsche would insist for the remainder of his career that the *Parsifal* affair "forced" him to reject Wagner, but this was not based exclusively on intellectual disagreement. For Nietzsche, the fateful break from Wagner came just as much from a need to succeed and even to surpass the cultural revolutionary. Nietzsche had a need to become a prophet—indeed the leading prophet—of nihilism.

Any account of Nietzsche's contribution to the rise of nihilism in modern Christendom must begin with atheism. He was well aware that he lived in a time when very few philosophers accepted the claims of Christianity. "Why atheism nowadays?" he asks in one of his works.

"The father" in God is thoroughly refuted; equally so "the judge," "the rewarder." Also his "free will": he does not hear—and even if he did, he would not know how to help. The worst is that he seems incapable of communicating himself clearly; is he uncertain? This is what I have made out . . . to be the cause of the decline of European theism; it appears to me that though the religious instinct is in vigorous growth,—it rejects the theistic satisfaction with profound distrust.

Here he notes the demise of theistic belief in the modern world but also claims that a religious spirit continues to animate culture. "Modern philosophy," he adds, "as epistemological scepticism, is secretly or openly anti-Christian, although (for keener ears, be it said), by no means anti-religious."[8] In other words, the moral and cultural order of modern Christendom had not yet responded to the radical consequences of atheism. Though self-consciously godless, it continued to function as if there were a transcendent absolute on which it was based.

It is this observation that led Nietzsche to make the paradoxical declaration that "God is dead." This statement, asserted in more than one of his writings, was a way for him to bring attention to the moral crisis of post-Christian Christendom. The rise of atheism resulted necessarily in the loss of moral absolutes. Without a transcendent God, there could be no point of reference for good and evil.

It was this historical condition that gave rise to nihilism, the conviction that there is no ultimate meaning to human life or the world. Man is confronted by a reality that is meaningless. However, rather than confront this terrifying reality, modern philosophers fell back on moral principles that they claimed bound human behavior and gave meaning to human life. Nietzsche rejected this as at best cowardly and at worst philosophically dishonest. Embracing the nihilistic consequences of the death of God, he claimed to be modern history's first truly consistent atheist.

By the late nineteenth century, atheists were certainly not rare among the cultural leadership of Christendom. In fact, it takes less time to list devout Christians than convinced atheists among the great thinkers who lived between the Enlightenment and the First World War. Atheistic philosophers included Jeremy Bentham, John Stuart Mill, Auguste Comte, Ludwig Feuerbach, and Arthur Schopenhauer. Atheistic social scientists included Herbert Spencer, Emile Durkheim, Max Weber, and Sigmund Freud. Atheistic revolutionaries included Pierre-Joseph Proudhon, Nikolay Bakunin, and Karl Marx. Atheistic novelists included George Eliot,

---

8   Friedrich Nietzsche, *Beyond Good and Evil*, trans. Helen Zimmern, in *The Philosophy of Nietzsche*, 439.

Charles Flaubert, Ivan Turgenev, and Thomas Hardy. And even many who were not atheists, strictly speaking, were, like Mark Twain in America, so turned off by Christianity and its historical legacy in the West that they functioned as if they were.

Nietzsche's rejection of a belief in God was therefore nothing new. What was different was its motivation. Before him, atheists and agnostics had lost their childhood faith (virtually all were baptized by believing parents at birth) because it failed, or at least appeared to fail, in the face of superior truth claims. Comte, for instance, became convinced that modern history produces an ever-increasing body of scientific knowledge that makes religious explanations of reality unnecessary. As progress advances, he claimed, Western culture will shed the primitive Christian superstitions that formerly kept it in darkness. This was not Nietzsche's experience with Christianity, however. While he was clearly influenced by the scientific rejection of Christianity (Darwin's theory of evolution affected him as much as it did others at the time), he was motivated more by the psychological effects of it.

To understand this, it is necessary to reflect briefly on the history of Western Christendom and its estrangement from Eastern Christendom. Nietzsche was limited in his understanding of Christianity by the forms it assumed following the eleventh-century Papal Reformation and the later sixteenth-century Protestant Reformation. He therefore suffered, as have all Westerners since the Great Division, from a deficit in the experience of Orthodoxy.[9]

For hundreds of years, Roman Catholicism and Protestantism were the only Christian options known to Western thinkers. The old Christendom of the first millennium was forgotten, and the new Christendom that evolved from the Great Division was separated from Eastern Christendom. This tendency toward occidental oblivion began at the ninth-century court of Charlemagne and then, after the Great Schism of 1054, became entrenched in papal supremacy and scholasticism. One of its most important outcomes was the loss of contact with Orthodoxy's comparatively affirmative

---

9   For an account of the cultural consequences of the Great Division between East and West, see volume 2 of the present work, *The Age of Division*.

anthropological and cosmological vision. In the early Church, man was called to participate in the kingdom of heaven while in this world, and through sacraments and worship he transformed it accordingly. This produced a paradisiacal culture. But after the Great Division, that culture began to wane as the transformational imperative was redirected from heavenly to reformational ends, such as the clericalization of society and the codification of repentance. As the doctrine of purgatory took hold, anthropological pessimism and cosmological contempt began to erode the experience of heaven. The human condition in this world, according to authorities like Pope Innocent III and Martin Luther, was increasingly characterized as one of misery. As theologians like John Calvin emphasized God's wrath, painters like Matthias Grünewald accentuated man's guilt.

It was this and not the revelations of modern science that motivated Nietzsche's rejection of Christianity. He experienced life in the modern world as a struggle against anthropological pessimism. The theme had appeared as early as the *Birth of Tragedy* in the two figures of Dionysus and Apollo. Each represents one of two fundamental tendencies in human experience. Dionysus, as we have seen, was the god of instinct, motivating men to celebrate life in this world without fear of the consequences of their actions. He was entirely affirmative. Apollo was the influence behind the world's first rationalist philosopher, Socrates, who instructed men to reflect critically on their actions and to avoid those that might result in harm or sorrow. The "Dionysian" man, Nietzsche claimed, says only "yes" to life; the rationalist is forever placing restrictions on it.

What Nietzsche was saying was that the only life worth living is one based on instinctive and fearless desire, what he would come to call "the will to power." This desire gave life its meaning, and in fact without it life was meaningless. The entire purpose of Christianity, as he understood it in its reformational form, was to stifle such desire. And in this sense he saw it as the heir to Socratic rationalism. Its purpose was to calculate salvation from an invented condition of "sinfulness" and to regulate life accordingly. This often meant placing one's life in the hands of the clergy, whose will to power generated a culture of degradation. The miserable condition of universal guilt was thus legitimated, leading to a system of moral repression and clerical supervision. Under such circumstances, man had learned only to say "nay" to life.

This critique was not limited to Christianity, however. It was also directed toward secular humanism. For Nietzsche, the atheistic unanimity of utopian Christendom served only to mask an effort to impose, in Christianity's absence, a new system of rules and restraints that were themselves genealogically tied to Christian morality. This was true even of revolutionaries, who planned to sweep away the old order. For instance, socialism and democracy, the two great political movements of the age, were each respectively traced to the Christian values of philanthropy and equality. Beneath a mask of atheism, therefore, proponents of these and other modern ideologies were really just crypto-Christians.

Real liberation required a total break from the legacy of Western values. In fact, it would come to demand the repudiation of values altogether—what Nietzsche called the "transvaluation of all values."

An Anti-Gospel

SO NIETZSCHE CHOSE THE WAY of a nihilist. It was by no means an easy path to take. Though he spoke rather too often about his suffering and isolation, he realized that very few convinced atheists had the resolve to plumb the deepest recesses of meaninglessness. From time to time he thought he had found such like spirits. The most important for him had been Wagner, whose music stirred up passionate desire and whose central hero, Siegfried, acted spontaneously without fear until he was finally stabbed in the back and killed. How different from traditional Christianity was the world-building mythology of the *Ring*, with its pagan gods and fearless heroes! It is no wonder that it was to Wagner that Nietzsche dedicated *The Birth of Tragedy*.

But as we have seen, the break with Wagner was due to more than intellectual differences. It was an act of enablement. It gave the megalomaniac Nietzsche a pretense for feeling "abandoned" by even the boldest of contemporary nihilists. After the *Parsifal* affair, Nietzsche claimed it was he who had "rejected" Wagner, and this claim would become a mania throughout the remainder of his life and would be underlined in nearly every one of his works. But in fact, his estrangement had a great deal to do with his own ego. It was important to him to break free from the influence of others, especially those like Wagner who subjugated everyone around themselves. "Friendship" with the Master inevitably led to abasement. Whenever Nietzsche had showed the temerity of straying from the topic of Wagner's current monologue, he was made to feel the Master's disapproval. The awkward young philosopher was even on occasion made the butt of jokes. More than once, he was actually sent on shopping errands.

To break free of this indignity, Nietzsche came to see in Wagner all that is weak in human nature and wrong with Christendom. The books that followed 1876 all record an effort to assert himself against the former master, to establish himself as a truly independent force in post-Christian myth creation. Wagner had revealed a world of godless desire but then wavered on the edge of the abyss. Nietzsche would take the plunge into the abyss and by doing so assume his rightful place as Christendom's ultimate nihilist.

And so he launched a project to dismantle Christianity more thoroughgoing than anything any atheist had ever undertaken. Not since Julian the Apostate's campaign to rid the Roman Empire of Christianity had anyone within Christendom so detested the faith and its influence. Nietzsche came more and more to set himself against Christ, coming finally by the end of his career to declare himself the Antichrist.

The term *antichrist* is used only four times in Scripture and is limited to the Epistles of Saint John. It can be interpreted as "the one who sets himself against Christ." But the prefix "anti" can also result in a rendering of "one who becomes an alternative to Christ." Both apply to Nietzsche, but it is perhaps the latter that better characterizes his life's work.

To leap to that work's conclusion: The fact that one of the final books produced by the philosopher bore the title *The Antichrist* tells a great deal about his purpose. Completed just months before his career came to its sudden end, the work is a relentless attack on Christianity from nearly every angle. The main argument, however, is that Christianity subverts human greatness, exhibited in its highest form by what Nietzsche had come to call the "superman."

Throughout the history of Christendom, he asserted, greatness has been despised. This is especially evident in secular humanism, which during the age of utopia placed such great hopes in progress. "Mankind surely does *not* represent an evolution toward a better or stronger or higher level, as progress is now understood," he wrote.

> *This "progress" is merely a modern idea, which is to say, a false idea. . . . True enough, it succeeds in isolated and individual cases in various parts of the earth and under the most widely different cultures, and in these cases a higher type certainly manifests itself; something which, compared to mankind in the mass, appears as a sort of superman. . . . We should not deck out and embellish Christianity: it has waged a war to the death against this higher type of man, it has put all the deepest instincts of this type under its ban, it has developed its concept of evil, of the Evil One himself, out of these instincts.*[10]

It is here that Nietzsche launches his attack on what Christendom—ancient and modern—considered one of the highest virtues, self-sacrificing love.

> *Christianity is called the religion of pity.—Pity stands in opposition to all the tonic passions that augment the energy of the feeling of aliveness: it is a depressant. A man loses power when he pities. Through pity that drain upon strength which suffering works is multiplied a thousandfold. Suffering is made contagious by pity; under certain circumstances it may lead to a total sacrifice of life and living energy—a loss out of all proportion to the magnitude of the cause (—the case of the death of the Nazarene).*[11]

Here for the first time in the book appears Nietzsche's main enemy, "the Nazarene."

As the anti-Nazarene—as the Antichrist—he undertakes the reversal of the very values that have shaped Christendom in its ancient and modern

---

10   Friedrich Nietzsche, *The Antichrist*, trans. H. L. Mencken (New York: Alfred A. Knopf, 1920), 44–45.

11   Ibid., 47.

forms. This supports his "transvaluation" of conventional morality and the conclusion that true greatness requires total indifference to the suffering of others. He even suggests actions that would lead to the elimination of inferior people.

> *What is good?—Whatever augments the feeling of power, the will to power, power itself, in man. What is evil?—Whatever springs from weakness. What is happiness?—The feeling that power increases—that resistance is overcome. . . . The weak and the botched shall perish: first principle of our charity. And one should help them to it. What is more harmful than any vice?—Practical sympathy for the botched and the weak—Christianity.*[12]

As we shall see in a later chapter, statements such as these would appeal to the Nazis, those heirs of Nietzsche most intent on post-Christian world building.

Written at the end of his career, *The Antichrist* was thus a summary of Nietzsche's project to demolish Christian morality. It was a philosophy of nihilism. Another book written in the same year, *The Twilight of the Idols*, had as its subtitle *How to Philosophize with the Hammer*. The author clearly intended his work to be an act of destruction, a message of nihilism.

The new morality of this "other Christ" could only be a kind of anti-Gospel, a reversal of most of what Christ had long ago proclaimed was ethically good and what modern philosophers, even atheistic ones, continued in one form or another generally to uphold. The *philosophes* of the eighteenth century, for instance, were well known for their rejection of Christianity. But they all praised Christ's call to love one's neighbor. In the Jefferson Bible, the Francophile former US president had expressed the deepest admiration for the Sermon on the Mount while rejecting as a matter of course the possibility of any of Christ's miracles.

Not so Nietzsche. In fact, his writing presents the Sermon on the Mount as a tremendous setback in the moral development of the West. Its attention to the kingdom of heaven was the wrong orientation for man. "Life

---

12 Ibid., 42–43.

terminates," he wrote in *Twilight of the Idols,* "where the kingdom of God begins."[13] Traditional Christianity regards the passions of fallen man as forces of spiritual enslavement. Christ, in the Sermon, spoke of the blessedness that is acquired through liberation from them. For the modern antichrist, there was nothing of value in human life that did not issue from the passionate faculty of man. He did not by any means endorse all passionate activity; for most people it led to coarseness and stupidity. But the possibility of greatness was to be found in the most elemental of human instincts, and to suppress them was folly.

> *Formerly, owing to the stupidity inherent in passion, men waged war against passion itself: men pledged themselves to annihilate it,—all ancient moral-mongers were unanimous on this point, "il faut tuer les passions." The most famous formula for this stands in the New Testament, in that Sermon on the Mount, where, let it be said incidentally, things are by no means regarded from a height. . . . The Church combats passion by means of excision of all kinds: its practice, its "remedy," is castration. It never inquires "how can a desire be spiritualised, beautified, deified?"— In all ages it has laid the weight of discipline in the process of extirpation (the extirpation of sensuality, pride, lust of dominion, lust of property, and revenge).—But to attack the passions at their roots, means attacking life itself at its source: the method of the Church is hostile to life.[14]*

In this attack on Christian asceticism, Nietzsche makes a very telling comment. He clearly regards Christianity as a monolithic moral system with an unnuanced record of hostility toward human desire. This indeed may have been the view from nineteenth-century Western Christendom. Again, the philosopher lived within an almost total oblivion about Orthodox Christianity. Only the anthropological pessimism of the West was known to him. Thus his lament: Christianity has never considered the possibility that

---

13 Friedrich Nietzsche, *The Twilight of the Idols: Or, How to Philosophise with the Hammer,* trans. Anthony M. Ludovici (Edinburgh: T. N. Foulis, 1911), 30.

14 Ibid., 26–27.

desire can be "spiritualized, beautified, or deified." In the ancient Church, of course, it had.[15] Nietzsche thus maintained a typically Western view of Christianity and used it as a foil for what he called "anti-Christianity."

There is a fascination to his anti-Gospel. He was a brilliant thinker, but he was also an excellent stylist. In fact, many who read his books are attracted to his philosophy by the sheer majesty of style, possessing as it does, both in the German original and in translation, a strong element of poetry. His use of aphorisms and surprising metaphors is an example of this. For instance, his opening sentence in *Beyond Good and Evil* is, "Supposing that Truth is a woman—What then?" Always the misogynist, his suggestion is that philosophers have always pursued knowledge of the truth the way seducers seek women, flattering the object of their attention and resorting to every dissimulation to win her. In other words, philosophy heretofore has been an exercise in duplicity driven by nothing less than the will to power.

Nietzsche's breathtaking style also comes through in his most famous work (in part because he proclaimed it as such), *Thus Spake Zarathustra*. This truly might be called the gospel of nihilism. It is filled with the same estranged, emphatically lonely tone of his other works, but on a much greater (or perhaps more convincing) level. This is due to the author's choice of hero: the mysterious quasi-divine figure of Zarathustra, modeled in part on the Persian god Zoroaster but really a voice for Nietzsche's personal god, Dionysus. As such, the book produces an air of divinity, chosen no doubt as a device with which to attack Christ. The style is mock biblical. Even in translation, the effect is striking.

What is perhaps most arresting about this nihilistic manifesto is the way it inverts Christ's teaching in the Sermon on the Mount to subvert it. Here Nietzsche boldly distances himself both from Christianity and from the humanism that had largely taken its place in the preceding centuries. In a

---

15 *Deification* is the prevailing term for salvation in the Orthodox tradition. The ancient Fathers spoke about the salvation of the whole human being, body as well as soul. While sinful passions were unredeemable, the passionate faculty of man could, like all other natural faculties, participate in the experience of salvation. In this sense, human desire could indeed be "spiritualized" and "beautified."

section entitled "Neighbor-Love," the philosopher turns two thousand years of moral teaching on its head. Emulating Jesus' use of antitheses ("Ye have heard it said of old . . . but I tell you . . .") to contrast his teaching with that of the past, Zarathustra proclaims:

> *Ye crowd around your neighbor, and have fine words for it. But I say unto you: your neighbor-love is your bad love of yourselves. Ye flee unto your neighbor from yourselves, and would fain make a virtue thereof: but I fathom your "unselfishness."*[16]

The suggestion is that the Christian virtue of unselfishness, or love of one's neighbor, is something other than it appears. It is really a flight from the reality of one's own ego, the only legitimate focus in ethics. "Do I advise you to neighbor-love," he continues questioningly:

> *Rather do I advise you to neighbor-flight and to furthest love! . . . But thou fearest, and runnest unto thy neighbor. Ye cannot endure it with yourselves, and do not love yourselves sufficiently: so ye seek to mislead your neighbor into love, and would fain gild yourselves with his error.*[17]

Likewise, when speaking about the enmity of warfare, Zarathustra reverses Jesus' praise for peacemakers:

> *Ye shall love peace as a means toward new wars—and the short peace more than the long. Ye say that it is a good cause which halloweth even war? I say unto you: it is the good war which halloweth every cause. War and courage have done more great things than charity.*[18]

It is often observed that Nietzsche had contempt for politics. Such statements as this one are, at least by Nietzscheans, therefore interpreted as being

---

16 Friedrich Nietzsche, *Thus Spake Zarathustra*, trans. Thomas Common, in *The Philosophy of Nietzsche*, 63.

17 Ibid.

18 Ibid., 47–48.

really about the inner, spiritual warfare of a great man. However, these claims sound rather like those of academic pluralists who dismiss the doctrine of jihad in Islam as a purely spiritual one. Nietzsche, it might be said, had only admiration for the mercilessness of the latter.

That he did in fact admire militancy can be seen in a statement made in the companion volume to *Zarathustra*. In *Beyond Good and Evil*, he applies the doctrine of the will to power to political developments in contemporary Europe. Reflecting on Russia, he anticipates much that Hitler would have to say later in *Mein Kampf*. The power of Russia's will, he writes, has long been growing and "waits threateningly to be discharged." He considers the possibility of a revolution forestalling its menacing growth, but adds:

> *I do not say this as one who desires it; in my heart I should rather prefer the contrary—I mean such an increase in the threatening attitude of Russia, that Europe would have to make up its mind to become equally threatening—namely, to acquire one will, by means of a new caste to rule over the continent, a persistent, dreadful will of its own, that can set its aims thousands of years ahead; so that the long spun-out comedy of its petty-stateism, and its dynastic as well as its democratic many-willedness, might finally be brought to a close. The time for petty politics is past; the next century will bring the struggle for the dominion of the world—the compulsion to great politics.[19]*

The claim that the doctrine of the will to power was intended by the philosopher as a merely internal mechanism of personal self-discovery cannot be seriously maintained with statements like this in the middle of his most representative books.

What was emerging from the nihilist's "transvaluation of all values" was a moral order in which good and evil no longer existed. Since God was dead, the world lacked a moral structure. It was meaningless. Since man was part of the cosmos, this meant human life was meaningless too. Abandoning the convictions of both Christianity and humanism, Nietzsche claimed

---

19 Nietzsche, *Beyond Good and Evil*, 509–10.

there is nothing that gives man a purpose apart from a will to power that flows through everything. Only this blind, indifferent, meaningless force could give human life a purpose. And since most human beings were not in Nietzsche's judgment worthy of the name, it fell to only a courageous few to realize the potential of the will to power.

This type of humanity was in fact a step beyond humanity itself. Nietzsche lived in the wake of the Darwinian revolution in biology, which claimed that every form of life—every species—is locked in a struggle for existence from which only the strongest would emerge alive. This process of natural selection yielded advances in each species and even led to the formation of new ones. *Homo sapiens*, man-the-animal, could perhaps himself advance to something higher.

To the atheists ready to make the historic transition "beyond good and evil," Nietzsche applied his famous term "superman" (*Übermensch*). For these few, he offered a new way of life called the "master-morality." This was worked out in its fullest form in a work entitled *The Genealogy of Morals*. The book is in some ways a history of Western culture. The worst event ever to befall the world, it claimed, was the rise of Christendom. Prior to that, the master morality of the pagan noble class enabled its leadership to enjoy a mastery over others without a bad conscience. Aristotle's legitimation of slavery was only the most elaborate expression of this. With the rise of Christianity, the slave class was able to impose a bad conscience on the master class, subtly forcing it to retreat. Instead of overthrowing their masters, slaves achieved something even more effective. They forced the world to embrace the virtue of mercy ("blessed are the merciful") and thereby brought it into submission to their will.

Nietzsche was convinced that Christian morality, either in its original form or in its denatured humanist form, would always seduce the weaknesses of the masses. But he did hope that a class of supermen might arise in the future and make use of his writings. As the Antichrist, he was convinced that he had something important to offer the generation of true atheists yet to come.

He always denied with the greatest emphasis that he was creating a new morality. At the end of the first part of *Zarathustra*, for instance, he has his hero declare:

I now go alone, my disciples! Ye also now go away, and alone! So will I have it. Verily, I advise you: depart from me, and guard yourselves against Zarathustra! And better still: be ashamed of him! Perhaps he hath deceived you.

The nihilist of the modern age must not follow anyone but himself, regarding even friends and loved ones with hostile suspicion. "The man of knowledge must be able not only to love his enemies," he adds coldly, "but also to hate his friends."[20]

Nevertheless, Nietzsche would prove to be obsessed with his own influence and legacy. After all, he was "another Christ."

"Behold the Man"

WE HAVE SEEN HOW THROUGHOUT his life Nietzsche was intently focused on his contribution to a post-Christian Christendom. That contribution he considered to be one of disjuncture, of repudiation, and of prophecy. He was aware, as many of his generation were, that modern science and philosophy appeared incompatible with traditional Christianity; that human greatness was being displaced by the coarse demands of a "herd instinct"; that secular humanism had failed to produce the superman; and that a new voice was needed to find a new way forward. He was that voice, he believed, and all his works were composed in the mode of one seeking the attention of a civilization in crisis.

Nietzsche was a man preoccupied with his own genius. He was aware of unusual powers of self-mastery similar to those of ancient Christian ascetics. The struggle against weakness and delusion runs throughout his life. An anecdote from his childhood tells of an electrical storm that suddenly broke when he was playing with other children. All fled but Nietzsche, who mastered his fear to stand defiantly in the middle of the street until the storm, finally defeated, had passed.

Another upwelling of self-mastery was his imperviousness to bodily

---

20 Nietzsche, *Thus Spake Zarathustra*, 82.

Nietzsche with Ree and Salome

discomfort. Never was an intellectual so chronically ravaged by sickness as was Nietzsche. The main form of it was migraine headaches that would last for days, accompanied by vomiting. Yet the genius worked on, often sitting in the darkness with the curtains drawn and composing the most joyous sections of his books. A letter describes the fateful year 1876, marked by the split from Wagner, as one in which two days out of three were spent "in torture." He praises the illness that marks this turning point in his life as "the greatest help" because it provided the physiological means to "set me free" and the encouragement "to be myself."[21] Such debilitating chronic illnesses may have paralyzed his body but served to spur intellectual creativity.

Nietzsche's sense of genius was also manifested in his social relationships, or lack of them. He was always conscious of being alone. This was certainly true of his scholarly status. It is estimated that during the course of his life, no more than five hundred copies of his many books were ever sold. As a professor of philology in Switzerland he was ridiculed for his (ingenious) revision of Greek classics. There he endured low enrollments and the snickering of students who, rightly or wrongly, took him for an eccentric homosexual.

In fact, his life was marked with few friendships and almost none with women. His one documented interest in the opposite sex was a stormy relationship with the freethinking Lou Salome, who records in her memoirs the halfhearted proposals of the socially inept philosopher. When she refused and showed instead an interest in Nietzsche's intimate friend Paul Reé, the professor lashed out with an abusive and insulting statement about her intellectual integrity and physical appearance. He never married and, the weird affair with Salome notwithstanding, never showed an interest in marriage.

---

21 Geoffrey Clive, ed., *The Philosophy of Nietzsche* (New York: New American Library, 1965), 36–37.

He considered the female sex hopelessly inferior to the male. The well-known statement "Thou goest to women? Do not forget thy whip!" is from *Zarathustra*.[22] It is the final message of a section of the work dedicated to the philosopher's "wisdom" about female humanity. The first is, "Everything in woman is a riddle, and everything in woman hath one solution—it is called pregnancy."[23]

Misogyny and self-mastery were not the only signs of Nietzsche's tendency toward megalomania. Nor was his uphill and ultimately futile competition with Richard Wagner. The most definitive record of it is to be found in the profuse statements about himself that fill his many books. Autobiography is always the temptation of a narcissist. The genre is not limited to them; Augustine invented it to expose his own moral weaknesses and to proclaim the greatness not of himself but of God. But in the nineteenth century, as the romantic cult of genius ripened to the point of putrefaction, self-reflection and introspection reached a high point. Wagner himself was an example, producing his monumental *Mein Leben* (*My Life*) in two volumes, and that covering only the period before the *Ring*. Nietzsche produced no fewer than eight different works of autobiography to document his creativity. He clearly delighted in every one. And he saved the best for last.

Ecce Homo is the final, definitive statement by Nietzsche about himself. Its tone was more shrill than that of earlier statements, but for that reason it is in a certain sense more direct and frank. Its first sentence trumpets the convictions of a self-isolated narcissist:

> *In view of the fact that before long I must confront my fellow-men with the very greatest demand that has ever yet been made upon them, it seems to me indispensable to declare here who and what I am. . . . The disparity between the greatness of my task and the smallness of my contemporaries is made plain by the fact that people have neither heard me nor seen me.*[24]

---

22 Nietzsche, *Thus Spake Zarathustra*, 70.

23 Ibid., 68.

24 Friedrich Nietzsche, *Ecce Homo*, trans. Clifton P. Fadiman, in *The Philosophy of Nietzsche*, 811.

To call the work a rant is an understatement. It is the furious cry of a man convinced of his genius and in agony that so few recognize it. In a sense this makes the allusion of its title ironic. "Behold the man" (*Ecce homo* in Latin) were of course the words of Pontius Pilate, directing the audience's attention to a man—Jesus Christ—who had, on that occasion, remained silent (Mark 15:3–5). Despite His humility, it was that man whose words had ruled the West for nearly nineteen hundred years, either directly in the form of Christianity or indirectly in the form of secular humanism. The reign of that man was now at an end, claimed Nietzsche. It was time for the Antichrist to speak.

What is particularly interesting in Nietzsche's choice of title is its suggestion that he is indeed worthy of comparison with Jesus Christ. Clever as always, his action is chilling in its audacity. Once he had written a book that supplanted the Sermon on the Mount. Now he pointed at himself, supplanting God.

In many ways it is the style of *Ecce Homo* that stands above the content. The now familiar assertions about Christianity, morality, and philosophy are all there, and little is new. But as he walks the reader through the library of his life's work, pointing to this or that remarkable doctrine, providing block quotes of his most illustrious teachings—all the while asserting the total bankruptcy of Christendom—his manner of speech is arresting. It knows no limits, going beyond even megalomania.

"Why I Am So Wise"; "Why I Am So Clever"; "Why I Write Such Excellent Books": these are the chapter titles that Nietzsche chose for presenting his life story to the world. The final one, "Why I Am Destiny," is a particularly remarkable expression of conceit, but also of foresight into the nihilism that Christendom would soon experience. "I know my destiny," it opens.

> *Some day my name will be bound up with the recollection of something terrific—of a crisis quite unprecedented, of the most profound clash of consciences, and the decisive condemnation of all that theretofore had been believed, required, and hallowed. I am not a man, I am dynamite.*[25]

"I am a joyful herald," he continues, "unparalleled in history;"

---

25 Ibid., 923.

I am acquainted with tasks of grandeur formerly inconceivable. Hope is reborn with me. Thus, I am necessarily a Man of Destiny. For when Truth engages in struggle with the falsehood of ages, we must expect shocks and a series of earthquakes, with a rearrangement of hills and valleys, such as has never yet been dreamt of. The concept "politics" is thus raised bodily into the realm of spiritual warfare. All the mighty forms of the old society are blown into space—for they all rest on falsehood: there will be wars, whose like have never been seen on earth before. Politics on a grand scale will date from me.[26]

The Nazis, seizing on these last words, would in fact bring some of them to realization. As the life of Nietzsche demonstrates, megalomaniacs inspire megalomaniacs.

As his creative work reached its conclusion, Nietzsche offered a final prayer, as it were, to his god Dionysus—the primordial nihilist—with whose identity he would soon merge:

I am by far the most terrible man that has ever existed; but, this does not negate the fact that I shall be the most beneficent. I know the joy of annihilation to a degree commensurate with my power to annihilate. In both cases I obey my Dionysian nature, which cannot separate the negative deed from yea-saying. I am the first immoralist, and thus I am the essential destroyer.[27]

Yet the destruction that did in fact follow was not totalitarianism and total warfare. That would come later.

What came right away was the destruction of his sanity. Just months or perhaps weeks after completing these words, Nietzsche went completely mad. The account that comes down to us is that one day early in January, 1889, he was on his way home to an apartment in which he was living in Turin, Italy. Across the street from the entrance he caught sight of a man with a horse. The man cruelly began to beat the defenseless creature.

---

26 Ibid., 924.
27 Ibid.

Nietzsche rushed to the horse, throwing his arms around its neck and sobbing uncontrollably like a little boy. This was the last moral action in the life of the great "immoralist." Within days he was an inmate in a mental hospital and would spend the remaining decade of his life as a dependent of others. The man who wrote "such excellent books" would lie helplessly on his bed, staring out the window and remaining totally mute. He would not even be able to write his name when given a piece of paper to do so.

What was the cause of Nietzsche's insanity? We will never know with certainty. The prevailing explanation is syphilis. In some cases, that venereal disease, which was not uncommon in the nineteenth century, results in the deterioration of the brain and the loss of sanity. This theory makes for a reasonable explanation. It might be noted, though, that Nietzsche, who unlike Wagner was never in his life known to lust after women, claimed only once to have visited a brothel, wherein, according to him, the only thing he touched "was a piano."

Another explanation is more psychological, even spiritual. It claims that the philosopher's mental collapse was due to the overwhelming strain that accompanied his wide-eyed gaze into the abyss of meaninglessness. His conviction that "God is dead" had brought him to the conclusion that morality is a fetter to the human spirit, that only the will to power makes life worth living. That instinct more often than not expresses itself in violence of one kind or another, and in the face of it the superman would assent to acts of cruelty. The philosopher had once commented in his study of morality, *The Genealogy of Morals,* that "the sight of suffering does one good, the infliction of suffering does one more good."[28]

Nietzsche, the self-styled superman who claimed to have traveled "beyond good and evil," had consistently railed against the Christian virtues of mercy and pity. Standing in the square of Turin, perhaps he saw, as it were mystically, the end result of his war against Christ. He had fancied himself a god, but in the end his soul broke and he proved to be "human, all-too-human" (to quote his degrading phrase for people who "suffer" from a moral conscience).

---

28   Friedrich Nietzsche, *The Genealogy of Morals*, trans. Horace B. Samuel, in *The Philosophy of Nietzsche*, 680.

Ironically, the fallen antichrist spent his long years of decline in the same female company that he claimed to have detested as a boy. He ended his life as the charge of his sister, but for many years after his collapse he was cared for by his mother. We know almost nothing about this quiet, pious woman, the widow of a Lutheran minister. But her act of taking the invalid into her home and enduring his catatonic silence, marked by occasional screaming fits, could only have been motivated by maternal love and Christian pity, two of the most debilitating values in what the philosopher had called the "slave morality."

It was observed that for a long time Nietzsche kept muttering the barely discernible phrase, "Mother, I have become stupid." Then he would begin screaming again. The only thing that consoled him was a small music box that some anonymous benefactor brought to him one day. When this was played, he lapsed back into catatonia.

The melody it played was Wagner's "Wedding March."

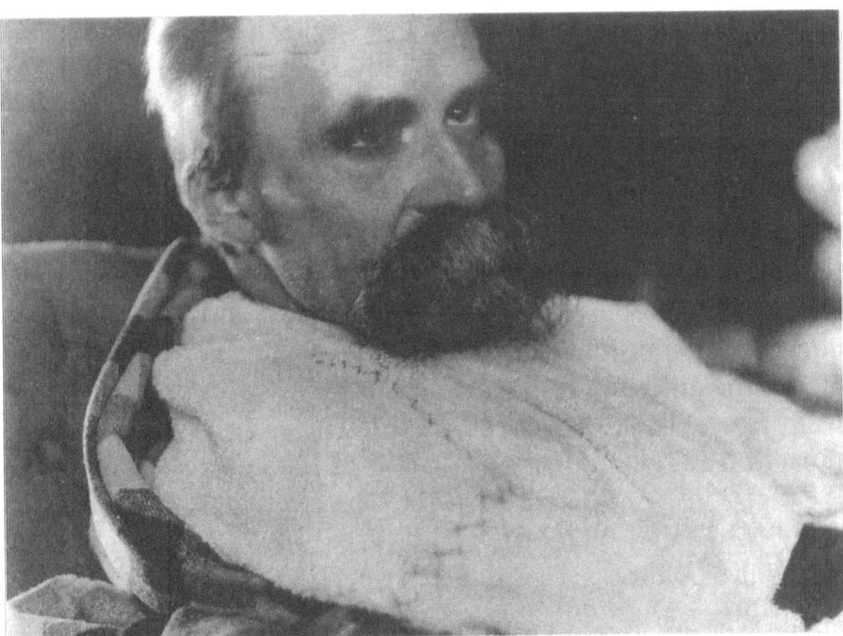

Nietzsche in his insanity

CHAPTER TWO

Dostoevsky

THE SPECTER OF NIHILISM PASSED across nineteenth-century Russia as it did across the Germany of Wagner and Nietzsche. Once a stronghold of Eastern Christendom, Russia had since the time of Peter the Great undergone a far-reaching process of westernization. Secular humanism established a permanent place in her culture. Peter was not much interested in cultural matters as such. His priorities were military and political. Later in the eighteenth century, however, Catherine the Great had finally opened the way to secularization, using the capital of St. Petersburg—dubbed Russia's "window on the West"—as an artistic point of entry.

Her most famous achievement was the Hermitage, a museum dedicated to displaying Western European painting exclusively. Native Russian works were scarcely permitted. Iconography, the form of painting in which Russians in past centuries had brilliantly distinguished themselves, was nowhere to be found behind its stylish baroque facade. Only humanist ideals were to inspire the new, secular awakening of modern Russia. The result was a kind of intellectual alchemy. From almost nothing, a secular culture erupted and soon distinguished itself as one of the West's brightest sources of the arts. As the sparks flew, some of the most distinguished works of literature, music, and painting were created.

The record is stunning. To take only one microcosmic example: In the year 1866, two important works of literature had begun to appear in serial form side by side in the same literary journal, *The Russian Messenger (Russky vestnik)*. Each author was working on his first large-scale novel, and no doubt many readers of the journal had never heard of either. A month would feature the latest installment of one work, and then, giving its author time to write more chapters, the following month would feature an installment from the other. So it went, month after month, in but a single journal in a single year of this amazing land of creativity. The first novel was *War and Peace* by Leo Tolstoy. The second was *Crime and Punishment* by Fyodor Dostoevsky.

Both writers would play an important role in the history of Russian literature. But it was Dostoevsky who would, better than any of his contemporaries, document through the use of fiction the growing crisis of utopian Christendom. More even than the composer Wagner or the philosopher Nietzsche, he realized that secular humanism had failed in its promises. And turning to the old Christendom for alternatives, he presented traditional Christianity—not nihilism—as the hope for what the West might once again become.

A Believer among Atheists

DOSTOEVSKY (D. 1881) WAS NEVER an atheist, but he liked to spend his time in the company of atheists. There was in them something that seemed authentic and even heroic. Perhaps he was drawn by the Russian atheist's tendency to go to extremes, something he observed in himself. "I have a vile and overly passionate nature," he once confided. "Everywhere and in everything I drive myself to the ultimate limit, all my life I have been overstepping the line."[1] As the most extreme expression of transgression, atheism appeared a compelling option for living an authentic life in the modern world. Dostoevsky believed that in any conversation about modernity, a place at the table must be held in reserve for the atheist. And one always appeared.

Dostoevsky's fascination with atheism is best understood in light of a youthful rebelliousness and the decade of suffering he experienced as a result of it. He was the son of a minor nobleman, like many intellectuals of

---

1   This he declared in 1867. *Selected Letters of Fyodor Dostoevsky*, ed. Joseph Frank and David I. Goldstein, trans. Andrew R. MacAndrew (New Brunswick, NJ: Rutgers University Press, 1987), 252.

his time. Like the others, any fortune he inherited was encumbered by an onerous debt of guilt. For until the middle of the nineteenth century, half of Russia's peasants were degraded by serfdom. The misery and resentment of the entire peasantry—nearly nine out of every ten Russians—continued even after the abolition of the cruel institution. Dostoevsky's father was an example of social injustice at its worst, possessing a brutal personality. His peasants finally rose up in rebellion one day and murdered him. When the event occurred, the future novelist was far away from home in the capital studying engineering, but knowledge of it affected him deeply. He was already dreaming of becoming a writer and using literature to explore the darkest depths of human experience.

It was nearly obligatory at this time for someone with literary ambitions to be in touch with the most progressive streams of Western thought. The young Dostoevsky was particularly impressed with a Russian radical named Vissarion Belinsky. This literary critic had helped form the emerging *intelligentsia* (the word was coined by Russians), a body of educated people who were deeply dissatisfied with contemporary society. A few of its members were known as Slavophiles and looked to pre-Petrine Russia and her Orthodox Church for inspiration. Most, however, were known as Westernizers. They celebrated the West and looked on the Orthodox Church, the autocracy, and native popular culture with contempt.

Belinsky was the leader of the Westernizers, and that made him an atheist. But on one occasion he found himself confronted by Dostoevsky, who resolutely defended the existence of God. Belinsky was probably amused by such naïveté, but after reading Dostoevsky's first novel, *Poor Folk,* he became an advocate for the young writer. He especially praised Dostoevsky's capacity for empathizing with the poor and plumbing their explosive psychological experiences. Ignoring Dostoevsky's "squeamish piety," Belinsky encouraged him to continue writing in a way that would stir dissatisfaction with the status quo.

As a believer, Dostoevsky was not impervious to the arguments against faith all around him. He found himself struggling against them. In one passage from an early letter, he speaks of his "thirst" for faith and his experience of its absence.

I can tell you about myself that I am a child of this century, a child of doubt and disbelief, I have always been and shall ever be (that I know), until they close the lid of my coffin. What terrible torment this thirst to believe has cost me and is still costing me, and the stronger it becomes in my soul, the stronger are the arguments against it. And despite all this, God sent me moments of great tranquility, moments during which I love and find I am loved by others; and it was during such a moment that I formed within myself a symbol of faith in which all is clear and sacred for me. This symbol is very simple, and here is what it is: to believe that there is nothing more beautiful, more profound, than Christ; and there not only isn't, but I tell myself with a jealous love, there cannot be. More than that—if someone succeeded in proving to me that Christ was outside the truth, and if, indeed, the truth was outside Christ, I would sooner remain with Christ than with the truth. . . . But it is better to stop talking about this.[2]

So in the end, Dostoevsky found his way through disbelief to a secure faith in God by contemplating the spiritual beauty of Christ. For him, love of God and love of man—the twin commandments of the gospel—remained intact and even expanded through his ongoing spiritual struggles.

But he remained rebellious in temperament, and this led him to join an intellectual group called the Petrashevsky Circle. It held secretive nocturnal meetings in which members discussed books by fashionable French socialists. Sometimes they fantasized about revolution. Their unquenchable thirst for progress impressed the nervous young writer. One day, however, the group's existence was discovered by the police and its members arrested. As in the twenty-first century, so in the nineteenth, the authoritarian Russian state treated dissent harshly. Along with other members of the circle, Dostoevsky was sentenced to execution.

The scene that followed on the parade grounds of Russia's capital in 1849 is famous. The twenty-one men who were brought out onto the winter snow were certain they would die that day. The first group was lined up in hoods

---

2   *Selected Letters of Fyodor Dostoevsky,* 68.

in front of the firing squad as the orders to prepare to shoot were initiated. Then, a soldier suddenly galloped up to the gallows to proclaim that Tsar Nicholas I (r. 1825–55), in an act of mercy, had issued a reprieve. The prisoners were "mercifully" consigned to hard labor in Siberia. Dostoevsky was fitted with ankle shackles that would not be removed for five years. Then he and most of the others were sent off to what he would later call "the house of the dead." Only one of the criminals did not make the journey. Having been among the hooded first group in the mock execution, he lost his mind at the shock of unexpectedly being granted his life back.

Before arriving in Siberia, the adult Dostoevsky had known only the company of the intelligentsia, the body of high-minded intellectuals who entertained lofty hopes for a progressive future. These men of culture, mostly from the nobility, had created a rarified atmosphere of social criticism and political conspiracy. They were driven, almost religiously, by what Belinsky had called the "burning questions" of progress. How was the intelligentsia to lift the peasantry up from the fetters of poverty? How was the intelligentsia to sweep away the oppressive autocracy of the tsar? How was the intelligentsia to eliminate the baneful influence of Christianity? The answers were elusive, but it was clear to all that they would come from secular humanism. And they would be motivated by a sense of moral indignation so intense as to constitute contempt for the existing order of things.

One early Westernizer, Alexander Herzen, tried to express the fervent, almost religious character of the questions by entitling a book *Who Is to Blame?* Years later another Westernizer, Nicholas Chernyshevsky, entitled a book *What Is to Be Done?* A later generation of Russian intellectuals, tired of utopia in its Communist form, would with typical Soviet political humor confront their society with the sarcastic question, "What is to be done and who is to blame?" But to the earnest and less jaded intelligentsia of the nineteenth century, locating guilt for Russia's backwardness and detailing revolutionary strategies against it remained a legitimate and burning question.

And it was answered, significantly, in well-furnished drawing rooms by men dressed in evening jackets living comfortable lives. In what were frequently all-night vigils of debate, intellectuals would assemble under the most polite circumstances to read selections from the latest Western author, apply his insights to the Russian situation, and propose action that would bring about a transformation of the world.

Dostoevsky breathed this atmosphere and even contributed to it. By the time of his arrest and exile, then, the promising young novelist was thoroughly imbued with utopian ideas. Denied the right to carry even part of his beloved secular library into exile, he must have been bemused when a charitable society with governmental support presented him with a copy of the New Testament. Nevertheless, he kept it under his pillow in the prison barracks for the next four years of his life.

In the prison camp, Dostoevsky encountered a very different kind of humanity from what he had seen in the drawing rooms of Saint Petersburg. Here his companions were hardened criminals—murderers, rapists, and child abusers. Every day for four years he slept on bunks next to these men, shared meals with them, performed hard labor among them. He was compelled to satisfy all his need for human companionship in conversation with them. Screaming arguments, beatings, drunken brawls, and deception became the normal experience of social interaction. All the while, the refined novelist pondered the character of human life. He also read from his New Testament.

With time he came to the conclusion that there was something fundamentally wrong with a purely humanist understanding of man. As inspirational as secular literature was, it somehow failed to grasp the whole of man. For even if the world could be transformed into utopia and everyone in the world given wealth, health, and freedom, in the end the kind of men who would inhabit it would still be the kind of men he was encountering now. The degree of moral depravity would not be as great, of course. But nothing about utopia could possibly heal altogether the brokenness that ruled in these men's hearts.

Dostoevsky later wrote about this broken humanity in a fictionalized memoir entitled *Notes from the House of the Dead*. In it, he described a complete absence of conscience, a built-in indifference to moral transformation.

In the course of several years, I never saw a sign of repentance among these people; not a trace of despondent brooding over their crimes, and the majority of them inwardly considered themselves absolutely in the right. This is a fact.[3]

Such an observation might have made him susceptible to the nihilism of Nietzsche. Both had discovered the limits of humanism and the illusion of utopia. Man was not fundamentally rational, and perfect human happiness was not attainable on earth. The human condition would never be free of moral transgression. Had he been literate, would not the kind of unrepentant child murderer that Dostoevsky met have been capable of appreciating the German philosopher's intoxicating accounts of the will to power? But there was a key difference between Dostoevsky and Nietzsche as they sat beneath the specter of nihilism, the one in the darkness of prison, the other in the splendor of Bayreuth. One was a believer and the other an atheist.

If Nietzsche's childhood faith was remembered as a disgrace, tainted by hypocrisy and pessimism, Dostoevsky's now came to him in a flash of beauty. A distant memory offered a way of transcending the broken world. It offered an alternative to the despair that came from nihilism.

The story is told in an autobiographical fragment later published in *The Diary of a Writer*. It relates to the same period chronicled in *Notes from the House of the Dead*. The story is set, significantly, within traditional Christianity's liturgical time. It takes place during the season of Pascha.

As the feast of Christ's Resurrection approached, the convicts were encouraged to attend liturgical services and receive the sacrament of Holy Communion. A passage from *House of the Dead* describes the experience in the first person. "I very much liked the week of the preparation for the sacrament," the narrator writes.

It was long since I had been to church. The Lenten service so familiar to me from the far-away days of my childhood in my father's house, the solemn prayers, the prostrations—all this stirred in my heart the far, far-away past, bringing back the days of my childhood. . . . The convicts prayed very

---

3   Joseph Frank, *Dostoevsky: The Years of Ordeal, 1850–1859* (Princeton, NJ: Princeton University Press, 1990), 95.

Dostoevsky after his return from Siberia

earnestly and every one of them brought his poor farthing to the church every time to buy a candle, or to put into the collection. "I, too, am a man," he thought, and felt perhaps as he gave it, "in God's eyes we are all equal."

The narrator brings attention to the prayers read at the Orthodox Divine Liturgy immediately prior to communion: "I believe, O Lord, and I confess, that thou art truly the Christ, the Son of the living God, who came into the world to save sinners, of whom I am first. . . ." The reflection on the equality of all men in Christ was itself paradisiacal. But more even than that, the prayer required each and every assembled member of the congregation to repeat the words of Saint Paul (1 Tim. 1:15) and regard himself as "first" among sinners. The narrator of the story states that at a later phrase in the same prayer, when the communicant prays "like the thief will I confess thee," the convicts, standing humbly in a line at the very back of the temple, "bowed down to the ground with the clanking of chains, apparently applying the words literally to themselves."[4]

On the day after the Sunday of Pascha, which in the Orthodox Church is called Bright Monday, Dostoevsky found himself back in the barracks

---

4   Ibid., 120–21.

meditating on this image and that of the risen Christ. But transformational peace was elusive. The convicts around him were drunken and quarrelsome, and frequently lewd songs or fistfights erupted among them. When a group of six men turned on another man and savagely began to beat him, the sensitive novelist fled outdoors into the prison yard. As he felt the demon of hatred rising in his own heart against the men who surrounded him, he bumped into another political prisoner like himself, who confided his own disgust for the uncultured peasants.

Suddenly and mystically, Dostoevsky's thoughts were taken away from the current scene and back to one from his childhood. He was nine years old and was strolling peacefully through his family's forest when a cry went out nearby that a wolf was at large. The boy was terrified and fled the wood, emerging from it into an open field where one of his father's serfs, a peasant named Marey, was laboring. Seeing the boy's desperate expression, Marey dropped what he was doing and ran to comfort him. Blessing the boy with the sign of the cross, he sent him toward the nearby house, promising to watch over him as he went.

Later in life, in his *Diary of a Writer,* Dostoevsky explained the significance for him of this event. It was not a matter simply of a grown-up offering momentary protection and comfort to a child. "Something entirely different had occurred." The "genuine love" that shone in the eyes of Marey was a revelation, an illumination, of the celestial beauty of the human condition in this world, overshadowed as it is by the darkness of enmity. It induced, in other words, a heavenly transformation of the world. After all, whose will had "forced" Marey to show such kindness?

> *He was our peasant serf, and I, after all, the son of his owner; no one would know how kind he had been and reward him for it. . . . The encounter was isolated, in an empty field, and only God, perhaps, saw from above what deep and enlightened human feeling, what delicate, almost womanly tenderness, could fill the heart of a coarse, bestially ignorant Russian peasant serf not yet expecting, nor even suspecting, that he might be free.*[5]

---

5   Ibid., 123.

With the sudden memory of this childhood experience, Dostoevsky was saved from nihilism in his Siberian exile. His Bright Week recollection of childhood enabled him now to look on his fellow convicts with sympathy rather than malice. Unconditional love, rooted in the Christian faith of the peasant Marey, now offered an alternative to nihilism.

That alternative was the paradisiacal culture disdained by Russia's elite since the time of Peter the Great. Despite the effects of westernization, this faith had been kept alive within the peasantry. As ignorant and coarse as the peasants were, those like Marey remained in contact with it. Against the failure of utopia and the specter of nihilism, traditional Christianity continued to promise a heavenly transformation of the world.

Confronting the Intelligentsia

INSIGHT INTO THE BENIGHTED SOULS of humanity's criminals, which he received by reading the New Testament, was the starting point for Dostoevsky's new approach to literature. Once his shackles were taken off and he was finally released from prison, he had much work to do. In 1859, he returned to the capital of Saint Petersburg and found there an intelligentsia animated with hope in the utopia he had come to mistrust. The reactionary Nicholas was dead, and following Russia's humiliating defeat in the Crimean War, the new tsar, Alexander II (r. 1855–81), promised to lead Russia in the direction of progress. The mood of the intelligentsia surged. The possibility of full-scale secular transformation had finally come.

From exile in London, the revolutionary Alexander Herzen actually praised his royal namesake when the latter began to discuss the liberation of the serfs—a reform he finally ordered in 1861. Other significant improvements to the Russian government followed in what came to be known collectively as the Great Reforms. But many within the intelligentsia were not content to await the outcome of Alexander's measures. They resolved to take action themselves, pouring into the countryside to agitate for a more radical form of progress. It was these populists, as they were known, who started down the road of mass mobilization that would ultimately lead to revolution.

While most members of the intelligentsia were content to continue secretive meetings and the discussion of utopian thought, a growing restlessness appeared. It produced more and more nihilistic solutions to the burning issues of progress. One fanatic named Sergey Nechaev went the furthest. Having obtained the financial backing of Nikolay Bakunin, another revolutionary known for the slogan "the act of destruction is a creative act," Nechaev arranged the murder of a fellow conspirator for no other reason than to solidify his domineering control over the movement.

Sergey Nechaev

In fact, Nechaev was part of a movement within the intelligentsia known to contemporaries as "nihilism." This was not the philosophical and moral nihilism we have already explored with Wagner and Nietzsche. In this case, the movement was assured of the possibility and value of progress. The term denoted rather a total contempt for Russia's traditional civilization. This included, foremost, the Orthodox faith and autocracy. But it extended to everything inherited from the more humanistic contributions of westernization, especially in the arts. With the exception of science and socialism, the existing order of Russian Christendom was meaningless to these nihilists. It must all be swept away and replaced with a completely new order.

The values embraced by Russia's nihilists were thoroughly utopian, and the expectation of progress would have made Nietzsche sneer. Though far more extreme in their trajectory, these values were the fruits of liberal utilitarianism and positivism. The first, based on the atheistic moral philosophy of Jeremy Bentham and John Stuart Mill, claimed that good and evil were determined exclusively by their social utility, that is, by the degree to which they advanced or impeded human happiness. Positivism was associated with the atheistic philosophy of Auguste Comte, who claimed that history moves inevitably in an upward progressive arc as religion is eliminated and scientific knowledge takes over.

Such values were advanced in Russia by the novelist Ivan Turgenev. In a work entitled *Fathers and Sons,* he created a protagonist named Bazarov, whom he described as a "nihilist." It was the first popularization of the term. Bazarov became immediately famous in Russian literary circles. He was a man of immense intelligence and total contempt for the existing social order. An atheist, he scorned all forms of knowledge not firmly grounded in logic and the scientific method. "Two times two equals four," he liked to say, "and the rest is nonsense."

To Dostoevsky, rubbing the scars on his ankles as he finally arrived by train in Petersburg, it appeared as though Russia's future still belonged to utopians. His first significant composition after his return, therefore, was designed as a challenge to the humanistic understanding of man. It was entitled *Notes from Underground,* and it would one day take its place as one of the most widely read classics of modern thought. The book had a strange structure, starting out as philosophical exposition and concluding as a collection of fictional anecdotes. The "underground man" who narrates it is a contemptible figure, yet his plaintive insights into social isolation and the tragedy with which his story concludes makes him strangely sympathetic. His first utterance, "I am a sick man . . . I am a spiteful man," sets the keynote for a tirade against modern society.

But it is not the opulent wealth of the nobility nor the poverty of the peasants about which the underground man complains. For him, society is rotten because under the influence of modern Western ideas it threatens to reduce man to the status of an animal. Utopians like Chernyshevsky (the author of *What Is to Be Done?*) were arguing from the basis of utilitarianism that the good of society depends on the enlightened self-interest of its individuals. For the nihilists, material comfort was, scientifically speaking, what any rational individual should desire and society encourage. But the underground man disagrees.

Isn't there, indeed, something that is dearer to almost every man than his very best interests, or (not to violate logic) isn't there a certain most advantageous advantage . . . which is more important and more advantageous than all other advantages, and for the sake of which a man is prepared, if need be, to go against all laws, against reason, honor, peace, prosperity— in short, against all those fine and useful things?[6]

What for Dostoevsky is more precious to a man than his rational self-interest?

One's own free, untrammeled desires, one's own whim, no matter how extravagant, one's own fancy, be it wrought up at times to the point of madness—all of this is precisely that most advantageous of advantages which is omitted, which fits no classification, and which is constantly knocking all systems and theories to hell.[7]

Mimicking Bazarov's complacent faith in science, the underground man declares that while he has "heard it said" that two times two makes four, in the irrational reality of human freedom, sometimes "two times two makes five."

Like Nietzsche, who had condemned the tendency of all moral systems to suppress the human will, Dostoevsky claimed the rational ordering of society threatens to destroy true human freedom. And while he saw no redeeming virtue in the will to power, he also shared Nietzsche's conviction that the good of human life is to be found in the innate dignity that is safeguarded by the will. *Notes from Underground* has been called the "philosophical preface" to Dostoevsky's great novels.[8] Indeed, it was this conviction about the innate dignity of the free will that defined some of the most memorable characters in literary history.

Two examples are Parfyon Rogozhin and Pyotr Verkhovensky. The first

---

6   Fyodor Dostoevsky, *Notes from Underground*, trans. Mirra Ginsburg (New York: Bantam, 1974), 24.

7   Ibid., 28.

8   Konstantin Mochulsky, *Dostoevsky: His Life and Work*, trans. Michael A. Minihan (Princeton, NJ: Princeton University Press, 1967), 254.

belongs to *The Idiot* (1868) and the second to *Demons* (1872). Rogozhin is the coarse-mannered heir of a vast fortune who squanders much of it and the opportunities that depend on it by pursuing the beautiful but disturbed Nastasya Filippovna. His is an especially grandiose example of the will to power—taking in this case the form of lust—overcoming all capacity for rational self-interest. Though completely secure in his fortune, he moves through the story like a cyclone of desire, pushing others aside (in some scenes literally) and attempting murder to acquire the young woman. In one unforgettable scene, he offers her the extravagant sum of one hundred thousand rubles to elope with him. Full of self-destructive self-loathing, she submits to the offer and then hurls the money into the fireplace to burn.

Verkhovensky is more complex. He is the son of a liberal landowner who, like many in the intelligentsia, consciously abandoned his faith in Christianity. The father plays with nihilistic ideas in the comfort of his estate; the son applies them to life. Verkhovensky is a revolutionary and seeks the overthrow of the whole political order. While claiming to serve the material interests of the suffering masses, however, in the end he is really interested in power for its own sake. This is revealed when he organizes the ruthless murder of another revolutionary, an act Dostoevsky took directly from news reports about the Nechaev affair discussed above.

In asserting an irrational will over rational self-interest, Dostoevsky's characters were not at all what the intelligentsia had in mind when it thought about the human condition. A figure like Verkhovensky appeared to most westernized intellectuals as grotesque, even offensive. To make matters worse, the novelist applied beliefs drawn from traditional Christianity to explain irrational and self-destructive behavior. One of the twin epigraphs of *Demons,* for instance, is a quote from the Gospel of Luke about the demons that enter the herd of swine and cause it to rush down the hill to self-destruction (Luke 8:32–36). When linked to the action that follows, this verse signals that nihilism lies below the surface of rationalism when the latter is divorced from the light of the gospel.

With its humanistic values, the intelligentsia could not tolerate such an insult. As a result Dostoevsky was a writer often as isolated as Nietzsche. When *Demons* was published, for instance, it was immediately attacked in the progressive press as the work of a retrograde fanatic.

Dostoevsky had the posthumous final word, however. His portrayal of a revolutionary movement falling into the hands of a megalomaniac obsessed with his own power and murdering members of his own circle to enhance that power proved to be, as we shall see in chapter 4, a literary prophecy of Stalinism.

The Dream of a Ridiculous Superman

THOUGH EQUALLY PREOCCUPIED WITH NIHILISM, Dostoevsky and Nietzsche had radically different responses to it. The contrast can be seen when aligning a fictional anecdote from a novel of the former with a nonfictional anecdote from the life of the latter. Strangely, few historians have ever made the comparison.

The fictional anecdote is contained in Dostoevsky's first large-scale novel, *Crime and Punishment.* It concerns the protagonist named Rodion Raskolnikov. This young man stands at the center of all action in the story. Scarcely a scene takes place in his absence. He consumes the action, as it were. And in the end he is consumed by it. The meaning of all this is revealed by the author when, in an early scene, Raskolnikov has a dream.

To understand its significance—especially in relation to Nietzsche—it is necessary to consider the way in which Dostoevsky's protagonist represents utopian Christendom. Raskolnikov is like many urban intellectuals, highly educated and eager to resolve the many problems of modern society. As a Russian intellectual, he comes from the minor social elite and is therefore never far from poverty. He is a student and lives in the most westernized of Russian cities, Saint Petersburg. His most important characteristic is that he is an atheist. He holds out hope, as many such radicals did, of a better life for himself and a better Russia through progress. But the story is not about the broken world around him, as it was for Belinsky, Herzen, and Chernyshevsky. It is about the broken world within him. And though he does not realize it, that brokenness stems from the influence of atheism.

In the early stages of the novel Raskolnikov appears to embrace the spirit of nihilism so completely that he goes well beyond the limits of his humanist contemporaries. In an article written before the action begins, for instance, he lays out his vision of morality. Though it displays respect for science and progress, the cerebral work asserts that the will of an individual is ultimately the only standard of morality. It is a call for the transvaluation of all values.

In this sense the article could have been written by Nietzsche. As we saw in the previous chapter, the German philosopher contrasted what he called the "slave morality" of Christians to the "master morality" of the superman. The essential feature of slave morality is its virtue of pity, of compassion for others. The superman, on the other hand, thinks only of himself and the enhancement of his power over all around him. He defines moral aims himself and pursues them ruthlessly, even cruelly, and with no concern for the harm they may bring to others. Living authentically by his conviction that God is dead, he is prepared to transgress moral boundaries that otherwise give life its meaning. He is prepared to travel "beyond good and evil." Here the ultimate inspiration is the image of Wagner's Siegfried, smashing Wotan's morality spear and fearlessly "crossing through the fire" to claim what is his by right of will.

Raskolnikov the atheist claims in his article to live by such a transvaluation of values. According to the article's elaboration by another character,

the whole point is that in his article all people are somehow divided into the "ordinary" and "extraordinary." The ordinary must live in obedience and have no right to transgress the law, because they are, after all, ordinary. While the extraordinary have the right to commit all sorts of crimes and in various ways transgress the law, because in point of fact they are extraordinary.[9]

As an extraordinary person—as a superman—Raskolnikov finds himself driven to murder an old, useless woman who, like Alberich in the *Ring*, is sitting on a hoard of treasure. Since this is a work of realism set in a nineteenth-century metropolis, her hoard is of course not the Rheingold. But it

---

9   Fyodor Dostoevsky, *Crime and Punishment*, trans. Richard Pevear and Larissa Volokhonsky (New York: Everyman's Library, 1993), 259.

is a no less mythical image, having been accumulated through a rapacious pawning operation. So, applying a master morality, Raskolnikov decides to kill the woman and take the money so that he may do something great in the world with his superhuman talents. Then, as he plans the well-reasoned if nihilistic deed, he has a "terrible dream."

Years later, Dostoevsky would publish a short story entitled "The Dream of a Ridiculous Man." That work is an account of a nihilist who, having lost confidence in the meaning of the world, resolves to kill himself. There is nothing "ridiculous" in such a state, of course. The author was using the word in an ironic sense to bring attention to a conviction that nihilism causes the disintegration rather than the liberation of the human personality. In *Crime and Punishment,* this tragedy is displayed even more vividly in another dream.

In Raskolnikov's dream, the protagonist is not an adult in full possession of his energies and aims in life. He is a child. What is more, a religious holiday is underway, and he is in the presence of his kindhearted father. They are walking down a street near a church they attend, and the child finds his thoughts dwelling on the beauty of the services there, the ancient icons, and the old, gentle priest. He sees the church graveyard where his beloved family members lie. He crosses himself piously.

But near this peaceful place there is something . . . evil. He keeps looking at it fearfully over his shoulder. It turns out to be a tavern in front of which drunken men are yelling, cursing, and brawling. Then he notices something more—a horse. It is a skinny old nag attached to a decrepit cart. The sight of the animal reminds the child painfully of how, from the security of his home, he would watch as such animals were often beaten cruelly,

> so painfully, so painfully, sometimes even on the muzzle and eyes, and he would feel so sorry, so sorry as he watched it that he almost wept, and his mother would always take him away from the window.

Now, in his dream, something more horrible occurs. The owner of the horse decides, with a bestial assertion of will, to kill the animal. "Whip the daylights out of her . . . I'll whip her to death!" he screams. "Have you no fear of God?" a bystander asks. No, he does not. The horse, he explains, is "my goods." As he proceeds to whip her, others standing by join in with their own weapons. The bloodbath finally ends when the meek animal collapses to the ground, dead. "'Papa, what did they . . . kill . . . the poor horse for!'" the boy Raskolnikov cries. "He throws his arms around his father, but there is such strain, such strain in his chest. He tries to take a breath, to cry out, and wakes up."[10] And that is how the dream of a ridiculous superman named Raskolnikov ends.

Dostoevsky, of course, intended the episode to serve as a mystical premonition of what was about to take place in the nihilistic plan of the protagonist. With amazing psychological insight (Sigmund Freud would himself later praise it), the author used the dream as an insight into the soul of a modern man who, captured by the spirit of atheism, begins to realize that without God there can be no limits on human behavior—that, as a character in a later novel will put it, "without God, anything is permissible."

For the moment, the shock of the spectacle is enough to cause Raskolnikov to reconsider his murderous design.

His whole body was as if broken; his soul was dark and troubled. He leaned his elbows on his knees and rested his head in both hands. "God!" he exclaimed, "but can it be, can it be that I will really take an axe and hit her on the head and smash her skull . . . slip in the sticky, warm blood, break the lock, steal, and tremble, and hide, all covered with blood . . . with the axe . . . Lord, can it be?"[11]

For a moment, the superman is humbled and in the face of his dream-revelation resolves not to commit the murder. He even resorts to a kind of prayer.

But for Dostoevsky, the spiritual realist, reason is not the only force that controls human behavior. As the protagonist walks home from the experience, he "chances" by a market where he overhears a conversation about the

---

10   Ibid., 54–59.
11   Ibid., 59.

pawnbroker and the fact that she will be alone in her home the following day. The demons take it from there.

Arriving at his own apartment,

He walked in like a man condemned to death. He was not reasoning about anything, and was totally unable to reason; but he suddenly felt with his whole being that he no longer had any freedom either of mind or of will, and that everything had been suddenly and finally decided.[12]

On the following day, he visits the old woman and murders her with an axe. Contrary to plan, he also murders her mentally disabled and innocent sister, who appears on the scene unexpectedly.

And this brings us to the second anecdote. It is nonfictional and relates to the life of Nietzsche. Dostoevsky almost certainly never read a work by Nietzsche, and nowhere in his correspondence is there a reference to the philosopher.[13] But we know Nietzsche read Dostoevsky. He mentions the Russian novelist more than once in his later writings and praises his psychological insights. Whether he had heard of *Crime and Punishment* we will never know.

But it is certainly amazing to consider that, as we saw in the previous chapter, Nietzsche went mad after witnessing someone beating a horse. It was a nearly identical scenario of cruelty to that experienced by Raskolnikov. In Raskolnikov, Dostoevsky's intention was obviously to reveal the spiritual reality of a self-proclaimed "extraordinary" man convinced that he has the right to defy divine law. Nietzsche was likewise convinced he was a superman. He celebrated rather than shrank from the thought of cruelty. "The

---

12 Ibid., 62.

13 Dostoevsky did hear the music of Wagner, however. And strangely, given the latter's spiritual extremities and violent psychological insights, Dostoevsky thought very little of "that tiresome German scoundrel." Alas, history often does not do what the historian would like it to do. Few other intellectuals of the nineteenth century were better poised than Dostoevsky to fathom the transgressive meaning of Wotan's cry, "Whoever fears the tip of my spear shall never cross through the fire!" Dostoevsky's comment is quoted in Geir Kjetsaa, *Fyodor Dostoevsky: A Writer's Life* (New York: Fawcett, 1987), 207.

sight of suffering does one good," we noted him in the first chapter as writing, and "the infliction of suffering does one more good." But when actually confronted with it, he too, like the purely fictional Raskolnikov, began a descent into madness. It turned out he was merely man and not a superman.

Nietzsche's loss of sanity was a kind of affirmation of what Dostoevsky had earlier claimed, under the influence of traditional Christianity, about humanity: Man cannot go beyond good and evil. He is a moral creature made in God's image and bound by laws established by God. Atheism is an anthropological delusion.

Repentance Will Save the World

THE SOLUTION TO NIHILISM THEREFORE becomes not mythological world building but repentance. Under the influence of traditional Christianity, first-millennium Christendom had inspired the transformation of the world through a "change of heart" (a literal translation of *metanoia*, the Greek word for repentance). From the time of the Papal Reformation, the new Christendom of the West—while maintaining strong emphasis on the value of repentance—elevated indignation as another means of bringing about the transformation of the world. Indignation had been the keynote of Gregory VII's seminal pontificate, from which flowed so much of normative Western civilization for the next half millennium. Within this development were included the great acts of militancy that occurred under the banner of the cross, such as the crusades and the wars of Western religion. Indignation at an untransformed world only intensified when paradise was replaced by utopia in the wake of the Renaissance.

By the nineteenth century, secular ideologies had gone beyond indignation in breeding contempt for any obstacles to progress, especially human ones. Dehumanization was loosed throughout the West. As we have seen, Russia's westernized intelligentsia thoroughly assimilated this tendency and in many ways brought it to its most extreme levels. Consumed by the burning questions of progress, its members considered moral indignation and ideological contempt to be cardinal virtues. As we shall see, Russian revolutionaries would set an example to the rest of the West in the great violence—and nihilism—that was to come. Dostoevsky saw this on the horizon. For him, only a radically different solution to the transformational imperative could possibly save utopian Christendom from the impending catastrophe.

For Dostoevsky, repentance would save the world. He would become famous for the statement—assigned to the most winsome of all his characters, Prince Myshkin—that "beauty will save the world." The statement is often quoted and has taken its place within debates about the problems of the modern West. However, the beauty in question is not just any sort of beauty. It is the transcendent beauty of Christ, which, as we noted above, had early in Dostoevsky's life become the principal defense against atheism and the nihilism to which it led. The world would be saved by such beauty, and it would do so by being transformed by it. Heavenly transformation thus required repentance—a change of heart.

Such beauty Dostoevsky located in the most paradoxical of sources. Orthodoxy, the theologian Thomas Hopko noted, is characterized by "paradoxy." Dostoevsky was only finding what had been retained by traditional Christianity for centuries. He was an avid reader of Isaac of Syria, who experienced the destruction of his native society by the Muslim Arabs. He also found mystical consolation in the Book of Job. The nearly total loss of everything good in this world and the resilient, defiant faith in God's love that this book expresses stirred his imagination. Job inspired a lifetime's reflection on suffering. As the author put it in a letter to his wife, the story of Job (which is read in the Orthodox Church during the course of Passion Week) "transports me to ecstasy. I put the book down and pace the room for as much as an hour. I almost weep."[14]

Mystical theologians and the long-suffering Job, regulated and illumined by his lifelong reading of the New Testament (which, as we noted, began earnestly in prison camp), filled Dostoevsky with a vision of spiritual beauty that was not of this world but was paradoxically accessible in this world. Only this, he believed, could rescue the West from its increasingly self-destructive tendencies toward nihilism.

---

14 *Selected Letters of Fyodor Dostoevsky*, 406.

His novels always present their protagonists with a challenge—or, perhaps better, an opportunity—to repent. A good example is the case of Raskolnikov. After the double murder, he fails utterly to live out the vision of self-mastery articulated by his notorious article. As we noted, his plan was to acquire the pawnbroker's hoard of treasure to use for his education and the betterment of society. However, he immediately buries the treasure under a rock, and that is the last the reader hears of it in the story. What remains during the great majority of the novel is his "punishment." The experience of this punishment, though, is entirely interior. It leads to repentance.

To reach this goal, Raskolnikov must encounter another character who represents traditional Christianity. Her name is Sonya, and she makes for a paradoxical witness to the gospel. She is a prostitute and an example of spiritual transformation in the face of the world's darkness. She is forced by her alcoholic father to sell her body to support the family that he has all but abandoned. When he finally dies of an accident in the street, her mother, whose surname, Marmeladova, translates absurdly as Mrs. Gumdrop, is forced to stand on the street corner to beg. Suffering from progressive tuberculosis, she teaches her horde of children to dance about ridiculously in hopes of attracting merciful passersby. Few stop to help.[15]

In the face of crushing circumstances, Sonya holds fast to her Christian faith. It is a statement about Dostoevsky's belief in redemption that he assigns to her the role of leading an atheist out of his moral delusion. She is an example of the suffering that Dostoevsky believed was at the heart of any sincere response to the nihilistic indignation of his time. Instead of lashing out at others or seizing on violent secular ideologies, Sonya, like Job, quietly but resolutely places all hope in God. Raskolnikov exhibits wild swings of

---

15 In this Mrs. Gumdrop's fate can be attributed in part to the rise of Social Darwinism and even Marxism, in that both humanistic counterfeits of traditional Christianity, while coming from opposite ideological points of view (liberal and socialist, respectively), served to abandon the poor and vulnerable. Social Darwinism scorned people consigned by "natural selection" to elimination, while Marxism taught that caring for desperate workers such as the Marmeladovs neutralized the "immiseration" necessary for them to become violently revolutionary. On these ironic fruits of secular humanism, see *Age of Utopia*, chapters 9 and 10.

temperament throughout the novel, but her character, even more crushed by sorrow, is spiritually adamant.

In a scene that represents a turning point in Raskolnikov's character development, the protagonist asks Sonya about her paradoxical faith. He then impulsively asks her to read to him from the Gospel of Saint John. The passage he desires to hear is the raising of Lazarus, which is assigned in the Orthodox Church to the Saturday before Palm Sunday, the beginning of Passion Week.

As she begins to read, it is clear that Dostoevsky is using the scene symbolically in an allusion to the liturgy and sacraments. These were, to repeat, the heart of the paradisiacal culture of the old Christendom. The theme in this case is spiritual resurrection through suffering and repentance. Sonya plays the symbolical role of a priest. She proclaims the Gospel as the priest or deacon would do at the Divine Liturgy on Lazarus Saturday. The reading leads to a change of heart in Raskolnikov, to whom the Nietzschean morality he formerly held now seems terribly mistaken. The analogue, of course, is the person who has spent forty days of fasting during the course of Lent and has arrived at Passion Week with "a broken and contrite heart." When the reading of the Gospel is concluded, Sonya—still functioning symbolically as priest—is the first to hear the murderer's confession. Then, after the penitent asks her what he must do to be saved, she urges him to undertake a healing act of penance. She sends him out into the marketplace—representing the ecclesial community within the world—to ask for forgiveness.

"Go now, this minute," she authoritatively commands,

stand in the crossroads, bow down, and first kiss the earth you've defiled, then bow to the whole world, on all four sides, and say aloud to everyone: "I have killed!" Then God will send you life again. Will you go? Will you go?[16]

Raskolnikov goes. And though it still takes time for him to gain the faith needed to bring his confession to the police, he finally does this as well.

The last scene of the novel is set, appropriately, during the liturgical

---

16 Dostoevsky, *Crime and Punishment*, 420.

season of Christ's Resurrection at Pascha. The place is also appropriate, given what we know about Dostoevsky's own journey of repentance. The scene takes place in a Siberian prison camp, where Raskolnikov has been sent as punishment for his crime. We are even told that he keeps a copy of the New Testament under his pillow. But the end of the story is also a beginning, for, like sacramental baptism, the desert of the prison colony opens to the penitent an entirely new life.

The radiant conclusion to the story of Raskolnikov's rise and fall and rise again could not be more different from the end of another character in the same novel, Svidrigailov. Dostoevsky used the latter as a device he called the "double," a character onto whom a protagonist's attributes are projected to reveal things about the protagonist that would otherwise remain obscure. In this case, Svidrigailov reveals what would have happened to Raskolnikov had he not repented.

Raskolnikov's name is rooted in the Russian word for "division." It brings to mind the schismatic Old Believers (*raskolniky*), who had separated themselves from the Orthodox Church in the seventeenth century. But it also signifies one who sets himself against the human community in general, as did the megalomaniacal Nietzsche. The superman's tendency toward nihilistic separation is manifested in Raskolnikov's double. Svidrigailov is to all appearances also an atheist. What is more, he appears in the story standing over Raskolnikov and eerily smiling at him when the protagonist awakes from a nap. At one point he even declares with conviction that the two men are really "apples from the same tree." The remark unsettles Raskolnikov, for his double turns out to be a rapist and a murderer. Yet Svidrigailov joins Raskolnikov in the self-described category of the "extraordinary." Instead of using murder for the advancement of progress, he simply uses it for the satisfaction of sensual desires.

Dostoevsky believed that atheism inevitably leads a human being made in the image of God to a point of self-destruction. All his great novels therefore contain an act of suicide. Svidrigailov is a case in point. Completely dead to God, separated by his passions from other men, he wanders from one lecherous encounter to another and in one case nearly rapes Raskolnikov's virtuous sister. There are for him no moral absolutes. There is only the will to power. And succumbing to the "nastiness" of a world in which he is separated from all other human beings by nihilism, Svidrigailov resolves to kill himself. Significantly, as he begins to commit the act with a pistol while standing on the Neva embankment, a passing policeman—instead of intervening with compassion—merely scolds him by saying "you can't do that here!"

Even more stunning than the case of Svidrigailov is the suicide of a character in the novel *Demons*. Kirillov is not just an atheist. He is so committed to the denial of God's existence that he actually concocts a plan to kill himself with the belief that doing so will prove the denial. The bizarre plan might be seen as a kind of variation on Nietzsche's theme that "God is dead." It is certainly an act of nihilism. But Kirillov's will toward self-destruction gets even stranger. He comes to the conclusion that by killing himself, he will in fact become god. Since suicide is the ultimate act of the will, its execution results in the overthrow of divinity. The suicidal superman deifies himself. The fact that this was a status that could be enjoyed only posthumously does not dissuade Kirillov from following through with the act.

The link between atheism and suicide—and the potential of repentance to heal both—is most dramatically represented by the protagonist of *Demons*, Nikolay Stavrogin. He is a shady figure throughout the book's narrative, inspiring other revolutionaries to acts of destruction yet remaining contemptuously aloof and separated from them. In the end, he too kills himself. But the most interesting element in his character development is found in a chapter that was removed by the censor due to its disturbing content. Happily, that chapter is usually interpolated into modern editions of the novel.

Stavrogin is the ultimate superman. He is, of course, an atheist. He is also in complete possession of his will, or so he believes. "I am always master of myself when I want to be," he declares.[17] Claiming that there is "no good or evil," he feels completely free to exercise his will to power over all others—from strong figures like fellow revolutionaries to weak ones like little girls. With his Nietzschean persona, he decides on a whim to rape

---

17 Fyodor Dostoevsky, *Demons*, trans. Richard Pevear and Larissa Volokhonsky (New York: Everyman's Library, 2000), 693.

an eleven-year-old named Matryosha. The event is described in horrifying detail, which resulted in the censorial removal of the chapter from the original edition. Dostoevsky uses his mastery of literary realism to relate it. One afternoon, Stavrogin finds himself alone with the girl, as he rents a room from her parents. He forces himself on her and then disappears for a number of days. When he returns to the home, he is met by the girl's concerned mother, who reports that little Matryosha has lost weight and is at death's door. Strangely, she reports, in her delirium the girl keeps on repeating the strange words, "I killed God!" Stavrogin is unmoved. He later finds himself in the sitting room, staring out the window, when suddenly Matryosha appears from behind a partition. He can scarcely believe his eyes. The eleven-year-old child, ravaged by guilt and self-hatred, is staring at him menacingly with the ferocity of a lioness. He is tempted to laugh at the apparition. But then she does something that fills the nihilist with unexpected dread. She raises her "little fist" in the air and begins shaking it at him in moral reproach.

Soon Matryosha withdraws from the room, and Stavrogin returns his attention to the window. Dostoevsky's command of psychological realism is here at its height. A fly buzzes about. Stavrogin perceives a small red spider spinning its web in the window frame. Then a faint sound is heard of a door opening and closing. The protagonist has a premonition that it was the girl who made the sound, and what she has left the apartment to do. He waits, exercising his iron will not to follow her too soon. When he has determined that it is finally time, he gets up, goes into the hallway to a closet door, and opens it. There, as he expected, he finds the dead body of Matryosha hanging from a rope.

This is not where Dostoevsky leaves one of his most intense and revealing accounts of nihilism, however. There is more to Stavrogin's story, just as there was for Raskolnikov after he committed the double murder. Yet Stavrogin's story does not involve repentance.

Years have passed, and the wandering superman has committed innumerable other acts of transgression. One day, however, he finds himself in a German town where a missed train forces him to spend time in a museum. He takes a particular interest in Claude Lorrain's *Acis and Galatea*, a baroque work representing a kind of utopia on the shores of the Mediterranean. That evening, back at his hotel, he has a dream. Like Raskolnikov's, it provides a mystical revelation of moral reality.

The dream starts out well. Stavrogin is graced with a vision of Lorrain's painting again, and this time with an intensified feeling of world harmony. He begins to weep as he meditates on the secular well-being that the painting's warm scenery communicates. Just as tears of joy begin to flow down his cheeks, however, the dream shifts into something different. As he gazes into the landscape of utopian happiness, he suddenly perceives, dropping down in front of him . . . the image of a small red spider. Suddenly, he is back in Matryosha's home, sitting by the window, watching her as she shakes her little fist at him in moral reproach. He nearly chokes in terror. And with this, the dream ends.

This story, which makes up the excised chapter of *Demons*, paradoxically takes place in a monastery to which Stavrogin has gone on an impulse to confess his transgression. But unlike Raskolnikov, he does not follow through with an act of repentance. The atheist never obtains forgiveness, because in the end he never repents. In the final scene of the novel he is discovered, as Matryosha had been, swinging from a rope with which he has killed himself.

For until the end, we are told, the man who believed he could go beyond good and evil had regularly seen the girl's pathetic little fist shaking itself at him, as if in an act of divine judgment. "This is what I cannot bear," Stavrogin confides, "because since [the day of Matryosha's suicide] it appears to me almost every day. It does not appear on its own, but I myself evoke it, and cannot help evoking it, even though I cannot live with it."[18]

Proclaiming the Godman

SO DOSTOEVSKY REJECTED THE UTOPIAN values of the intelligentsia and what he considered their monstrous outcome, moral nihilism. But his challenge to post-Christian Christendom also had an emphatically affirmative

---

18 Ibid., 704.

element. Drawing instead on the traditional Christian values of the Orthodox Church, he presented an image of modern man that was modeled on Jesus Christ.

Known in theology as the "Godman" (*Theanthropos* in Greek), Christ is proclaimed to be both God and man. Since the time of Pentecost, the Church has taught that through the Incarnation the divine nature was joined inseparably to human nature. This dogma has long nourished the anthropology and cosmology of Eastern Christendom. For instance, iconography, the practice of depicting divinely transfigured humanity with painted images, was defended on incarnational grounds at the Seventh Ecumenical Council. Hesychasm, too, the ancient practice of prayer of the heart resulting in participation in God's immediate, divine energies, was defended on incarnational grounds by Saint Gregory Palamas. These themes were also found in the Latin West, especially during the first millennium, but they began to recede in connection with the Great Division. Frankish theologians—the leading voice of Latin Christendom—all but rejected the incarnational doctrine of iconography during the ninth century. Centuries later, their scholastic successors in the new Christendom looked on the incarnational vision of hesychasm with great suspicion. Orthodox Christianity, on the other hand, continued after the Great Division to nourish the old Christendom of the East with an incarnational doctrine of salvation known widely as *deification*.

Dostoevsky drew on this as he searched for a solution to modern man's moral and spiritual plight. In addition to reading Eastern fathers such as Isaac of Syria, he took an interest in the revival of ancient monasticism in places like Optina Pustyn, where the practice of hesychasm, largely in abeyance since the time of Peter the Great, was being revived. Dostoevsky made a pilgrimage to Optina soon after the death of his firstborn son and used his experience speaking with the elders there to develop characters for his last two novels. The most famous of these characters was Elder Zosima in *The Brothers Karamazov*. He expresses a radiant love for the beauty of the world. But his characteristically Eastern affirmation of the cosmos did not blind him to the terrible darkness that also pervades it.

That darkness can reach an unbearable peak. In *The Brothers Karamazov*,

Optina Pustyn

for instance, the reader endures scene after scene of misery and despair, culminating, perhaps, in the images of human cruelty that Ivan presents to his brother Alyosha as a prelude to the famous "Legend of the Grand Inquisitor." To explain why he is an atheist, Ivan assembles a catalog of anecdotes that document the way people have tortured the innocent over the ages. He brings attention to cases such as Turkish soldiers impaling infants on their bayonets before the eyes of mothers; Protestant clergymen convincing a condemned youth that his execution is the happiest day of his life because it will bring an end to his sinfulness; Orthodox parents flogging their seven-year-old daughter with a barbed stick as she cries out in terror, "Papa, Papa, dear Papa!"; a five-year-old girl who is locked in a freezing outhouse all night as punishment for wetting her bed, and whose mother then smears her face with excrement while she prays to a "dear God" for protection; a Russian landlord who takes revenge on a peasant boy who accidentally injures his hunting dog by having him torn to pieces before the eyes of his mother.

And so on. Because of these and other examples of the darkness of the human condition in this world, Ivan declares himself in rebellion against God. It is not a doctrinal atheism so much as a moral atheism, an act of will. He accepts that intellectually he is flawed and may be wrong about the nonexistence of God. But that is beside the point. He cannot accept God as He is defended by what is called Christian "theodicy." This technical term was an invention of Western Christendom. It was introduced during the eighteenth century to justify the existence of a good God who allows evil to take place in His creation. Theodicy was parodied by the famous deist Voltaire in his novel *Candide*. It is highly significant that Dostoevsky had long spoken of the intention to write a "Russian *Candide*," and that *The Brothers Karamazov* is the culmination of the project. For the atheistic Ivan, there is simply no moral justification for a belief in God. For Ivan, as for Nietzsche, God is dead.

His pious brother's response to such nihilism is profound but paradoxical: There is no "answer" to the problem of human suffering, but only silence and love. Alyosha's mystical rather than rational faith enables him to see beyond the world to the kingdom of heaven and there to find the strength and inspiration to live with both joy and suffering. Otherwise, rationalism and the egoistical will that drives it produce only atheism. And from this is born nihilism. "Without God," his brother Dmitri famously observes, ". . . everything is permitted."[19]

Out of the darkness of human suffering and under the shadow of atheistic despair, Dostoevsky provided one of the most convincing witnesses to Christianity in modern thought. It was a totally different approach to suffering and the shortcomings of the world from that which progressive intellectuals found in secular ideology. It was a witness that is gentle, lacking assertions and polemics. It was neither morally indignant nor ideologically contemptuous. Dostoevsky, as we have seen, was a believer among atheists all his life. Though he was personally subject to strident convictions and regarded many of his contemporaries with deep disdain, in a hero like Alyosha a mystical confidence in Christ prevails.

Another affirmative example of faith in Christ is found in *The Idiot*. Its protagonist, Prince Lev Myshkin, was designed by the author to be an example of a Christlike figure within a world torn apart by egoism and self-destruction. Interestingly, the author refers to him in his notebooks as "Prince Christ," and he spoke of him as representing a "truly beautiful human being." In this sense, the book is a statement of Dostoevsky's anthropology, grounded as it was in the incarnational piety of the Orthodox Church. Indeed, the very name of the prince is an allusion to Christ as the Godman. Lev is the Russian equivalent of Leo, meaning "lion." *Mysh* is the Russian word for "mouse." Prince "Lion-Mouse," then, is really a manifestation, in literary form, of the two natures of Jesus Christ.

---

19 Fyodor Dostoevsky, *The Brothers Karamazov*, trans. Richard Pevear and Larissa Volokhonsky (New York: Everyman's Library, 1990), 589.

Throughout the novel, the prince encounters only brokenness. The most poignant example perhaps is that of Nastasya Filippovna. When she is a girl, first her mother and then her father are tragically killed in accidents. Dostoevsky actually paraphrases the Book of Job when narrating the sudden loss of her family. Orphaned, she is taken in by a philanthropic capitalist, who sends her to his summer estate and then, as she begins to bloom in her early beauty, becomes much less philanthropic. He begins to rape her on a regular basis. When the novel begins, he is in the process of "selling her off" to an associate's friend in order to be rid of her and escape responsibility for his immoral actions. But then the violent and lustful Rogozhin enters the story. Himself cruel and irrational by nature, he tries to win Nastasya in order to dominate her himself. In the end Rogozhin, having finally gained possession of the tragedy-plagued girl, murders her with a knife on their wedding night.

The prince enters into this drama as a fool, a veritable "idiot." Guided by compassion and selfless love for others, he regularly witnesses to the values of traditional Christianity.

One example is his views on art. When visiting Rogozhin's house, he notes a painting on the wall that contrasts with traditional iconography. The painting is a work of the Renaissance, Hans Holbein's *Christ in the Tomb*. This famous work, like others from the dawn of utopian Christendom, was composed in the naturalist style. Hailed as the rebirth of the pagan painting of antiquity, naturalism celebrated the world in its spiritually untransformed state. Emphasizing fleshy bodies, three-dimensional space, and shadows, it deviated significantly from the painting of Byzantium and Russia before Peter the Great.[20]

As Myshkin himself notes, traditional Christian iconography never depicts the Crucifixion of Christ without expressing hope in the Resurrection. An icon of the deposition of Christ in the tomb, for instance, typically shows a dead Christ whose body is radiant and beautiful, symbolizing the victory over death that is to come. In the case of Holbein, however, Christ is pictured as a cadaver. His body is stiff with rigor mortis, his cracked lips

---

20 For an account of Renaissance painting in the context of traditional iconography, see *Age of Utopia*, 62–73.

gape wordlessly, and his dead eyes stare vacantly at nothing.

"I like looking at that painting," the godless Rogozhin mutters. Myshkin's reaction—filled with mysticism—serves as a statement by the author about the whole trajectory of utopian Christendom: "At that painting!" the prince exclaims. "A man could even lose his faith from that painting!"[21]

Dostoevsky, along with Wagner and Nietzsche before him, was fascinated by the possibility of a Christendom without Christ, though in a radically dif-

Dostoevsky at the time of writing The Brothers Karamazov

ferent way. Together, the three prophets of nihilism contemplated the end of utopia. They were before their time, to be sure. Wagner's "music of the future" was scorned by the contemporary musical establishment. Nietzsche was likewise largely disdained. In the preface to *The Antichrist*, for instance, he conceded that his philosophy belonged to "the day after tomorrow." Dostoevsky was often condemned by the progressive leadership of the intelligentsia as an irrelevant reactionary. In his case, the forward-looking solution to utopia was found not in nihilism but in the paradisiacal culture of Eastern Christendom.

Alyosha, the hero of *The Brothers Karamazov*, longs for the kingdom of

---

21 Fyodor Dostoevsky, *The Idiot*, trans. Richard Pevear and Larissa Volokhonsky (New York: Everyman's Library, 2001), 218.

heaven, and his ecstatic words about its presence in this world express the convictions of the author. At a turning point in the novel, Alyosha has a vision of the heavenly transformation of the world while standing over the dead body of his departed teacher, Elder Zosima. Leaving the temple, he suddenly finds heaven coming down upon the earth. The experience is profoundly mystical and no different from that cultivated for nearly two millennia by the paradisiacal culture of the old Christendom.

Filled with rapture, his soul yearned for freedom, space, vastness. Over him the heavenly dome, full of quiet, shining stars, hung boundlessly. From the zenith to the horizon the still-dim Milky Way stretched its double strand. Night, fresh and quiet, almost unstirring, enveloped the earth. The towers and golden domes of the church gleamed in the sapphire sky. The luxuriant autumn flowers in their flowerbeds near the house had fallen asleep until morning. The silence of the earth seemed to merge with the silence of the heavens, the mystery of the earth touched the mystery of the stars . . . Alyosha stood gazing and suddenly, as if he had been cut down, threw himself

The study in which Dostoevsky wrote The Brothers Karamazov *and in which he died*

to the earth. . . . It was as if threads from all those innumerable worlds of God all came together in his soul, and it was trembling all over, "touching other worlds." He wanted to forgive everyone and for everything, and to ask forgiveness.[22]

---

22 Dostoevsky, *Brothers Karamazov*, 362.

CHAPTER THREE

Dehumanization

CHRISTENDOM'S INCREASINGLY POST-CHRISTIAN CULTURAL ELITE proved ill equipped to appreciate Dostoevsky's vision of man and the cosmos. Wagnerian transgression and Nietzschean transvaluation were more to its taste. Both, after all, gave expression to a mounting contempt for the surrounding society. The achievements of utopia may have been impressive on economic and political levels, but on a cultural level things were different. The apparent smugness of the growing middle class and the limitations it imposed on the transformational imperative caused grave disappointment among those in the business of critical reflection and cultural creativity.

Nietzsche was the most celebrated among them. With his genealogical approach to values, he had argued that humanism was nothing more than a counterfeit of traditional Christianity. He had exposed religiously rooted epistemological assumptions behind Descartes's statement "I think therefore I am" (*cogito ergo sum*), the basis for modern rationalism. He had exposed religiously rooted political assumptions behind Rousseau's "social contract," the basis for modern democracy. In "old Kant," he had exposed religiously rooted ethical assumptions behind the concept of "intuition," the basis for modern individualism. Philosophizing with his hammer, Nietzsche left few of his predecessors standing and little in their humanistic philosophies that was free of suspicion.

It was becoming increasingly evident that utopia was threatened by the very beliefs and values that inspired it. Secular humanism had reoriented

Western culture toward the saeculum—the spiritually untransformed world—and made a place for humanity within it. Man, less a descendant of Adam than the unrestrained offspring of Prometheus, was now autonomous in his capacity to cultivate a perfect world. This secular form of the transformational imperative provided a way of reorienting the beliefs and values of the West, especially after reformational Christianity disgraced itself in the wars of Western religion. But by the beginning of the twentieth century, it was clear there was something wrong with secular humanism.

With utopia sinking into mediocrity and paradise long forgotten, the transformation of the world no longer demanded promethean autonomy—let alone reformational indignation or penitential humility. It demanded annihilation. Nietzsche's "transvaluation of values" would not occur on a mass scale for another century. But for the generation of elites that lived before the First World War, nihilism offered cultural renewal.

The Solvent of Modernism

NIHILISM'S FOUNDING FATHERS WERE ALREADY being venerated at the dawn of the twentieth century. In a newly united German Empire, for instance, sculptors and architects were erecting Götterdämmerung Towers in city after city, demonstrating publicly the influence of Wagner's spiritually subversive art. For his part, the composer Richard Strauss—an enthusiastic Wagnerian—composed a musical monument to Nietzsche's *Thus Spake Zarathustra*. In an eponymous "tone poem" (then considered an innovative form of music), he envisioned the moment when the superman appears on earth. And he did so by appropriating Wagner's intoxicating orchestral technique. The opening of the work is called "Dawn," and its rousing use of brass would become famous long afterward when used in Stanley Kubrick's *2001: A Space Odyssey*. In that film's opening scene, a group of apelike hominids assembles near a watering hole when suddenly one clubs another to death, marking the appearance of the will to power—the defining characteristic of the biological species known as *Homo sapiens*.

Other composers were inspired by less violent elements of *Zarathustra*. Gustav Mahler, romanticism's last great symphonist and another Wagnerian, incorporated a famous poetic aside known as "Zarathustra's Roundelay" into the fourth movement of his Third Symphony. The results were exquisite but decidedly ominous. Interestingly, both musical homages to the raving philosopher's magnum opus premiered during the same year—1896—on the very cusp of Christendom's most terrible century.

To be sure, not all intellectuals fell under Wagner's or Nietzsche's spell. In the field of classical music, Johannes Brahms (d. 1897) continued to build on the conventions of early romanticism, as did less prolific composers like Antonin Dvorak (d. 1902) and Sergey Rachmaninov (d. 1943).

But a nihilistic tendency was gaining ground in the arts, even when allusions to Wagner or Nietzsche remained only implicit. An example is the extraordinarily rebellious music of Igor Stravinsky. He produced a triad of ballets in the years before the First World War that radically subverted utopian Christendom's musical legacy. As Nietzsche had taken a hammer to metaphysics, so Stravinsky took one to the received tonal system of Western music. *The Rite of Spring* (1913) went the furthest.[1] It actually caused a riot when it premiered in Paris, bringing to mind the comparable reception of Wagner's *Tannhäuser* there a half century earlier. Stravinsky's self-conscious assault on bourgeois taste included the celebration of pre-Christian sexuality (in this case the bacchanalia of *Tannhäuser* found a successor in pagan fertility dances). The ballet reached its climactic end when, in the middle of the stage, the human sacrifice of a virgin was enacted. The work's most flamboyant innovation was its chaotic mix of tonal structures. Apollonian proportionality, to paraphrase Nietzsche, gave way to dithyrambic dissolution. Stravinsky even employed a frenetic drumbeat inspired by native African dance to make his point. The melodic tradition of classical music, born five centuries earlier in the Renaissance, had been shattered.

So had that most famous of Renaissance art forms, painting. It all started with something called Impressionism. This was the forerunner of a cacophony of styles that came to be known as modernism. Impressionism appeared first in France after her defeat in the Franco-Prussian War. A work shown in 1874 by Claude Monet entitled *Impression, Sunrise* provided the style

---

1   The other two works were *The Firebird* (1910) and *Petrushka* (1911).

with a name. Its adherents preferred outdoor settings to the confines of a studio. Shifting patterns of light and the play of shadows enabled them to emphasize the transitory character of human existence. They preferred spontaneity to study and ephemerality to eternity. Not only were depictions executed swiftly, but the brush strokes used to represent objects grew broader and less precise. By the end of his life, Monet was painting water lilies that scarcely looked like water lilies.

Portrait of Igor Stravinsky, *1920, by Pablo Picasso*

But that was the point. Since the Renaissance, the world had been represented in Western painting with naturalistic techniques. The goal had always been objectivity. Yet in the wake of romanticism, painting began to emphasize subjectivity. German landscape artist Caspar David Friedrich had declared the painter should not paint what lies before him but rather what lies within him. This principle, a by-product of romanticism's cult of the creative genius, now found fuller expression among the Impressionists. They suggested that reality was contingent on perceptions, such as those that reveal water lilies one way at noon and another at sunset. This ephemeral approach to the world was an insight paralleling Nietzsche's claim in *Ecce Homo* that truth is but a matter of optics.

The most successful Impressionist, Auguste Renoir (d. 1919), linked this insight to eroticism. More preoccupied by female nudes than any other great painter since Boucher, he once responded to a question about his technique by stating it was not his hands that adorned the canvas but his genitals. Perhaps Freud would have approved. It seems appropriate that a painter with this attitude was commissioned to paint the portrait of Richard Wagner just a year before the composer's death. The work was not particularly memorable, but it did exhibit the same dissolution of reality that occurred in Renoir's more famous compositions. One study, entitled *Torso of a Woman in the Sunlight* (1876), depicts a nude girl whose face is a blur and whose body is a mixture of fleshy pinks and almost cadaverous greens. Experimental use of colors and open-air subjects were the keys to Renoir's overwhelming charm. Liberated from the confines of nature yet delighting in the senses, his canvases, whether of solitary debutantes or gatherings of merrymakers, exude with their brightness and color a sense of moral weightlessness.

The gaiety of the bourgeoisie could seem frivolous to more earnest painters. Vincent van Gogh (d. 1890), for instance, was inclined to explore society's shadows. One of these was rural poverty. Another was mental illness. Van Gogh struggled with the latter affliction himself, and as he descended ever deeper into the depression that would eventually lead him to suicide, his brush strokes became increasingly unnaturalistic by Renaissance standards, expressing an inner life at odds with external reality. Subjectivity is apparent in his fascination with the self-portrait, a genre to which he turned

Tree Roots, *by Vincent van Gogh*

no fewer than forty-one times. Even landscapes revealed his crisis of objectivity. In the case of *Starry Night* (painted within an insane asylum), the effect is almost hallucinatory. Its swirling representation of moon and stars amid a color-saturated deep-blue sky is so arresting as to be auditory. At the time of his death, Van Gogh was at work on a study called *Tree Roots*. The stylistically gnarled and twisted representation of his subject in this case serves as a memorial to one of modern Christendom's most tormented and sympathetic geniuses.

Van Gogh is called a post-Impressionist because his bold use of colors and lines went much further than that of Monet or Renoir. But this school was itself soon superseded by one called Expressionism. Its early advocates included the Norwegian painter Edvard Munch, whose *Scream* (1893) remains an emblem not only of the dissolution of objective reality but of the promethean autonomy of modern man. Munch was a disciple of Nietzsche, and another of his works depicts the brooding father of nihilism with colors and brush stokes that make Monet's water lilies look almost naturalistic.

Even the Expressionists were soon divided among themselves. Visionaries declared the formation of subschools like so many Protestant confessions breaking away from one another in the heat of reformational zeal. By now, however, few of Christendom's artistic elite adhered to their culture's primordial faith. In fact, the most influential of them consciously looked to destroy Christianity. They were miserably restless and dissatisfied with the West.

But as tradition disintegrated, no style could withstand critical assault very long. Artists resorted to inflammatory (but seldom convincing) invectives called "manifestos." Modeled on revolutionary pronouncements of the nineteenth century—Marx's *Communist Manifesto* chief among them—they were really just febrile visions of a utopian culture on the brink of collapse. Apart from flourishes of rhetoric, artists' manifestos provided little in the way of values with which to inspire a new, post-Christian culture. Their indignation—inherited from Thomas More's original sixteenth-century *Utopia*—was in fact the long-term legacy of the eleventh-century Papal Reformation. But now, following Nietzsche's example, they transmuted indignation into contempt. With great vehemence, artist-agitators declaimed the decadence of Western society. But their calls for progress remained indeterminate. If they offered anything new, it was only the rejection of what the West had once been.

In 1905, for instance, a new school of German artists called the Bridge (*die Brücke*) declared their intention to transform society by eschewing all previously existing conventions—not only artistic but sexual. They turned leader Ernst Kirchner's apartment into a studio in which painting and sexual activity occurred simultaneously. With time they set up what was effectively a nudist colony at a forest lake outside Dresden. The goal was a total way of life that, inspired by Wagner's vision of the "total work of art," centered on free-floating aestheticism. Taking their cue from earlier nihilists, they hoped to subvert what they considered a bourgeois culture in which authentic transformation had become impossible. They found nothing of value in the present, and the only inspiration they found in the past was the affective painting of German masters like Matthias Grünewald (whose ghastly Isenheim altarpiece represented the demise of iconography during the Renaissance).[2]

The group claimed to offer a "bridge to utopia," but theirs was a very different utopia from that introduced by More during the Renaissance—or elaborated by his post-Christian heirs. Their vision of transformation was Nietzschean. One of their members, Ernst Heckel, created a primitivistic woodcut of the philosopher who had once commented that man is only a "bridge" to a higher form of biological life. Nietzsche's hero Zarathustra declares in one place,

> *Man is a rope stretched between the animal and the Superman—a rope over an abyss. . . . What is great in man is that he is a bridge and not a goal: what is lovable in man is that he is an over-going and a down-going. . . . I love the great despisers, because they are the great adorers, and arrows of longing for the other shore.*[3]

---

2   As Peter Gay aptly put it, "Brücke artists were intent on blowing up bridges to the past" rather than crossing them. Peter Gay, *Modernism: The Lure of Heresy* (New York: W. W. Norton, 2008), 125.

3   Nietzsche, *Thus Spake Zarathustra*, 8–9.

Bridge artists claimed their movement would be the means toward a surpassing of "the human, all-too human." As the superman became visible across the abyss, existing man—whether in the form of *Homo sapiens* or *Imago Dei*—was to be negated. As indignation turned to contempt, the imperative toward progress degenerated into the call to annihilate.

This is what explains Cubism. The most radical approach to art prior to the First World War, as a school it did to representational painting what Stravinsky did to tonal music: it annihilated tradition. The art movement had several advocates, but none so determined its course as did Pablo Picasso (d. 1973). A phenomenally creative painter, he contributed to a variety of styles during the course of his long career. Living the life of a bohemian artist in Paris, one day he was commissioned by the expatriate American collector Gertrude Stein to paint what would come to be a landmark of modernism. His patroness herself was heavily invested in the movement and used it as the context in which to publish some of the West's earliest examples of homoerotic literature. She appears to have helped establish the term "gay" as a synonym for "homosexual."

Picasso's *Portrait of Gertrude Stein* (1906) produces an image more masculine than feminine, with the subject's heavyset and inelegant figure hunching forward unselfconsciously. But the portrait's most notorious element is the face. More than the Expressionists, Picasso intentionally distorted the eyes so much that one is actually larger than the other and stares in a slightly different direction. Together these eyes occupy disparate planes on the canvas's surface. The effect is to destroy naturalistic objectivity.

Remarkably, that very effect is in a certain sense similar to one created by an ancient icon of Christ Pantocrator located at Saint Katherine Monastery on Mount Sinai. The latter work, produced in the sixth century, also features a subject with asymmetrical eyes. However, the purpose in that case seems to have been to emphasize the Godman's two natures, divine and human.

Picasso was an atheist and had no interest in exploring the doctrine of the Incarnation or the long-lost paradisiacal culture that sprang from it. But if this put him in league with secular humanists, his subversion of physical reality radically opposed him to humanistic naturalism. Picasso was announcing a vision of man never seen in the West since the onset of the Renaissance. Cubism, as foreseen in *Gertrude Stein*, would declare that man is neither dignified nor autonomous.

Picasso's artistic revolution was even more forcefully announced a year later in a work entitled *The Young Ladies of Avignon* (*Les Demoiselles d'Avignon*). Its subject was a collection of prostitutes. Sexual perversity was a key element in the world envisioned by the avant-garde. The Bridge group had mixed free love with painting, and Picasso himself maintained a long series of mistresses whose favors proved indispensable for his creativity. But rather than depict his *Demoiselles* in an alluring way, as Boucher would have done, Picasso represents the scene with awkward, geometrically exaggerated faces and bodies. Asymmetrical eyes again prevail. In one case, the prostitute's naked body ceases to be flesh and merges strangely with an abstract background. The effect is of a cartoon, not a celebration of natural beauty. This may have been a statement of ambiguity about the human value of the women in the artist's eyes. Having himself renounced virginity at a brothel when only thirteen years of age, he used and discarded scores of lovers and a couple of wives throughout his life. Among them, two suffered nervous breakdowns and two others committed suicide. Picasso once acknowledged that for him women were nothing more than a means of creative inspiration—either "goddesses or doormats."

A couple of details in the cultural significance of *Demoiselles* are of interest to any narrative about Christendom's descent into nihilism. Picasso produced numerous sketches in preparation for the final work. In these, two male figures appear. One, standing outside the circle of women, is a medical student—an allusion perhaps to the practice of having prostitutes examined by physicians for venereal disease. The other figure sits at the center of the circle and is a sailor—representing perhaps a self-destructive disdain for the risks of promiscuity. These two figures have been seen by art historians as clues to how the work was to be viewed. Knowing Picasso's interest in the *Birth of Tragedy*, they can be seen to express Nietzsche's concept of an Apollonian-Dionysian tension in Western culture: the student represents reason and order whereas the sailor represents untamable desire. What is interesting is that Picasso was himself undoubtedly drawn toward the latter "virtue," and this is why he places the sailor on the inside of the circle. He once declared his art to be a nihilistic "sum of destructions." Like his life, it was intended to produce a chaotic state unrestrained by reason or morality.

Another element of interest is the relationship *Demoiselles* thus has with earlier painting in Western civilization. Unlike painting since the Renaissance, the work gives little attention to content and concentrates its energies rather on form. The work is not about five prostitutes, or even, in the final version, their impact on the now absent sailor. It does not represent any reality at all. By geometrically dissolving the natural images of the women and exchanging the sailor for the viewer, it suggests man's autonomous personality—the key to secular humanism since the time of Petrarch—was disappearing. All that is left is desire.

And this links it in a very interesting way to traditional Christian iconography. Though of a totally different character with completely incompatible beliefs and values, first-millennium painting likewise did not seek to enhance personal autonomy. It emphasized both content and form, linking the content of an icon (such as Christ) with the viewer through an anagogic understanding of form. Incarnational theology, at odds with the counterfeit claims of naturalism, had protected Western art from the specter of nihilism.

But in the wake of Nietzsche, Cubism brought the dream of the Renaissance to an end. Naturalism had over the course of a half millennium killed iconographical transcendence, despite the heroic efforts of romantics to "supernaturalize" it. Beholding the counterfeit project of secular humanism with contempt, Nietzsche had announced the "death of God." Mocking transcendence, he looked to a purely immanent alternative called the will to power. Surging through humanity but offering no salvation, this force assured the West's longed-for transformation by annihilating man in an ecstasy of "self-overcoming." This, as we have seen, was the destiny of the superman. And the result was the dehumanization of man.

As with music and painting, so literature expressed a strong dissatisfaction with the culture of utopia. Here too rebellion in taste was closely connected to rebellion in moral conventions. The Frenchman Charles Baudelaire established a precedent. According to a contemporary, "he abhorred

Charles Baudelaire

philanthropists, progressists, utilitarians, humanitarians, utopists."[4] As a
poet he subverted everything a bourgeois reader would have expected in art.

---

4   Quoted in Camille Paglia, *Sexual Personae: Art and Decadence from Nefertiti to
Emily Dickinson* (New Haven, CT: Yale University Press, 1990), 429.

He was to poetry what Wagner was to music. He transformed it and by doing so inflicted on it a mortal wound. It is therefore not a coincidence that he was a self-proclaimed Wagnerian, defending the composer in the aftermath of the infamous Parisian staging of *Tannhäuser* in 1861. As Nietzsche himself put it, Baudelaire was simply "Wagner without the music."

In *Flowers of Evil,* published first in 1857, the poet managed to take the reader even deeper into the madness of Venusberg (the scene of exuberant sensuality in the opening of *Tannhäuser*). His choice of title suggested an effort at redefining beauty by merging the delightful and the demonic. Here Baudelaire goes beyond Wagner in negating good and evil. He actually commends Satan and not the goddess of erotic love as the symbolic source of human vitality. As he heartily declares in the opening, "It is the Devil who pulls the strings that move us!" An overwhelming and impersonal will to power, he suggests, drives man ever deeper beyond conventional boundaries of morality.[5]

Each day we go down one more step toward Hell,
Without horror, through the darkness which smells rank.

Just as a lustful pauper who kisses and bites
The martyred breast of an aged whore,
We steal, as we move along, a clandestine pleasure
Which we squeeze hard like an old orange.

Packed tight and swarming like a million maggots,
A crowd of demons carouse in our brains,
And, when we breathe, Death into our lungs
Descends, an invisible river, with heavy wailings.

---

5   Though Nietzsche knew of Baudelaire, the obverse was not the case due to their offset lifespans. But the vision of an impersonal force that takes possession of the individual subject in violation of humanistic autonomy is abundantly documented in the poet.

If rape, poison, the knife and arson
Have not yet woven with their pleasing patterns
The banal canvas of our pitiful fate,
It is because our soul, alas, is not bold enough.[6]

It is only through transgressive acts that man escapes the "boredom" that modern bourgeois life inflicts on him. These acts might be rape or murder. They might also be transgressive sexuality. Baudelaire originally intended his radical collection to bear the title *The Lesbians,* and indeed several individual poems within it address that subject.

The themes of sacrilege and homosexuality were soon taken up by other modernists. They inspired the work of Paul Verlaine (d. 1896), who, after abandoning wife and child to live with lover Arthur Rimbaud (d. 1891), shot the latter in a fit of jealousy. But the most public example of a new, post-Christian sexual morality was the case of Englishman Oscar Wilde (d. 1900). Married with two sons, he turned to a same-sex relationship that, in the legal atmosphere of Victorian England, resulted in a public trial and imprisonment. Even before this drama unfolded, he had published a work entitled *The Picture of Dorian Gray* (1890). It celebrates "art for art's sake"— that is, the primacy of aesthetical experience over spiritual truths and moral absolutes. The novel was a declaration of a new vision of Western values— one unrestricted not only by traditional Christianity but also by secular humanism.[7] It contributed to a new school in literary modernism, known variably to historians as the Aesthetic or Decadent movement. For its elitist membership, all values inherited from Christendom's distant and recent past were to be abandoned in exchange for a life of sensuality and rebellion.

These twin goals were, of course, the respective core virtues of Wagner and Nietzsche. And indeed, modernist authors in every corner of Europe drank heavily from those fathers of nihilism.

For instance, in Italy Gabriele D'Annunzio produced a work (derivatively

---

6   Charles Baudelaire, *The Flowers of Evil and Paris Spleen,* trans. Wallace Fowlie (Mineola, NY: Dover, 2010), 3.

7   Aestheticism, after all, had been Nietzsche's way of dismissing all claims to moral and spiritual absolutes.

entitled "The Case of Wagner") in which composer and philosopher were fused for fellow Italians into a single ideal. A novel entitled *The Triumph of Death* (1894) featured a protagonist who was "determined to lift himself above Good and Evil through the sheer energy of his will."[8] In another called *The Flame* (1900), D'Annunzio applied this vision to advance a Dionysian "transfiguration of life."

Nihilistic vitality excited other Italian literary figures as well. The most significant was Filippo Tommaso Marinetti, through whom modernism, in one historian's words, decisively "canceled [its] debt to humanism."[9] Like D'Annunzio, Marinetti could not evade the haunting influence of Wagner and Nietzsche. The two Germans provided the "two poles" between which he developed a new vision of life called Futurism.[10] The premise of this latest school of modernism was that the West had entered inescapably into a condition of decadence. Following Nietzsche's rebellion against tradition and history, it claimed authentic forms of life could be realized only when directed toward an as-yet incomplete future. Wagner's destabilization of artistic convention was also an inspiration.

In what is probably the most read and celebrated art manifesto of modernism, Marinetti "rejected autonomy as the category that defines art in bourgeois society." Since the rise of humanism during the Renaissance, art and the humanity it defined had idealized self-determination. It was in many ways a reaction against centuries of accumulated pessimism about the human condition.[11] Now man was surrendering to external forces once again, casting off the illusion of *autonomy* ("self-rule") and accepting an inescapable *heteronomy* ("other-rule"). Traditional Christianity had always proclaimed that man is not self-determined but rather a creature faced with the awesome responsibility of choosing to cooperate with the will of another—either God or the devil. But instead of opening man to the rule of God, as

---

8   Mark Thompson, *The White War: Life and Death on the Italian Front, 1915–1919* (New York: Basic Books, 2010), 41.

9   Ibid., 233.

10   Luca Somigli, *Legitimizing the Artist: Manifesto Writing and European Modernism, 1885–1915* (Toronto: University of Toronto Press, 2003), 106.

11   For the rise of humanism, see *Age of Utopia*, chapters 1–2.

the old Christendom of the first millennium had done, the new Christendom in its posthumanist phase assigned another "other" to rule man. In the case of Marinetti, this "other" was the will to power.

Nietzsche's posthumous influence extended even to Russia—especially into her capital city, known as a "window on the West." There the novelist Andrey Bely longed for a "ruthless and undeviating" morality to replace Christianity and found it in the concept of the superman. An essay of 1907 promoting the philosopher spoke of the coming death of existing morality and the birth of a "new man." Before the war, Bely planned a trilogy of novels entitled *East or West* to contrast a decrepit rationalism—the fruit of utopia—with a Dionysian culture free of humanism. He considered Western Christendom the source of the former and a neopagan (rather than Christian) East the promise of the latter. He never completed the project, but the second volume, entitled *Petersburg* (1913), is by all critical accounts emphatically Nietzschean. It features a revolutionary son named Nikolay Apollonovich planning the murder of his father, Apollon Apollonovich, a bureaucrat in the government of Nicholas II. The son is assisted by a Zarathustra type named Dudkin, who furnishes a bomb for the deed. Both father and son have a name taken from Apollo, Nietzsche's archetype of order and reason. The son, however, breaks the family mold. Surrendering to the will of Dudkin, he casts aside conventional morality and comes to realize "that he himself was a bomb." Like Nietzsche, Bely's hero becomes an agent of nihilism, the personification of moral dynamite.[12]

Across the continent in France, André Gide published a novel entitled *The Immoralist* (1903), in which the protagonist rejects the spent morality of his time and turns to a self-consciously Nietzschean vision of life. The

---

12 This is not to say the author himself was a nihilist. He was one of many contemporary Russians seeking what came to be called "a new religious consciousness," a vision of reality that was spiritual yet unconcerned with the doctrinal integrity of traditional Christianity. Deeply affected by the "myth-creation" advocated in *Birth of Tragedy*, he syncretized (among other elements) Dionysus and Christ. And as one scholar has noted, "in *Petersburg*, we find this dual figure in the character of . . . Dudkin." Edith W. Clowes, "*Petersburg* and Russian Nietzscheanism," in *A Reader's Guide to Andrei Bely's Petersburg*, ed. Leonid Livak (Madison: University of Wisconsin Press, 2018), 70–84.

work had an autobiographical quality to it, for the novelist himself was fascinated with the philosopher's call for a transvaluation of Western values. Only by destroying the traditional values of Christendom could personal authenticity be achieved. Interestingly, for Gide the opportunity to live such an "authentic" life arose after being initiated into the sexual nihilism of Oscar Wilde. He met the Irishman a year after the publication of *Dorian Gray*. Almost immediately, Gide became an exponent of Wilde's decadent aestheticism, or division of art from all standards of morality and truth. In his autobiography, Gide relates how, when the two found themselves in French Algeria together, Wilde hired boy prostitutes for their entertainment. Gide claims the experience turned him into a lifelong pederast. He used Nietzschean language of the will to power to explain his experience of an ecstasy liberated from any feelings of compassion for his underaged male servant-lovers.

In Germany, a young Rainer Maria Rilke (d. 1926) fired a generation of Germans with strange poetry expressing a Nietzschean sense of the personality's ecstatic dissolution. In "The Panther" (1902), he suggests man is a powerful beast caged within tradition and convention. Beyond the bars of this cage there is "no world," that is, nothingness. Nihilism also haunts Rilke's greatest work, the *Duino Elegies*. Begun in the years leading up to the First World War, its ethereal poems menace the reader with words like "dissolution," "evaporation," and "annihilation." Even the powerful angels that now return to the consciousness of Christendom—since the Renaissance they had been reduced to emasculated, winged babies—do not offer man any consolation. Rilke was not a Christian and had no interest in restoring traditional Christian anthropology; his angels have nothing to do with those of the Bible. They are "deadly birds of the soul" that impose on *Homo sapiens* the specter of annihilation. They are merely agents of the superman.

Across the English Channel in Britain, George Bernard Shaw (d. 1950) composed a drama entitled *Man and Superman*. Its title was a cue to the playwright's conviction that utopian values had exhausted themselves within the bourgeois culture of the Victorians. Shaw would later become a dedicated socialist—that is, something Nietzsche hated—but at an early stage in his writing career he was magnetically drawn to the archenemy of everything bourgeois. It helped that Nietzsche had been a fellow atheist. Shaw was also a lover of Wagner, and he had enthusiastically presented the amoral hero Siegfried as a superman years earlier when advocating for the *Ring of the Nibelung* to a still hesitant British public. His play follows the pathologically verbose Wagner's example by requiring nearly five hours to perform in its entirety (which in production history has rarely happened). Its message about man is that he is fading as a species, sure to be superseded one day by a more evolved being.

But as Christendom lurched ever closer to total warfare, it was in Austrian literature that the nihilistic vision of modern man loomed most starkly. There Franz Kafka (d. 1924) brought modernism's theme of dehumanization to its most extreme limit. And he did so by inverting Christendom's ancient imperative toward the transformation of the world.

The history of human dignity had been a long one. Born at Pentecost in the Church's optimistic anthropology, for a thousand years it had shaped Christendom's experience of divine participation. It was grounded in traditional Christianity's claim that man is the image of God, and that God, by becoming man, had enabled man to participate in divinity. However, after the eleventh century this culture of paradise had, in the new Christendom of the West, undergone constriction. Penitential pessimism emerged from a series of reformational innovations, not least of which was the doctrine of purgatory. Pope Innocent III articulated this new anthropology in a work entitled *On the Misery of the Human Condition*.[13] Only in the quattrocento was such a view decisively opposed and Christendom's original optimism restored. But the vindication of man came at a price. Renaissance humanists restored human dignity but locked it within the saeculum—that is, the spiritually untransformed world. Heavenly immanence began to fade. Liturgical worship and sacramental communion were swallowed up by secular glory. For five hundred years, a parade of promethean humanists, post-Christian deists, philosophical idealists, and, finally, unapologetic atheists betrayed Christendom's original conviction that heaven and earth had been united

---

13 On the posthumous legacy of Pope Innocent III's treatise *On the Misery of the Human Condition*, see *Age of Utopia*, 88–97.

by the Incarnation. Utopia promised to supersede the experience of paradise. But under the disintegrative effects of modernism, that promise was now shown to be a falsehood.

In the first sentence of Kafka's short work "Metamorphosis," the hero awakes one morning in a modern city to find that he has been transformed into a "monstrous insect." It is an absurd and disturbing opening, but the story amasses an ever-growing series of setbacks to demonstrate that utopian man is anything but what the humanists had once proclaimed. Prometheus has become a cockroach. The title of the radical work means in Greek "transformation," indicating how the metamorphocentric promise of the old Christendom had now been completely reversed.

In another work entitled *The Trial,* man's powerlessness and incapacity to comprehend the world reach an even more terrifying level. Now the hero is unexpectedly charged with a crime he did not commit. Indeed, the crime is never even named. In this way, Kafka joins the prophetic Dostoevsky in foreseeing the totalitarian terror rising just beyond the horizon of the First World War. His hero is persecuted, arrested, put on trial, and finally, in the last scene, "shot like a dog."

Thus, as Nietzsche had suggested, not only God but even man was fading away as the center of Western values. Man was becoming dehumanized.

And the worst of it was still to come.

Dismal Sciences

IN THE MEANTIME, MODERNIST ART was not the only agent of utopian Christendom's cultural dissolution. Various fields of scientific inquiry were exposing man as less—even much less—than Renaissance humanists had claimed him to be.

A half century earlier, Thomas Carlyle had coined the phrase "dismal science" to characterize the many gloomy aspects of modern economics. By the dawn of the twentieth century, this discipline had been joined by other fields of knowledge whose claim to objectivity was matched by somber and even pessimistic views of the human condition. And in these other dismal sciences, the ghost of Innocent III appeared yet again.

But now, neither reformational Christianity nor even its bastard utopian offspring had any real purchase on Christendom's intellectual elite. The program of anti-evangelical benightenment launched during the eighteenth century had gone too far. True, it had been briefly suspended by the romantics, whose idealism sought the reunion of heaven and earth. But their counterfeit experience of transcendence had never been convincing—even to themselves. In any case, belief in man's ability to commune with an impersonal "Absolute" had now been thoroughly discredited. In the absence of traditional Christianity, the only compelling way toward an effective transformation of the world was full-throated atheism and the anthropological nihilism it necessarily entailed.

As with the artistic avant-garde, so with the emerging academic establishment, this conviction led to a view of man in the world—what can be called anthropo-cosmology—that was even more pessimistic than that born of the Great Division. And as the multiplication of Western monastic orders had once contributed to competing schools of theology, so the diversification of academic disciplines contributed to competing schools of human science.

Among these was sociology. Its founder was Emile Durkheim (d. 1917). He was a student of Auguste Comte, the philosopher who had determined history inevitably moves to higher and higher stages of human achievement as religious beliefs give way to science. In an elaborate system called positivism, Comte argued that man will acquire happiness when Christianity finally dies out. His disciple, however, was not so sure. Though an atheist himself, Durkheim discovered through groundbreaking studies of modern society that something very important was being lost in the progressive march of secularization. One of his studies was entitled *Suicide*. Building on an earlier analysis of industrialization and its corrosive effects on social structures, the father of sociology concluded that rising rates of self-harm would become an inevitable part of modern life. He turned out to be right.

Durkheim linked his dismal prognosis to what he called *anomy* (or *anomie*), a condition in which the individual, cut off from traditional morality, falls into a state of moral boundlessness. Severed from organic communities like family, village, or confessional church, modern man is unable to position himself morally within society and as a result becomes afflicted by unregulated passions and despair. Durkheim's concept of anomy (literally "without rule") can be contrasted to the humanist ideal of moral *autonomy,* in which the individual achieves "self-rule." It can also be contrasted to traditional Christianity's model of deified *heteronomy,* in which man participates in the divine "rule of another."

In a famous work on the sociology of religion, Durkheim linked anomy even more directly to secularization. There, the atheistic social scientist dryly proclaimed with a vocabulary similar to that of Nietzsche that God is dead.

The great things of the past which filled our fathers with enthusiasm do not excite the same ardour in us, either because they have come into common usage to such an extent that we are unconscious of them, or else because they no longer answer to our actual aspirations; but as yet there is nothing to replace them. . . . In a word, the old gods are growing old or already dead, and others are not yet born.[14]

Durkheim was not a Nietzschean as such, though he was familiar with the philosopher's writings. The sociologist was far too invested in utopia. Following in the footsteps of Comte, he framed his obituary for God within the hopes and dreams of positivism. Indeed, in the very passage cited he goes on to express optimism that one day a new religiosity will spring up within post-Christian Christendom, and he cites with approval the world-building example of revolutionary France's reign of terror. It is fitting, perhaps, that Durkheim died the very year an even more ambitious—and violent—campaign to fill Christendom with a new mythology was born in Russia. But in the absence of Communism, Durkheim met the end of his life wondering when, exactly, the anomy caused by secularization would be alleviated. For his twenty-first-century successors measuring suicide rates in the sociology departments of modern universities, the question is still being asked.

A fascination with the effects of secularization was shared by Durkheim's German counterpart in sociology, Max Weber (d. 1920). Also an atheist,

---

14 Emile Durkheim, *The Elementary Forms of the Religious Life*, trans. Joseph Ward Swain (New York: Free Press, 1915), 475.

Weber did not celebrate unequivocally the apparent victory of secularization. He realized a post-Christian Christendom had lost an important source of human fulfillment. Interestingly, he chose a term for the process that was negative. Whereas the positive term "enlightenment" had been employed by secularists from Voltaire to Comte, Weber instead chose to speak of "disenchantment." The emphasis was on loss as much as on gain. Progress was unmistakable in the rise of modern science and social organization. But because of this transformation, a once sacred cosmos had been desecrated.

It is noteworthy that the model of the world to which Weber's term "disenchantment" alluded was not that of traditional Christianity. Little interested in the old Christendom and its role in the formation of the West, the sociologist took as his point of departure the new Christendom that arose only after the Great Division. There cosmology had become notably contemptuous (to apply the word used by Innocent III). It was comparably stavrocentric ("cross-centered") in relation to the metamorphocentric ("transformation-centered") piety fostered during the first millennium. From disasters like the plague to doctrines like purgatory, the fourteenth-century West was a society trapped in pessimism. And since for Weber society determines the form religion takes (and not the other way around), pessimism was the normative form of Christianity. In *The Sociology of Religion,* he declared Christianity a "religion of world-rejection."[15] Its founder, Jesus, preached as his central tenet "an absolute indifference to the world."[16] The paradisiacal culture of first-millennium Christendom was thus totally ignored in Weber's analysis. Naturally, for him the disenchantment process was a good thing in that it freed the world from a contemptuous cosmology. But, as we have seen, in affirming utopia Weber was also compelled to acknowledge its spiritual costs. Had he known better the character of traditional Christianity and the cultural record of the old Christendom, he might have envisioned a "re-enchantment" of the West on terms that were both spiritually authentic and cosmologically affirmative.

---

15   Max Weber, *The Sociology of Religion,* trans. Ephraim Fischoff (London: Methuen, 1963), 270.

16   Ibid., 273.

By far the most profound yet culturally subversive human science to appear at this time was psychology. Its chief advocate was Sigmund Freud (d. 1939), who founded a specific scientific branch of it called psychoanalysis. He too was an atheist. With brilliant insights based on clinical research, he offered post-Christian Christendom a way of understanding the "soul" (*psyche*) that would complete the process of secularization begun in the eighteenth century.

The irony of the philosophes had been that they assimilated various features of Christianity in their anti-evangelical program of secular transformation. After all, they were filling the transformational gap that reformational Christianity and the wars of Western religion had opened. So too Freud. A positivist by nature and training, he made of psychoanalysis a kind of doctrine-specific cult. Presenting radical views of humanity to a stunned and sometimes hostile society, he attracted the most progressive physicians to his home in Vienna for Wednesday evening assemblies. Attendees, basking in the glow of ingenious theories about the human personality and its explanation of all existence, went through something like a conversion experience. Speaking for the whole, one declared himself an "apostle of Freud who is my Christ."[17] In 1908 the Viennese Psychoanalytical Society formed, with a format for meetings that followed "a definite ritual":

> *First, one of the members would present a paper. Then, black coffee and cakes were served; cigars and cigarettes were on the table and were consumed in great quantities. After a social quarter of an hour, the discussion would begin. The last and the decisive word was always spoken by Freud himself. There was an atmosphere of the foundation of a religion in that room. Freud himself was its prophet.[18]*

Like Zarathustra surrounded by fellow supermen, the founder of psychoanalysis enjoyed what Nietzsche had craved but never achieved.

---

17 Quoted in Peter Gay, *Freud: A Life for Our Time* (New York: Doubleday, 1988), 173.
18 Ibid., 174.

Sigmund Freud

Nevertheless, his disciples were not always faithful. As Freud dispatched them to the capitals of the West to plant local chapters of an International Psychoanalytical Association, many developed doctrines of their own and fell away. The most grievous apostasy was committed by Freud's anointed successor and the president of the association, Carl Jung. Even so, enough of the original Freudian inner circle remained faithful to carry the new science through the First World War and beyond. When Freud died (of mouth cancer caused by cigars like those "consumed in great quantities" at the Vienna gatherings), he left behind an empire of academics convinced that the West's anthropo-cosmological questions would be resolved by science and not religion.

Nevertheless, as with sociology so with psychology, the answers were painfully ambivalent. On the one hand, there was in psychoanalysis enough nineteenth-century positivism—with its faith in the empirical method and its hope in the future—to convince adherents that they were the avant-garde of progress. But Freud's vast writings also contained deeply pessimistic elements.

One was his model of the human personality. Unlike the rationalists of the eighteenth century, he considered man to be fundamentally irrational. Here he found inspiration in the thought of Nietzsche and of Dostoevsky. Though he claimed never to have studied the former, he owned a copy of the philosopher's collected works, and biographers agree there is little doubt he read them. Russia's great novelist also provided insight into the irrational, especially when writing about his characters' dreams and their transgressive impulses such as parricide.

Nietzsche's emphasis on the will to power as a destructive, elemental drive that defies reason and well-being found a parallel in Freud's concept of the *libido,* or sexual instinct. In a scientifically reductionist manner reminiscent of Marx's theory of dialectical materialism, Freud claimed that libidinous desire drives virtually all human behavior. Not only sexual acts but politics and art are the result of its influence. This provided him with a mechanism with which to explain the development of the personality from the earliest stages of childhood. In what may have been a reaction to the naive views of sexuality held by his Victorian contemporaries, he claimed human beings are preoccupied with the body's "erogenous zones" from the moment of birth.

The mechanism of libido also equipped him to introduce one of the most outrageous theories of the human personality ever. He eventually called it the "Oedipus complex" (after the Greek myth of a son who kills his father and then unknowingly mates with his mother). This theory claimed that children are universally and without exception determined by a psychosexual attachment to the mother, leading boys to desire the death of their father in order to mate with her. Girls are governed by the same law, though a condition Freud called "penis envy" made them turn away from the mother (whom girls came to see as emasculated) and direct their desire toward the father. Jung called this the "Elektra complex" (alluding to another Greek myth about a woman who avenges her father's murder at the hands of her mother), but by the time he did so, Freud considered him a heretic and rejected the term.

Freud considered healthy child development to depend on these ignoble psychodynamics. Otherwise, he claimed, boys and girls would grow up to identify with the same-sex parent and the result would be homosexuality (or bisexuality). In an age when deviant sexual behavior was becoming increasingly common among Christendom's intellectual elite, such scientific explanations had the effect of legitimating new—and, for humanists and Christians alike, nihilistic—values.[19]

But the sexual conventions of two millennia were not the only cultural casualty of Freudianism. Psychoanalysis made broad use of a concept known as the "unconscious." During the Renaissance, great value had been placed on rational autonomy. Individuals were ennobled by their ability to make rational decisions in navigating their lives toward principled ideals. The so-called Enlightenment only amplified this. In Freud's hands, the concept of the unconscious fundamentally threatened humanistic autonomy. Now the human personality was an unstable balance of often undetected forces competing for dominance. Freud created a tripartite model to explain them. An *id* (literally "the it") provided instinctual desires that included not only

---

19 Freud himself, interestingly, seems never to have acted in anything but a morally conventional way and remained faithful to his lifelong wife.

the libido but a destructive "death instinct." Each of these was met by a *superego* (literally "the über-I"), which sought to stifle them through the workings of conscience and social expectations. These competing forces were synthesized within the *ego* (literally "the I"), which represented the conscious personality. Because so many of these inner conflicts were immersed within the unconscious, managing a healthy life was fraught with difficulty. This, of course, is why Freud recommended psychotherapy for all who took an interest.

And if Freud's theory of the human personality was degrading, that which he assigned to the human collective left little opportunity to tout human dignity. In *Totem and Taboo* (1913), he used the Oedipus complex to explain the origins of civilization. Like his sociological counterparts in the dismal sciences, he was fascinated with the cultural force of religion, even as that force was waning in the early twentieth century. In his fanciful narrative, religion and the civilization that springs from it are reducible to a primordial event of psychosexual violence. Here one is reminded of Kubrick's scene in *2001* depicting the first act of the will to power as Strauss's *Thus Spake Zarathustra* plays. For Freud, at the dawn of human civilization a group of brothers, desiring sexual gratification with their mother, spontaneously rise up against their father and commit parricide. They then devour his body in a ritual act, joining incest to cannibalism. Because of their guilt, however, they internalize their absent father's authority, which takes the place of a collective superego. From that moment on, human civilization has worked to suppress the libidinal will to power in men by repressing desire and transferring it to more "sublimated" activities. All religions—but especially Christianity with its doctrine of God the Father—are compensations for this primordial act of parricide. They can all be traced back to this scientifically formulated (and completely theoretical) act of original sin.

The psychoanalytical view of man—at once anti-evangelical and anti-humanistic—was becoming thoroughly morbid. It was reverting to a kind of Innocentian pessimism. The thirteenth-century architect of the new Christendom had, after all, located human conception in an act he considered disgusting and demoralizing. Freud did the same for the origins of civilization. But for Freud, science partly obscured the specter of nihilism the way reformational Christianity had shielded the great pope. And, as Freud would later claim in *The Future of an Illusion* (1927), science in the form of psychoanalysis would eventually eradicate Christianity by enabling modern man to see the primordial faith of Christendom as an "obsessional neurosis" dating from its infantile stages of development.

> *Religion would thus be the universal obsessional neurosis of humanity; like the obsessional neurosis of children, it arose out of the Oedipus complex, out of the relation to the father. If this view is right, it is to be supposed that a turning-away from religion is bound to occur with the fatal inevitability of a process of growth, and that we find ourselves at this very juncture in the middle of that phase of development.*[20]

But even as Freud struggled to sound optimistic about the human condition, the West around him was running ever faster toward the abyss.

The Great War and Its Consequences

IF MODERNIST ART AND THE human sciences had been dissolving the West's cultural foundations for decades, the First World War brought the utopian structure down like an edifice demolished. It was the deadliest conflict ever waged. Some ten million soldiers were killed by the fighting, and another ten million civilians perished from hunger and disease.

Numbers like these had never been recorded, and important features of the new utopian civilization erected during the past century were responsible for the carnage. Ideological nationalism, which was the direct cause for the outbreak of war, was foremost among these. It pitted a Central Alliance (Germany and Austria) against an Entente Alliance (France, Britain, and Russia). The conflagration had erupted when Serbian nationalists assassinated Archduke Franz Ferdinand, heir to the throne of Austria. Once armies were mobilized, the efficiency of the bureaucratic state (about which Weber

---

20 Sigmund Freud, *The Future of an Illusion*, trans. and ed. James Strachey (New York: Norton, 1989), 55.

had had so much to say) also played a role. Governments—increasingly representative and constitutional—cynically used propaganda to sustain the slaughter of their constituents. They also enacted mass conscription, a relatively new practice that had originated only in the Napoleonic Wars. Britain with her ideal of individual liberty held out as long as she could, but in 1916 was finally compelled to adopt the practice. Even women were mobilized in a way by being impelled to occupy factory floors vacated by conscripted workingmen.

The new industrial economy was a key agent in producing the unprecedented death toll. It not only provided the trains that rushed soldiers to the front lines; it mass-produced the weaponry that cut them down. A new invention called the machine gun did much of the work. But science opened even wider frontiers for violence. The U-boat and poison gas, for instance, would have been impossible without recent advances in the respective fields of physics and chemistry. In all, some sixty million soldiers were mobilized to the fronts, and they, together with civilians on the "home fronts," experienced a form of total warfare unimaginable without the advances of utopia.

Hostilities erupted in August 1914. Germany, ruled by Kaiser Wilhelm II, had shown the greatest disposition to war. She launched an ambitious invasion of France that was halted the following month at the First Battle of the Marne. From that point until the end of hostilities, the western front was fixed in a state of immobilized trench warfare. All that was needed to stop infantry attacks effectively was a line of machine gun emplacements and enough factory-produced ammunition to feed them. Between assaults, artillery pummeled the enemy at a longer distance. At the Third Battle of Ypres (1917), for instance, the breaches of British cannon devoured an entire year's production of shells. No fewer than 322 trains were required to deliver them. All of this resulted in a mere 45 square miles of conquered German territory. The cost in British lives was 8,222 soldiers for each one of those pitiful square miles.[21]

The territory between the lines came to be known as "no-man's land," a

---

21 Theodore Ropp, *War in the Modern World* (London: Collier-Macmillan, 1962), 250.

landscape marked to the horizon by interminable shell craters. Men unfortunate enough to be trapped within this area had little hope of survival. The wounded might cry out for help, but rarely could they be rescued in the face of enemy sniper fire. Their helpless cries probably did more damage to the souls of their comrades than did the shelling. When they finally fell silent, swarms of "corpse rats" would emerge from rain-flooded trenches and bomb craters to feed on the remains. Among the living, combat was marked by mud and fear and was utterly devoid of dignity. Snipers rarely saw the faces of the men they killed. Victims of chlorine and mustard gas attacks, crouching in the trenches, died slowly of asphyxiation.

For their part, generals calculated victories based on the mathematics of attrition. In 1916, the greatest battles on the western front, at Verdun and the Somme, were fought on this principle. The results were more than two million casualties. The eastern front proved more fluid, but there also no decisive breakthrough ever occurred. In 1917, revolution weakened Russia's resolve to fight, and by early 1918 war in the east came to a stop. In the west, fighting continued until Germany agreed to an armistice in November of that year. In 1919 the Treaty of Versailles formally ended the deadliest war then known in history. Survivors simply called it the Great War.

The effects on utopian Christendom were devastating. In some lands, revolutions broke out. The first was the Russian Revolution. Tsar Nicholas II had been forced to abdicate early in 1917 due to an insurrection caused by war disruptions, and by the end of the year Vladimir Lenin had formed a Communist dictatorship. A civil war followed, killing twice as many Russians as the Great War. Another revolution occurred in Germany, where a republic was declared in 1918. Centered in Weimar, it declared universal suffrage for both men and women. Economic security was promised to workers. Many considered the Weimar Republic to be the most progressive in history. But the economic terms of the Versailles Treaty and the postwar contraction of capital severely weakened it. In 1924 the relatively unscathed American economy was tapped to provide capital through the Dawes Plan. But in 1929 the collapse of Wall Street terminated this support, and the German economy plummeted into the Great Depression. As it did so, antidemocratic political parties grew in popularity. On the left were the German

Communists. On the right were the National Socialists. Neither had any investment in the ideal of liberal democracy. Weimar politics, according to one historian, became a "candle burning at both ends."

In the meantime, total warfare had thoroughly subverted the beliefs and values of utopian Christendom. As we have seen, modernism had prepared the way for cultural despair. During the war, a group of radical artists took refuge in neutral Switzerland to form the movement's latest school, which came to be known as Dada. This word was virtually meaningless, and for adherents that was precisely the point. In their opinion, the entire culture and civilization of the West was completely devoid of value. It was itself meaningless. One of the leaders, the Romanian Tristan Tzara, composed a manifesto in 1918. In it he confirmed, first of all, that "Dada means nothing." He then went on to utter nihilistic statements including:

The new artist protests; he no longer paints.
All pictorial or plastic art is useless.
There is no ultimate truth.
Logic is always wrong.
Let each man proclaim: There is a great negative work of destruction to be
accomplished.

By the end of the war, Dada had spread far beyond Switzerland. It found a home in New York City, where a perverse French émigré named Marcel Duchamp entered an art competition with a "composition" entitled *Fountain* (1917). The object was nothing more than a discarded urinal bearing an artistic signature. By showing it, Duchamp was declaring that art is meaningless. Two years later, he presented a simple black-and-white reproduction of Leonardo's celebrated *Mona Lisa* under the title *L.H.O.O.Q.*, which when pronounced in French mimics the phrase "She has a hot ass." The artist even defaced the venerable image—a monument of humanism—with a moustache.

Back in Europe, Dada exhibitions looked forward to what would come to be known as the "art installation," in which the public is provoked into an interaction with the artwork. One such exhibition held in

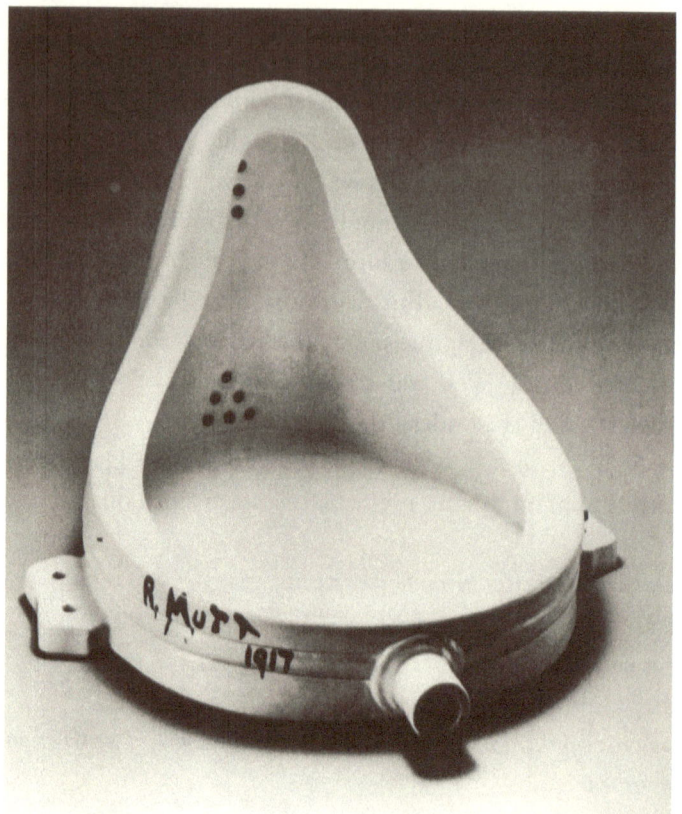

Fountain *by Marcel Duchamp*

Cologne in 1920 was situated in the courtyard of a pub. Viewers entered through the establishment's public toilet room. They were then required to walk past a girl dressed in a revealing "first-communion dress" reciting lewd poetry. At the center of attention was a bust carved from wood in a natural-istic style resembling something the great Michelangelo might have inspired. However, a hatchet was buried in its forehead, and a sign instructed viewers to hack off a piece of the face before moving on for a beer. The message, it would seem, was that Christianity's hypocritical desire for divine commu-nion had led the West to a belief in man's promethean autonomy. But since the Great War had exposed this, too, as counterfeit, a "great negative work of destruction" (to quote Tzara) was needed. And when it was completed, nihilistic Christendom would promise modern man nothing more than an ephemeral pursuit of inebriated pleasure.

The sculptor of the Cologne exhibit was Max Ernst. Like Tzara, he was beyond indignant at the waste of human life caused by the Great War. He was also heir to the avant-garde's hatred for the bourgeoisie. During the war, Dada seemed to him the most effective means of leading the long rebellion against Christendom's values. But after the war, he wearied of Dada's inability to do more than destroy. He would therefore go on to help found a new school of art called Surrealism, which we will explore in chapter 8.

For now, the broader cultural consequences of total warfare deserve attention. These were felt as much by common men and women as by the intellectual elite. In 1918 an obscure schoolteacher named Oswald Spengler released the first volume of a history entitled *The Decline of the West*. Drawing on Nietzsche and even Dostoevsky, its declension narrative contrasted culture with civilization. A vibrant religion is necessary for the former, he asserted, but when convictions about it begin to fail, an uncreative civilization begins to form. This process grows out of efforts to reform the primordial religion and the culture that springs from it. Rationalism arises among elites in an effort to compensate for the loss of religious convictions. Though common people react to secularization by trying to revive the old religion, and authoritarian political leaders arise to assist them, an ossified civilization will inevitably replace a vital culture. Spengler audaciously claimed this is the pattern of all world civilizations, the West included. During the decade that followed the Treaty of Versailles, he seems to have struck a nerve as his book became widely distributed and discussed throughout Europe.

An even more popular book was written at the end of the decade by another German, Erich Maria Remarque. *All Quiet on the Western Front* (1929) was a best seller that went through several editions and was translated into numerous languages. It sold millions of copies within only a few years, and in 1930 a film version made in Hollywood was awarded the Academy Award for best picture. It tells the story of a common soldier who goes off to fight, leaving behind a youthful love of art and science. Paul Bäumer is an amateur poet and avid butterfly collector. However, his years of service in the German army destroy all prewar humanistic ideals. When he returns home for a brief leave, he cannot bring himself to spend time with his parents or to feel at peace in the home of his childhood.

Meanwhile, life in the trenches subjects him to hunger, degradation, and harrowing encounters with death. In one famous scene he is trapped with a French soldier in a crater in no-man's land. Hand-to-hand combat results in victory over his enemy by the use of a bayonet. There ensue hours of watching the man die slowly of the wound. Gurgling in his own blood and staring in terror at Paul, the enemy executes a devastating judgment against the war and all of Paul's generation. In vain Paul tries to bandage his victim and help him, and in doing so he stumbles across photographs of the man's wife and children. These cause him to realize he has been caught up in a fundamentally deceitful culture. When death finally comes to the Frenchman, Paul pathetically cries out to him:

> *Comrade, I did not want to kill you. If you jumped in here again I would not do it, if you would be sensible too. But you were only an idea to me before, an abstraction that lived in my mind and called forth its appropriate response. It was that abstraction I stabbed. But now, for the first time, I see you are a man like me. I thought of your hand-grenades, of your bayonet, of your rifle; now I see your wife and your face and our fellowship. . . . Forgive me, comrade; how could you be my enemy? If we threw away these rifles and this uniform you could be my brother.*[22]

There is no evidence that Remarque was motivated by traditional Christianity in framing this scene. Yet under different cultural circumstances he might have been. The Sermon on the Mount, after all, commanded men to love their enemies, and before the Great Division of the eleventh century, Western Christendom had not tried to justify the killing of fellow Christians.

But secularization had advanced too far for the gospel to be seen as an alternative to the moral abyss into which Paul stared. The only barrier that

---

22 Erich Maria Remarque, *All Quiet on the Western Front*, trans. A. W. Wheen (New York: Fawcett Crest, 1958), 223.

separated him from despair was the secular humanism in which he was raised. And now it had collapsed. Remarque's oft-quoted preface to the novel about a generation of men being "destroyed by the war" can thus be taken to refer to their utopian culture as well.

Losing Faith in Godlessness

BUT A FEW INTELLECTUALS WERE casting their thoughts back to a time when the science of killing was less advanced and the gospel of love more influential. The specter of nihilism loosed by the Great War gave a new voice to Christian apologetics. Suddenly, the arguments for atheism seemed to lose their strength.

Already by the time of the war, certain eminent writers were advocating traditional Christianity as a solution to the impending problems of a godless utopia. The best-known among them in Anglophone Christendom was G. K. Chesterton. He had been raised a Unitarian but after marrying an Anglican he accepted her trinitarian faith. Eventually he became a Roman Catholic. In 1908, while still an Anglican, he published *Orthodoxy*. With little knowledge of the Orthodox Church, he meant by the title simply a form of Christianity free of the accretions of theological liberalism. His foil was the utopian Christianity that since the time of Friedrich Schleiermacher had cooperated so closely with secularization and facilitated its ends.

Indeed, when war broke out in 1914, a cluster of German theologians with these tendencies had signed their names to a notorious "Manifesto of Ninety-Three German Intellectuals to the Civilized World." The eminent Lutheran Adolf von Harnack, for instance, placed his name alongside those of such figures as Fritz Haber (the father of poison gas) to defend Germany's military "struggle for existence." German church leaders were not the only ones guilty of militancy. In England, the Anglican bishop of London, Arthur Winnington-Ingram, infused the war with a spiritual purpose. On learning of the Armenian genocide committed by the Turks in alliance with Germany, he called on British soldiers "to kill the Germans: to kill them not for the pleasure of killing, but to save the world, killing the good and the wicked, the young and the old."[23] Needless to say, as the sentiments of writers like Remarque gained circulation throughout the West in the aftermath of total warfare, utopian Christianity's susceptibility to secular ideologies like nationalism made it an unappealing option.

More attractive was the resolute witness of traditional Christianity in the full variety of its Orthodox, Roman Catholic, and Protestant forms. Apologists for it began to appear in the immediate aftermath of the war. Some were reacting directly to liberal theology of the Harnack variety. Among these was Karl Barth. Himself a Protestant, he looked to Calvinism as a defense against the decline of theology in modern times. In *Epistle to the Romans* (1922), he attacked any who suggested that human culture could aid divine revelation in any way. One observer characterized the book's appearance as a bomb landing in the "playground" of modernist theologians. Barth's views influenced the revival of Calvinism in what is sometimes called "neo-orthodoxy"—again a term, like Chesterton's, expressing a built-in ignorance of the Orthodox Church. Indeed, by turning to Calvin, Barth was reviving the reformational Christianity of the sixteenth century, which was in significant ways very different from the Christianity of the first millennium. But while it did not, in following Calvin, offer a sacramental vision of culture to the war-torn West, it did place strong emphasis on returning to traditional theological convictions.

Barth was never anything but a zealous Christian. But many intellectuals were discovering the Christian faith as if for the first time. Among these were a group of Russian émigrés who appeared in Belgrade, Berlin, and Paris after being driven from their homeland during the Russian Civil War. Like the Jews in Babylon whose exile from Jerusalem was related in Psalm 136 (137), they remembered Zion with great love and hope. They also felt bitter disappointment, for they were forced by circumstances to live in a society that had little respect for traditional Christianity and that, evidenced by books and movements like those of Chesterton and Barth, knew little or nothing about Orthodoxy.

---

23 *Daily Lives of Civilians in Wartime Twentieth-Century Europe*, ed. Nicholas Atkin (Westport, CT: Greenwood, 2008), 32.

One of these émigrés was Nicolas Berdyaev (d. 1948). He had been a revolutionary and in the years before the war rubbed shoulders in Petersburg with modernists like Bely. He too had worked to assimilate Marx and Nietzsche into a modern vision of culture. However, he eventually lost confidence in the science of Marxism, and this led to a loss of faith in godlessness. Under the influence of Dostoevsky, Berdyaev returned to his childhood faith in Orthodoxy. His strong Christian convictions led him to contribute to a collection of essays, entitled *Landmarks* (1909), that called on Russia's intelligentsia to repent of its atheism.[24] Finding himself in exile in France, he published a work entitled *The End of Our Time* (1924) that called on his Western European contemporaries to repent of the utopian values that had led to the modern catastrophe of war and revolution. Claiming that the Renaissance had actually led directly to the dehumanizing experiences of capitalism, total warfare, and modernism, he claimed to discern the onset of a "new middle ages." Utopia had spent itself, he argued. The solution was not to return to the lost civilization of premodern Christendom, but to reestablish a Western culture in which humanity and the cosmos were restored to their former dignity. Interestingly, Berdyaev took issue with Barth's vision of culture and the world, claiming that its pessimistic anthropo-cosmology would prevent the renewal of a paradisiacal culture. Instead of neo-Calvinism, he drew on historical Orthodoxy.

The intellectual environment within which Berdyaev moved was not altogether unsympathetic. Many who had entered the Great War as atheists or agnostics were returning to Christianity in the years that followed it. Among them were many British, such as the literary scholar C. S. Lewis, the novelist Graham Greene, and the poet T. S. Eliot (who was born in America but adopted England as his homeland). We will return to the first of these in a later chapter, since much of Lewis's apologetical work belongs to the period during and after the Second World War. As we reach the end of part one of our narrative, however, the case of Eliot is interesting in that it highlights a dissatisfaction with utopia and at the same time points to a

---

24   For the contribution to the collection by another former atheist, Sergey Bulgakov, see *Age of Utopia*, 337–39.

T. S. Eliot

Christian solution to the West's cultural problems.

T. S. Eliot will always be remembered as a titan of literary modernism. In his debut poem, *The Love Song of J. Alfred Prufrock* (1915), he called the promethean model of humanity created by the Renaissance into question by placing a sexually frustrated protagonist in a society that neither notices nor speaks to him. Amid a singsong refrain of "In the room the women come and go / Talking of Michelangelo," the man in question stumbles around within a dreary city—or perhaps only within his mind. Disorientation is the dominant mood. Instead of rising up like the romantic figure of a Caspar David Friedrich landscape, he occupies a modern cityscape paralyzed by vulnerability, "like a patient etherised upon a table." He lacks the ability to make decisions: "In a minute there is time / For decisions and revisions which a minute will reverse."[25] The poem's epigraph, significantly, is taken from Dante's *Inferno* and alludes to the shame of one who is condemned to eternal punishment.

Eliot is most famous for "The Waste Land" (1922), a statement about the West in the aftermath of the Great War. There can be no doubt about such an interpretation, though the work is extremely complex and intentionally confusing. Again, allusions are made to Dante, but in this case an epigraph intones an ominously pessimistic note by alluding to a sybil who ages but cannot die—rather like the once-glorious Christendom of the West. Even more noticeable is the theme of the Fisher King, the mythical figure at the heart of the Arthurian legends about sin and healing (something that also attracted Wagner). Eliot, by evoking Dante and Arthurian legend, was turning away from the horrifying state of modern Christendom, stifled by its nihilism, and looking to the distant past for meaning. He was gazing toward Zion.

The poem features two important themes in Eliot's vision of a nihilistic Christendom. First, the West has lost its fertility: it is a "dead land" (the first stanza is entitled "The Burial of the Dead"). April, instead of being a time of rejuvenation as it had been in the vigorous culture that produced the fifteenth-century *Canterbury Tales* (to which the famous first line alludes), is "the cruellest month" because it reminds one that the West is dying. This impression is reinforced by the images of dead people—most notably a corpse buried by a soldier, incongruously, in a garden. After the deadliest war in history, Christendom has become a land barren of life. Sexuality is featured everywhere, but it is always sterile: a wealthy woman spends her afternoons dreaming of committing adultery; a poor woman recounts

25   T. S. Eliot, "The Love Song of J. Alfred Prufrock," in *The Complete Poems and Plays* (New York: Harcourt Brace Jovanovich, 1971), 3–7.

taking abortion pills (which have the side effect of making her teeth fall out); a typist tolerates the lustful advances of a man she does not know; and a homosexual pursues lurid seductions.

Second, as a consequence of its sterility, the West has become prone to forgetfulness. In contrast to the painful light and warmth of spring, the narrator pathetically remarks, "Winter kept us warm, covering / Earth in forgetful snow."[26] Trapped by a transformational imperative limited exclusively to immanence, the West has lost the capacity to remember its heavenly myths. Allusions to a dizzying range of religions fill the poem, for having lost its confidence in traditional Christianity, the West now exposes itself to anything that will rescue it from spiritual oblivion. The poem actually ends by quoting the Hindu Upanishads.

But it is to the mythography of Christendom that Eliot is most drawn. As noted, the poem is organized around the myth of the Fisher King, who stands at the center of the Arthurian legends. This figure was a tragic ruler who, having suffered an incurable wound, awaits the knight who will restore him to health by bringing him the healing Grail. Since, mythically speaking, a realm is identified with its king, Eliot appears to be suggesting that all of Christendom likewise awaits a healing that can only come from a remembrance of Zion, from a recovery of the Grail of paradise.

When he composed "The Waste Land," Eliot was an agnostic. However, he soon began to repent of the values that had made the West unfruitful and forgetful. By the time he composed his next major work, he was beginning to look to traditional Christianity for a solution to his own despair and by extension that of his civilization.

"The Hollow Men" (1925) is much shorter and more accessible than "The Waste Land" but no less profound. Much of its content is the same. It describes the vacuous character of its protagonists, the men who populate the modern West. They live under the specter of nihilism: "Our dried voices, when / We whisper together / Are quiet and meaningless." They represent a "paralyzed force." They have lost not only the ability to communicate with each other but, significantly, the ability to communicate with God.

---

26 T. S. Eliot, "The Waste Land," in *Complete Poems and Plays*, 37–55.

This is the dead land
This is cactus land
Here the stone images
Are raised, here they receive
The supplication of a dead man's hand
Under the twinkling of a dead star.

By now, the poet saw in the prayers of the past a means of deliverance from the despair of the present. But still, authentic faith is difficult to will in the aftermath of modernity's assault on Christianity. "Lips that would kiss / Form prayers to broken stone."

What was certain was that two alternatives now faced the West: either it would continue on its course of nihilism, or it would return to the paradisiacal culture that centuries ago had made it what it properly was. In either case, the poem suggests, utopia has been proven a failure.

In the final verses of "The Hollow Men," Eliot can be heard struggling to make the transition from one alternative to the other. A children's nursery rhyme opens the section, suggesting the meaninglessness of the world. After this, philosophically profound questions are raised. Then fragments of the Our Father appear. But they are still tentative, and the poem ends with an ominous prophecy of the West's alternative to paradise:

Life is very long

Between the desire
And the spasm
Between the potency
And the existence
Between the essence
And the descent
Falls the Shadow

For Thine is the Kingdom

For Thine is
Life is
For Thine is the

This is the way the world ends
This is the way the world ends
This is the way the worlds ends
Not with a bang but a whimper.[27]

In 1927, Eliot finally converted to traditional Christianity in the form of Anglicanism. The next poem he published, "Ash Wednesday" (1930), marked his return to Zion. Its theme was repentance, the same taken up by his traditional Christian literary predecessor Dostoevsky. And like that of Dostoevsky, its Christian message caused scandal to the agnostics and atheists of the avant-garde.

As the age of nihilism dawned, literary modernism's greatest poet broke the cardinal rule of creativity: Thomas Sterns Eliot exorcised rather than surrendered to the specter of nihilism.

---

27 T. S. Eliot, "The Hollow Men," in *Complete Poems and Plays,* 56–59.

PART II

The Ideological Search for Meaning

CHAPTER FOUR

Communist World Building

B EFORE THE GREAT WAR, MOST people living in Christendom were not haunted by the specter of nihilism. Its presence had been divined by intellectuals and artists because they, as representatives of utopia's elite, were the most sensitive to the shortcomings of secular humanism. Our narrative so far has therefore been limited to what is usually called high culture. But after the war, the age of nihilism came to popular culture as well.

Total warfare opened an abyss for nearly everyone. Millions of men were slaughtered by the weapons of progress, and millions more—along with wives, mothers, daughters, and sisters—were forced to adjust to the horror. In the aftermath, the capitalist economy sank into a depression, and political stability dissolved. As certainty about the upward trajectory of history faded, so did confidence in utopia. The problem of meaninglessness had ceased to be an exclusively elite concern.

If one were to look for a symbolic moment in the demise of utopia's mass appeal, it would perhaps be the Christmas truce of 1914, when, after several months of trench warfare, common soldiers suddenly turned from secular humanism to traditional Christianity. On Christmas Day they proclaimed an evangelical "peace on earth"—and in, of all places, no-man's land. Scorning the claims of the nation-state, German and French soldiers spontaneously gathered together around bomb craters, singing hymns and reciting the Our Father. For a moment they remembered the old Christendom's experience of divine participation, of union with the incarnate God "on earth as it is in heaven." But the fleeting glimpse of paradise ended with the holiday. When the soldiers reluctantly resumed firing the following day, the guns seemed to annihilate not only the men in front of them but the beliefs and values of paradise and utopia. The West no longer knew what it had once been or what it was supposed to be.

The result was a civilization without a stable culture to support it. Oswald Spengler, in his *Decline of the West,* argued at this time that an important difference exists between civilization and culture. The former depends on the latter, drawing from culture the beliefs and values that sustain it. But when culture dies out, it leaves civilization in a state of rootlessness. A once flourishing garden becomes desiccated and pale. When this happens, civilization inevitably puts forth new roots—it searches for a new culture to give it life. Applying this Spenglerian principle, it can be said that something like this had happened centuries earlier in the aftermath of the Great Division. In the West the paradisiacal culture of the old Christendom became desiccated, its transformational imperative being diverted toward and exhausted by institutional reformation. The outcome of that process was a pessimistic anthropology that fundamentally threatened a civilization dependent on transformation. The crisis was resolved during the Renaissance, when the new beliefs and values of humanism reoriented a new Christendom toward the saeculum. But now, as the utopian culture of humanism reached its own crisis of meaning, the West began to seek an even newer culture to sustain it.

This was provided by secular ideology. Rather than look to Christendom's primordial faith and the repentance it prescribed, advocates for renewal looked to the intoxicating doctrines of ideologues. Communists, National Socialists, and liberals all promised to cure utopia of its despair through a therapeutic regime of ideological world building.

But as we shall see, this therapy could not be accomplished without purgatives and amputations equal in many cases to the effects of the Great War. As the masses now joined elites in an ideological transformation of the saeculum, the West was drawn even deeper into the abyss of nihilism.

When Marx Met Nietzsche

IN RUSSIA, THE IDEOLOGICAL SEARCH for meaning reached an important turning point in 1927. That year marked the decennial of the October Revolution. For ten years the Communists had been engaged in a self-defined project of "building socialism," of realizing the utopia that Marx had promised through the violence of the proletarian revolution. Much had been accomplished during this decade, but much also remained to be done.[1] Lenin had died in 1924, leaving the Communist Party (known earlier as the Bolsheviks) to find its way forward without the leader who created it. The decennial of 1927 gave the party an opportunity for a new start. Though frequently at odds with each other over the question of policy, Lenin's successors were united in their resolve to build a new world on the ruins of the old. They used the anniversary celebration to define Communism as a great world-building project.

At the heart of the celebration was a parade staged on Red Square in Moscow. There, on Revolution Day (November 7), Joseph Stalin stood atop a monumental tomb dedicated to Vladimir Lenin. He had by this time positioned himself as the true successor to Lenin, greater even than Leon Trotsky (whom most had considered the leader's likely successor). Stalin had waged a ruthless struggle against other so-called Old Bolsheviks, the party members who supported Lenin ten years earlier during the seizure of power. Stalin stood among some of them, but conspicuous by his absence was Trotsky himself. By this time, the latter had been cast out of the party by Stalin and was awaiting a sentence of exile that would permanently isolate him from power. Stalin was not yet done with his fallen rival, but for now he enjoyed unparalleled authority within the Soviet state. As he looked down on the workers and peasants marching beneath him, he was no doubt contemplating the next step to take in the pursuit of what Nietzsche had called the will to power.

The decennial celebration of 1927 was also marked by less elaborate but no less memorable artistic compositions. One commission was given to a

---

1   For an account of the first ten years of Soviet history, see *Age of Utopia*, chapter 12.

brilliant cinematographer named Sergey Eisenstein. It resulted in a film called *October*. The action featured scenes of the storming of the capital's Winter Palace and the arrest of a cowering "bourgeois" Provisional Government found therein. The film greatly exaggerated the heroism and scale of these events, but such after all is propaganda. Made to order for the Soviet government, *October* nevertheless was a work of art. Employing the modernist technique of "simultaneity," in which time collapses into the present—an imitation of liturgically mediated heavenly immanence—one interesting image shows a child sitting on the vacant throne of the discarded tsar. He is intended to symbolize worldly renewal through revolutionary politics, and as he laughs ecstatically, a series of montage frames flash images of clocks around the world recalibrating to Russian time. Eisenstein's masterpiece declared that the transcendent kingdom of posterity, the counterfeit of paradise unsuccessfully sought by the humanists of the nineteenth century, had finally been established in an act of ideological theurgy. And as this pseudo-eschatological event occurs, the film's ultimate hero, Vladimir Lenin, is shown stepping forward at a nearby assembly of revolutionaries to declare that all power now rests with the soviets (the name for democratically elected socialist councils).

A great man thus stood at the center of the decennial parade and Eisenstein's officially sanctioned representation of the Russian Revolution. This is significant. Communist culture, of course, was grounded in the philosophy of Karl Marx, but his philosophy assigned very little importance to the role of great men in history. Revolutions, after all, are supposed to be the expression of class forces. Having come to power under the leadership of Lenin, however, the Communists were compelled to draw from other sources of inspiration.

One of these was the philosophy of Friedrich Nietzsche. Aligning Marx with the father of nihilism is not, on first glance, an intuitive thing to do. Nietzsche was a critic of socialism, seeing it as a secular mask for Christianity's odious rejection of life. He celebrated the individual's freedom from the collective. He considered purely economic concerns a burden on the human spirit, however naturalistically he defined the latter. And he despised what he considered the herd instinct of collective welfare.

Yet there were in Nietzscheanism certain virtues and principles that found their way into the Communist ethos, either directly or indirectly. This fact has only recently received the full notice of historians, who, during the course of the Cold War, had been accustomed to seeing the Soviet Union as a product of Marxism alone. Marxism was the primary philosophical influence, to be sure. But a more nuanced interpretation of Communism reveals elements that are better explained by the force of nihilism, even those articulated by its most sophisticated advocate. As Bernice Glatzer Rosenthal has concluded, "the Soviet obsession with creating a new culture stemmed primarily from Nietzsche, Wagner, and their Russian popularizers."[2]

One example of this is the role of the individual leader in Communism. In Nietzschean language, Lenin was a superman. For Communists he was simply the "leader" (*vozhd*). *October* certainly made him look that way. Singlehandedly, he had forged the Bolshevik Party and looked down with contempt on fellow revolutionaries—many of them fellow Marxists. Issuing manifesto-like statements and using the language of modernism, Lenin created a "vanguard party" that dehumanized its opponents. The only goal of its militant program was to obtain power with which to transform the world into the socialist utopia outlined by Marx. As leader, Lenin managed the party with an iron will that would have impressed the "self-overcoming" creator of Zarathustra. He overwhelmed his rivals with an intellectual brilliance and violent contempt lacking any pretense of human sympathy. His recurring expression was "who-over-whom" (*kto-kogo*), that is, who will destroy whom in the inevitable struggle for power? Like Zarathustra, he knew how to hate his friends. Lenin had not been alone in the Nietzschean disdain for others. Leon Trotsky was also present when the Communist utopia was founded in 1917. When a large number of revolutionaries objected to the formation of the dictatorship by marching out of the hall where Lenin announced the seizure of power, Trotsky leaped to the podium. In a brilliantly conceived ideological statement, he attacked the deserters as cowards, declaring them nothing more than agents of the

---

2   Bernice Glatzer Rosenthal, *New Myth, New World: From Nietzsche to Stalinism* (University Park: Pennsylvania State University Press, 2002), 3.

Lenin giving a speech in the presence of Trotsky (at right of podium)

counterrevolutionary bourgeoisie. If they should dare to turn their backs on the party leader, he warned, they were turning their backs on all hopes of true progress. Communism's socialist transformation of the world was the only hope for the West, and no other option was acceptable. "You are pitiful, isolated individuals," he sneered in conclusion. "You are bankrupt. Your role is played out. Go where you belong henceforth, into the dustbin of history!"

The famous speech could not be a more articulate expression of the Marxist vision of revolutionary progress. What is more, it expresses a relativistic morality in which human life has value only insofar as individuals belong or contribute to a more progressive society.

But there is something more to Trotsky's "dustbin of history" speech, something that goes beyond even a Marxist standard of good and evil. Issued at the very inauguration of Communist power, it begins to abandon moral standards altogether. Utopian indignation was giving way to nihilistic contempt. When an entire category of the human race is dismissed as refuse, as a worthless obstacle to progress, then good and evil no longer have any meaningful social referents. Only power—or rather the will to power—has value. The rest is meaningless.

This Nietzschean tendency continued beyond 1917. Trotsky himself proved to be one of the most ruthless architects of the process called "building socialism." His talents were recognized when he was made commissar of war during the Russian Civil War, which followed inevitably from the formation of a Communist dictatorship. He was merciless in his policies, introducing the death penalty for stragglers in the Red Army and subjecting potential enemies to what he called the Red Terror. During the course of the conflict, he contrasted Communism with more humane and democratic forms of socialism by declaring that history shows "no other way of breaking the class will of the enemy except the systematic and energetic use of violence."[3]

Such views were the context for the creation of the first of a series of variants of the Soviet secret police force. It was known as the Cheka. Its founder was a close associate of Trotsky named Felix Dzerzhinksy, a ruthless advocate for the use of nihilistic terror in building utopia. An article in one Chekist newspaper published during the Civil War made the case in terms that fused Marx and Nietzsche. It even contained a Dostoevskian aside worthy of Ivan Karamazov.

> *For us there do not, and can not exist the old systems of morality and "humanity" invented by the bourgeoisie for the purpose of oppressing and exploiting the "lower classes." Our morality is new, our humanity is absolute for it rests on the bright ideal of destroying all oppression and coercion. To us all is permitted, for we are the first in the world to raise the sword not in the name of enslaving and oppressing anyone, but in the name of freeing them from all bondage. . . . Blood? Let there be blood, if it alone can turn the grey-white-and-black banner of the old pirate's world to a scarlet hue, for only the complete and final death of that world will save us*

---

3   Leon Trotsky, *The Defense of Terrorism: Terror and Communism* (Oxford: Routledge, 2014), 52.

from the return of the flag of the old jackals![4]

After the war, the need for violent destruction of the people and institutions of the old order did not abate. In the case of Trotsky, it turned into a struggle for leadership within a party that resembled the otherwise fictional drama of *Demons*. Demons, it turned out, were real.

Anatoly Lunacharsky

Nietzscheanism was also influential in Communist cultural policies. One self-conscious advocate was Anatoly Lunacharsky (d. 1933). Soon after the October Revolution, he was appointed commissar of enlightenment—an office on which the world-transforming ambitions of the Communists were sure to depend. In fact, his decade-long tenure proved comparatively ineffectual in an atmosphere that always subordinated culture to power. His Nietzschean education might have prepared him for this. The artist, he once observed,

> *works primarily in order to sense his own strength, for the freedom of his creative genius. Can the social activist not work in the same way? To him the people, society are a lump of marble from which he creates a beautiful humankind in accordance with his ideal. . . . Is he an altruist? He is not interested in your happiness, reader. It may be that he would not sacrifice a fingernail for your happiness. On the contrary, if you get in his way he will destroy you.*[5]

---

4   Quoted in Robert Gellately, *Lenin, Stalin, and Hitler: The Age of Social Catastrophe* (New York: Vintage, 2007), 66–67.

5   Quoted in A. L. Tait, "Lunacharsky: A 'Nietzschean' Marxist?" in *Nietzsche in Russia*, ed. Bernice Glatzer Rosenthal (Princeton, NJ: Princeton University Press, 1986), 275–92.

Prepared by an education in both Marx and Nietzsche, Lunacharsky brought to his office a vision of an entirely new culture for Christendom.

It was a vision rooted in utopian socialism, but it was also shaped by nihilism. It is no coincidence that Lunacharsky was the leading Bolshevik advocate of Wagner, arranging on several occasions to have the composer's music performed publicly. In his efforts to build a new culture, he was drawn to the concept of the total work of art that would release creative energy in a mass experience of political ceremony. The increasingly histrionic character that Soviet festivals assumed in cases such as the October Revolution decennial is, as we will see, evidence of this.

The early Nietzsche, in *Birth of Tragedy,* advocated corporate participation in myth-making ceremony. This was attractive to some of the early Bolsheviks, since prerevolutionary Russia, under the influence of Orthodox Christianity, followed a rich tradition of public worship. The last tsar, Nicholas II, had in some ways raised public Christian ceremony to heights it had not seen since before the time of Peter the Great. Innumerable churches were built during his reign in styles predating westernization. Many of these were expressly located in the capital of Saint Petersburg, Peter's "window on the West" and the center of secularization. Here baroque architecture adopted from Roman Catholic and Protestant lands had always predominated. The most famous new liturgical construction was the Cathedral of the Resurrection, visually reminiscent of the sixteenth-century St. Basil's Cathedral on Red Square and popularly known as the Church of the Savior on Spilled Blood because it was built on the site of Tsar Alexander II's assassination in 1881. Every year, millions traveled to local churches in Petersburg and every Russian city to commemorate annual feasts and to venerate miracle-working icons and saints' relics.

All of this was ended by Communism, and Lunacharsky, as a dedicated but intellectually sensitive revolutionary, was thus confronted by the specter of cultural nihilism. He realized that "God is dead and the universe is without meaning. Where is man to find a firm foundation on which to build? How is he to retain his dignity in an empty cosmos?"[6]

---

6   These are his biographer's words in ibid.

The solution, he concluded, was to foster a new religion for the proletariat, one that would emulate the old religion but support purely atheistic values. This, as we have seen, was something the sociologist Emile Durkheim had been anticipating at the same time at the opposite end of Europe. Lunacharsky explored the matter in a two-volume study entitled *Religion and Socialism*—a work the sober materialist Lenin derided as an effort at "God-building."

Lunacharsky was supported by other Marxists, however. One was his brother-in-law and a rival to Lenin's leadership of the Bolshevik Party, Alexander Bogdanov (d. 1928). Though also a dedicated Marxist, the latter was dissatisfied with the prospect of a new society in which the spiritual and cultural experience of man remained untransformed. Marx and Engels had only touched on this question in passing, and Bogdanov resolved to settle it definitively.

His point of departure was anthropological. In one of his earliest works, *The Gathering of Man,* he juxtaposes a triad of relevant epigraphs about the human condition: "God created man in his own image" (Gen. 1:27); "Social existence determines consciousness" (Marx); and "Man is a bridge and not a goal" (Nietzsche). The first of these statements had been, along with the doctrine of the Incarnation, a touchstone for the paradisiacal culture of the first millennium. The second had been designed to replace Christian anthropology during the age of utopia. The third was a step into the unknown, where the human race is no longer fixed by any permanent characteristics.

So, as the revolution liberated man from the prison house of capitalism, a new religion would transform him into a new creation over which the limitations and boundaries of the past would have no influence. Bogdanov was convinced along with Lunacharsky that Nietzsche's vision of the superman could be adapted to inspire the proletariat with a model of this new humanity. What was needed, as Nietzsche indicated, was a new mythology to replace the bankrupt mythologies of Christianity and humanism. His word for this mythology, as Rosenthal has shown, was *ideology*. For Bogdanov, "myth would function as a religion, that is, as an integrating ideology."[7]

---

7   Rosenthal, *New Myth, New World,* 89.

In the wake of the October Revolution, Bogdanov used his relationship with leading Bolsheviks to create a specifically Communist ideology to define what was increasingly being called "the new Soviet man." His influence extended to Nikolay Bukharin, whose *ABC of Communism* provided a framework for social transformation during the Dionysian excesses of the Civil War. The policy of "War Communism" with which the book is forever associated was in fact coined by Bogdanov.

With the support of his brother-in-law, now the commissar of enlightenment, Bogdanov helped launch a new school of modernism called Proletarian Culture, known by the abbreviation Proletkult. In some ways it was an extension of Futurism. The latter had found a strong base in Russia prior to the war, where complete disdain for the past appealed to revolutionaries. However, Proletkult tried to keep its distance from the bourgeois affiliations of the Futurists. Boasting a membership of a half million men at its height, it created networks of workers' clubs where literacy and science were taught. Its fearless leadership envisioned a transvaluation of values by which a totally new culture would emerge. This culture, founded on Communist ideology rather than morbid Christianity or its defunct humanist variants, was grounded in a violent imperative toward social transformation. Though Proletkult was disbanded with the termination of the Civil War, its ideals continued to guide Communist mythology in the decades that followed.

One of these ideals was the figure of a proletarian superman. It was promoted strongly in literature. An example is Gleb Chumalov, the hero of Fyodor Gladkov's novel *Cement* (1925). Set during the economically uncertain period of the New Economic Policy, when the extremes of War Communism were relaxed, the novel depicts a Bolshevik worker's return to his hometown after the Civil War. There he finds his cement factory closed and his wife, Dasha, changed into a new woman. She wears a red kerchief (the symbol of revolution) and refuses to nurture Gleb or to sleep with him. Her aversion for the self-indulgent pleasure of sex did not prevent her, however, from giving herself to Red Army soldiers during the recent conflict in order to spur them to victory. Now she is never at home, preferring to spend her time among fellow workers and organizing the local women's section of the Communist Party. Dasha is so dedicated to building socialism, in fact, that her daughter Nurka is sent to an orphanage and dies there of neglect. Gleb slowly learns to accept Dasha as a new Soviet woman transformed by revolution, and he recovers his will to participate in the social transformation. By the end of the novel, it is he who dramatically climbs atop a reopened cement factory to proclaim economic victory to all the common people.

Such myths were intended to provide Russians with the collective values of a proletarian utopia. Yet they had a nihilistic side as well. Individuals who did not contribute to the building of socialism were represented in the new culture as subhuman and expendable. A scene in *Cement,* for instance, depicts a Communist Party purge, anticipating the dark days that lay ahead. One character, a representative of the prerevolutionary bourgeoisie, finds himself displaced and isolated because of his class loyalties. Even the innocent child Nurka is sacrificed for the cause.

Bogdanov's influence would continue to thrive in the form of another myth, which would continue until the end of Soviet history. Lenin died in 1924, and immediately the nascent Communist ideology created a cult around his memory. An important step in creating the cult was a decision to embalm the leader's body for scientific study and popular veneration. It would be placed on display in a mausoleum built in the modernist style on Red Square. Bogdanov had by this time become fascinated with the idea of natural immortality. He obtained state funds to establish a clinic for research into life extension through blood transfusions. He would ultimately die from being transfused with the tainted blood of a proletarian donor (being of inferior bourgeois provenance, he had long desired to share the genetic material of the world's most progressive class). But his experiments excited those placed in charge of Lenin's embalming project. Some of the specialists held out hope that the day would come when science would actually enable the reanimation of the dead. In the meantime, Lenin's transcendent presence within Soviet culture was declared by modernist poets like Vladimir Mayakovsky, who penned a work with the refrain "Lenin lived, Lenin lives, Lenin shall always live!" Working with such inspiration, morticians were able to drain Lenin's body of its blood, and chemists were able to concoct a combination of fluids that promised to preserve it for all eternity.

The Bolshevik superman who had seized power in the name of a new humanity thus became the object of a new religious ritual. By now, Russia's Orthodox Christians were being put to death by the thousands. Churches were being closed, icons were being smashed, and relics were being destroyed. But the new men and women of the Soviet Union, as beneficiaries of Lenin's transvaluation of values, were learning to live by secular ideology. Centered on the cult of Lenin, it would eventually draw millions to it. And its most emphatic public ritual was to travel on a nihilistic pilgrimage to venerate the superman's relics at Lenin's Tomb. It was something of which the author of *Ecce Homo* could only have dreamed.

It was at the top of this mausoleum that Stalin, during the October Revolution festival of 1927, stood watching columns of Communists marching below him and brooding over a future even more nihilistic than Lenin's.

A Final Solution to the Peasant Problem of Russia

AFTER A DECADE IN POWER, the Communists were growing restless with the limitations of the New Economic Policy (NEP). Lenin had only introduced the measure in 1921 as a compromise with those who opposed the world-transforming ambitions of the revolutionaries. War Communism had been the economic arm of the Red Terror, and almost everyone in the land had suffered horribly from it. The most afflicted were peasants, who according to the vision of the *ABC of Communism* could expect a ruthless expropriation of grain by the government. Marx had viewed the peasantry as an historically retrograde element since it was preoccupied with acquiring private property in the form of land. Peasants thought like individuals, he declared, like "petite bourgeois," and their economic interests were limited to amassing higher and higher "piles of dung." Nevertheless, under NEP villages were mostly left alone. Some peasant families were able to grow enough grain to sell a surplus at a profit, though some who did so were labeled "kulaks" (from the Russian word for clenched fist). To the Communists, such a situation represented a return to capitalism rather than a step forward in the march of progress.

More intolerable, perhaps, was the fact that it was the peasantry that continued to make up the bulk of the Soviet Union's inhabitants. It constituted about 85 percent of the population—little different from the situation under the tsars. This meant that the industrial proletariat, the supposed demographic base of Communism, remained tiny. After a decade of trying to build socialism, Russia remained a backward society in comparison to her more progressive industrial rivals to the west.

What was needed was a process of mass industrialization to solve this ideologically defined demographic "problem." But to accomplish this, millions of peasants would need to move from villages to the cities. What is more, financial resources—known to economists as capital—would need to be extracted from agriculture and reallocated for the construction of factories and apartments. Yet after years of ceding autonomy to the wealthiest peasants through NEP, it was obvious this would never occur naturally.

There arose, therefore, a fierce debate within the Communist leadership about how to interpret Lenin's last great contribution to the building of socialism. Should the party maintain NEP indefinitely, or, having secured its dictatorial position after the Civil War, should it return to the severity of War Communism? Lenin himself had allowed for both views to take hold. By the end of the 1920s those advocating the status quo, such as Bukharin (ironically, in light of his ruthless attitude in the *ABC of Communism*), believed the time for a violent confrontation with the peasantry had still not come. Those advocating a return to the use of "the old Bolshevik iron," such as Lev Kamenev and Grigory Zinoviev, opposed Bukharin. They sided with Trotsky in advocating an end to NEP and a return to fulfilling the ideological myth of economic transformation. This situation gave Stalin an opportunity.

The least scrupulous of the Old Bolsheviks was the odd man out in intraparty debates because of his comparatively unsophisticated economic training. Most of Lenin's lieutenants had been professional intellectuals who learned the skills of government as an avocation. Stalin, on the other hand, had little intellectual training but a strong native capacity for management. He had embraced the office of party general secretary when no one else wanted it because of its tremendous political potential. He had used the office to enroll large numbers of new party members soon after Lenin's death, thus creating a power base personally loyal to himself. These became his creatures. And with his control over the party apparatus, he decided the time had come to eliminate rivals—real, potential, and imagined.

Stalin had already isolated his archrival Trotsky by labeling him a factionalist after the latter formed a group within the party known as the "left opposition." To this Kamenev and Zinoviev decided to link a group of their own called the "united opposition." Stalin's use of antifactional rhetoric was effective since the party had always prioritized unity and a collective approach toward policy. Trotsky himself had articulated a principle about "the will of the party" taking the place of moral absolutes.

> *Clearly, the Party is always right. . . . We can only be right with and by the Party, for history has provided no other way of being in the right. . . . And if the Party adopts a decision which one or another of us thinks unjust, he will say, just or unjust, it is my party, and I shall support the consequences of the decision to the end.*[8]

The end would come for Trotsky soon enough, but as the decennial approached, Stalin played the antifactionalist card to clear the party of his Old Bolshevik rivals. He used the party machine he had created since becoming general secretary.

First, he turned on the left oppositionists and their allies and had them expelled from party membership. Soon the only one who remained was Bukharin, still to the right of Stalin in supporting continued adherence to the principles of NEP. So early in 1928, Stalin turned against what he labeled a "right opposition," a party faction headed by the author of the *ABC of Communism*, who, he declared, opposed Lenin's long-term wishes and was thereby resisting the proletariat's demand for revolutionary transformation.

With Bukharin thus isolated, there was only one thing left to do. Stalin needed a state of emergency to justify the creation of a personal dictatorship. An opportunity arose when, in the spring of 1928, several dozen bourgeois engineers—some of them foreigners—were accused of deliberately trying to

---

8   Quoted in Robert Conquest, *The Great Terror: A Reassessment* (Oxford: Oxford University Press, 1990), 112.

wreck the coal industry in the North Caucasian town of Shakhty. In what became "the curtain raiser of the Stalin era's show trials," the men were found guilty by the judge, a creature of Stalin's named Andrey Vyshinsky.[9] Stalin used the trial to establish a climate of fearful indignation—a precondition for the new revolution he was planning. "We have internal enemies," he warned. "We have external enemies."[10] In the wake of the Shakhty trials, Stalin was prepared to launch what he himself came to call a Revolution from Above.

The concept was perfectly Leninist. Instead of a popular movement, the party would assume militant leadership of the revolution. To be sure, this was a deviation from Marx's vision of revolution, which was supposed to arise from below. But by applying a Nietzschean sense of superhuman will, the Communists under Stalin were convinced they could pull it off. With Zarathustrian flair, Stalin contemptuously dismissed "Bukharin's childish formula about the peaceful growing of capitalist elements into socialism." A truly Leninist approach to progress, he asserted, could never be peaceful.

> *Our development has proceeded and continues to proceed according to Lenin's formula—"kto-kogo." Either we will overcome and crush them, the exploiters, or else they will overcome and crush us, the workers and peasants of the USSR—that's how the question stands, comrades.*[11]

This opened the way for what can be called the final solution to the peasant problem of Russia—to allude to Hitler's chilling formula for the annihilation of Europe's Jews. This solution would be achieved through a merciless application of Communist ideology.

The plan all centered on an application of class violence—which, after all, the *Communist Manifesto* had in its opening sentence declared the engine of progress. When grain procurements fell short in the North Caucasus late in 1928, Stalin ordered forced requisitions. Such measures had not been

---

9   Robert C. Tucker, *Stalin in Power: The Revolution from Above, 1928–1941* (New York: W. W. Norton, 1990), 76.
10 Ibid., 78.
11 Ibid., 87.

seen since War Communism. They achieved the desired results. Grain quotas were met, and Stalin used the case to justify unlimited collectivization the following year. The results were stunning. Overnight, Soviet agriculture went from almost completely private to predominantly collective. It seemed as though Stalin was a second Lenin, a superman who could channel the proletariat's will to power.

The process of collectivization was of course unspeakable in its brutality and costs. It was premised on the Marxist science of class division and conflict. The Communists used the presence of kulaks in the countryside to justify the need for violent acts of expropriation. But in all cases they blurred the distinctions between truly wealthy peasants (who made up a small minority of the population) and others who simply did not want to join the new collective farms. Why would they, when it meant surrendering their family's property to party cadres who appeared in the village from nowhere to demand compliance? Only the poorest peasants saw an advantage to joining, and the Communists used this element as the face of the "laboring masses." When armed cadres of party activists arrived in a village, they ordered all inhabitants to turn out on a given day to declare their compliance or face consequences. Those who resisted or stayed at home were arrested and sent off to labor camps—that is, if they weren't shot on the spot. Those peasants who complied often did so with deep resentments that were often expressed through the slaughtering and consumption of their existing livestock. In many cases they destroyed their grain reserves.

The result of these disruptions was a famine unique in the history of the world. In the first case, it was caused entirely by human agency and not, as is usually the case, by climate or disease. The recalcitrant peasants simply destroyed a large percentage of Russia's food supply. What is more, the state greatly exacerbated the situation through its methods of seizing what was left. Here it is important to recall the progressive ideology that guided the Communists. The chairman of a given collective farm would extract grain supplies and lock them in a warehouse under armed guard until they could be shipped away from the village to a point of market for the purpose of raising capital to invest in industrialization. If doing this resulted in the deaths of the surplus peasantry, party leaders reflected, the cost was worth the benefit. Factories would be built, cities would grow, and the industrial proletariat would take its rightful place as the dominant class in history's first socialist utopia.

As for the peasants, Stalin ordered "the liquidation of the kulaks as a class." The secular values of Communist ideology, following Marx, denied to certain categories of humanity any value at certain stages of historical progress. The peasantry had long been understood as inferior in its value to the proletariat, and within it the kulaks were seen as especially subhuman. It was exactly this kind of secularized anthropology that would guide the Nazis in the Holocaust. The Communists were not racists, but they applied the same morality in a different way.

By 1932, as the Soviet Union prepared to celebrate the completion of the first five-year economic plan for building socialism, almost all agriculture had been collectivized. Because of this, capital had been successfully transferred to the cities and superindustrialization had produced the first fruits of a modern economy. Along the way, in 1930, Stalin had even written an article in the Communist Party newspaper *Pravda* entitled "Dizzy with Success." Significantly, he used the occasion to distance himself from the horrendous effects of the collectivization drive, which were already obvious to everyone. But he hailed collectivization as a victory in economic development.

The famine it caused killed millions. The death toll from this "harvest of sorrow" (as one historian has called it) will never be known with certainty—such was the effectiveness of Communist propaganda—but estimates range from five to fifteen million people.[12] Almost nothing like it had been inflicted on a society before, and it was all the result of Stalin's Revolution from Above and the broader utopian ambitions of the Communists. But because Marx had declared morality relative to the goals of progress, and Nietzsche had declared it merely a function of the will, the Communists considered the costs justified.

Through a transvaluation of values, the Communists had opened the way

---

12   Robert C. Conquest, *Harvest of Sorrow: Soviet Collectivization and the Terror-Famine* (Oxford: Oxford University Press, 1986).

for building a socialist society. As utopian supercities like Magnitogorsk in the Urals sprang up and elements of the backward peasantry were wiped out, a gathering of party leaders was organized in 1934 to discuss the way forward. The event was the seventeenth congress of the Communist Party. It was one of many held over the years, and on this occasion it was convened to assess the achievements of collectivization and crash industrialization. Its background also included the ongoing starvation of millions of Soviet citizens. Nevertheless, in a typically utopian manner, it was immediately dubbed "the Congress of Victors."

During the course of it, one speech after another hailed the success of Stalin's policies. And each time the general secretary's name was uttered, the hall resounded with waves of standing ovations. A representative speech was given by none other than Bukharin, forced into isolation by Stalin yet still intent on supporting his party.

> *By his brilliant application of Marx-Lenin dialectics, Stalin was entirely correct when he smashed a whole series of theoretical premises of the right deviation which had been formulated above all by myself. . . . It is the duty of every party member to rally round Comrade Stalin as the personal embodiment of the mind and will of the party, as its leader.*[13]

One can imagine deafening explosions of applause interrupting the penitent Old Bolshevik as he stumbled through his fervent confession.

The scenes of ecstasy that surrounded the sequence of speeches about socialist success changed dramatically, however, in the hallways between plenary sessions. Nearly two thousand delegates were present at the congress. They came from throughout the Soviet Union, and it is certain that among those from regions hardest hit by the famine—such as Ukraine and the North Caucasus—reality began to superimpose itself on fantasy. Yes, they may have agreed, Comrade Stalin has led us to achievements Lenin only promised. But with industrialization in high gear and enemy elements

---

13 Quoted in Dmitri Volkogonov, *Stalin: Triumph and Tragedy*, trans. Harold Shukman (London: Forum, 1996), 197.

like the kulaks in flight, would it not be better to find a more moderate leader capable of guiding us through the nightmare of mass famine?

These whispered discussions appear to have yielded a proposal to replace Stalin with Sergey Kirov, the comparatively amiable head of the Leningrad party headquarters. The latter, upon learning of this, actually approached Stalin to inform him of the idea. Stalin, puffing his pipe, no doubt nodded and thanked his comrade for such party-minded openness. Then, when the counting of ballots for the office of general secretary was concluded, Stalin was informed that his name had been crossed out by at least one hundred of the delegates. He quietly ordered those ballots to be destroyed. But since they had been anonymous, he could not know who had cast them. As a result, standing at the podium at the end of the gathering, he would have surveyed a field of adoring faces without knowing which among them were in fact traitors to his cause.

As delegates of the Congress of Victors departed from Moscow, they must have felt that a great event in Communist world building had occurred. However, as the nearly two thousand zealous party members parted company with smiles and kisses, none realized that nearly half would soon be arrested as enemies of the Soviet Union. Moreover, among those who had been elected to the party's central committee, more than 90 percent would within only a few years be shot to death.

The Congress of Victors, one historian noted, was to become a "congress of victims."[14]

"Cultural Revolution"

IN THE MEANTIME, THE COMMUNIST dictatorship was overseeing the creation of the world's first totalitarian system of life. The term "totalitarianism" is an invention of the twentieth century used to describe the unprecedented forms of statecraft found in Communist Russia and Nazi Germany.[15]

---

14   Tucker, *Stalin in Power*, 238.

15   Some have extended totalitarianism to include states like Fascist Italy and even Franco's Spain, but these and lesser forms of authoritarianism did not rise to the same levels of comprehensiveness in their ideologies, especially insofar as

It expresses ideologically liberal values, yet as we shall see in Part III, liberalism would itself eventually exhibit certain totalitarian tendencies. In its original rendering, totalitarianism included four key elements of the Soviet and Nazi states: a political monopoly by a single party; a secret police force to destroy rivals to the party; a command economy to manage and distribute resources for the sake of the party; and a system of communications to establish ideological uniformity as defined by the party.[16] All of these had been introduced to Russia at some level in 1917, but now, under Stalin, they were brought to full development in the wake of the first five-year plan.

The last on the list is particularly important for understanding the age of nihilism. Ideologies of various sorts had entered Christendom toward the end of its age of utopia. The three most influential were liberalism, nationalism, and socialism. All arose in the wake of the French Revolution when the transformation of the state remained unresolved. To various degrees, all pursued the task of building a new state that would serve the interests of a particular element in society: liberalism was dedicated to the individual; nationalism was dedicated to the national community; and socialism was dedicated to the working class (either industrial or agrarian). By seeking to rebuild the state around one or another of these social priorities, ideologies contributed to the ongoing secular transformation of the world begun during the Renaissance.

But they were more than mere agents of secularization. They actually served to compensate for its effects. Chief among these was the desecration of the world, the process by which heavenly immanence had been eliminated in modern Christendom. This is what Weber had called "the disenchantment of the world."

Under the influence of traditional Christianity, as we have seen, the West inherited a culture built on a transcendent experience of paradise. Secular humanism had subverted this. Following the most extreme period of

---

they accommodated the continued existence of traditional Christianity.

16 See, for instance, Carl J. Friedrich and Zbigniew K. Brzezinski, *Totalitarian Dictatorship and Autocracy* (New York: Frederick A. Praeger, 1956), 9–10. The authors identify a total of six elements, but for the sake of simplification I have used only four.

cosmological desecration, the eighteenth-century benightenment, romantics had tried rather desperately to restore transcendence to their culture. The lasting beauty and power of their music, poetry, and painting can be attributed to this characteristically Western impulse toward spiritual transformation. But they failed. Their means of transcendence proved futile because it was counterfeit. They established communion with an idol called the Absolute rather than with the God who, through the Incarnation, established a Church in which sacramental liturgy provided an objective grounding for the kingdom of heaven in the world. Thus they could not produce a lasting way of life. As compelling as romanticism was (and still is), it was not a religion but a movement. It offered only an escape from rather than a transformation of the world.

Ideology was different. Unlike romanticism, it was progressive. It abandoned the romantic search for transcendence in the present moment and redirected it toward the future. Liberalism, nationalism, and socialism in their original nineteenth-century forms defined eschatology in their own way according to the social priorities they embraced. But they all shared one thing in common: their eschatology was a kingdom of posterity. They promised transcendence through progress, and this became Christendom's new myth.

As the specter of nihilism began to loom with the coming of the twentieth century, however, the myth of progress became unstable. Then, during the Great War, it all but collapsed. In its secular form, the transformational imperative was once again in crisis. This time, resolution was found in the reconfiguration of ideological myth. Instead of promising a future experience of transcendence, new expressions of the old ideologies claimed that progress was immanent. To use theological language, ideological eschatology became "realized."

This happened first with Communism, the cultural basis of Soviet totalitarianism. As we have seen, eschatological experiences of Communist ideology had accompanied the Bolshevik seizure of power in 1917. Trotsky's "dustbin of history" speech was one example. Another was the policy of War Communism. The cult of Lenin was probably the most emphatically transcendent element in Communist world building. But it was not until the rise of Stalin after the October Revolution decennial that the "cultural revolution" reached its completion. And it could not do so until the state had done its best to eradicate all vestiges of Communism's great alternative, traditional Christianity.

Obliteration and not "enlightenment," nihilism and not humanism—this is how the Communists prepared their myth-driven reconfiguration of the West. If the nineteenth century had seen positivists like Auguste Comte anticipate the withering away of religion with the advance of science, in the Soviet Union secularization "was not the goal of the revolution but only the precondition for birth of the new Communist order."[17] The October Revolution had tentatively established a legal separation of church and state along the lines of republican France, but during the Civil War such policies were dismissed as insufficiently transformative. In 1919, the eighth party congress adopted a program by which members would pursue "the complete destruction of the ties between the exploiting classes and the organization of religious propaganda, [by] effecting the liberation of the masses from prejudices and organizing the broadest scientific-enlightenment and antireligious propaganda."[18] Like all Communist rhetoric, this statement obfuscated reality with ideological jargon. But its significance is clear: progress must be accelerated, and a nihilistic policy toward existing reality was the way to make it happen.

The annihilation of the Church and other religious bodies hinged on a significant ideological principle. Marx had famously asserted that religion is the "opiate of the masses." What he and his followers meant by this aphorism is that religion serves to induce in the oppressed a false sense of well-being similar to that produced by narcotics. With this function, religion serves the class interests of the oppressing class. Communists concluded that the continued existence of religion after the proletarian revolution is therefore a sign that true progress, measured ideologically, has not yet been achieved. By definition, as long as religious faith exists so does class

---

17 Victoria Smolkin, *A Sacred Space Is Never Empty: A History of Soviet Atheism* (Princeton, NJ: Princeton University Press, 2018), 32.

18 Ibid., 40.

oppression. The cultural revolution therefore demanded an end to religion.

This led to a wholesale assault on the Orthodox Church, though Roman Catholics and Protestants—as well as Jews, Muslims, and Buddhists—were persecuted in smaller numbers. Innumerable Orthodox proved themselves up to the challenge, though some did not. At the time of the revolution, Russian Orthodoxy was in many ways beleaguered. The most significant trouble came from the effects of westernization. Since the seventeenth century, scholastic and pietistic patterns had overtaken parish life. A legalistic approach to confession and communion was joined to an individualistic and excessively emotional experience of salvation. Most debilitating was the inability of the hierarchy to offer vigorous leadership. With the abolition of the Moscow patriarchate under Peter the Great, an increasingly secularistic state reduced episcopal authority in many cases to a passive minimum. The restoration of the patriarchate in 1917 was a great improvement, but it was obvious by then that many other troubles beset the Church. Village clergy were insufficiently educated to address the great social problems of the time, and the laity, who received communion infrequently, were insufficiently evangelized by services and scriptural readings conducted in an archaic language (Slavonic rather than modern Russian) they could not understand.

The tragedy for the Orthodox Church was that the threats and opportunities brought about by the fall of the autocracy caused widespread division. One temptation was to throw off traditional Christianity in an effort to "rescue" the Church. This was what lay behind a schism called Renovationism. Inspired partly by reformational Christianity and partly by utopian Christianity, it radically challenged traditions like fasting and episcopal celibacy while proclaiming enthusiastic support for the revolution. Other demands, such as calls for the use of a vernacular form of Russian in the services, were not in violation of church tradition. But whether demoralized or inspired, the Living Church, as its adherents styled themselves, set itself against the newly restored Moscow Patriarchate and used the Communists (and was used by them) to bring about the destruction of canonical order. The leader of the Renovationists, Alexander Vvedensky, in 1923 betrayed Patriarch Tikhon and assembled a schismatic council at Christ the Savior Cathedral in Moscow.

Far more destructive to the Orthodox Church were the actions of the government. Within a week of the October Revolution, Communists murdered an Orthodox priest named John Kochurov. It was the first act of a persecution that soon exceeded in deaths and desecrations all the persecutions carried out in pagandom during its three centuries of struggle against the early Church. More than a million faithful Orthodox Christians may have been put to death primarily for their faith. The murky record of totalitarianism prevents us from knowing exactly how many there were. The vast majority of them were common peasants and townspeople. Some resisted the closure of village churches during collectivization and were shot. Some resisted the seizure of valuable holy objects in city cathedrals and were shot. Some were shot for participating in outdoor icon processions. Some were shot because they were members of a monastic community. Villagers were shot for refusing to betray their priests, and village priests were shot for refusing to betray their parishioners. We will never know all the details or even all the names of these new martyrs, though heroic efforts are being made today in a post-Communist Russia to learn more.[19]

We do know about the most visible members of the clergy and laity. Among the first was Patriarch Tikhon. He was a missionary hierarch in the United States before the revolution and distinguished himself by defending traditional Christianity's affirmative cosmology there. He commissioned translations into English and exhorted the American laity to participate in the spiritual transformation of their world. Back in Russia, he was arrested on multiple occasions. He was threatened, mistreated, and tortured until he finally died of exhaustion and grief.

Among the many martyrs who died directly at the hands of the Communists were Metropolitan Vladimir of Kiev (who resisted the influence of Ukrainian nationalism in church policy); Priest Constantine of Merkushino (who sang his own funeral service while being marched to his death because he knew no one from his parish church would survive to bury him

---

19 Among the most prolific researchers is Father Damascene Orlovsky, whose indefatigable work has been published in Russia and contributed to decisions by the Moscow Patriarchate to canonize numerous new martyrs.

New Martyr John Kochurov

properly); Nicholas II and the Imperial Family (later canonized for their dignified faith when shot while prisoners living in the Urals); Grand Duchess Elizabeth (a convert from Lutheranism who gave her great wealth away to become a nun and a caretaker of the Moscow poor); Metropolitan Benjamin of Petrograd (who supported efforts to use church wealth for relieving famine but insisted parishes do so voluntarily); and Archpriest Alexander Khotovitsky (who served at Christ the Savior Cathedral before it was seized by the Renovationists).

To repeat, not only the Orthodox suffered. The Communists persecuted people of all faiths. Roman Catholic and Protestant Christians were slaughtered for their faith. Jews, Buddhists, and even animists were put to death for theirs. All believers whose faith witnessed to an anthropology at odds with Communism were subject to repression.

But it was certainly the Orthodox Church that suffered the brunt of antireligious policy. And in addition to the arrest and execution of her faithful, her properties and her holy objects were violently desecrated. As we have noted, Nicholas II sponsored the construction of hundreds of parish churches before the revolution. Those whose non-Western architecture most symbolized Russia's roots in Eastern Christendom were mostly blown up by the Communists. Churches built in baroque or other Western styles, on the other hand, fared better. But these too were frequently desecrated. Those that were not destroyed were converted to "economically productive" workshops, "culturally enlightened" museums, "publicly healthful" gymnasia, and "popularly entertaining" cinemas. The enormous Christ the Savior Cathedral in Moscow was blown up in 1931 to accommodate the construction of a grandiose Palace of Soviets. According to plans, the structure would be taller than the Empire State Building, and its peak would be surmounted by a statue of Lenin nearly the height of the Statue of Liberty. Costs made the project impossible, however, and in the end the Communists settled on installing the world's largest heated outdoor swimming pool instead. As for the Soviet Union's churches, of the fifty thousand that operated at the time of the revolution, only some five thousand or so were still doing so two decades later. Tens of thousands of clergy and monastics were shot, and among the hierarchy only a handful survived.

A microcosm of the new martyrdom was found at the Solovetsky Monastery located on a group of islands in the White Sea known as Solovky. It was quickly expropriated by the revolutionaries and became the Soviet Union's first concentration camp. With a large number of Orthodox Christian inmates, it represented a kind of clerical Auschwitz (though many anti-Communist figures were sent there for reasons unrelated to religious faith). In 1929 it was visited by the famous writer Maxim Gorky (d. 1936). Another of the Soviet Union's Nietzschean Marxists, he had gotten his literary start writing stories about rootless wanderers among Russia's peasantry. Remaking Zarathustra in Marxist terms, he described his heroes as "super-hobos." One biographer has noted that the writer's

> conviction that the Russian people needed strong, aggressive leaders, his intolerance for "weak" intellectuals, and his belief that harsh actions were justifiable in man's struggle to create a better future, help to explain both Gorky's admiration for Lenin and his later cooperation with Stalin. Gorky's quest for a Russian superman—a quest that bore strong resemblance to the Bolsheviks' own determination to create a new Communist man—may be traced back to Gorky's childhood, but its philosophical rationale derived from his reading of Friedrich Nietzsche.[20]

Gorky's Nietzscheanism certainly influenced his attitude toward the men and women he met at Solovky. Returning from the frigid north, Gorky penned a glowing travel journal of their lives of "rehabilitation" there. "There is no impression of life being over-regulated in the prison camp," he reassured his readers. "No, there is no resemblance to a prison, instead it seems as if these rooms are inhabited by passengers rescued from a drowned ship."[21] Significantly, Gorky had come to the forsaken place on tour to observe the newly constructed White Sea Canal. Rather than being rescued from anything, the inmates of nearby Solovky were actually being used as

---

20   Mary Louise Loe, "Gorky and Nietzsche: The Quest for a Russian Superman," *Nietzsche in Russia*, 251–74.

21   Quoted in Anne Applebaum, *Gulag* (New York: Doubleday, 2003), 43.

slave laborers to build this, one of the most ambitious economic projects of the first five-year plan.

Having torn down a large part of traditional Christianity's human and material infrastructure, the Communists were ready to start building a new culture. This included institutions designed to break the attachments of the old culture. The League of Militant Atheists, for instance, conducted anti-religious agitation in the countryside but also sponsored a journal dedicated to what the historian Victoria Smolkin calls secular "world building." Its founder, Yemelian Yaroslavksy, attached the Lenin cult to an anti-religious yet transcendent myth.

> *Marx has died. Lenin has died. But we say: Marx lives in the minds of millions of people, in their thoughts, in their struggle; Lenin lives in each Leninist, in the millions of Leninists, in the entirety of the proletariat's battle, in the Leninist party fulfilling Lenin's testament and leading the working class in its battle for the construction of the new world. This is immortality.*[22]

The league acquired an impressive membership with the onset of Stalin's Revolution from Above. But as its popularity was a function of state initiative, so was its influence. In fact, as an historian notes, it was ultimately little more than a "nationwide Potemkin village of atheism."[23]

Another institution was the Komsomol (Communist Youth League), designed to sever bonds between young adults and their parents. When its members were not swimming at summer camps or socializing with peers, they were expected to study Marxism and volunteer to harvest grain on collective farms. Komsomol's feeder organization was the Young Pioneers, one of whose thirteen-year-old members was celebrated for denouncing his father as a kulak. The episode inspired an unfinished film by Eisenstein entitled *Bezhin Meadow,* in which the heroic lad breaks from his father after the

---

22 Smolkin, *Sacred Space*, 43.
23 Daniel Peris, *Storming the Heavens: The Soviet League of the Militant Godless* (Ithaca, NY: Cornell University Press, 1998), 9.

latter resists the desecration of a village church and its conversion to a peasants' clubhouse. In one pseudo-iconographic image, a burly peasant resembling Samson pushes over the church's iconostasis with a liberating crash.

The new culture was regulated by a system of communication designed to impose utopia and to do so even when reality proved defiant. Its most important propaganda organ was *Pravda* (*The Truth*), the official newspaper of the Communist Party. The paper is a monument to falsehood. In a Kafkaesque way, it reflected the truth as accurately as a circus mirror. It was *Pravda,* for instance, that published Stalin's "Dizzy with Success" article claiming that collectivization had proven wildly popular with the peasants and that local cadres, and not the central government, were alone responsible for any excesses. When famine struck, the newspaper was silent about it. But the party line was taken up by a sympathetic British reporter named Walter Duranty, who traveled to the Soviet Union and claimed in articles published in *The New York Times* that any talk of famine was the result of western conspiracies to stain the utopian society's reputation.

Pravda readers did learn of the great industrial achievements of the period, like the construction of Magnitogorsk, but nothing of the death toll they exacted. Instead, editors sounded a drumbeat of militant resistance to omnipresent enemies to motivate ever more heroic sacrifices. In 1932 the front page featured a photo of the newly completed Dnieper Hydroelectric Dam with a statement warning that "neither the frenzied opposition of class enemies, nor the base work of opportunist agents can halt the victorious expansion of socialist industrialization."[24] The newspaper directed Soviet culture to embrace purely secular values. One historian has noted that though its editorials gave only limited attention to science and technology prior to 1928, the number of such mentions exploded after that.[25] Heroic figures like Alexey Stakhanov, a coal miner who during one particular shift greatly exceeded his quotas, were held up as examples of the highest virtue. *Pravda* quoted Stalin on the matter in its front page editorial for the

---

24 Quoted in Jeffrey Brooks, *Thank You, Comrade Stalin! Soviet Public Culture from Revolution to Cold War* (Princeton, NJ: Princeton University Press, 2000), 56–58.
25 Ibid., 80.

New Year in 1935: "The founding of the Stakhanov movement," the leader declared,

> *served most of all to improve radically the material condition of the work-ers. Life has become better, Comrades. Life has become merrier. And when life is merry, work goes quickly. Hence high norms of production. Hence heroes and heroines of labor.*[26]

Heroic many Soviet citizens were undoubtedly becoming under the weight of totalitarian hardships, but only by reconfiguring the experience of time could anything like happiness—the promise of Communism—be claimed.

We have seen how culturally sensitive Marxists like Lunacharsky and Bog-danov had turned to Nietzsche for inspiration when building new myths for the secular society. They were aware that traditional Christianity approached time mystically, claiming that in liturgical acts both the past and the future are united in the present. As Communists sought the destruction of Chris-tendom's ancient sacramental culture, they created a new eschatology along ideological lines. Like earlier socialists, they deferred human fulfillment to the future. But they also claimed that due to the revolution, the present now participates in that future. As one historian puts it, "the gaps between past, present, and future vanished in the press's near mystical account of Soviet life."[27] To be sure, the temporal continuum favored the future over the past (though in Stalin's time a glance toward the glories of Russian ancestry also began to occur).

A sign of temporal mystification was a slogan introduced to support an accelerated tempo for the economy's shock workers: "Two plus two equals five!" This was an allusion to the five-year plans that regulated the pace of Communist world building. But the expression brought to mind Dosto-evsky's famous statement in *Notes from Underground* about the primacy of the human will over science and mathematics. The Communists applied the equation to the early completion (after four years) of the first five-year plan.

---

26 Quoted in ibid., 89.
27 Ibid., 79.

Poster advertising the Five-Year Plan

Another expression of the union between present and future was found in novels about the pseudo-sacramental experience of collective labor, such as *Time, Forward!* (1933). This novel features the efforts of a group of eager concrete pourers in Magnitogorsk to outdo earlier records of production. As they achieve their goal, they feel a transcendent bond not with the workers they surpassed, but with other workers who will soon set new records.

Perhaps the most impressive example of such efforts was found in the decoration of the Moscow subway. Built like so many projects through a crash program, when it opened it featured stations with extraordinarily elaborate murals and paintings of the new society. Kiev Station is a good representative. Mosaics depict in winsome ways such subjects as collective farmers, steel workers, metallurgists, agronomists, chemists, and university students. Contemporaries called such subway stations "palaces of transport," and so they were. But in addition to treating Moscow commuters to sumptuous architecture formerly reserved for the oppressing classes, such pseudo-iconography, located within a pseudo-liturgical space in which the proletariat regularly assembled and moved, served to unite the present with the utopian future.

As the totalitarian system was being expanded after the October Revolution decennial, nowhere was eschatological nihilism more in evidence than in the cult of Stalin. Lenin—the initial Soviet leader—had sincerely shunned the rare efforts Bolsheviks made to laud him. Nevertheless, he did leave behind an example of the revolutionary superman, a figure of towering ambition and will, which became the basis of a transcendent cult upon his death. In addition to pilgrimages to Lenin's Tomb, statues appeared on the squares of all self-respecting cities, and odes to his genius dominated the output of writers.

Stalin had always been dedicated to his predecessor but had not really distinguished himself in either the October Revolution or the Civil War. During the intraparty debates about building socialism that followed, he remained likewise relatively irrelevant. It was only his use of political intrigue, as we have seen, that opened the way to real leadership. With most of the other Old Bolsheviks humbled in the aftermath of the first five-year plan, he was finally free to satisfy his megalomaniacal craving for attention.

What is remarkable is that it was some of his rivals within the party who were the most abased—despite having credentials more illustrious than Stalin's—who advanced the new cult. We have already heard from Bukharin. Another was Karl Radek (d. 1939), a Polish Communist who traveled with Lenin in the famous sealed train that delivered the leader back to Russia in 1917. He was not a stranger to the new mythology of Marxist hero worship. As Rosenthal has observed, "Radek moved in circles that were suffused with Nietzsche."[28] During the decade that followed the revolution, he issued a string of myth-creating articles on the most ruthless of the Old Bolsheviks. Lenin (of course) as well as Trotsky and Dzerzhinsky received his praise for their contributions to the eradication of "counter-revolutionaries." Interestingly, though Radek was ideologically an antifascist, he was impressed by the emerging cult of nationalist heroes in troubled Weimar Germany, discussing its cultural implications in an article entitled "Hitler" (1932). Having studied Nietzschean myth-building, Radek honed his panegyric skills with other Old Bolsheviks when praising the late Lenin. He also became one of Stalin's most effusive advocates, despite suffering temporary exclusion during the Revolution from Above. After being readmitted to the party, he joined other rehabilitated Old Bolsheviks in showering praise on the new leader at the Congress of Victors in 1934. Later that year, he advocated for the ideological aesthetic known as "socialist realism." At the First Soviet

---

28 Rosenthal, *New Myth, New World*, 376.

The cover of a 1930 issue of Bezbozhnik (The Atheist)

Writers Conference, he rhetorically joined Stalin to the Lenin cult when describing the world-building obligations of art.

Old Bolsheviks might shower Stalin with praise, but Lenin's successor seems to have felt nothing but emptiness. His restlessness turned quickly on real and imagined enemies. From the beginning, he had shown a strong inclination toward retribution against others. An anecdote was later told by his estranged daughter that illustrates this. It has been called the case of the "purged parrot."

> *There was a caged parrot in one of the rooms of the Kremlin apartment. Stalin, whose custom it was to pace back and forth puffing on his pipe as he thought things out, regularly did so in that room. By uncouth habit, he would spit on the floor now and then as he paced. Once, the parrot imitated him spitting. Incensed rather than amused, Stalin reached into the cage with his pipe and killed the bird with a blow to its head.*[29]

It is not possible to psychoanalyze people posthumously (though some historians have tried). What can be said, though, is that Stalin clearly exhibited a need for recognition and praise within the Nietzschean atmosphere of Communist leadership, and that the manner of his rule can not be separated from this passion.

This explains why he decided, in 1934, to purge the Soviet Union of all his real and imagined enemies—beginning with members of the Communist Party itself.

The Great Terror

IN THE AFTERMATH OF THE Congress of Victors, Stalin's megalomaniacal thoughts were racing at phenomenal speed. He was obsessed with losing his hard-won ascendancy within the party. The key link in the problem appeared to be Kirov.

As we have seen, the Leningrad chairman had fully supported forced

---

29 This is Tucker's retelling of the daughter's account. *Stalin in Power*, 147.

collectivization, but now he had become a magnet for those who opposed the general secretary and his place as the successor to Lenin. As summer turned to fall, Stalin therefore called on a secondary figure in the secret police named Genrikh Yagoda. The general secretary elevated Yagoda to the head of the Cheka's successor organization, known as the People's Commissariat of Internal Affairs or NKVD. Stalin's orders must have taken Yagoda's breath away: the new head of the secret police was tasked with the murder of Kirov. Accordingly, on December 1, 1934, an assassin recruited by the NKVD infiltrated the Leningrad party headquarters and shot Stalin's friend and imagined rival through the back of the head. The action was the prologue to what came to be known as the Great Terror.

Its first victims, like its last, were agents of the secret police. The assassin responsible for Kirov's death was easily apprehended, and along with him scores of alleged "Kirov assassins" were rounded up and shot. Stalin had landed on a brilliant means of elevating his power and prestige in the affair. Not only had he eliminated a potential rival in Kirov, but because no evidence for the assassination was made public (the entire team recruited by Yagoda perished almost immediately), he was able to use the affair as a pretext for additional bloodletting. In fact, he created a state of emergency by claiming in *Pravda* and other propaganda organs that Kirov's death was the result of a broad conspiracy to overthrow Communism. Dysfunctional collective farms, disorderly factory production, and the horrendous grief and anger caused by the famine all offered, ironically, justification for these otherwise outrageous claims. Throughout 1935, Stalin directed his inner circle and the NKVD—which he called the "unsheathed sword of the revolution"—to lay the groundwork for what became the deadliest political repression in history.

Among the party's top leadership, those Old Bolsheviks who had not, like Vyacheslav Molotov, ingratiated themselves with Stalin were most immediately in danger. Trotsky was long gone from the Soviet Union, having finally settled in Mexico after his deportation. But almost all of Stalin's early colleagues remained.

Stalin turned first on two of Trotsky's erstwhile allies in the so-called left opposition, Zinoviev and Kamenev. Both had been arrested in connection

Stalin during the Great Terror

with the Kirov affair but had escaped with their lives. In 1936 they were rearrested and placed on trial for serving Trotsky's alleged efforts to assassinate Stalin from abroad. They were also accused of seeking, unbelievably, the destruction of Communism. Yagoda was still in charge of the NKVD, but Stalin assigned a subordinate named Nikolay Yezhov the task of interrogation. When it finally dawned on the two bewildered Leninists that capital punishment was a real possibility, they wrote to Stalin begging for their lives. An earlier letter by Zinoviev reveals the confused and even hysterical tone they would have taken.

> *I am guilty of nothing, nothing, nothing before the party, before the Central Committee and before you personally. I swear to you by everything that is sacred to a Bolshevik. I swear to you on Lenin's memory. I cannot even imagine what could have aroused suspicion against me. I beg you to believe my word of honour. I am shaken to the depths of my soul.[30]*

---

30 Quoted in Volkogonov, *Stalin,* 277.

The Old Bolshevik's conception of the "soul" was of course very different from that of the many victims of the anti-Christian terror he had been advocating since 1917. Zinoviev's letter in no way reverses his fulsome support of political violence in the past. But clearly, something extraordinary was now happening at the very core of totalitarian government.

Zinoviev and Kamenev were among those first placed on what came to be known as a "show trial," a tribunal designed to reinforce publicly the propaganda of the state. Reporters were invited to attend, and not only those of *Pravda* but those of liberal western states as well. The chief prosecutor was Vyshinsky, who had made such a good impression on Stalin at the Shakhty trial in 1928. He was the Cicero of totalitarianism, fiercely committed to the legal annihilation of its reputed enemies and convincing in his use of extravagant rhetoric. The main defendants had been twins in policy throughout the years, and now, in their final act of building socialism, they spoke with a single progressive voice. Kamenev, from the prisoner's dock itself, declared that whatever sentence he received was "just" and called on his sons to carry on and "follow Stalin." Zinoviev, more emotional than his comrade, admitted "my defective Bolshevism became transformed into anti-Bolshevism, and through Trotskyism I arrived at Fascism." Drowning in ideology, he then added cryptically (and incoherently), "Trotskyism is a variety of Fascism, and Zinovievism is a variety of Trotskyism."[31]

The defendants were by no means innocent of inflicting totalitarian terror on millions of fellow countrymen, but they were innocent of the actual charges laid against them. This is obvious to all historians. Even to contemporaries the trial was a charade. One newspaper in Denmark noted that a hotel at which, according to the prosecution, the defendants had established contact with Trotsky had been demolished ten years earlier. Reality did not matter, however. Progressive ideology, now in the strong hands of Stalin, demanded blood.

How the pair of defendants could have confessed to such absurd charges is explained in part by the fact that they realized that in doing so they were advancing the cause of Communism against its enemies. For as Leninists

---

31 Quoted in Conquest, *Great Terror*, 103.

they understood that progress always has enemies. More practically, they had also been promised by Stalin that if they confessed they would not be executed. Progress, he reminded them, simply needs scapegoats. So they confessed. Immediately afterward, they were transported to the Lyubyanka, the headquarters of the NKVD in Moscow. There they were conducted into a holding cell and, after a brief period of uncertainty, taken into the basement and shot. All accounts report that Zinoviev, before the fatal shot was fired, dissolved in a fit of hysteria and begged for Stalin to relent.

Karl Radek, Stalin's enthusiastic panegyrist, was the next to go. Then, after his trial in early 1937, all hell broke loose. The military was another center of potential resistance to Stalin's dictatorship, for it possessed both leadership and weaponry. Marshall Tukachevsky was a Civil War hero, but he was one of the first to be executed. In a period of months, the Soviet Union lost the majority of its generals and admirals. The Red Army was decapitated.

Stalin next moved against members of the former right opposition. At their head was Bukharin, another faithful Leninist and the chief advocate (and propagandist) for War Communism. In 1938 it was his turn to be placed on trial. But he was not alone. At his side in the dock was Yagoda, former head of the NKVD. On Stalin's orders, the overseer of the Kirov assassination had by now been replaced by Yezhov. The latter was an attractive replacement not only because he was likewise prepared to do Stalin's will, but because the leader was short of stature and Yezhov even shorter. Indeed, this and another virtue of the new NKVD head—that he was unscrupulously violent—earned Yezhov the nickname of the "bloodthirsty dwarf."

By now, Vyshinsky was in top form as state prosecutor, even if it took little effort on his part to exact the prisoners' confessions. In the case of Bukharin, Stalin had already taken care of that. The author of the *ABC of Communism* realized he would be shot; this outcome was obvious in light of the case of Zinoviev and Kamenev. What Bukharin hoped was that his wife and son would not also be shot. Stalin, on visiting him in his cell, agreed to these terms. Thereafter, Bukharin and his "accomplice" Yagoda were found guilty. Vyshinsky's closing argument was set in the mythology of Communist world building. "In our country," he declared, *rich in resources of all kinds, there could not have been and cannot be a situation in which a shortage of any product should exist. . . . It is now clear why there are interruptions of supplies here and there, why, with our riches and abundance of products, there is a shortage first of one thing, then of another. It is these traitors who are responsible for it.*

In conclusion, Vyshinsky demanded that the defendants be

shot like dirty dogs! Our people are demanding one thing: crush the accursed reptile! Time will pass. The graves of the hateful traitors will grow over with weeds and thistles. . . . Over the road cleared of the last scum and filth of the past, we, our people, with our beloved leader and teacher, the great Stalin, at our head will march as before onwards and onwards, towards Communism![32]

The accused were found guilty and were indeed shot to death. Contrary to his assurances, Stalin ordered the arrest of Bukharin's wife. Only after twenty years would she emerge from prison.

The annihilation of Stalin's Old Bolshevik rivals was only a microcosm of the Great Terror. Throughout the Soviet Union, hundreds of thousands of innocent people were swept "into the whirlwind," as one chronicler put it. In factories, where abrupt changes of policy flowed from the haphazard policies of shock industrialization, endless accusations against managers were made. A complete turnover of personnel resulted as Stalinist bureaucrats at Gosplan, the state economic planning agency that set production targets and prices, replaced a nascent industrial leadership. By far, however, it was the military that was the hardest hit. By the end of the decade, the decimated officer corps was scarcely able to manage the armed forces that would be needed if the Soviet Union were to be attacked by real enemies.

Even Stalin was aware of this problem. As the clouds of war gathered on the western horizon in 1939, therefore, he decided to suspend the terror campaign. But he needed yet one more scapegoat. So during preparation for

---

32 Quoted in ibid., 390–91.

the eighteenth party congress that occurred early in the year, the final act of the Great Terror was played out at that man's great expense.

Elections to the Central Committee were held as usual, and in this case Yezhov received, as an unfailing servant of the leader, the necessary votes. However, Stalin suddenly appeared from the shadows, smoking his pipe and accusing his subordinate of all the unjustified killings that had sullied Communism during the past five years. An eyewitness later recounted the scene.

> *Yezhov turned pale and in a broken voice answered that his whole life had been devoted to the party and to Stalin, that he loved Stalin more than his own life and didn't know anything he had done wrong that could provoke such a question. "Is that so?" Stalin asked ironically. . . . Stalin went on to accuse Yezhov of working too feverishly, arresting many people who were innocent and covering up for others. "Well? Go on, get out of here! I don't know comrades, is it possible to keep him as a member of the Central Committee? I doubt it. Of course, think about it . . . As you wish . . . But I doubt it!"*[33]

The bloodthirsty dwarf thereafter disappeared from party meetings, and a few days later he was shot through the back of the head. The greatest chapter in Communist bloodletting thus reached its macabre conclusion.

Even so, Stalin remained unsatisfied. One other Old Bolshevik remained alive and beyond the reach of the secret police. In 1940, therefore, Stalin arranged for a Spanish Communist to travel to Mexico City. There, in a simple domestic office, the agent pulled an icepick out of his jacket and buried it in the forehead of Leon Trotsky. With this act, Stalin finally destroyed the last and greatest of his rivals.

Yet even as he did so, closer to home, across the Soviet Union's western border, another great rival was rising in the person of Adolf Hitler.

---

33 Quoted in Robert Conquest, *Stalin: Breaker of Nations* (New York: Penguin, 1991), 208–9.

CHAPTER FIVE

Nazi World Building

I F IN RUSSIA THE DECENNIAL celebration of the October Revolution marked a resurgence of Communist world building, an insurrection in Germany four years earlier announced the emergence of an even more transformational Nazi alternative. In 1923 Hitler organized the Beerhall Putsch, so named for the crowded Munich tavern in which it was launched. As party militants stormed the hall, their leader leapt onto a chair and fired a pistol into the air. Theatrically, he declared the beginning of a "national revolution." In the end, the event came to nothing. Hitler was arrested for sedition and jailed.

But if the Beerhall Putsch proved a farce, there was nothing ridiculous about the ideology that inspired it. National Socialism was the most bestial vision of the West ever concocted. More even than Communism, it promised to replace decrepit humanism and moralistic Christianity with a totally new moral order unrestrained by reason or mercy. Utopia could be reclaimed, its founder Hitler declared, but only through a transvaluation of values so complete as to nullify what the West once was.

When Darwin Met Nietzsche

THE THEATRICAL YOUNG REVOLUTIONARY WHO tried to seize power in the Beerhall Putsch had not always been interested in politics. Adolf Hitler began his career as an art student in Vienna before the Great War. But failing to make his way within the academy there, he spent some five years studying architecture, attending performances of Wagner's operas, and reading aimlessly in municipal libraries (for which he held multiple memberships). As he cultivated a sense of alienation equal to that of the modernists, he took particular notice of the growing power of anti-Semitism. He too was prone to a nihilistic view of the West's bourgeois establishment, and anti-Semitism offered a grand narrative of decline.

Here not only Wagner's contempt for the Jews but the composer's operatic narratives provided inspiration for passing from art to politics. Hitler later related how profoundly a performance of *Rienzi,* based on the life of the fourteenth-century Italian revolutionary, affected him.[1] "In that hour it began," he declared, alluding to the ideology of National Socialism.[2] Convinced the West had not grown greater with secular humanism but weaker, Hitler became fascinated with the possibility of creating an entirely new world grounded in ideological myth.

After fighting for Germany during the Great War, Hitler decided to enter politics. Drawn to the extreme right of the Weimar political spectrum, he joined a preexisting but struggling National Socialist Workers Party and helped turn it into a movement with strong popular support. He assumed leadership in 1921 and began to mount a relentless and ultimately victorious challenge to everything leftward. His party attacked the moderate socialism of the Social Democratic Party and the liberalism of the Center Party. But it was especially hostile toward the German Communist Party. Above all, Hitler had one driving goal—the destruction of Weimar's democratic constitution and the creation of a Nazi dictatorship. The Beerhall Putsch was his first effort to achieve this.

As with Communism in Russia, the ultimate success of the Nazi movement took advantage of unresolved revolutionary aspirations arising from

---

1 On the place of Cola di Rienzo in the history of utopian Christendom, see *Age of Utopia,* 41–45.

2 Quoted in Alex Ross, *Wagnerism: Art and Politics in the Shadow of Music* (New York: Farrar, Straus and Giroux, 2020), 427. The author here acknowledges the fact that the accuracy of Hitler's reminiscence, made only in 1939, has been subjected to skepticism. But it otherwise conforms well with the dictator's many other attributions of influence to Wagner.

the outcome of the Great War. Five years before the Beerhall Putsch, the once-mighty German Empire had collapsed in abject defeat. More perhaps than other belligerents, her subjects had been living with the conviction that their national culture was greater than any other in the West. After all, it had produced the likes of Luther, Kant, Beethoven, and Bismarck. But overwhelming military losses at the Battle of the Somme and a terrible, war-induced famine known as the "turnip winter" had destroyed German morale and brought the army to its knees. In 1918, the Empire surrendered to the Allies. Kaiser Wilhelm II abdicated, and a November Revolution created a new form of government known as the Weimar Republic.

Initially, the new Germany was lauded as the most progressive state in Europe. Its constitution was the fruit of liberal and socialist ideals stretching back decades. It was fully democratic, granting all adult citizens the right to vote. Significantly, this included women. It also provided unemployment insurance and other benefits to the working class. Members of the Social Democratic Party prided themselves on the fact that German socialism was not following the radical example of the Russian Communists. There was no terror and no violent expropriation of the middle class. Nevertheless, postwar political conditions soon deteriorated, and the shadow of extremism began to fall on Weimar democracy.

The economy was largely to blame. Germany had been crushed by postwar financial obligations. War reparations were built into the Treaty of Versailles (1919), which formally ended the war. These all but assured German insolvency. In the decade that followed, there was really no way forward as the exhausted economy floundered. In 1924 the American Dawes Plan provided temporary stability, but this collapsed with the American stock market in 1929. As Wall Street disintegrated, the United States proved unable to prop up the European economy. Hyperinflation returned to Germany, causing Weimar's moderate majority to hold its breath in anticipation of what would follow.

The political order soon turned to chaos. Insolvency made government support of the unemployed workforce impossible, causing many workers to lose confidence in the system. Political liberties encouraged demagogues to radicalize the disaffected workers. Two opposing ideological poles soon appeared. One was German Communism, inspired and assisted by the Soviet Union. Its advocates demanded an end to the "sham" welfare state of bourgeois democracy and the creation of a proletarian dictatorship. At the other extreme was National Socialism. Its membership, known as the Nazis, also intended to replace the constitutional order with dictatorship. Thus, as one historian has described the situation, Weimar Germany became a "candle burning at both ends."[3]

Hitler learned from the failed insurrection of 1923 that his party would need to obtain legitimacy within the democratic system before it could overthrow that system. He realized that his vision of a new order for Germany and the rest of Europe would need to be explained to voters. Above all, he was convinced the disenchanted cosmology of humanism could be replaced with myths about racial transcendence. The decade that followed the Beerhall Putsch provided the time needed to accomplish these goals.

Hitler had been convicted of treason and sentenced to confinement at Landsberg Prison, yet he found himself inundated with letters of support and admiration. Clearly, National Socialism had a promising future. One letter was from a stranger who saw in Hitler's movement the only hope of restoring transcendence to a post-Christian Christendom. "You gave a name," Joseph Goebbels declared, "to the suffering of an entire generation who were yearning for real men, for meaningful tasks. The words you spoke [during your trial] are the catechism of a new political faith amid the despair of a collapsing, godless world."[4]

Hitler appreciated such letters (and would soon learn more about the author of this one). But he did not need them. He was already convinced he was a man of destiny similar in stature to two of his greatest sources of inspiration, Richard Wagner and Friedrich Nietzsche. The composer had been for him a revelation of modern myth creation. The philosopher, on the other hand, had modeled contempt of the modern world and provided a vocabulary with which to plan its destruction. What is more, both fellow

---

3   Robert O. Paxton, *Anatomy of Fascism* (New York: Vintage, 2004), 92.

4   Quoted in Anthony Read, *The Devil's Disciples: Hitler's Inner Circle* (New York: W. W. Norton, 2003), 138.

Germans were models of a megalomaniacal approach to world building.

Having settled into a comfortable routine in Landsberg, Hitler set out to write *Mein Kampf* (*My Struggle*), a political counterpart to Wagner's *Mein Leben* and Nietzsche's *Ecce Homo*. On the one hand it laid out a vision of utopia based on the secular ideologies of nationalism and (to a lesser extent) socialism. But on the other hand, it called for a transvaluation of the political values that would build the new order. In particular, it repudiated the humanistic values that had earlier given rise to those ideologies. The West was so sick, he claimed, that it could be saved only by eliminating or radically reconstituting the legacy of the Renaissance.

Mein Kampf is important for understanding Hitler's mind and the plans he had for Christendom. Nevertheless, it is a tiring book to analyze both for its length (a thousand pages) and for its turgid style. It also frustrates analysis with its minimum discussion of the author's life and intellectual formation. It is clear that beneath the surface great ideas are at work, but the subterranean influence of writers like Hegel, Marx, Darwin, and Nietzsche is never really documented. In the end, *Mein Kampf* is a massive rant, or, as one biographer has put it more cautiously, "a statement of prejudice expressed in a series of assertions."[5]

These assertions, as poorly expressed as they are, culminate in three nihilistic convictions that lay at the heart of National Socialism: the existence of a master race, the inferiority of other races, and the need for a war of racial annihilation. Each of these dreadful convictions would be acted on, Hitler promised, when the Nazis finally came to power.

The first nihilistic conviction is that Christendom in general and Germany in particular depend for their health and even survival on the supremacy of something Hitler called the Aryan race. In asserting this supremacy, he was drawing on the views of nationalistic writers from the late nineteenth and early twentieth centuries. The most prominent of these in Hitler's mind was Houston Stewart Chamberlain, an expatriate Englishman who settled in Germany after falling in love with the mythological vision of Richard Wagner. For Chamberlain the composer of the *Ring* offered a way of seeing

---

5   Michael Lynch, *Hitler* (New York: Routledge, 2013), 63.

modern civilization in a new light, free of scientific and economic determinism. Nietzsche,
too, seemed to offer a vital alternative to the
deadening experience of modernity. Mixing
Wagnerian nationalism with Nietzschean worship of the will, Chamberlain declared in a
work entitled *The Foundations of the Nineteenth
Century* that the West was built by a master
race called the Aryans. Since the rise of Charlemagne in the eighth century, it was the German nation that preserved Aryan supremacy
through morally unflinching expansion and
conquest. This had been the genius of a nation
ruled by the long line of Charlemagne's successors stretching from Frederick Barbarossa

Houston Stewart Chamberlain
Bundesarchiv, Bild 119-1600-06
/ CC-BY-SA 3.0, CC BY-SA 3.0
DE <https://creativecommons.org/
licenses/by-sa/3.0/de/deed.en>, via
Wikimedia Commons

to Wilhelm II. However, when under the last kaiser the German military
collapsed in 1918, Chamberlain was thoroughly confounded.

The rise of racist nationalism such as Chamberlain's was an outcome of
secularization in which new ideologies replaced not only traditional Christianity but the secular humanism that had, since the Renaissance, served as
its counterfeit. Christendom's core values—paradise and utopia—could not
sustain a civilization with a supporting culture that directed its members
toward the racial transformation of the world. Traditional Christianity had
always declared that all races—both "Greek and Jew"—are one in Christ
(Col. 3:11). Race, like gender and class, does not mediate in any way the
experience of paradise. However, secular humanism, with its interest in a
natural rather than supernatural anthropology, greatly weakened Christendom's harmonious vision of man. True, eighteenth-century deists like Rousseau thought humanity would be united one day by natural reason. But this
unity totally failed to materialize during the French Revolution, which the
deists inspired. In fact, it was precisely in the wake of that cataclysm that
nationalism arose in a post-paradisiacal and post-utopian Christendom. And
it did so most virulently in Germany.

Hitler devoured evolutionary ideas about an Aryan master race and used them to argue that individual human beings have no innate value. They certainly do not possess the image of God assigned to them by Christian anthropology. Instead, nature stands autonomously against traditional forms of religion and morality. But this also fundamentally undermined humanism as it had been defined since the Italian quattrocento. Natural selection now began to negate the autonomous individual celebrated by Pico della Mirandola. As race subverted individuality, man lost his capacity for both divine and promethean dignity. "A stronger generation will drive out the weaklings," Hitler claimed, "because in its ultimate form the urge to live will again and again break the ridiculous fetters of a so-called 'humanity' of the individual, so that its place will be taken by the 'humanity' of Nature which destroys weakness in order to give its place to strength."[6] In this increasingly nihilistic form, nationalist ideology reduced humanity to a function of genetics.

The Aryan, Hitler declared, has shown himself throughout history to be the master of all other races, "for he alone was the founder of higher humanity as a whole, thus the prototype of what we understand by the word man. He is the Prometheus of mankind, out of whose bright forehead springs the divine spark of genius at all times."[7] However, the Aryan has begun to surrender his mastery by interbreeding with lower races. "The Aryan gave up the purity of his blood and therefore he also lost his place in the Paradise which he had created for himself." Hitler concludes that "all that is not race in this world is trash."[8]

It is interesting to note that the nationalism on which Hitler drew reworked the secular myth of progress in racial form rather as Marx reworked it in economic form. Here the intellectual and mythical influences on National Socialism and Communism are closely related. Both replaced heavenly immanence with secular ideology. Both replaced heavenly transformation with a secular counterfeit. And by doing so, both offered to their successors a nihilistic transvaluation of values with which to condemn their

---

6   Adolf Hitler, *Mein Kampf* (New York: Houghton Mifflin, 1939), 171.
7   Ibid., 397–98.
8   Ibid., 406.

reputed enemies. We have seen how the Communists sought to annihilate an entire category of humanity in the form of class enemies. We will soon see how the Nazis did the same to what they considered racial enemies.

The second nihilistic conviction in *Mein Kampf* is that the Aryan race, preserved almost exclusively by the German nation, is surrounded by inferior races that must be displaced, conquered, or eliminated. Since the West now lived by secular rather than heavenly patterns of transformation, nationalists like Hitler looked to science to sustain the utopian myth of progress. They found validation in the evolutionary theory of Charles Darwin and his followers. The agnostic father of evolutionism had claimed in *The Descent of Man* that *Homo sapiens*—like all animal species—was not a creation of God but the accidental product of "natural selection." A violent "struggle for existence" became the model for thinking about humanity among Darwin's followers.

Scientists like Herbert Spencer and Francis Galton applied the biologist's principle of "survival of the fittest" to human society broadly. They concluded, for instance, that charity for the poor threatened humanity by sustaining inferior individuals nature had selected for elimination. Others, observing the West's imperial expansion across the globe, applied Darwinian principles to international relations. Karl Pearson declared in a book entitled *National Life from the Standpoint of Science* that "history shows me one way, and one way only, in which a high state of civilization has been produced, namely, the struggle of race with race, and the survival of the physically and mentally fitter race." One of Darwin's most influential German publicists was Ernst Haeckel (Darwin actually endorsed him personally). He claimed the world was divided into multiple races that functioned almost as distinct species. One of these, the Caucasians, was superior to all others. This radical division of humanity by race led the German evolutionist to declare that science should assign to members of inferior races—"psychologically nearer to the mammals (apes and dogs) than civilized Europeans"—a "totally different value to their lives."[9]

---

9   On the contributions of Pearson and Haeckel to the rise of nationalism, see *Age of Utopia*, chapter 11.

Hitler's enthusiasm surged as he pored over such writings during his frustrated years in Vienna. As Richard Weikart has demonstrated, "for Hitler the Darwinian struggle for existence was more than a phrase to justify violent competition. It lay at the heart of his world-view, coloring almost every dimension of his ideology and policy."[10] Though we will never know all the authors he read directly, it is certain Hitler encountered dehumanizing accounts of "inferior races" by social Darwinists in newspapers and the lending libraries he frequented.

At the top of the list was the case of the Jews. Chamberlain, whom we know Hitler read directly (he indicates as much in *Mein Kampf*), identified the Jews as the greatest enemy of the Aryans. *Foundations of the Nineteenth Century* argued that Aryan supremacy was threatened by miscegenation, or inbreeding with inferior races. Hitler actually made a pilgrimage to Bayreuth to meet with the English expatriate to discuss such views only months before the Beerhall Putsch. He was particularly impressed with Chamberlain's conviction that a Jewish conspiracy had been the cause of Germany's defeat in 1918. As he digested these ideas, the two anti-Semites even enjoyed a performance of *Parsifal* together.

But it was not ideas alone that influenced Hitler. The Austria in which he spent his youth was in fact a laboratory for applying such ideas in the transformation of the world. Political anti-Semitism as a movement had been launched there by Georg Schönerer, a member of the Austrian legislature who scuttled religious affiliations (he was a notorious enemy of Roman Catholicism) and replaced them with racial ones. Another anti-Semitic politician was the Viennese mayor Karl Lueger, who combined vehement rhetoric against the Jews with far-reaching efforts to modernize the Austrian capital. Hitler praised both of these men in *Mein Kampf*, though he faulted them for depending on a fainthearted middle class and failing to make use of the more easily radicalized "masses."[11] His vision of the future was indeed radical, and it would require nothing short of a transvaluation of values.

---

10 Richard Weikart, *Hitler's Ethic: The Nazi Pursuit of Evolutionary Progress* (New York: Palgrave Macmillan, 2009), 33.

11 Hitler, *Mein Kampf*, 131.

Hitler's experience with both intellectual and political anti-Semitism led him to the conclusion that without severe measures against the Jews, Germany and all the West would face extinction. As we have seen, he had been an aspiring artist who was strongly affected by painting, architecture, and music. His difficult years in Vienna were eased somewhat by the rapture he experienced when attending the operas of Wagner. Under the spell of Wagnerian totality, for instance, he is reported to have once declared that "whoever wishes to comprehend National Socialism must first know Richard Wagner."[12] Following the composer's anti-Semitic theorizing about culture, Hitler asserted that modernism's dissolution of the arts was the result of Jewish influence. He specifically cited Dada as an example of the West's current cultural malaise. In contrast to the "culture-bearing" Aryan, he claimed, the Jew is "only a parasite in the body of other peoples."[13] Jewish assimilation within Christendom—what many considered the great achievement of secular humanism—was for Hitler an impossibility. The Jew was to Western culture what the "vampire" is to his victim. The racial core of Western culture would be preserved only when Jews were driven from influence.

But the Aryan race was threatened by more than the Jews. The second most dangerous racial enemy for Hitler was the Slavs. He often blurred the distinction between Jews and Slavs by speaking of "Jewish-Bolsheviks." As he put it in *Mein Kampf*, "in Russian bolshevism we must see Jewry's twentieth-century effort to take world dominion unto itself."[14] Many Soviet leaders did in fact have Jewish ancestry, and he made the most of this. These included Trotsky, Zinoviev, Kamenev, Radek, and Yagoda. Hitler also made much of the fact that Marx himself was of Jewish lineage. But the Slavs were in the end to be distinguished from the Jews. They were a "mongrel race" that were, in the classification of Darwinists like Haeckel, of much less value than purebred Aryans. In Hitler's mind, they were nothing but potential slaves in the coming new order.

This brings us to the third nihilistic conviction of *Mein Kampf*: Germany,

---

12 Gerald Fleming, *Hitler and the Final Solution* (Berkeley: University of California Press, 1984), 7.

13 Hitler, *Mein Kampf*, 419.

14 Ibid., 960.

becoming the bastion of Aryan civilization, must launch a war of conquest, enslavement, and extermination toward the east. Here he drew on nineteenth-century discussions of the need for racial *Lebensraum,* or "living-space." He did so for two reasons. In the first case, the majority of European Jewry inhabited lands outside Germany. Only half a million Jews lived within the borders of the Weimar Republic—scarcely one percent of its population. If the National Socialists were to act on the goal of eliminating the Jews from Europe as a whole, they would need to occupy both Poland and the Soviet Union, for it was there that the majority of Jews lived. Both states had Jewish populations of about three million souls.

In the second case, a war of eastward expansion was necessary because only that would enable the Nazis to build a racist utopia. Such an undertaking was a challenge to be sure. Poland's population consisted of 35 million, most of whom were Slavs. The Soviet Union, though ethnically more diverse, had a population of 170 million. Germany, by comparison, possessed only about 87 million people, or half the population of the Soviet Union. Nevertheless, Hitler was convinced that Germany's concentration of Aryan blood assured her of an advantage in the coming and inevitable war.

Indeed, he blended a Nietzschean vocabulary of "lords of the earth" with a Darwinian vocabulary of evolutionary struggle. *The Will to Power* had envisioned a master class of supermen who would exercise dominion over the earth. Abandoning a slave morality that taught compassion and mercy, they would follow a "master morality" of cruelty and exploitation. On the other hand, *The Origin of Species* envisioned all animals—including humans—being locked in an unending struggle with others to survive. For Hitler, a vaguely conceived divine mandate had decreed that "we are placed in this world on condition of an eternal struggle for daily bread, as beings to whom nothing shall be given and who owe their position as lords of the earth only to the genius and courage with which they know how to struggle for and defend it." Hitler's blending of Nietzsche and Darwin in this passage is obvious. But the appeal to a transcendent mandate for conquest is augmented by an equally transcendent experience of communion with posterity. "The soil and territory on which a race of German peasants will some day be able to beget sons," he declared, "sanction the investment of the sons of today, and will some day acquit the responsible statesmen of blood and guilt and national sacrifice" that racial warfare demands.[15]

On his release from prison, Hitler resumed the struggle for power put forward in *Mein Kampf.* He undertook a significant change in tactics, however. Instead of overthrowing the Weimar Republic with an insurrection, he would do so with the power of democracy. The National Socialist Worker's Party was reformed to compete effectively with other parties for leadership in the parliamentary Reichstag. Thus, as the Great Depression grew worse following the withdrawal of the United States from the Dawes Plan, the radicalism of the Nazis grew more attractive to the electorate.

In the Reichstag elections of 1928, when American aid was still flowing into Germany, the Nazis received only 2 percent of the vote compared to the moderate Center's 12 and the Social Democrats' 31 percent. In 1930, after the American financial crash and the end of foreign aid, Nazi support leapt to 19 percent as the Center remained at 12 and the Social Democrats shrank to 25 percent. Then, after two more crushing years of mass unemployment and runaway inflation, democratic elections gave the Nazis 38 percent of the vote, by far the highest in the Reichstag.

Hitler, now elevated to the office of chancellor, realized the time had come. The German Communists had also seen their fortunes rise along with economic anxieties, and they appeared as another extremist alternative. So in the following year Hitler decided to turn on them. In February 1933 a fire gutted the Reichstag building, and the new chancellor used this as a pretext to outlaw the Communists. He then declared a state of emergency. Under these circumstances, he had an Enabling Act passed in March that canceled parliamentary oversight of the government and gave Hitler the dictatorial powers he had been seeking since the Beerhall Putsch a decade earlier.

Nazi world building could finally begin.

---

15 Ibid., 948.

"Cultural Coordination"

AS STALIN HAD DONE IN the Soviet Union, the new Nazi leaders of Germany used ideology to transform Christendom's former culture. Needless to say, a new morality was needed for this. Hitler held the values of the average German citizen in contempt, despite the fact that so many had recently voted for his party. He understood that few would support the racist order he planned without undergoing a transvaluation of values. After all, as much as the nihilistic specter of total warfare, economic collapse, and artistic modernism had haunted German culture, it had not fully obliterated Christianity or humanism.

One of the most important priorities was to lay the basis for a policy of violent racism. Germany was by no means naturally disposed toward the extremes of National Socialism. As one historian has noted, "Germans did not become Nazis because they were antisemites; they became antisemites because they were Nazis."[16] Here "anti-Semites" could be broadened to "racists," since, as we have seen, the Nazis intended to do great harm not only to the Jews but to the Slavs. Neither of these, nor any other races, had historically been hated by Germans. Biological racism was in fact something new. For while Christendom had a long history of anti-Judaism, which sometimes took the form of violent persecution, hatred of the Jews and others as races rather than as religious communities required the existence of a specifically secular ideology.

But National Socialism provided much more than a license to commit genocide. It was a way of establishing meaning for a generation no longer rooted in the transcendent experience of paradise. It solved, or at least endeavored to solve, the transcendence crisis created by the secular culture of utopian Christendom. By the twentieth century humanism had desecrated the world so thoroughly that the West had little beyond rationalist philosophy and empirical science with which to establish the meaning of its civilization. As Nietzsche, Dostoevsky, and a range of modernists and social scientists revealed, humanism was not enough for a civilization with a

---

16 Claudia Koonz, *The Nazi Conscience* (Cambridge, MA: Belknap, 2003), 10.

supporting culture that had once directed its members toward the heavenly transformation of the world.

Ideology filled the void created by secular humanism. In the case of National Socialism it was supported (as we noted in the case of *Mein Kampf*) by a science of racist anthropology. But it went beyond mere science, because science cannot provide solutions to the ultimate problems of meaning, such as death and immortality. National Socialism, in the words of a scholar named Detlev Peukert, was designed to solve "the problem of legitimation in a secularized world."

> *A secularized world no longer provided final answers: it had no way of pointing beyond itself. Once the facade of nontranscendent everyday mythology had been shattered by [Weimar Germany's economic, political, and cultural] crisis, the search was on for "final solutions." The "death of God" in the nineteenth century gave science dominion over life. For each individual human being, however, the borderline experience of death rebuts this claim to dominion. Science therefore sought its salvation in the specious immortality of the racial [national body], for the sake of which mere real, and hence imperfect, life could be sacrificed.[17]*

As a secular ideology, National Socialism was designed to restore utopia while transcending its secular limitations. It was designed to provide Christendom with a new culture. To advance this new culture, the party leadership from the very start introduced a policy called *Gleichschaltung*, or "coordination." The German word was taken from the vocabulary of scientific engineering, but the Nazis assigned to it a broader significance. It can also be translated simply as "Nazification." As a necessary process in ideological world building, cultural coordination formed a "Nazi conscience."[18] As a new morality it would replace Christianity and humanism, enabling average Germans to tolerate what would formerly have been considered blasphemies

---

17 Detlev Peukert, "The Genesis of the 'Final Solution' from the Spirit of Science," in *Reevaluating the Third Reich*, ed. Thomas Childers and Jane Caplan (New York: Holmes and Meier, 1993), 234–52.

18 Koonz, *Nazi Conscience*.

and inhumanities. The goal of cultural coordination was the total reengineering of German beliefs and values so that they would conform to the ideology of National Socialism.

This policy produced the most determined propaganda system Christendom has ever seen. It was run by Joseph Goebbels (d. 1945), who had welcomed the Beerhall Putsch and joined the party after his correspondence with Hitler when he was at Landsberg. Goebbels was no mere brownshirt thug. He held a PhD in romantic literature and spent his early years writing novels and plays, though unsuccessfully. From the start, he felt an obligation to dedicate all his talents to Hitler and the cause of National Socialism. Though Hitler initially kept him at arm's length, Goebbels soon became one of his most trusted henchmen. His diaries from the early years of party activity read like confessions of love for the great "leader" (*Führer*). His devotion resulted in his being elevated to the office of minister of public enlightenment and propaganda. The assignment was similar to that of Anatoly Lunacharsky in contemporary Russia, and like his Communist counterpart, Goebbels used it to transform the culture of the West.

Goebbels hated the culture of modern Christendom. An ambitious but frustrated writer himself, he looked on the monuments of literary modernism with disgust. Following Hitler's lead, he blamed Jews and Marxists for everything he considered wrong with the modern world.

And indeed, some of the most notorious works of Weimar modernism had been inspired by Marxism. The plays of Bertolt Brecht, for instance, employed a device their author called "alienation-effect." Its purpose was to disturb rather than charm the audience—to stir it into class-conscious revolutionary indignation rather than lull it into satisfaction with the contemporary status quo. As such it could not be further from the goals of Nazi propaganda. A famous example of alienation-effect was a song incorporated into Brecht's *The Threepenny Opera* (1928) by Brecht's Marxist collaborator Kurt Weil. Entitled "The Ballad of Mack the Knife," the song uses a catchy melody that in the context of a romance might bring a complacent smile to the faces of a middle-class audience. But in this case the song tells the narrative of a serial killer. And though the bloody images the song brings forth would certainly have alienated the contemporary bourgeoisie, with time the melody would be coopted—in a victory for nihilism—by the capitalist establishment itself. In America, renditions in the form of jazz songs (Louis Armstrong) and even fast-food commercials ("It's a good time / For the great taste / At MacDonald's / It's Mac tonight!") brought Brecht's and Weil's subversive song to a complacent rather than alienating end.

But none of this would have satisfied the anti-bourgeois indignation of Goebbels. So much did he detest modernist art that in 1937 his ministry organized an exhibition of paintings deemed "decadent." They featured many of the Expressionists we discussed in chapter 3, including van Gogh and Picasso. The founder of Bridge, Ernst Kirchner, on learning that hundreds of his paintings had been purged from German galleries and some selected for the exhibit, committed suicide. Ironically, it was left to the most destructive regime of the twentieth century to bring attention to and condemn artists whose work served to negate the humanistic legacy of modern painting. Apparently, it took a nihilist to know one.

Through the ministry of propaganda Goebbels resolved to change the culture of the West, beginning in Germany. All forms of communication—including the newly invented radio—were coordinated to advance the Nazi definition of "enlightenment." Professors were driven out and newspaper editors sacked. Along the main thoroughfares of every city appeared Nazi banners and the omnipresent image of the party leader. The swastika was placed on the facade of every governmental building.

Perhaps most ambitiously, an organization called the Hitler Youth was created. Like the Soviet Komsomol, its purpose was to separate impressionable children from their traditionally minded parents. Like its Communist counterpart, it featured events such as camps and agricultural programs that gave teenagers a sense of purpose and liberated them from traditional morality. It also gave them unwanted pregnancies. In 1936, for instance, no fewer than nine hundred girls conceived at the annual Nazi party rally—with only half of them knowing the identity of the child's father.[19] Finally, as in the Komsomol, there were cases in which zealous youths—both male

---

19 Michael H. Kater, *Hitler Youth* (Cambridge, MA: Harvard University Press, 2004), 108.

and female—denounced their parents to the authorities.[20]

All beliefs and values that did not serve Nazi interests were to be eradicated. One of Goebbels's first acts upon being made minister of enlightenment was a public book-burning in Berlin. As volumes of Marx, Freud, and Remarque went up in flames, he announced "the collapse of the intellectual basis" of a decrepit humanism.[21]

But he and other Nazis knew the destruction of secular humanism was not enough. The coordination of the new culture would also require the destruction of Christendom's primordial faith. The regime's leadership was universally contemptuous of traditional Christianity's doctrinal integrity. In the case of Roman Catholicism (to which about a third of the population adhered), the principles of universality and international leadership through the office of the papacy were totally unacceptable. On the other hand, in the case of Protestantism (to which about two-thirds of the population adhered), there was more to work with. Luther himself, for instance, was not only a national hero but had expressed notoriously anti-Jewish views. Calvinism was another major force in German Protestantism, and its comparative disregard for a sacramental culture also provided an accommodation to Nazi world building. On balance, however, reformational Christianity's long-term priority of elevating society to the standards of the gospel was deeply subversive to the Third Reich.

The new government realized Christianity and National Socialism could not coexist. In public, Hitler feigned support for the historical churches of Germany, but privately he made his intentions very clear. Within his inner circle he asserted the day would come when an elimination of Christianity would be necessary. "When National Socialism has ruled long enough," he declared, "it will no longer be possible to conceive of a form of life different from ours."[22] Because Nazi world building, when completed, would negate—even annihilate—all rival beliefs and values, the leader frequently

---

20 Ibid., 38–39.

21 Peter Longerich, *Goebbels*, trans. Alan Bance, Jeremy Noakes, and Lesley Sharpe (New York: Random House, 2015), 224.

22 *Hitler's Secret Conversations, 1941–1945*, trans. Norman Cameron and R. H. Stevens (New York: Signet, 1953), 36.

spoke the language of Nietzsche when articulating religious policy. This enabled him to dismiss Christianity's (as well as humanism's) concern for individual persons out of hand. "To the Christian doctrine of the infinite significance of the individual soul," Hitler announced, "I oppose with icy clarity the saving doctrine of the nothingness and insignificance of the individual human being, and of his continued existence in the visible immortality of the nation."[23] Nietzsche had deplored the rise of Christianity more than any other event in Western history. The gospel, after all, stifled the will to power by teaching love of one's enemies and the practice of mercy. "The heaviest blow that ever struck humanity," Hitler likewise asserted, "was the coming of Christianity."[24]

Surrounding the leader were religious convictions ranging from confidence in a kind of divine non-Christian providence resembling deism to a full-blown neopaganism. Goebbels belonged to the first group. He had begun to apostatize from his native Roman Catholic faith as a young man, though a nihilistic comment made in his diary from the period suggests an elastic definition of religion: "It doesn't matter what we believe in, as long as we believe." As one of his biographers has noted, such statements reveal that "Goebbels was urgently seeking an ideology to which he could commit himself."[25] Significantly, he was working at the time on a play entitled *Prometheus,* the mythical symbol of modern man liberated from a transcendent God.

Similar views were held by Martin Bormann (d. 1945), Hitler's private secretary and close advisor. With appeals to modern science, he claimed that "National Socialist and Christian conceptions are incompatible."[26] He advanced the policy of cultural coordination at every corner, promoting the removal of crucifixes from classrooms and discouraging the distribution of Christian writings in the Hitler Youth and the army. So radical and

---

23 Quoted in Michael Burleigh, *The Third Reich* (New York: Hill and Wang, 2000), 256.

24 *Hitler's Secret Conversations,* 37.

25 Longerich, *Goebbels,* 31.

26 Richard Steigmann-Gall, *The Holy Reich* (Cambridge: Cambridge University Press, 2003), 245.

persistent was his campaign of dechristianization that more than once other leading Nazis and even Hitler himself had to intervene to mitigate the resistance he provoked among common Germans.

Many Nazi leaders were actually neopagans. The most elaborate beliefs were held by Alfred Rosenberg (d. 1946), who in the early years was informally named by Hitler chief intellectual and spiritual authority of the Third Reich. A Baltic German refugee from the Russian Civil War, Rosenberg cultivated a deep hatred for both Communism and Jewry. He combined these animosities with one for Christianity. After he joined the Nazis, his philosophical pretensions soon earned him the editorship of the official party newspaper. He was also appointed temporary leader of the party by Hitler during the latter's imprisonment.

Rosenberg's greatest single contribution to world building was his massive *Myth of the Twentieth Century* (1930), which drew on a variety of inspirations but most notably on Chamberlain's *Foundations of the Nineteenth Century.* The similarity in titles was not coincidental; Rosenberg intended to bring his predecessor's racist vision of Christendom to its neopagan completion. Chamberlain had held Christianity in contempt, but Rosenberg adds a plan for a post-Christian religion. This explains the use of "myth" in elaborating it. The book draws heavily on the vocabulary of Nietzsche and sympathizes with Wagner for longing to create, through art, a "new world." Rosenberg was intoxicated by Wagner's operatic universe of promethean Siegfrieds shattering the moral spears of Wotans in order to slaughter Semitic Mimes. The transvalued neopaganism of *The Ring of the Nibelung* offered him and other Nazis an important key to utopia.

Rosenberg's *Myth* would sell more than a million copies in the Third Reich. But like *Mein Kampf* it was a book seldom read and even more seldom understood. One historian characterized it as "a ludicrous concoction of . . . half-baked ideas on Nordic supremacy palmed off as the fruit of what passed for erudition in Nazi circles."[27] Goebbels called it an "ideological belch." Though it expressed well the darkly mythological ways in which Germany

---

27 William Shirer, *The Rise and Fall of the Third Reich* (New York: Simon and Schuster, 1960), 149.

and the West were being reimagined, it does not seem to have had much direct impact on the Nazi new order.

But another neopagan Nazi did. Heinrich Himmler (d. 1945) competed with Goebbels in serving as Hitler's right-hand man. The head of the Schutzstaffel, or SS, he would oversee the mass murder of millions in the coming war. His organization was originally created to serve as the personal bodyguard for Hitler, but after 1933 it hypertrophied into the leader's personal army. Until just days before committing suicide in his Berlin bunker, Hitler considered Himmler his truest disciple, his "faithful Heinrich."

As Himmler's biographer has noted,

in order to arm [National Socialists] for the forthcoming epochal conflict between "humans and subhumans" Himmler wanted to direct the SS to one task above all: it was to act as the vanguard of overcoming Christianity and restoring a "Germanic" way of living. As he understood it, this was the actual mission of his Schutzstaffel; it was to this task that it owed its identity and the justification for its existence. Christianity seemed to him so dangerous because its sexual morality stood in opposition to the biological revolution he planned, and because the principle of Christian mercy contradicted his demand for unwavering severity in dealing with "subhumans."[28]

So, to complement the transvalued values of *Mein Kampf*, Himmler enhanced Nazi myth with neopagan beliefs and rituals.

He was assisted in this by a quack archeologist named Karl Maria Wiligut, whose life mission was to uncover the pre-Christian religious basis of Germanic civilization. Fascinated by the rise of a cult of Wotan among Wagnerian intellectuals, he joined the SS with the hope of seeing the organization reestablish pagandom in the Third Reich. His fascination with Viking civilization contributed to Himmler's decision to use runes and the death's head image as emblems of the Schutzstaffel.

---

28 Peter Longerich, *Heinrich Himmler*, trans. Jeremy Noakes and Lesley Sharpe (Oxford: Oxford University Press, 2012), 265.

But Himmler was not satisfied with mere emblems. He actively supported the reintroduction of purported pagan rituals and festivals. Himmler, to be sure, was no atheist. In fact, he expressly barred atheists from serving in the SS, which he regarded as the religious successor to the crusading order of Teutonic Knights (emphatically without papal oversight). Schutzstaffel officers were expected to be true believers in the neopagan alternative to Christianity. For example, men were instructed to honor the winter solstice instead of Christmas and were given special yule candles to burn at home. As Himmler observed, "the wife in particular, when she loses the myth of the church, will want to have something else to fill her mind and the mind and heart of her child."[29]

As with Communist festivals and rituals, National Socialist ones were self-consciously mythological. During the Soviet cultural revolution the children of Communists were "octobered" and not baptized. In Nazi Germany, newborn SS children were to be "name-consecrated" on an altar draped with a swastika placed beneath an image of Adolf Hitler. Instead of Soviet "red weddings," young SS soldiers and their brides, after documenting their Aryan ancestry, received instruction on their duties to the race with solemn readings from *Mein Kampf* and *Thus Spake Zarathustra*. Instead of a cross to wear (as remained the custom for many German Christians), SS elites received from Himmler the death's head ring. They were instructed that the neopagan image of death was a

> *sign of our loyalty to the Führer, of our unchanging obedience towards our superiors, and of our unshakable solidarity and comradeship. The death's head admonishes us to be ready at any time to commit our individual life for the life of the whole community. The runes on the opposite side of the death's head are the sacred symbols of our past, with which we are reconnected through the ideology of National Socialism.*[30]

---

29 Longerich, *Himmler*, 287.
30 Ibid.

A more pseudo-transcendent definition of the nihilistic world building of the Nazis could scarcely be found.

With their hatred of Christianity and reverence for the militant naturalism of Nordic pagandom, it is no surprise that the Nazis persecuted Germany's historical churches. Their primordial enemy after the Jews and the Slavs was the pope of Rome. They inherited Bismarck's nationalistic disdain for the universal community of Roman Catholicism and were intent on destroying its political influence. Initially, their methods were intended to appear conciliatory. A concordat in 1933 granted the Roman Catholic Church freedom from party intervention provided her clergy abstained from political interference.

But Hitler never intended to honor the concordat's terms. Cardinal Eugenio Pacelli, the future Pope Pius XII (r. 1939–58), was the one who signed the concordat on behalf of the reigning Pope Pius XI. Attacked by some later historians as "Hitler's pope," Pacelli was in fact by no means compromised by the Nazi regime. He actually used the concordat and his subsequent authority as pope to defend traditional Christianity against the cunning of the Nazis. That he favored negotiations with the Nazis can be understood by recalling that the papacy was then under constant intimidation by Hitler's ally, the Fascist dictator Benito Mussolini. In fact, in 1937 Pacelli's predecessor Pius XI actually issued a bold challenge to Nazi world building, smuggling into Germany an encyclical entitled *Mit brennender Sorge* (*With Burning Concern*) to be read from every Roman Catholic pulpit on Palm Sunday. It was an heroic defense of traditional Christianity. By such measures, the papacy openly resisted anti-Christian persecution in a way that the contemporaneous Moscow patriarchate under Sergy—appointed by Stalin in the face of German invasion—never did. Needless to say, in retaliation Goebbels arranged for the arrest of hundreds of German priests. In all, a third of all Roman Catholic clergy in Germany suffered some form of repression.[31]

Protestants fared only slightly better. Since Luther was a national hero,

---

31   Ian Kershaw, *The Hitler Myth: Image and Reality in the Third Reich* (Oxford: Oxford University Press, 1987), 115.

the Nazis were inclined to view his followers with more tolerance. Indeed, the very year the Roman Catholic concordat was signed, a congress of Protestants formed a German Evangelical Church that incorporated Lutherans, Calvinists, and other Protestants into a single national body. What is most significant is that it was formed under the influence of a movement known as Positive Christianity. This movement had roots in a utopian Christianity that dated to the time of Friedrich Schleiermacher. However, its adherents (known also as "German Christians") are best understood as adherents of a sort of paradoxically nihilistic Christianity. For they adopted many of the racist views that shaped National Socialism. They were fiercely anti-Semitic and promoted the claim, advanced by writers like Chamberlain (who had been a close friend of the liberal theologian Adolf von Harnack), that Jesus was not a Jew but an Aryan. It was an incredible claim, but these were incredible times. Led by Ludwig Müller (d. 1946), the Evangelical Church's first Reich Bishop, they provided strong support for the Nazi policy of cultural coordination.

However, the rise of Positive Christianity alienated many Protestants who held non-negotiable commitments to traditional Christianity. And so a schism soon followed. In 1934 a Barmen Declaration by Karl Barth and other Calvinists rejected categorically any submission by the clergy to the Nazis. At about the same time, the Lutheran Martin Niemöller joined with Barth and Dietrich Bonhoeffer to form something known as the Confessing Church. These theologians and pastors were adamantly opposed to the Evangelical Church's adoption of an Aryan paragraph that denied pastoral authority to Christians of Jewish or Slavic ancestry. Needless to say, Goebbels's ministry of propaganda was furious. Barth was driven from Germany, Niemöller was thrown into prison, and Bonhoeffer, after suffering for years in a concentration camp, was martyred only days before the Third Reich finally collapsed. As for Reich Bishop Müller, he remained a committed Nazi to the end, and, when confronted with the inevitable, acted like a true Viking priest by killing himself.

With significant resistance raised by both Roman Catholics and Protestants, the Nazis realized traditional Christianity could not be eliminated right away.[32] This was, perhaps, the sole instance in which Hitler and his regime were forced to concede at least temporary defeat in cultural coordination. But they had no doubts that resistance was only temporary. We have already quoted the Nietzschean predictions of Hitler about the inevitable destruction of Christianity. During the war, Rosenberg laid out a plan for transitioning to a nihilistic form of Christianity. Among the points relating to a fully coordinated church were:

The National Church declares that to it, and therefore to the German nation, it has been decided that the Führer's Mein Kampf *is the greatest of all documents. It . . . not only contains the greatest but it embodies the purest and truest ethics for the present and future life of our nation. On the altars there must be nothing but* Mein Kampf *(to the German nation and therefore to God the most sacred book) and to the left of the altar a sword. On the day of its foundation, the Christian Cross must be removed from all churches, cathedrals, and chapels . . . and it must be superseded by the only unconquerable symbol, the swastika.[33]*

Yet as in the Soviet Union, Nazi Germany would ultimately fail to destroy what still remained of traditional Christianity.

For now, they had to make do with the myth-bearing beliefs, symbols, and festivals they could control. The most sensational demonstration of these was the national party rally that recurred every year at Nuremberg. As the harvest season commenced, the nation made a pilgrimage to this medieval town, at once a symbol of transcendent ancestry and of Wagnerian modernity (for it was here that Hitler's favorite opera, *The Meistersingers of*

---

32 An argument has been made that, contrary to the vast majority of assessments, the Nazis retained a nominal affiliation with Christianity and that their program of cultural coordination should therefore not be seen as a fundamentally anti-Christian movement. However, such a view ignores the fact that insofar as the Nazis occasionally spoke in favor of Christianity, they did so cynically and with gross disrespect for its traditional rather than utopian or nihilistic forms. For this mistaken view of Nazidom, see Steigmann-Gall, *Holy Reich*.

33 Quoted in Shirer, *Rise and Fall of the Third Reich*, 240.

Nazi rally at Nuremberg, 1934

Nuremberg, had been set). The Communists had set a precedent of sorts by organizing their own festal party congresses, but these had been intermittent and were never open to the general public. Goebbels put Nazi party meetings to much more effective propaganda use.

The one held in 1934 was the most spectacular, if only because it was memorably documented by the Eisenstein of Nazi cinematography, Leni Riefenstahl (d. 2003). It is remarkable that within the hyperpatriarchal society of the Third Reich a woman could rise to great heights in the profession of filmmaking—and a non-party member at that. But such was the surreal world of Nazidom.

In *A Triumph of the Will,* Riefenstahl used Nietzschean language to portray the 1934 party rally at Nuremberg as an experience of nationalistic transcendence. As the film opens, aerial footage of the town's medieval cathedrals and marketplaces is backed by the exquisitely serene prelude to act 3 of Wagner's opera. Suddenly, as if in a counterfeit experience of divine participation, viewers realize they are seeing these unprecedented views from the perspective of Hitler, who is descending through the clouds in an airplane. As the leader alights from his aircraft, crowds of Germans throng to greet him with the standard salute of *Sieg heil!* (Hail, victory!). As the days of festivity advance, thousands of Aryan townspeople, workers, peasants, and soldiers are shown in national costume marching and shouting in joyful affirmation of communion with Hitler. Innumerable speeches culminate in the one great speech—that of the leader—which reviews necessary acts of repression against enemies of the *Volk* (people). In fact, Hitler had just completed the bloody purge of his old party comrade Ernst Röhm, head of the militant Storm Troopers (SA), in an event known as the Night of the Long Knives. In light of this, fictional images of unity were more important than ever. The film therefore also features a sequence in which Hitler, flanked by Himmler, solemnly approaches a monument to the fallen soldiers of the Great War, and, as if repudiating the sign of the cross, commemorates them with the Nazi salute. Behind rises neither stained glass cathedral windows nor the image of the Crucifixion but the "twisted cross" of the swastika.

Every year in September these myth-propagating ceremonies were repeated among ever-growing crowds of attendees. Eventually hundreds of thousands massed to hear the leader speak of the recovery of Christendom's transformational imperative. "All of them," Hitler declared at one of the rallies, "will be able to come to the same conclusion: we are truly the witnesses of a transformation more tremendous than any the German nation has ever experienced."[34] The experience may not have been the heavenly transformation of the old Christendom, but within the secularized and disintegrating culture of the new Christendom it was still a marvel to behold.

The special theme chosen by Goebbels's propaganda ministry for the Nuremberg Rally of 1939 was "Peace." The designation was ironic. For a day before the grand opening, word came from Berlin that the event had to be canceled. Hitler had finally decided to bring peace to an end and go to war.

A "War of Annihilation"

THE PURPOSE OF CULTURAL COORDINATION had in fact always been the preparation of Germans for total warfare. From the start, Hitler intended to abrogate the Treaty of Versailles and resume the conflict that had, for him and other nationalists, only been suspended with the ignominy of 1918. After coming to power, he therefore committed a series of aggressive actions including remilitarizing the Rhineland, launching a full-scale production of armaments, and, early in 1938, forcibly incorporating Austria into the Third Reich. As fears of war spread through democratic France and Britain, Hitler offered a deceptive olive branch in the form of the Munich Agreement in September 1938. By its terms, he was granted the German-speaking Sudetenland of Czechoslovakia in exchange for promises to expand the Nazi state no further. Prime Minister Neville Chamberlain returned to London from the meeting waving Hitler's promise in the air and declaring his policy of appeasement a success. In the Soviet Union, Stalin, who had so far been encouraging a tougher international stance toward Germany, interpreted the agreement as a sign he could not count on Western democracies in opposing Nazism.

The Munich Agreement was in fact a shameful failure. The following

---

34 Burleigh, *Third Reich*, 211.

spring the Third Reich, along with Hungary and Poland, completed the annexation of all Czechoslovakia. Hitler now began to make noises about ethnic Germans "suffering oppression" in the Polish city of Danzig. As it became clear this would be his next target, an alliance was formed between Poland and a slowly wakening France and Britain.

Hitler's generals greatly feared another two-front war. But the evil genius had a solution. Late in August he sent to Moscow his foreign minister, Joachim von Ribbentrop, to negotiate a nonaggression pact with the Soviet Union. The move was as brilliant as it was unexpected. As we noted in the previous chapter, Stalin had killed off most of his military high command during the recently suspended Great Terror. Seeing he now had no military support in the west, he realized he was in no condition to fight Germany. He therefore had his commissar of foreign affairs, Molotov, sign the Nazi-Soviet Pact. By doing so, the Soviet Union acquired a much-needed breathing space to prepare for a conflict that promised to dwarf the Great War.

On September 1, 1939, Germany invaded Poland and by doing so triggered declarations of war by France and Britain. This was the beginning of the Second World War. Germans were terrified at the prospect of another interminable conflict, as were Hitler's generals. Had the leader's reckless militarism doomed the nation once again to military encirclement and economic asphyxiation? Miraculously, the answer was no.

The Nazis had been working hard ever since 1933 to rearm the *Wehrmacht* (armed forces) with weaponry that would prevent another war of immobility. First among these was the battle tank, or *Panzer*. It could drive directly into defensive machine-gun positions and return fire in kind, ultimately using its cannon to destroy the enemy. Fast, heavily armed fighter planes and dive bombers were other new weapons. Among the latter was the Stuka, which could target defensive positions from more than 10,000 feet in the air and swoop down—often with sirens mounted to the fuselage for terror effect—to destroy them. This highly mobile form of warfare soon earned the name *Blitzkrieg,* or "lightning war."

Hitler's Wehrmacht proved unstoppable during the first two years of the conflict. The comparatively primitive Polish armed forces were no match for it. In some cases they even sent cavalry into battle, which were decimated by roaming German panzers. Poland was simultaneously invaded from the east by the Soviet Union, an outcome of the nonaggression pact. In little more than a month, the Polish state ceased to exist. Germany's eastern flank was secure, and Hitler now turned on France.

Neither she nor Britain had raced into action after their declaration of war in September, freeing the Wehrmacht for operations against Poland. After a lull in fighting—a period known as the "phony war"—in May Germany attacked the west in full force, enveloping the French and driving their British allies to the English Channel. Proud France had withstood German arms for more than four years during the Great War. She now fell in six weeks. What is more, the British army that had been sent to defend her only narrowly escaped destruction through an unprecedented civilian-coordinated seaborne evacuation at Dunkirk. Demoralized and retreating across the English Channel, Britain was the only enemy that remained. During the Battle of Britain in the summer and fall, Germany's *Luftwaffe* (air force) sought to degrade the Royal Air Force enough to free the channel for a massive invasion. But armed with the famous Spitfire and forewarned of Luftwaffe sorties by newly invented radar, the British were able to stave off the invasion. Nevertheless, the new prime minister, Winston Churchill, realized that Britain was in no position to fight back.

The year 1940 thus came to an end with images of Hitler everywhere victorious. One photo showed him making the Nazi salute over troops marching through Warsaw. Another showed him gathered with generals beneath the Eiffel Tower. Still another showed him back in Berlin, reviewing a throng of grateful Germans from the balcony of the German chancery. He had led Germany to military glory against all odds. The Third Reich built by his Nazis seemed invincible. Yet the restless erstwhile artist and miracle-working warlord was not finished. In fact, the most ambitious act of Nazi world building was yet to come.

In *Mein Kampf* Hitler had made it abundantly clear that the long-term plan of National Socialism was the elimination of the Jews and the enslavement of the Slavs. Both goals were contingent on the conquest of the Soviet Union. Since a large percentage of European Jewry lived within her borders and those of Poland, a war in the east was necessary. Poland had now

Hitler before the Eiffel Tower

fallen, and German military forces were already sweeping through the country rounding up its Jewish citizenry. But the Soviet Union—the heart of "Jewish-Bolshevism"—remained untouched. To overcome the Aryans' greatest racial enemy and subdue the Slavs, a full-scale invasion was necessary. As 1941 opened, then, Hitler prepared for what came to be known as

Operation Barbarossa. Bringing Nazi ideology to fulfillment, it proved to be the greatest invasion in history.

Hitler's plans for the invasion of Russia were laid out in a series of meetings and reports during the spring. They were defined by a combination of utopian vision and nihilistic contempt. Gathering his generals before him on March 30, the leader declared that the coming struggle was not merely one of army against army but of culture against culture. It would be a "clash of two ideologies," he explained. The Communists and Nazis had erected their states on the ruins of Christendom. Both Christianity, with its principle of charity, and humanism, with its celebration of autonomous individual dignity, were bankrupt. Wars in the past, he observed, had accommodated such values. But mercy and chivalry were now dead. Between opposing armies, he declared "we must forget the notion" of sympathy.[35] The coming conflict will be "a war of annihilation."[36]

Hitler's generals got the message. One, Erich Hoepner (d. 1944), subsequently declared to his men with a combination of Darwinian objectivity and Nietzschean ruthlessness:

> *The war against Russia is an essential phase in the German nation's struggle for existence. It is the ancient struggle of the Germanic peoples against Slavdom, the defense of European culture against the Muscovite-Asiatic tide, the repulse of Jewish Bolshevism. That struggle must have as its aim the shattering of present-day Russia and therefore be waged with unprecedented hardness. Every combat action must be inspired, in concept and execution, by an iron determination to ensure the merciless, total annihilation of the enemy.[37]*

Another order known as the Barbarossa Directive provided blanket protection to German soldiers who committed atrocities against unarmed Soviet citizens. Its provisions authorized the execution of civilians in cases where a

---

35 Quoted in Gellately, *Lenin, Stalin, and Hitler*, 422.
36 Mark Mazower, *Hitler's Empire: How the Nazis Ruled Europe* (New York: Penguin, 2008), 139.
37 Quoted in ibid., 428.

German officer approved the measure. When individual enemy saboteurs evaded arrest, German officers could order reprisals against local communities. The directive protected all German soldiers from court-martial in cases where they executed noncombatants. Since the stakes were so high for civilization, Nazi thinking went, international military law simply did not apply in the "barbaric east."

Indeed, defending the civilization of the West demanded nihilistic dehumanization. To prevent the possibility in the future of a revival of Communism, Russia's entire intellectual leadership "must be liquidated." The plan of extermination applied even to "bourgeois-aristocratic" elements that remained from before Stalin's Revolution from Above. Such priorities led Hitler, shortly before the invasion, to issue an infamous directive known as the Commissar Order. In a hair-raising instance of projection, it declared that

> in the struggle against Bolshevism, we must not assume that the enemy's conduct will be based on principles of humanity or international law. In particular, hate-inspired, cruel, and inhumane treatment of prisoners of war can be expected from all grades of political commissar who are the leaders of real resistance.[38]

In other words, the Nazi plan to inflict "hate-inspired, cruel, and inhumane treatment" on the Slavs was blamed on the enemy. Accordingly, all captured Red Army commissars "are to be shot immediately."

Such orders, however chilling in their details, dissolved into a much broader policy known as General Plan East, an elaborate design for establishing the Nazi new order among the Slavs. It was commissioned by Heinrich Himmler, whose Schutzstaffel assumed broad oversight of military conduct. One historian has summarized the General Plan's intentions in the following way:

---

38 Quoted in ibid., 426.

Germans would deport, kill, assimilate, or enslave the native popula-
tions, and bring order and prosperity to a humbled frontier. Depending
upon the demographic estimates, between thirty-one and forty-five mil-
lion people, mostly Slavs, were to disappear. In one redaction, eighty to
eighty-five percent of the Poles, sixty-five percent of the west Ukrainians,
seventy-five percent of the Belarusians, and fifty percent of the Czechs were
to be eliminated.[39]

Himmler with architects of General Plan East
Bundesarchiv, Bild 183-B01718 / CC-BY-SA 3.0, CC BY-SA
3.0 DE <https://creativecommons.org/licenses/by-sa/3.0/de/
deed.en>, via Wikimedia Commons

Conspicuously absent from these figures are the ethnic cleansing quotas assigned to the Russians. The plan left this category of Slavdom open, presumably with the expectation that the further the Wehrmacht advanced eastward, the more completely those easternmost Slavs would be eliminated. Such was suggested by Himmler, who in the full heat of war would later declare, "How the Russians . . . fare is absolutely immaterial to me. . . . Whether [such] nations live in prosperity or starve to death interests me only insofar as we need them as slaves for our culture, otherwise, it is of no interest to me."[40] Himmler's allusion to hunger was not mere rhetoric, as we shall soon see.

On June 22, 1941, Hitler threw more than three million German, Romanian, Hungarian, Italian, and other Axis soldiers across the borders of the Soviet Union in the long-prepared surprise attack. They were supported by thousands of tanks and hundreds of dive-bombers. The unprecedented front stretched nearly two thousand miles from the Baltic Sea to the Black Sea.

---

39 Timothy Snyder, *Bloodlands: Europe between Hitler and Stalin* (New York: Basic, 2010), 160.

40 Gordon Wright, *The Ordeal of Total War, 1939–1945* (New York: Harper and Row, 1968), 117.

Stalin, who had been ignoring signs of the impending attack, was taken totally by surprise. So was the Red Army. Within days, it was in full retreat as three major German army groups drove deeply into Soviet territory. One great city after another fell. Hundreds of thousands of Red Army soldiers were killed or captured at Minsk in July. Greater losses occurred at Smolensk in September. And then at Kiev an even greater number were encircled. When the city fell (also in September), three-quarters of a million soldiers were dead, wounded, or captured. Operation Barbarossa had succeeded in stunning the Soviet Union, decimating her armed forces, and placing her western territories almost entirely under Nazi rule.

And yet the invasion turned out to be a complete failure. From the start, its organizers realized it could produce two very different outcomes: either it would result in swift surrender by Stalin, or it would open the door to a war of attrition the Germans, in light of the Great War, knew they could not sustain. By the autumn, German generals realized that a sudden collapse of the Soviet government was not going to occur. And as long as new reserves of Red Army soldiers appeared on the horizon, the Wehrmacht would have to continue fighting. What made things difficult was the fact that unlike the French, Soviet soldiers fought fanatically and in many cases to the death. Outside Moscow, the Red Army was finally in a position to take a stand. In December it launched a counterattack under Marshall Georgy Zhukov that drove the Germans backward. By this time, German lines were terribly overextended, and soldiers lacked adequate clothing for the winter conditions. What is more, the onset of frigid temperatures was immobilizing tanks and aircraft as sump oil froze and tracks became encased in muddy ice. Under such conditions, Blitzkrieg was impossible. Two years into its war of annihilation, the Wehrmacht had come to a stop.

It would still be years before the war machine collapsed, but in the meantime the Nazis were building the new order in earnest. Their actions were guided by the genocidal principles of the General Plan East. Himmler and his SS assistant Reinhard Heydrich made full use of the control Germany now had over the bulk of the Soviet and Polish populations. Implementing the terms of the plan included efforts to starve cities to death. Such was the fate of Leningrad, known once as Saint Petersburg before being renamed after the October Revolution. The Wehrmacht's northern army group surrounded the city with the help of allied Finland and subjected it to nearly three years of siege. Stuka pilots targeted bread factories and fuel depots in order to cause general starvation. Hitler was not interested in conquering the city; his goal was to annihilate it. Orders were given that under no circumstances was its surrender to be accepted. In fact, Hitler planned to raze the city to the ground when it finally fell. But Leningrad never fell. A million unarmed men, women, and children perished from starvation and cold, but the city remained defiant. Its resilience was expressed by the composer Dmitry Shostakovich, whose Seventh Symphony (nicknamed *Leningrad*) was partly composed and even performed in the city during the blockade.

Mass starvation was not limited to Leningrad but was general Nazi occupation policy everywhere in the east. Plan organizers were motivated in part by the practical consideration of providing adequate food supplies to Germany's armies and civilian population. There were, of course, only so many calories to go around, and obviously the master race was given primary access to them. Not only were "mongrel races" expendable, but a policy of starvation could be used as a supplement to mass executions. So, in the massive prison camps set up in open fields after the early victories of Barbarossa, hundreds of thousands of Red Army soldiers were given only enough food to keep the strongest alive. In all, more than three million captive Slavs were systematically murdered this way.

Those who survived were transported to Germany to work as slaves in armaments factories. There they encountered their civilian counterparts who, according to the General Plan, were likewise forced to serve the master race. One of the myriad personal stories was that of a ten-year-old boy deported from Kiev in 1941. As the Wehrmacht approached his native city, Communists executed his father, who had been known for criticizing Stalin's rule. After Kiev fell, the boy and his mother were placed in a cattle car to be transported to Germany. But along the way, overcrowding led the Nazis to take the mother off the train and shoot her before the boy's eyes. Soon afterward, the child—orphaned in accordance with the twin ideologies that created totalitarianism—found himself in a German city making bombs that would be used to kill his people back in the Soviet Union. By

the end of the war, more than seven million slave laborers—nearly a quarter of the
labor force—toiled on the brink of death
in German factories.

But application of the General Plan was
not restricted to prison camps and slave
factories. Behind Operation Barbarossa's
three advancing army groups—and in
full coordination with them—Himmler
dispatched a secondary army consisting
of innocuously designated *Einsatzgruppen*
(special task forces). Their "task" was the
mass murder of civilian Jews and Slavs
living in occupied territories. One of their
largest single operations occurred at Babi

Soviet slave boy in Nazi factory
Bundesarchiv, Bild 183-H26334 /
CC-BY-SA, CC BY-SA 3.0 DE <https://
creativecommons.org/licenses/by-sa/3.0/
de/deed.en>, via Wikimedia Commons

Yar, a ravine outside Kiev. There tens of thousands of people, mostly Jews,
were driven naked into a gully and shot to death. Most killings were on a
smaller scale than Babi Yar, making the history of the genocide difficult to
detail, but the overall death toll reached some two million people.

Naturally, even National Socialist propaganda could not fully prepare SS
agents for the carnage they were ordered to inflict. Machine gunners passed
out during the killings, while others lost their minds. Some resorted to suicide. Even Himmler himself nearly suffered a nervous breakdown on the out-
skirts of Minsk, where he first witnessed the act of genocide. Clearly, mere
death squads could not meet the ambitious quotas set by the General Plan.

Which brings us to the ultimate emblem of Nazi world building, the
death camp. Concentration camps had already been used in the Soviet
Union. But there the purpose was largely to isolate and punish the victims
of totalitarianism. In Hitler's new order, some concentration camps were
designed for simple extermination. Auschwitz is the most terrible example.

Well before Operation Barbarossa, the Nazis had been exploring ways
of eliminating "inferior races" and further strengthening the imaginary one
they called Aryan. One was a 1933 law requiring mandatory sterilization
of the physically and mentally unfit. Goebbels's propaganda office strongly

supported the production and release in 1937 of a film entitled *Victims of the Past: The Sin against Blood and Race.* It opens with a Darwinistic narrator explaining in a matter-of-fact way, "All that is non-viable in nature invariably perishes. . . . We humans have transgressed the law of natural selection in the last decades."

The authoritative words—attributed in the opening credits to a medical doctor—conclude that Germany will be overrun by "drooling imbeciles," whose individual value is "lower than any beasts," unless the charitable programs in place to help them are shut down. Such is the hard reality of science.

The Nazis were not only inspired by Darwin. Appropriating the trans-valued values of Nietzsche, they developed a world-transforming vocabulary of eugenics. They distinguished, for instance, between *Übermenschen,* or "supermen," and *Untermenschen,* or "subhumans." One way of eliminating the latter was the introduction of legal measures against miscegenation. Accordingly, the 1935 Nuremberg Laws not only deprived Jews of citizenship but prohibited their intermarriage with Aryans. It turns out that Nazi policy development was inspired in part by the example of the legal system of the United States, where laws against blacks marrying whites had long been codified.

Even more ominous was the Nazis' introduction of euthanasia. Darwin had seen the death of the weak individual as a benefit for the species. Nietzsche had advised supermen "to know when to die." A science of enacting "good death" had its origins in the broader civilization of an explicitly post-Christian Christendom. It can be traced to the late nineteenth-century work of the English Darwinist Francis Galton, who founded the British Eugenics Society. His twentieth-century successors extended eugenics to actual proposals for selective killing of the physically and mentally "unfit."

On the eve of war, the Nazis began killing deformed children and other people they considered "unworthy of life." But once the conflagration of total warfare was underway, it was possible to expand such activities enormously. A program known as Aktion T4, introduced in occupied territories, resulted in the murder of more than a quarter of a million "defects," many of whom were children. Simultaneously, involuntary medical experiments were

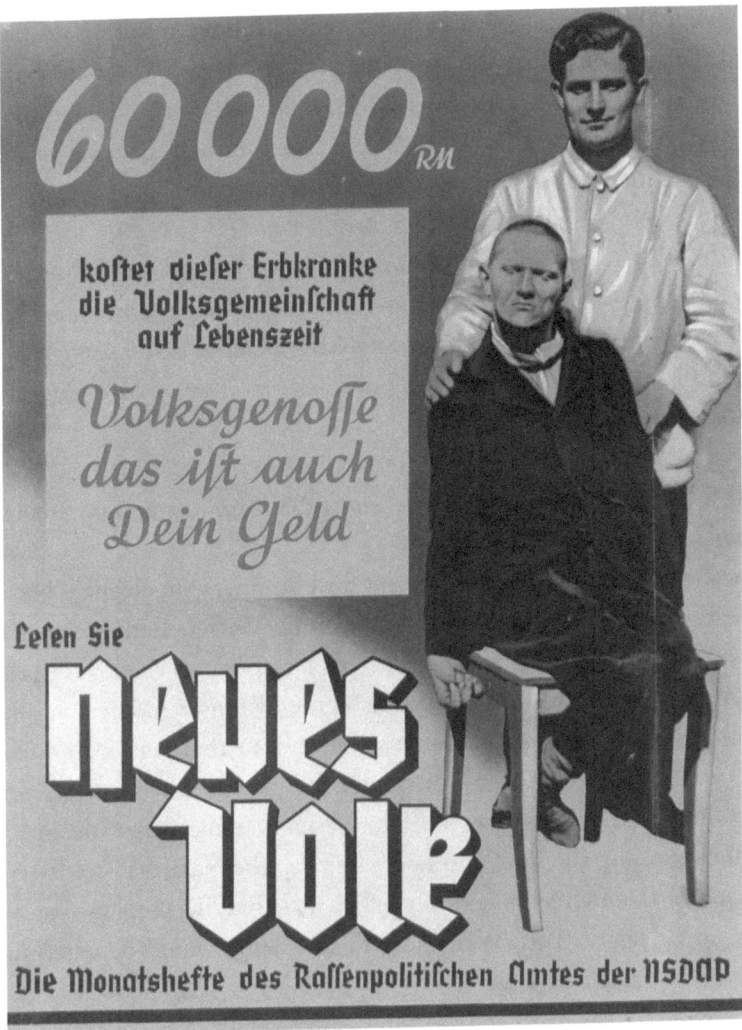

Nazi eugenics poster, 1937

undertaken on the helpless victims. Josef Mengele, who held doctorates in both philosophy and medicine, was given funding for a clinic within Auschwitz where he performed experiments including unnecessary amputations of limbs, removal of organs without anesthesia, and random killings for the sake of dissection. If a victim of the sadistic doctor happened to survive, he was in most cases soon exterminated in the camp gas chamber.

The word *extermination* actually takes on a unique meaning in the context of the age of nihilism. For millions of people were now, thanks to Nazi ideology, seen as biological pests that required the intervention of specially trained exterminators. This is the way the leader himself spoke of the matter. Even before the war got underway he once declared:

> *Nature is cruel; therefore we also are entitled to be cruel. When I send the flower of German youth into the steel hail of the coming war without feeling the slightest regret over the precious German blood that is being spilled, should I not also have the right to eliminate millions of an inferior race that multiplies like vermin?*[41]

On this matter Himmler and the entire SS administration were in full agreement.

Therefore it was perfectly consistent for Himmler's subordinate Heydrich to assemble a group of Nazi officials at Wannsee outside Berlin early in 1942 to discuss what participants called the "final solution to the Jewish problem of Europe." Based on decisions made at the Wannsee Conference, a plan was implemented that would subject the Jews to thorough extermination. Gone was a reliance on legal restrictions. Gone was a reliance on emigration to other parts of the world. Gone even was the use of death squads machine-gunning the Jews into nonexistence. The Nazis had settled on the most rational and technologically efficient—that is, utopian—means of annihilating Jewry. Their designated racial enemy would be exterminated like vermin, using a pesticide.

The weapon was hydrogen cyanide, a by-product of a chemical that had been developed in (of all places) the orange groves of late nineteenth-century California. During the Great War, German chemical firms took an interest in the deadly substance for use as a poison gas, and by the opening of the Second World War it was remarketed under the brand name Zyklon B. It required a good deal of managerial leadership to bring the substance into

---

41 Quoted in Joachim C. Fest, *Hitler*, trans. Richard and Clara Wilson (New York: Harcourt, Brace, Jovanovich, 1974), 679–80.

large-scale production. Rudolf Höss proved the man for the job. He had been made commandant of Auschwitz by Himmler in 1940 and then, in the wake of the Wannsee Conference, ordered to expand the concentration camp to make it a center for the Final Solution. Höss had first used Zyklon B in 1941 on a group of Slavs captured on the eastern front. Sure that he had landed on the means of annihilating the Jews, he suggested that Himmler commission IG Farben, Germany's leading capitalist chemical conglomerate, to begin mass production. The firm was even given a lease at Auschwitz to build a factory that used slave labor.

In all, more than one million people were murdered at the death camp, the great majority being Jews. Auschwitz became the principal symbol of the Holocaust, the ideologically motivated murder of about six million Jews. Along with the Solovetsky prison camp, Auschwitz was a monument to the age of nihilism.

But by the time the gas chambers and crematoria of Auschwitz were fully operational, the Third Reich was already beginning to crumble. By the summer of 1942, hopes among Hitler's generals that the Red Army would capitulate had been all but lost. Nevertheless, the superhuman leader continued to express great confidence in the Wehrmacht and demanded unconditional submission from those around him. In August he ordered a full-scale attack on the city of Stalingrad, significant for both its control of the Volga and its ideologically offensive name. The ensuing battle became the turning point of the war. Though the Germans made much initial progress, reducing the city to rubble and nearly reaching its eastern perimeters on the riverside, a massive counterattack across the Volga from the east made German victory impossible. Street fighting continued for months, but finally the entire German Sixth Army under Friedrich Paulus was forced to surrender in February of the following year. Losses on both sides were horrifying, but for the Germans they were simply catastrophic.

As the Wehrmacht began its long retreat westward, another battle erupted near the Ukrainian city of Kursk in July 1943. In all, two million men fought with six thousand tanks and two thousand aircraft. By now the Germans were using the advanced Tiger tank, and, for the first time, the even more sophisticated Panther tank. Nevertheless, weapons are measured by their effectiveness, and neither stood up to the Soviet T-34. This tank was a clunker dating to the earliest stages of the war, yet it outperformed everything engineered by the Germans. As a result the greatest tank battle in history resulted in another Soviet victory.

By the following summer, the Red Army had driven the Wehrmacht almost entirely from the Soviet Union. It was at this moment, in June 1944, that a coalition of American and British armies invaded from the west at the beaches of Normandy in an operation called D-Day. The United States had entered the war six months after Barbarossa in response to the surprise attack by Germany's ally Japan on Pearl Harbor. Despite huge battles in the Pacific, American President Franklin Roosevelt established the strategic principle of "Europe first." Long-range B-17 bombers were sent to England from factories in Seattle and began the relentless destruction of German cities from the air. In a single three-day raid in early 1945, the medieval town of Dresden was reduced to rubble in a bomb-induced firestorm that killed some twenty-five thousand unarmed civilians. By now the Red Army was moving swiftly through Poland and entering eastern Germany. In April, Berlin itself was about to fall.

The age of nihilism is in some ways epitomized by what happened in that city as the infernal new order came to an end. Hitler had built a vast chancery for his government in the heart of the capital. Below it was a bunker in which he spent his final days. From the stuffy, unnaturally illuminated recesses of this lair the superman screamed orders that his generals fight to the last man. That there was now no chance of victory was irrelevant. When told that continued fighting would result only in the destruction of the city and the unnecessary loss of more lives, the leader declared he did not care. The German people had failed to rise to the world-historical occasion, and nature had selected even them for annihilation.

One after another, Hitler's inner circle began to abandon him. Hermann Göring (d. 1946) was first. He committed treason by sending the leader a telegram in which he all but usurped leadership of the failing Reich for himself. When Hitler learned of the act, he suffered a paroxysm of despair. "Now nothing remains," the megalomaniac shrieked. "Nothing is spared to me. No allegiances are kept, no honour lived up to, no disappointments that

I have not had, no betrayals that I have not experienced—and now this, above all else. Nothing remains."[42] The word "nothing"—the root word for nihilism—was one that came naturally in these final days.

Hitler immediately ordered Göring's execution. Though the paralyzed condition of the chancery at this last hour prevented the order from being carried out, Göring would eventually commit suicide. Other betrayals soon followed. Albert Speer, minister of war production and Hitler's artistic soulmate, came to the bunker to confess he had disobeyed Hitler's order to reduce to nothing—to annihilate—all of Germany's industrial infrastructure in the face of the Allied advance. Next appeared "faithful Heinrich," who on leaving the bunker immediately abandoned Hitler and opened negotiations with the Americans. Himmler too would eventually commit suicide. Yet his failure to collaborate in the total destruction of Germany, when Hitler learned of it, was perhaps the final straw. The founder of the "Thousand-Year Reich" now made plans to kill himself.

Hitler had always seen the empire he built as a realization of Wagnerian mythology. So perhaps his last act was inspired by the composer. Speer, intellectual that he was, had somehow managed to stage the final scene of *Götterdämmerung* in Berlin only a few days before the end. As we noted in chapter 1, the action features the fiery destruction of the divine order as the heroine Brünhilde suicidally casts herself upon the funeral pyre of Siegfried. Her final aria contains the haunting curse *Ruhe, ruhe, du Gott!* (Rest thou, rest thou O God!). The statement is her condescending dismissal of an irrelevant Wotan and a paraphrase of Nietzsche's later declaration that God is dead.

The symbolism of the scene was appropriate. A half century after the rise of nihilism, millions had now perished in the godless utopia of Nazidom. Perhaps the spectral presence of nothingness had never been so prominent— at least not since the dark day of the Crucifixion. Some accounts report that after the performance of the final scene of the *Ring,* cyanide capsules were distributed to the departing audience in preparation for the Red Army's final assault.

---

42 Quoted in Alan Bullock, *Hitler: A Study in Tyranny* (London: Odhams, 1964), 789.

Back in the devil's lair, cyanide was in high demand. This seems an irony, considering the fact that this very poison had been involuntarily administered to the innumerable victims of the death camps. Now even Goebbels partook. His wife and six children came to the bunker to join in the Third Reich's death vigil. After murdering his children by forcing the capsules on them, the minister of propaganda killed his wife and himself rather than live in a desecrated world, as he put it, without the hope of National Socialism.

Hitler's own death by suicide went almost unnoticed. After killing his longtime mistress and new wife Eva Braun, he bit down on one of the capsules and simultaneously pulled the trigger of a pistol he held against his head. An adjutant disposed of the body by burning it to ashes. When the Red Army finally arrived, nothing of the superman or the racist utopia he had built remained.

CHAPTER SIX

Liberal World Building

SELF-DESTRUCTION PROVED TO BE THE natural outcome of Nazi world building; eventually, genocide led to suicide. But the West's victorious political systems—Soviet totalitarianism and transatlantic democracy—would themselves eventually face problems. The former, after Stalin's death, would undergo fitful efforts at humanistic reform and finally, in the face of its absurdity, descend into a death spiral. Liberal democracy, touting itself as a bastion against totalitarian Communism during the Cold War, would, after the loss of its Soviet rival, change into something very different from what it had been during the decades following the Second World War.

Neither Communism nor liberalism was untouched by the stain of nihilism. This was manifest even before the end of the war. So consuming was the struggle against Nazism that the armies of Soviet Communism and American liberalism committed their own acts of transvalued depravity. In liberating Eastern Europe, for instance, the Red Army denied assistance to desperate Polish resisters in the Warsaw Uprising of 1944, and thereafter subjected the German civilian population to actions so atrocious as to drive it into chaotic westward flight.

In liberating Western Europe and Asia, the United States military for its part firebombed German cities into virtual nonexistence. Then, on the feast of Christ's Holy Transfiguration (August 6) in 1945, it annihilated a hundred thousand unarmed Japanese civilians at Hiroshima with the dropping of a single atom bomb. Unperturbed by the unprecedented carnage, America dropped a second bomb on Nagasaki three days later. Defeating the most nihilistic powers to threaten Christendom since the Mongol invasions provoked, in turn, acts of barbarity.

Total warfare had exposed the shortcomings of utopia to all Christendom. Formerly discerned only by intellectuals like Nietzsche, the specter of nihilism was becoming ever more visible as the tragedy of the twentieth century played itself out. Instead of turning to traditional Christianity in repentance, however, the West seized on the easier solution of building states with political ideologies that falsely promised to evade the specter.

So the ambiguous march of progress continued.

When Mill Met Nietzsche

A CLUE TO THE IDEOLOGICAL self-image of America and her non-Soviet allies during the Second World War is found in a series of propaganda films commissioned by the US War Department, entitled *Why We Fight*. Its creator, three-time Academy Award–winning director Frank Capra, was known for popular movies like *Mr. Smith Goes to Washington* and, after the war, *It's a Wonderful Life*. He had been deeply impressed with Riefenstahl's *Triumph of the Will* and modeled the series in part on that great work of cinematography. But as propaganda, of course, *Why We Fight* opposed Nazism with the ideology of liberalism.

The opening film of the series speaks of "two worlds"—rather like the cosmology of early Christianity, which, in the case of the *Didache*, spoke of "two ways": that of life and that of death. In Capra's view, America and her allies represent the "free world." Nazi Germany and her allies represent the "slave world." But the question is still one of life or death. At the end of the first film, the narrator declares that in the great struggle then unfolding, one of the two worlds "must live" and "one must die." Instead of horizons defined by the kingdom of heaven and the darkness of sin, then, the twin horizons of modern Christendom are entirely secular: democratic freedom or totalitarian slavery. Ideology has come to replace Christianity, and because the problems are ideological, so are the solutions.

For America and her democratic allies, the solution was liberalism. Defending democracy from Nazi totalitarianism depended on the liberal values of individual autonomy and rationality. These had been elaborated with particular urgency during the eighteenth century and were the core values of the American revolutionaries. Such values certainly guided the framers of the constitution, who looked to John Locke's *Second Treatise on Government*—the most famous expression of liberal political philosophy— as a foundational text of the new republic.

But as a post-Christian myth designed to fill the vacuum of secularization, liberal ideology had its own totalitarian tendencies. As the political scientist Patrick Deneen has argued,

> *liberalism was the first political architecture that proposed transforming all aspects of human life to conform to a preconceived political plan. [Americans] live in a society and increasingly a world that has been remade in the image of an ideology—the first nation founded by the explicit embrace of liberal philosophy, whose citizenry is shaped almost entirely by its commitments and vision.*

It is not surprising, then, that the myth of a free world in which individual liberty is the highest good became the trademark of the United States during the Second World War. This is what fueled propaganda like *Why We Fight*. However, as Deneen notes, "unlike the visibly authoritarian regimes that arose in dedication to advancing the ideologies of fascism and communism, liberalism is less visibly ideological and only surreptitiously remakes the world in its image."[1] Though this was not always apparent (especially in its early development), liberalism pursued a world-building project comparable to those being undertaken by Communists and Nazis. How could it not do so? After all, like totalitarian regimes across the Atlantic, liberal democracy was a thoroughly secularized solution to humanism's desecration of the world and the specter of nihilism that appeared as a result.

Like its ideological cousins, liberalism was from the beginning a counterfeit of traditional Christianity. The original civilization and culture of

---

1 Patrick J. Deneen, *Why Liberalism Failed* (New Haven, CT: Yale University Press, 2018), 5.

the West had, since Pentecost, sought the total transformation of the world through sacraments and liturgy, through asceticism and repentance. "Be not conformed to this world," Paul had enjoined the early Church, "but be ye transformed by the renewing of your mind" (Rom. 12:2). For a millennium, traditional Christianity trained the old Christendom to "seek first" the kingdom of heaven. The world could never become paradise, but it could, through the life of the Church, participate in that eschatological reality. Having entered the world through the Incarnation, the transcendent God filled the world with heaven. The result was a paradisiacal culture. Nevertheless, after the eleventh century this culture was weakened and eventually was superseded by a utopian one. Beginning with the Renaissance, a new Christendom looked to secular transformation as the measure of human dignity, freedom, and prosperity.

Secular ideals were all that mattered for the nineteenth-century English philosopher John Stuart Mill (d. 1873).[2] In certain ways, Mill's vision of man and the world brought the Renaissance to its fulfillment. At a time when Marx and Darwin were calling man's promethean autonomy into question by emphasizing the respective determinism of class and biology, Mill defended the individual's ability to define life for himself. And this made him an unwitting collaborator with Nietzsche.

To be sure, had Mill lived long enough to read Nietzsche's work, he probably would not have seen a similarity. But neither would Nietzsche. Living after the Englishman, the German expressed explicit disdain for liberalism. Nevertheless, Mill's dedication to the individual created a significant point of contact between these two architects of modernity. In fact, as we shall see, by the end of the twentieth century Nietzschean nihilism became an almost inevitable outcome of liberalism.

Like Nietzsche, Mill was an atheist. And like Nietzsche, he considered philosophical atheism one of the greatest achievements but also greatest problems of modernity. With Wotan's spear in pieces, a new morality was needed—one no longer anchored in Christianity or transcendent absolutes.

For Nietzsche, no objectivist morality was legitimate; man—or rather

---

2   For a brief account of Mill's philosophy in context, see *Age of Utopia*, 287–91.

the superman—must, in the wake of God's death, go beyond good and evil to create a completely autonomous morality. The only good was the will to power, and man should enhance its ultimately meaningless flow through him, regardless of outcomes.

The Victorian Mill was not so radical. His ethical system was equally atheistic in principle, but it was governed by the mundane values of pleasure and happiness. He called it utilitarianism. This philosophy was grounded in the humanistic conviction that man's purpose is fulfilled in a spiritually untransformed world. And if man suffered from egotistical tendencies, these were stabilized by a famous "harm principle," by which no acts are considered moral if they infringe on the pleasure or happiness of (that is, cause harm to) other individuals. In this sense, utilitarianism was in stark contrast to the views of Nietzsche, who saw no value in altruism and frequently presented cruelty as a virtue.

But beyond this significant difference, both philosophers insisted that morality be uprooted from Christian tradition and be transvalued entirely by the individual on a case-by-case (rather than transcendent) basis. And since for both it was the extraordinary individual who was most capable of appreciating and exercising authentic liberty, a disdain for the masses and the customs they lived by found a place in both Mill's *On Liberty* and Nietzsche's *Thus Spake Zarathustra*. For Mill, according to Deneen, "extraordinary individuals—the most educated, the most creative, the most adventurous, even the most powerful—freed from the rule of Custom, might transform society."[3] For Nietzsche, so might the superman.

Such individualism, divorced from Christendom's moral tradition, was joined to and in some ways came to depend on a new order in which all truth claims are contingent. Mill was a rationalist and believed that the culture of the future would be generated by a free exchange of ideas, in the same way the capitalist marketplace exchanged commodities. As a laissez-faire state abolished censorship and ceased encouraging traditional values, departing from what Christian statecraft since the time of Constantine had done, individuals would reach conclusions about right and

---

3   Deneen, *Why Liberalism Failed*, 145–46.

wrong on their own. This would yield a utopia of individual liberty.

Nietzsche suffered from no such optimism. However, he also placed great emphasis on the importance of every person establishing his own convictions without the influence of others. Even a model superman like Zarathustra emphasized this. The anti-Christian hero actually tells his disciples to disregard what he has taught them: "I now go alone, my disciples! Ye also now go away, and alone! So will I have it. Verily, I advise you: depart from me, and guard yourselves from Zarathustra! And better still: be ashamed of him! Perhaps he hath deceived you."[4]

In *Ecce Homo,* as we have seen, Nietzsche likened truth claims to optics. Reality is determined solely by one's perspective. Mill's marketplace of ideas and Nietzsche's perspectivism both served, therefore, to open the door to a culture of pluralism.

There was another way in which Nietzsche complemented Millian individualism. This became particularly visible in America after the Second World War. Having watched the destruction of Europe by the Nazis only to see a rival Soviet Union emerge vigorously from the rubble, the liberal American establishment needed intellectual inspiration more potent than that provided by the mild-mannered Locke or Mill. With his contempt for "herd morality," Nietzsche offered such inspiration. The "philosopher with a hammer" had, it is true, a tarnished reputation because of the use the Nazis made of his extremist doctrines. But in postwar years a young émigré professor at Princeton University named Walter Kaufmann (d. 1980) set out to free Nietzsche of those associations and turn him into an advocate of wholesome if nonconformist individualism. Through Kaufmann's translations and a widely read biography, Nietzsche became "a towering thinker uniquely poised to address many of the pressing intellectual concerns of the cold war era: anxieties about the psychic costs and social dangers of mass society, hostility to collectivist ideologies, and longing for new sources of redemption after the horrors of the recent past."[5] The disappointing side effect of this,

---

4   Nietzsche, *Thus Spake Zarathustra*, 82.

5   Jennifer Ratner-Rosenhagen, *American Nietzsche: A History of an Icon and His Ideas* (Chicago: University of Chicago Press, 2012), 222.

for one critic, was to make of Nietzsche a "King-Kong-in-chains . . . under heavy sedation."[6]

Nevertheless, an "American Nietzsche" began to influence the cultural mainstream. In academia this presence did much to advance the nihilistic values of epistemological suspicion and ethical solipsism. What would be called postmodernism was based, as we shall see, on such values. In popular culture, too, Nietzschean terminology and concepts began to appear. There are many examples. The term "superman," for instance, was popularized through the eponymous superhero of the DC Comics universe and became a household term (even as his altruistic feats defied the transvalued values of Nietzsche). Then, in 1954, the editorial of the inaugural issue of *Playboy* called every man "between the ages of 18 and 80" to shake off conventional morality and join "a female acquaintance for a quiet discussion on Picasso, Nietzsche, jazz, sex."[7] In 1966 *Time* featured a stark black cover with the unsettling words, "Is God Dead?"

For the time being, the answer of the American establishment was "no." Too many citizens of the new republic identified with the West's Christian heritage, and since the constitution granted the right to adhere to Christianity, no governmental campaign to eradicate it (as Communist and Nazi ideologues had undertaken) was possible. Not yet, at least. For Americans defined their liberal values against those of the rival Soviet Union, where religion was spurned as "the opiate of the masses" and atheism hailed as the key to progress. As long as the Communist "other" defined what America was not, Christianity would be an important element in liberal world building.

However, as we shall see, when Russia shook off Communism and restored elements of traditional Christianity to her civilization, the liberal American establishment would begin to see things differently.

---

6   Ibid., 224.
7   Ibid., 252–53.

The American Way

FOR NOW, WITH GERMANY IN ruins and the Soviet Union looming in the east beyond her, the postwar United States set out to build a new world in her own liberal image. Her ambitions can be seen in a growing interest in something historians call "American exceptionalism." The nationalistic concept of a form of life unique to the United States had a long provenance. It can be traced to the Puritan colonists, whose "city on a hill" was intended as a beacon of reformation to the new Christendom of the old world. After the American Revolution, national messianism was secularized, finding expression in the antislavery movement, the settlement of the western frontier, and the doctrine of "manifest destiny," by which the entire continent was seen as the home of a great progressive civilization.

This early vision of American exceptionalism found expression in a painting by John Gast entitled *American Progress* (1872). The painting depicts the restless expansion of American Christendom through the westward colonization of North America. As the sun rises behind her, a towering Lady Columbia carries symbols of utopia—a school primer and a telegraph line—and gazes benignly in the direction of the Pacific Coast. Beneath her, Euro-Americans build a new civilization while Native Americans scatter.

Since Gast was an immigrant, his painting also speaks to the multitude of ethnic groups using the myth of progress to stake their claim on liberal democracy. He very likely had fellow immigrants in mind when painting the pioneers and farmers advancing beneath Lady Columbia. Two broad waves of European relocation to the United States preceded the Great War: an "old immigration" including English and Germans was followed by a "new immigration" including Italians, Irish, Poles, and Russians. Those belonging to the first wave were mostly Protestant and found it comparatively easy to blend into the nation's "melting pot." Those from Italy, Ireland, and Poland tended to be Roman Catholic and would find assimilation more challenging. And the Russians, being mostly Orthodox, would have the greatest challenge of all.

By the turn of the century, an Irish immigrant named Archbishop John Ireland (d. 1918) had begun the process of "Americanizing" the Roman

Catholic Church through cooperation with the government and the settlement of immigrants in the West. In addition, waves of Orthodox and Uniates (Roman Catholics following the Byzantine rite) were arriving by the end of the century from Eastern European lands. For his part, Ireland alienated the Uniates by disparaging them and imposing restrictions on their clergy. In response, a priest named Alexis Toth led an exodus of Ruthenians (known also as Carpatho-Russians) into America's still small Orthodox Church. Once there, they joined immigrants from Russia, who mostly remained behind the walls of ethnically defined parishes. This would leave the Orthodox more culturally isolated than their Protestant and Roman Catholic fellow Christians. But by avoiding Americanization, the Orthodox would at the same time be better prepared for the confrontation with ideological liberalism when it assumed an anti-Christian form on the other side of America's postwar horizon.

In any case, religious diversity did not subvert national unity and in some ways even seemed to strengthen it. This had been the conclusion of Alexis de Tocqueville, whose famous *Democracy in America* had seen in the various churches the resources needed to sustain liberty and to protect against tyranny.[8] It was a happy coincidence that the nation's official motto was, for the time being, *E pluribus unum* ("out of many, one").

Yet as the twentieth century began, Lady Columbia, in her westward progressive march, began to look back over her shoulder uneasily toward an old world being dimmed by the clouds of militarism. When the Great War broke out, most Americans preferred isolation. President Woodrow Wilson (1913–21) was able only with difficulty to persuade the nation to join the liberal democracies of Britain and France against Imperial Germany. America had merged Christianity with secular progress, and Wilson was both the son of a Presbyterian minister and an advocate for the period's progressive movement. An idealist at heart, he declared the conflict would make the world "safe for democracy." What is more, he claimed that under liberal American influence the conflict could be transformed from a war of conquest into "a

---

8   For a brief description of de Tocqueville's views in context, see *Age of Utopia*, 224–27.

war to end all wars." It was Wilson who, at the Treaty of Versailles, proposed the creation of a utopian League of Nations that would assure conflict resolution and peace in the years ahead. The league eventually disintegrated, and the treaty, despised by the Nazis, later proved (to appropriate one historian's phrase) "a peace to end all peace."[9]

As authoritarian alternatives to liberal democracy began to proliferate in the old world after the First World War, Americans were forced to reassess their national way of life. This became critical after Black Friday, the day the stock market crashed in 1929. The Great War, the Great Depression, and the culture behind a contemporary novel entitled *The Great Gatsby* (depicting the disintegration of Victorian morality during the Roaring Twenties) all revealed the specter of nihilism and the need for a new myth to escape it.

This myth was called the "American Way." Inspired by the Declaration of Independence's "pursuit of happiness" and the Bill of Rights' protections of individual liberty, it provided an alternative to totalitarian collectivism. The American Way represented a renewal of the nation's sense of exceptionalism, but with an increasingly ideological rather than religious character (as had been the case in de Tocqueville's assessment). The concept of a uniquely American approach to civilization was designed not only to shore up liberal democracy but to revive the flagging capitalist economy. In this sense it was the product of the Great Depression, a genealogy discernible in the way the term became normalized. One historian, by using the *New York Times* as an index, has observed that while the phrase "American Way" appeared only 722 times from the Civil War to 1932 (when Franklin Roosevelt was elected president in the midst of the Depression), it occurred some 2,230 times during the decade that followed.[10] At a time of domestic economic crisis and foreign threats, Americans were eager to find a new way of thinking about their civilization.

---

9 The historian is David Fromkin, who used the phrase for the related outcome of the war in the Middle East: *A Peace to End All Peace: The Fall of the Ottoman Empire and the Creation of the Modern Middle East* (New York: Henry Holt, 1989).

10 Wendy L. Wall, *Inventing the "American Way": The Politics of Consensus from the New Deal to the Civil Rights Movement* (Oxford: Oxford University, 2008), 15.

The nation's renewed sense of exceptionalism brought into existence a related myth known as the "American Dream." This term was first coined by James Truslow Adams in 1931. Its content was designed to energize liberalism at a time when an individualistic basis of utopian Christendom was faltering. "The dream," wrote Adams,

> *is a vision of a better, deeper, richer life for every individual, regardless of the position in society that he or she may occupy by the accident of birth. It has been a dream of a chance to rise in the economic scale, but quite as much, or more than that, of a chance to develop our capacities to the full, unhampered by unjust restrictions of caste or custom. With this has gone the hope of bettering the physical conditions of living, of lessening the toil and anxiety of daily life.*

For Adams, the American Dream imparted to every individual an "inherent right to be restricted by no barriers."[11]

This last detail is significant. Patrick Deneen for his part has noted how liberalism, as an ideology originating from the promethean fountainhead of the Renaissance, has progressively sought the overthrow of all limits and boundaries for humanity. In his analysis we see the strange but undeniable influence of both Mill and Nietzsche: "Liberal philosophy rejected [the] requirement of human self-limitation. It displaced first the idea of a natural order to which humanity is subject and later the notion of human nature itself." Here we might recall that Nietzsche had proclaimed man to be but a "bridge" to a higher being.

> *Liberalism inaugurated a transformation in the human sciences and humanity's relationship to the natural world. The first wave of this revolution—inaugurated by early-modern thinkers dating back to the Renaissance—insisted that man should employ natural science and a transformed economic system to seek mastery over nature. The second wave—developed*

---

11   Quoted in Lawrence R. Samuel, *The American Dream: A Cultural History* (Syracuse, NY: Syracuse University Press, 2012), 13–14.

largely by various historicist schools of thought, especially in the nineteenth century—replaced belief in the idea of a fixed human nature with the belief in human "plasticity" and capacity for moral progress.[12]

Thus defined, liberalism found partial fulfillment in the American Dream. Mill's confidence in an inevitable, open-ended, and unending march of progress was closely linked to the Nietzschean subversion of a stable human condition—that is, to what Adams called "the inherent right to be restricted by no barriers."

Deneen's recent insights here are not dependent on the "postmodernist turn" that has occurred in recent decades (which we shall consider in a later chapter). Indeed, they were anticipated a half century ago by James Burnham, who likewise noted the "plastic" nature of liberal anthropology. That philosopher asserted that "liberalism believes man's nature to be not fixed but changing, with an unlimited or at any rate indefinitely large potential for positive (good, favorable, progressive) development."[13]

It is interesting to note that Burnham contrasted liberal anthropology with a "traditional" Christian one, in which man is both fixed by God in his essence and subject to the limitations of original sin. In making this contrast, he failed to accommodate the Eastern Christian vision of man's potential for deification in this world, instead characterizing traditional Christianity in anthropologically pessimistic terms. The only alternative to such a model thus becomes the Renaissance one: man, to flourish in this world, must be an autonomous being. Like Petrarch, then, Burnham and other Western philosophers—uninformed as they are about Orthodox Christianity—have tended to define secular humanism against an historically contingent and relatively modern form of Christianity introduced by the Papal Reformation and defined by its Protestant outcome. Measured against the paradisiacal culture of the old Christendom, humanism would thus have failed to offer an alternative worth pursuing.

---

12 Deneen, *Why Liberalism Failed*, 35.
13 James Burnham, *The Suicide of the West: An Essay on the Meaning and Destiny of Liberalism* (Washington, DC: Regnery Gateway, 1985), 49–50.

But in the new Christendom born of the eleventh century and secularized in the eighteenth, deification had ceased to be an option. Forgetting about paradise, modern man became disoriented, turning away from the kingdom of heaven and pursuing worldly transformation within the saeculum. As the West reoriented itself this way, transcendence became impossible. Neither the incarnate God nor deity substitutes like those concocted by nineteenth-century romantics anchored humanism's promethean anthropology. However, ideology did. Its only alternative was a form of Christianity that seemed, from this side of the Great Division, almost impossible to restore.

So Lady Columbia continued her benighted march toward progress. As she went, she sowed ideological liberalism along the American Way, and it brought forth great confidence in man's plasticity. Grown in the soil of individual rights, fertilized by consumers' appetites, liberalism produced a bumper crop in the years following the Second World War.

The role of free-market capitalism is, again, crucial in explaining the origin of the American Dream. And once the Second World War had passed and America found herself at the center of a global economy, her ideological self-image as "the land of opportunity" was cemented in place. For this reason, one historian has dubbed postwar America "a consumers' republic."

> In reconstructing the nation after World War II, leaders of business, government, and labor developed a political economy and a political culture that expected a dynamic mass consumption economy not only to deliver prosperity, but also to fulfill American society's loftier aspirations: more social egalitarianism, more democratic participation, and more political freedom. In their ideal America, a mass consumption–driven economy would provide jobs, purchasing power, and investment dollars, while also allowing Americans to live better than ever before, to participate in political decision-making on an equal footing with their similarly prospering neighbors, and to exercise their cherished freedoms by making independent choices in markets and politics.[14]

---

14   Lizabeth Cohen, *A Consumers' Republic: The Politics of Mass Consumption in Postwar America* (New York: Alfred A. Knopf, 2003), 403.

As a world-building myth, then, the American Dream helped increase freedom and consumption by uniting them.

In doing so, it reasserted the anthropological optimism of the Renaissance. Like humanism in its primordial form, liberalism celebrated the individual's self-mastery to a point of near infinitude. Horizons began to vanish. A "new American man" matched or even exceeded the utopian potential of the "new Soviet man." And as the values of Mill and his now domesticated collaborator Nietzsche were assimilated, the road to human fulfillment was not narrowly defined by the collective.

At the same time, the benefits of individualism were distributed widely to society as a whole. American liberalism released hopes and expectations more multitudinous than totalitarianism could ever offer—or tolerate. Members of a sizeable middle class could rise higher in the social and economic hierarchy. Members of the working class, protected by the New Deal welfare state, could enter the middle class. Even racial, ethnic, and religious minorities—many of them second-generation immigrants—were invited to live the American Dream.

A decade after the defeat of Nazi Germany, the American Way appeared to have succeeded in countering the utopian promises of Communism. And it had done so without the four elements of totalitarianism discussed in chapter 4 (a single-party state, a secret police force, economic control, and enforced ideological uniformity). The American Way seemed the fulfillment of promethean autonomy, promising unlimited progress through a union of political freedom and material prosperity.

This can be seen in the generations that produced the dream. If a benchmark "Lost Generation," born around 1890, witnessed the destabilization of utopia during the Great War, its successors proved liberal democracy could be rebuilt on an even grander scale. The "Greatest Generation" (born c. 1910) joined with its offspring the "Silent Generation" (born c. 1930) to find solutions to the Great Depression and to participate in the defeat of fascism. By 1950 a "Baby Boomer Generation" had emerged, and its enormous size was matched by an enormous appetite for everything from commodities to college educations. Its future, like its vision of man, seemed open-ended indeed.

Yet as we will see, these Baby Boomers and their own "Generation X" offspring were to become skeptics of the liberal utopia. Themselves offspring of generations that searched the saeculum for the meaning of the West, they would begin to call off the search.

Anticommunism

THE WORLD IN WHICH AMERICANS lived was now a bipolar one. Even before the defeat of the Third Reich, a Cold War had erupted in which two ideological antagonists—the United States and the Soviet Union—faced off across the heartland of Christendom. Nevertheless, these states and the blocs they controlled were in a real sense rather similar. Both operated according to the myth of progress.

It is important to emphasize this. Too often the Soviet Union and her client states have been set apart as "the East," contrasting them to a "West" defined by liberal democracy. In fact, Communism was thoroughly Western and in certain ways carried the new Christendom born in the eleventh century to its most logical point of development. Ideology in the Soviet bloc may have been undisguised and unsophisticated. It certainly pursued a blatant method of world building, whereas liberalism (to quote Deneen again) "surreptitiously remakes the world in its image." But issuing from long-term developments within the new Christendom, it continuously sought the secular transformation of the world. Not only was Communism grounded in the philosophy of Karl Marx (a German educated in the Western humanities and sciences), but the industrial economy generated by Stalin's Revolution from Above, the bureaucratic nature of the Soviet state, and a high level of education and scientific research all had profoundly Western origins. It was Soviet scientists, after all, who designed Sputnik, the first satellite to orbit the Earth in 1957. The Soviet Union was decidedly not part of an East defined by the old Christendom, however resolutely her catacomb dissidents and new martyrs held to traditional Christianity.

The point was well made by Samuel Huntington. "By adopting Western ideology and using it to challenge the West," he wrote, Soviet

Russians in a sense became closer to and more intimately involved with the West than at any previous time in their history. Although the ideologies of liberal democracy and communism differed greatly, both parties were, in a sense, speaking the same language. . . . The conflict between liberal democracy and Marxist-Leninism was between ideologies which, despite their major differences, were both modern and secular and ostensibly shared ultimate goals of freedom, equality, and material well-being. A Western democrat could carry on an intellectual debate with a Soviet Marxist. It would be impossible for him to do that with a Russian Orthodox nationalist.[15]

And yet, as we shall see, the day would come when Communist ideology would disintegrate and Russia would once again look to traditional Christianity and the possibility of rebuilding the old Christendom.

For now, the Soviet Union was firmly within the West—however bipolar that civilization happened to be. And since the US State Department realized engagement on common secular values was possible (as Huntington indicated), a network of liberal propaganda was directed toward the adversary. As we have seen, the War Department had been busy building support at home with films like *Why We Fight*. The State Department, supported by the newly created Central Intelligence Agency (CIA), now launched a policy of "cultural diplomacy" to assist in efforts to contain and even push back Communism in foreign lands where it had taken hold. Since films and printed materials could not easily be disseminated behind what Churchill called the "Iron Curtain," radio became the principal medium of influence. With faith in the superiority of liberalism, intelligence officers like Averill Harriman were certain "the USSR could not win a radio war with the USA." The most emphatic anticommunist diplomat was George Kennan, author of the famous "containment policy" that guided American diplomats throughout the Cold War. "We must formulate and put forward for other nations," he declared, "a much more positive and constructive picture of the

---

15 Samuel P. Huntington, *The Clash of Civilizations and the Remaking of World Order* (New York: Simon and Schuster, 2011), 142.

sort of world we would like to see than we have put forth in the past."[16] Liberal world building would now become international, and state-directed propaganda was a key to realizing it.

Thus was founded Voice of America, the state-run agency for broadcasting within the Soviet Union news and other programming bearing a liberal narrative. It was affiliated with Radio Free Europe, which dedicated itself to the client states of Eastern Europe. Together these state-run media enterprises did their best to export the American Way.

American diplomacy did not of course stop with propaganda. A series of military commitments was also introduced to project liberalism throughout the world. These represented a complete reversal of the nation's earlier preference for isolation. One was the Truman Doctrine. Under this policy any democratic state threatened with socialist insurrection was promised military assistance from Washington. Even more strident was the formation of the North Atlantic Treaty Organization (NATO), which provided an overwhelming military deterrent to Soviet interference. Bolstered by nuclear weapons, its Article 5 declared that an attack on any one member of the alliance was an attack on all.

To provide financial backing for these diplomatic and military measures, the United States also sponsored the Marshall Plan. This was a project of economic reconstruction breathtaking in its scope. Many of Germany's cities had been flattened by Anglo-American bombing during the war. With national economies exhausted, there was little hope of recovery. Yet the material devastation of total warfare was now reversed as billions of dollars poured into western Europe from an America that had (as in the First World War) entered the conflict late and never suffered invasion or significant bombing. Needless to say, the plan helped reestablish free-market capitalism in nation-states that, following the American Way, merged individual political rights with consumerism. As a result, Britain, France, West Germany, and other lands on the liberal side of the Iron Curtain established closer ties to and dependence on the White House and Wall Street.

---

16   Laura A. Belmonte, *Selling the American Way: U.S. Propaganda and the Cold War* (Philadelphia: University of Pennsylvania Press, 2008), 15.

American-sponsored realignment and reconstruction fundamentally remade postwar western Europe. They not only thwarted the influence of revolutionary socialism (Greece, Italy, and France all had substantial Communist insurgencies after the war) but prevented radical nationalism from rearing its ugly head again. Memory of the Nazis was so strong, in fact, that an effort was soon launched to unify western Europe into a single, liberal-democratic bloc.

One of the visionaries to promote this idea was the French statesman Robert Schuman (d. 1963). A native of the contested borderland between France and Germany, he had twice endured total warfare and was painfully aware of the destructive potential of nationalism. He was also a pious Roman Catholic and saw Christendom before the rise of the nation-state as inspiration for a post-nationalist Europe. Nevertheless, the civilization he envisioned was not paradisiacal but utopian. Under his influence, a Council of Europe was created in 1949 to institutionalize peaceful relations between Europe's liberal democracies. In 1957 the European Economic Community (EEC) was created using the American Way as one of its models. This and the European Union (EU), which later evolved from it, merged individual democratic liberties and consumer capitalism to prevent future conflict rather than turning to

Robert Schuman

the gospel. Because of his success in finding a nonviolent means of rebuilding a liberal Europe, Schuman came to be considered the "father of European unity." The procedure for his canonization as a saint was even set in motion. But despite his conviction about the importance of a shared Christian heritage, western Europe drifted ever further from the old Christendom because, in the end, the architects of liberal democracy were averse to institutions that recognized—let alone served—transcendent values.

Indeed, as R. R. Reno has noted, the entire postwar political system established under American influence was designed to eradicate the "strong gods" of any collectivist ideology. Communism and Nazism had both appeared to show that the transcendent values of such an ideology—however counterfeit—lead inevitably to persecution and mass murder. In the place of totalitarianism, American political theorists designed an "open society" that cultivated "a negative piety which gives priority to critique and self-questioning over conviction." Such an approach, Reno states, "guards against resurgent authoritarianism by renouncing metaphysical claims. There can be no substantive end or purpose to life."[17]

In the aftermath of total war, then, liberalism offered a way of life fundamentally detached and suspicious. However, as we shall see in Part III, this could not last forever. In Reno's language, human nature would ineluctably abandon "weak gods" for strong ones when the memory of collectivization and genocide began to fade.

Nevertheless, the postwar ideological consensus of which Reno speaks did in fact have strong convictions when it came to Communism. This was due in part to liberalism's resistance to authority. Liberty as Mill defined it was largely negative—that is, it was freedom from external restraints such as the state. The individual was thus set against the community—the source of majoritarian tyranny. Communism's overwhelming state repression of individuals in the name of community naturally offended such ideological sensibilities. But American exceptionalism also played a role. Having resolved on an internationalist rather than isolationist course, the American Way

---

17 R. R. Reno, *Return of the Strong Gods: Nationalism, Populism, and the Future of the West* (Washington, DC: Regnery, 2019), 18.

demanded that alternative ways—especially the totalitarian one that survived the war—be negatively objectified, isolated, and eventually eliminated.

Anticommunism erupted spectacularly during the presidential administration of Dwight Eisenhower (1953–61). By the time the former Supreme Allied Commander of Europe was elected in a landslide, numerous threats to America's mission to defend liberal democracy had appeared around the globe. In 1948, Stalin ordered a blockade against West Berlin. Only a bold American airlift prevented the Allied section of the city from falling to the Communists. In 1949, Communist Mao Zedong took control of China. In 1950, Communist Kim Il Sung of North Korea launched an invasion of South Korea and, with Chinese and Soviet support, nearly prevailed until a United Nations coalition led by America stopped him. Then, in the second year of Eisenhower's administration, Communist Ho Chi Minh gained power in North Vietnam and announced his intention to subjugate the South. Communism seemed to be on the move everywhere.

America's role as leader of the "free world" demanded that the United States contain Communism not only abroad but at home. To this end, a series of actions was taken to root out domestic subversion. The most notorious was the campaign of Senator Joseph McCarthy, launched in 1950 with a raving speech in which he waved a piece of paper containing the names of numerous Communists he claimed were working within the State Department. During the years that followed, the Wisconsin senator railed against elements in the government he considered either "soft on Communism" or outright treasonous. As with the diversity statements required at a later stage in the history of liberal democracy, federal, state, and local governments followed McCarthy's lead and demanded oaths of ideological correctness from employees. Soft persecution in the form of public humiliation and job termination was directed against those who refused.

McCarthy anticommunist hearing, 1954

John Edgar Hoover used the newly created Federal Bureau of Investigation to spy on suspected Communists and harass them. In Hollywood, a nest of leftists was "discovered" by Congress's House Committee on Un-American Activities, with conservative filmmaker Walt Disney and actor Ronald Reagan eagerly cooperating. This postwar "red scare" was not the work of conservatives alone, however. Hubert Humphrey, a progressive northern Democrat renowned for supporting civil rights, helped draft the Communist Control Act of 1954, by which the Communist Party of America was banned and membership in it criminalized. As Humphrey declared when advancing the legislation on the Senate floor, "I want Senators to stand up and answer whether they are for the Communist Party or against it. I am tired of reading headlines about being 'soft' toward Communism. . . . I do not intend to be a half patriot."[18] Whether Republican or Democrat, then, the anticommunist establishment was united in defining the American Way in ideologically liberal terms.

That definition also accommodated something called "civic religion." We have seen how the totalitarian tendencies of secular ideology led inevitably to religious persecution in the Soviet Union and Nazi Germany. And for limited periods, those totalitarian regimes also supported utopian forms of Christianity such as the Renovationists (in Russia) and Positive Christians (in Germany). These were, to use the Nazi term, "coordinated" to support the ruling ideology. In America, open religious persecution was not possible because of the first amendment. In this case liberalism protected religious practice and prevented state-sponsored confessionalism. Nevertheless, at this stage in the history of liberal democracy, virtually no American within the establishment believed public statements of religion were subversive to the liberal order. In fact, most seemed to believe that the liberal order depended on them.

So in a way comparable to that employed by the ideological rivals of the United States, favor was shown by the government to those faiths that were most fully "coordinated" with the American Way. This included mainline Protestant churches, such as Episcopalians, Lutherans, Presbyterians, and

---

18 Jonathan Michaels, *McCarthyism: The Realities, Delusions and Politics behind the 1950s Red Scare* (New York: Routledge, 2017), 141.

Methodists. These bodies continued to hold distinct teachings rooted in reformational Christianity but found their boundaries increasingly fluid by midcentury. Their middle-class adherents, after all, had long been assimilated within the cultural melting pot. Roman Catholicism was less assimilated, and not simply because its membership had grown out of the new immigration. Nevertheless, efforts at Americanization by Archbishop Ireland had had an effect, and by midcentury the faith was widely recognized as a major element in American Christianity. It would become even more so in the aftermath of the forward-looking council known as Vatican II. Finally, with the arrival of large numbers of Jews from Eastern Europe, Judaism, at least in its liberal forms, claimed a place within what was increasingly called America's "Judeo-Christian tradition." This term is arguably a self-contradiction. To merge Christianity and Judaism—two of the world's great religions—into a single tradition does justice to neither. But such was the intentionally blurry character of America's emerging civic religion. What was valued was not an orientation toward the kingdom of heaven but confidence that America offered a utopian alternative to it.

All of this was on display during the 1950s, a decade dominated by the Eisenhower administration. The president himself set the tone. During his electoral campaign he proclaimed that the Declaration of Independence, with its statement about Creator-endowed rights, demonstrates that America was built on a foundation of the Christian faith—"and," he immediately added, "I don't care what it is."

Indeed, Eisenhower was no dogmatist. As a young man he had failed to live up to the pacifistic standards of his Mennonite parents. He fought in the Second World War. Upon his election, he remained unbaptized. He remedied this a week after his inauguration by having a Presbyterian minister perform the rite. But he made it clear that the denomination in question meant nothing to him, insisting he did not identify with any one "sect or organization." In fact, shortly before the private ceremony, on learning that his new pastor had boasted of being the first in history to baptize a sitting American president, Eisenhower exploded to an assistant, "You go and tell that goddam minister that if he gives out one more story

President Eisenhower leaving church on Inauguration Day

about my religious faith I won't join his goddam church!"[19]

Because of his indifference to the confessional and doctrinal bases of traditional Christianity, Eisenhower made an excellent high priest for the liberal establishment. He came to preside over what has been called a uniquely American form of "ceremonial deism." He appears to have been perfectly sincere in his promotion of it. His presidential inauguration was soaked in references to God. The institution of the National Prayer Breakfast, held annually thereafter with participation by America's political and economic elite, was itself inaugurated with his blessing and attendance during the second week of his tenure in office.

The prayer breakfast was held in a Washington, DC, hotel ballroom

---

19 Kevin M. Kruse, *One Nation under God: How Corporate America Invented Christian America* (New York: Basic, 2015), 73.

beneath a monumental canvas depicting a bare-headed Uncle Sam on his knees with hands clasped fervently together. The image was named *America at Prayer*. After the meeting Eisenhower commissioned a reproduction and had it hung in the Oval Office. The event convinced Eisenhower that in the ideological struggle against Communism, religion—scorned in the Soviet Union—would play a central role. As he himself later put it, "Without God, there could be no American form of Government, nor an American way of life. Recognition of the Supreme Being is the first—the most basic—expression of Americanism."[20] A patriotic young evangelist named Billy Graham agreed. Having himself attended the inaugural prayer breakfast, he went so far as to say the event "could very well be the turning point in the history of western civilization."[21]

As Kevin Kruse has argued, it was certainly a turning point in Eisenhower's administration. The event, significantly, had adopted the political theme of "government under God." Eisenhower now applied this to the presidency. He regularly opened staff meetings with prayer and frequently peppered public statements with allusions to God. Later the same year, in response to prodding by the Roman Catholic televangelist Fulton Sheen, he rededicated Independence Day as a Day of National Prayer. The Declaration of Independence—the original event marked by the civic liturgical calendar—was thus said to be infused with "God's transcendent power."

In 1954, Eisenhower was attending a church in the capital when the pastor proposed augmenting the pledge of allegiance to acknowledge such a power. A day later the president had legislation introduced that resulted in a new version of the pledge with the qualifying phrase "under God" added to "one nation." This addition would become a flashpoint in America's future culture wars, but for now it occurred to no one that religion and liberalism might not always go together. In 1956, Eisenhower also supported the decision by Congress to change the national motto from *E pluribus unum* to *In God We Trust*. Within a year, all paper currency was being printed with the new motto (which had already been added to coinage).

---

20 Ibid., 75.
21 Ibid., 78.

A decade after the inception of the Cold War, then, American liberalism was standing strong against Communism. And its strength was increasingly attributed to a vaguely defined but emphatically transcendent civic religion. The American Way was not only progressive. It was godly.

Fading Echoes of Paradise

IT WAS PRECISELY AT THIS time that one of the great examples—perhaps the greatest—of America's ideological capacity for justice occurred. In 1955, the civil rights movement took its place within the mainstream of liberal world building. But within a decade, its evolution would reveal the limits of liberalism's capacity to remake the world in its own image.

Prior to the Second World War, efforts at racial justice had been largely minimal and unnoticed despite the fact that African Americans constituted some 10 percent of the nation's population. What came to be known as the civil rights movement was fueled by a century of injustice dating from the outcome of the Civil War. During Reconstruction, the thirteenth, four-teenth, and fifteenth amendments to the constitution abolished slavery and granted to freed blacks the rights of citizenship. However, in the South, measures known as Jim Crow laws were passed by a resentful white elec-torate which effectively barred blacks from the democratic political process. Furthermore, blacks were segregated from whites in public schools and other areas of society. The effect was to reduce African Americans to the status of second-class citizens, restricting their rights and degrading their humanity.

Efforts to alleviate racial discrimination had been undertaken for decades by a series of black leaders such as W.E.B. Dubois. In 1909 he helped found the National Association for the Advancement of Colored People (NAACP). The association's means of opposing Jim Crow restric-tions was largely judicial—that is, shaped by the ideology of liberalism. Lawyers such as Thurgood Marshall (who would go on to be the nation's first black Supreme Court justice) mounted challenges to existing laws and in some cases succeeded in overturning them. The most famous of these actions was against schools in Topeka, Kansas, that segregated black and white children. In the name of one of the parents, a pastor named Oliver

Brown, the NAACP sued the Topeka Board of Education and lost. However, this defeat enabled Marshall and other lawyers in the association to appeal. In *Brown v. Board of Education* (1954), the US Supreme Court ruled in favor of the plaintiffs. The long-standing policy of "separate but equal" racial segregation of schools thus became illegal. It was a great victory for liberalism, but without mass support it was likely to be bogged down by local resistance in the South.

Then, a year after the ruling, an event occurred so outrageous and painful in its details that when publicized it provoked mass support for the civil rights cause. A fourteen-year-old black boy from Illinois named Emmitt Till was visiting relatives in Mississippi when he came into contact with endemic white supremacy. Till had been patronizing a small-town general store in which a young white woman was working. Upon leaving, he was alleged to have made a wolf whistle at her. The woman's husband and his brother-in-law, who were violently opposed to federally ordered desegregation, looked on the incident as a result of the policy. What is more, Till's alleged insult was an affront to their racist conception of a social order in which black men were barred from amorous contact with white women. In the middle of the night, they abducted Till at gunpoint and carried him off in the back of their pickup truck to a river's edge. There they murdered him. The lynching was preceded by a beating so terrible that when Till's face was photographed later at his funeral, the ghastly image galvanized a public outcry. The cause of desegregation, until then held back in political obscurity, began to be a mass movement.

One of those shocked by the Till lynching was a black woman named Rosa Parks. She was an activist working with the local chapter of the NAACP in Montgomery, Alabama, and sought an opportunity to challenge segregation there. One local form was the policy of requiring blacks to remain at the back of city buses and to yield seats when whites ran out of their own seats in the front. On December 1, 1955, she refused to comply and was promptly arrested. Association lawyers eager to foment mass opposition to segregation had been looking for a case to publicize, and now they clearly had one. The spectacle of a well-mannered married woman being arrested under such circumstances was a shock to anyone who took the values of liberal democracy seriously.

But the desegregationist cause was not limited to secular ideology. Christianity retained its purchase on the values of many who otherwise might have followed Mill or even Nietzsche into a secular resolution to racism. We have seen how anticommunist world building inspired a patriotic civic religion. This proved largely powerless against segregation. But another form of utopian Christianity did have the power to change America's racial order.

It was known as the social gospel. It had its origins among liberal Protestants in the early twentieth century who could not ignore the growing inequalities of industrial capitalism. A Baptist theologian named Walter Rauschenbusch, for instance, reinterpreted the central message of the New Testament as a challenge to bring the kingdom of heaven into the world through progressive social reforms. Throughout the first millennium, traditional Christianity had emphasized an affirmative cosmology but without advocating social reform. The world was transformed through liturgical and sacramental experience, and the effects of this included the transformation of society (through Christian marriage) and the state (through Christian statecraft). Only after the Great Division in the West did Christendom's transformational imperative become institutionalized, and during the Protestant Reformation that tendency only increased.

Rauschenbusch was, as a Protestant, not only heir to this but a critic of it as well. Heavily influenced by secular humanism, especially in its socialist forms, he dismissed Christianity's emphasis on guilt and repentance as too individualistic. The fullness of the gospel, he claimed, would be achieved only when the salvation of the individual was subsumed within the salvation of the collective. And instead of looking to sacraments or saints in which a transcendent and corporate communion was available immediately to all, he projected salvation into a future struggle against social injustice. "The new thing in the social gospel," he claimed, "is the clearness and insistence with which it sets forth the necessity and the possibility of redeeming the historical life of humanity from the social wrongs which now pervade it."[22]

---

22 Walter Rauschenbusch, *A Theology for the Social Gospel* (New York: Macmillan, 1917), 95.

Such a view seemed naive to other Protestant theologians likewise struggling to find a Christian response to social injustice. One of these, Reinhold Niebuhr, drew from the "neo-orthodoxy" of Karl Barth to advocate greater realism in recognizing that even Christian reformers are limited in the good they can do by the effects of original sin. But such critics of Rauschenbusch's optimism did not jettison the hope that Christianity would assume a largely liberating function within modern society.

These views were thoroughly digested by a young black preacher named Martin Luther King Jr. He had arrived in Montgomery to assume leadership of the Dexter Avenue Baptist Church only a year before Rosa Parks made her courageous stand against segregation. King electrified his congregation with rousing sermons about personal salvation and the social evil of racism. Soon after Parks's arrest, he was asked to help lead a boycott of the city's bus system. During the course of the year that followed, he ignited a mass movement to advance civil rights.

By turning to the social gospel, King introduced utopian Christianity into the burgeoning movement. However, his vision went well beyond that. He also turned to traditional Christianity. Under his leadership, blacks and their white sympathizers sought not only to abolish segregation but to do so with a paradisiacal vision of interracial harmony grounded in sacrificial love and forgiveness. The principle of mercy, largely absent in secular ideology since its appearance in the nineteenth century, became the heart of his program.

Evangelical forgiveness of one's enemies applied even when he himself was threatened. Soon after the boycott began, white racists bombed his house, nearly killing his wife and children. When an enraged black crowd appeared at the site with guns in their hands, King ascended the demolished front porch to dissuade them from violence. "We believe in law and order," he declared. This was to remind them of the values of liberal democracy. But then he continued:

Don't get panicky. Don't do anything at all. Don't get your weapons. He who lives by the sword will perish by the sword. Remember, that is what

God said. We are not advocating violence. We want to love our enemies. We must love our white brothers no matter what they do to us.[23]

For a black man whose family had nearly been killed by white racists, the commandment to forgive was a truly heavenly response. Originating in the old Christendom under the influence of traditional Christianity, even now, mixed within the social gospel, it reshaped liberalism.

Not all blacks joined Martin Luther King in this paradisiacal approach to social justice. But as long as he lived, he managed to steer the civil rights movement away from the violence that many, following the lead of secular ideology, would otherwise consider the only path to liberty.

King's most famous act of leadership was a speech delivered on the steps of the Lincoln Memorial at the National Mall during a civil rights rally called the March on Washington for Jobs and Freedom in 1963. By then King had helped create an ancillary organization to the NAACP called the Southern Christian Leadership Conference, which he served as president. Its goal was to surpass the judicial scope of the NAACP and make civil rights a populist cause.

Surrounded by leaders of the movement and facing a crowd containing a quarter of a million black and white faces, King made a memorable contribution to America's project of liberal world building. He brought attention to the American Way and reviewed some of what he considered its most elemental liberal expressions. These included the Declaration of Independence and the US Constitution. He also spoke about the Emancipation Proclamation. Not only was he standing in front of a national monument to its author, but the year marked the centennial of its issuance. These documents were necessary to the myth of liberal democracy, but with his rhetorical genius he turned them against the white establishment. To disenfranchised and impoverished blacks, he argued, they were only a "promissory note" yet to be honored. In fact, King declared, the check issued in the name of "life, liberty, and the pursuit of happiness" was now being returned by African

---

23 Quoted in David Levering Lewis, *King* (Urbana: University of Illinois Press, 2013), 70.

Martin Luther King Jr. delivering "I Have a Dream" speech

Americans due to "insufficient funds." As liberal as the American Way was, he suggested, real freedom required more than documents and laws. It required a cultural transformation. For the Baptist preacher, this could be offeed only by Christianity.

King's utopian vision of interracial harmony was "rooted," as he put it, "in the American Dream." But as he approached the culmination of his most famous speech, he joined liberal ideology to traditional Christianity. "I have a dream," he elaborated, that one day the sons of slaves and the sons of slavers will sit together in Georgia at a "table of brotherhood"—as if in paradise itself. "I have a dream," he continued, that one day in Alabama "little black boys and black girls will be able to join hands with little white boys and white girls as sisters and brothers." Such images were more heavenly than secular.

And so was his ecstatic final sentence. The advance of the civil rights movement, he declared eschatologically, will "speed up that day when all of God's children, black men and white men, Jews and Gentiles, Protestants and Catholics, will be able to join hands and sing in the words of the old Negro spiritual, 'free at last, free at last, Great God a-mighty, we are free at last!'"

Coretta Scott King remarked on the paradisiacal effect of hearing her husband's words at the March on Washington. "At that moment it seemed as if the Kingdom of God appeared," she later recalled. "But," she added, "it only lasted for a moment."[24]

Indeed, oratory alone would not free America's black (or Hispanic, or Asian) population from the evils of racism. But until the cultural transformation King looked for occurred, laws and other governmental interventions could help. One of the many whites watching the "I Have a Dream" address in stunned admiration—before a television screen in the White House, it turned out—was President John F. Kennedy. In alliance with other progressive Democrats such as Vice President Lyndon Johnson and Senator Humphrey, he was an advocate for civil rights legislation. In no small part because of the national prestige gained by King during the march, efforts were now made to prepare a Civil Rights Act, which was signed into law the following year. This was succeeded in 1965 by a Voting Rights Act.

That same year the tension between Washington and the South had been displayed when King led a march from Selma, Alabama, to the state courthouse in Montgomery. The march drew large numbers of religious leaders representing both traditional and utopian Christianity. The most senior among the former was Archbishop Iakovos of the Greek Orthodox Archdiocese of America. Among the latter, a Unitarian-Universalist pastor named

---

24 Gary Dorrien, *Breaking White Supremacy: Martin Luther King Jr. and the Black Social Gospel* (New Haven, CT: Yale University Press, 2018), 352.

James Reeb was beaten to death by segregationists for his stand against racism.

Despite such violence, King remained firmly committed to a movement driven by civil disobedience and not by revolutionary insurgency. Nonviolent protest (which he had partly adapted from the policies of Mahatma Gandhi) not only fulfilled Christianity's commandment to love but proved effective among an American populace still defined by high rates of church attendance.

Hence King's demand that protestors in Birmingham, Alabama, in 1963 not resist the authorities when marching in streets and occupying lunch counters with "sit-ins." And when he found himself arrested and jailed for violating laws he considered unjust, he wrote a "Letter from Birmingham Jail" to a group of critical white pastors. In it he used Christian authorities such as Augustine and Thomas Aquinas to argue for a society free of racial dehumanization. He even flourished an allusion to Nazi anti-Semitic legislation to remind his audience of the primacy of divine over human law. He used the occasion to argue for divine-human synergy—a cornerstone of traditional Christian anthropology—in resolving America's racial injustice. "We must come to see," he asserted, "that human progress never rolls in on wheels of inevitability. It comes through the tireless efforts and persistent work of men willing to be coworkers with God, and without this work time itself becomes an ally of social stagnation."

And in answer to the charge of being an extremist, he reminded his Christian readers of the illustrious examples of evangelical maximalism. "Was not Jesus an extremist?" he asked rhetorically, following the question by quoting the Sermon on the Mount on love of one's enemies (Matt. 5:44).

In fact, King never publicly succumbed to the violence and hatred that confronted him and his cause. We have noted his call to forgiveness for the murderous attack on his home in Montgomery in 1956. Two years later, he was stabbed in the chest (by a schizophrenic black woman, of all people) and narrowly escaped death. In the hospital, he issued a statement of his continued dedication to nonviolence and forgiveness of his attacker.

But not all blacks were content with King's Christian approach to the movement. One, Malcom X (d. 1965), had emerged with a militant alternative. He was the son of a Baptist lay preacher. During time in prison he renounced Christianity and converted to the radical African American religious body Nation of Islam. Because American Christianity—even in its populist black forms—was associated with white enslavement, he decided that a religion indigenous to Africa made a preferable moral basis for black liberation. The piety of the ancient Church of Ethiopia was thoroughly African, of course, but it did not support his new conviction that white men are "devils." Echoing Nietzsche, he declared that Christianity could not be a means of racial justice because the commandment to sacrificial love stifled the black will to power. Accordingly, he held the SCLC in contempt. In his autobiography he scoffingly characterized the March on Washington as a "Farce on Washington," dismissing King and other SCLC leaders as "Uncle Tom Negroes." Malcolm X would be murdered by members of the Nation of Islam after his decision to leave the body, but his contempt for American liberalism lived on among other dissatisfied members of the civil rights movement.

Huey Newton (d. 1989) was a good example. A disciple of Malcolm X, he founded the militant Black Panther party in 1966. A native of impoverished Oakland, California, Newton was familiar with the exclusion of blacks from mainstream American society. Against a liberal ideology that united political rights with material consumption, he advocated what he called "black power." This would serve as a counter-ideology to the American Way. The political and religious writings of Marx, Lenin, and Durkheim provided inspiration. So did Nietzsche. Black Panthers were encouraged to carry weapons and be prepared to fight against the white oppressor. In 1967, Newton shot and killed a white police officer after being detained during a traffic stop. Convicted of the killing, he nevertheless succeeded in having the sentence overturned. He then returned to the work of racial struggle.

Before he was himself murdered by a rival black revolutionary, Newton published his autobiography, with the appropriately nihilistic title *Revolutionary Suicide* (1973). In it he described how the philosophy of Nietzsche influenced Black Panther ideology. It assigned formative influence to what the author considered the bane of Christian morality, the imperative of the will to power, and the promise of the superman. According to one historian, Newton

> *offered a Nietzsche who encouraged a self who could listen to its inner voice and not mistake the white man's voice for his own conscience. Nietzsche could teach African Americans to no longer be supplicants to "vacated mythologies" about an open society or black racial inferiority. . . . Newton transfigured* Thus Spoke Zarathustra *to animate his vision of an America after the death of the "white man's . . . God." He stressed that the slogan "All Power to the People" was more than something catchy to shout at marches or to inscribe on Black Panther Party memos. Instead, it expressed quite explicitly a "metaphysical" claim about "man as God," animating the Panthers' vision for the movement.*[25]

Newton felt contempt for reformational Christianity—perhaps the only kind with which he, as the son of a Baptist, was familiar. He described it as anticosmological rather than cosmologically affirmative (as had been the case with traditional Christianity). Newton, in his own words, wanted to create a black power movement in which "rewards were due in the present" and one could hope in an eschatological "Promised Land *here and now.*"[26] What he was describing was a secular counterfeit of the old Christendom's principle of heavenly immanence. But about this, of course, he knew nothing.

And so black power militancy continued to gain adherents, especially as the SCLC began to lose traction in the wake of the progressive but still ineffectual Voting Rights Act of 1965. Martin Luther King kept militating for non-militancy, but even his eloquent baritone voice was being drowned out by radicals calling for black empowerment at the expense of their white enemies.

In 1968 the growing crisis became apparent during a march in Memphis, Tennessee. The city's black sanitation workers had gone on strike after two of their members had been accidentally crushed in trash trucks. But

---

25 Ratner-Rosenhagen, *American Nietzsche*, 258.
26 Ibid., 259.

no sooner had the SCLC organized nonviolent protest marches than radical black power organizations interfered and incited a riot. King was dismayed. Nevertheless, he reluctantly agreed to organize new protests on strictly nonviolent terms. The black men who participated were to wear sandwich boards declaring "I Am a Man"—a poignant expression of anthropological dignity inspired by Paul's statement that "there is neither Jew nor Greek, there is neither slave nor free, there is neither male nor female; for you are all one in Christ Jesus" (Gal. 3:28).[27] As we saw in chapter 2, Dostoevsky had used almost the same phrase when describing the paradisiacal experience of Lenten worship in a Siberian prison camp.

Before the second march was set to occur, King gave a speech at a local Pentecostal church. By this time, death threats from white racists had begun to occur on an almost daily basis. In the speech, he disclosed this fact but alluded to the failed assassination attempt a decade earlier as a source of encouragement. And though he recognized he might yet fall in the struggle for civil rights, he expressed certainty that the movement would survive him. For though there might be many difficulties ahead, he declared, "I have been to the mountaintop." This was an allusion to Moses' ascent of Mount Nebo shortly before his death, when the prophet was blessed to see the land promised to the Israelites—a chosen people delivered from slavery in Egypt. And though King hoped like any man to live a long life, he admitted, as with Moses the most important thing was to put his trust in God.

I just want to do God's will, and He's allowed me to go up to the mountain, and I've looked over and I've seen the Promised Land. I may not get there with you, but I want you to know tonight that we as a people will get to the Promised Land. So I'm happy tonight, I'm not worried about anything, I'm not fearing any man.

---

27 The phrase "I am a man" also alludes to the racist practice of addressing black men as "boy." It was this practice that jazz musicians tried to subvert by speaking to one another as "man"—a mannerism that was later assimilated into the hippie counterculture.

"Mine eyes," he concluded paradisiacally, "have seen the glory of the coming of the Lord."

The next day—April 4, 1968—King was standing on the balcony of his motel when a shot rang out. An assassin's bullet pierced his face and killed him.

The civil rights movement, at least as King had defined it with nonviolent principles of Christian mercy, died with him. Now, secular ideologies—sometimes violent and nihilistic—would drive efforts to alleviate American racism. Stokely Carmichael, a former advocate for nonviolent protest who had recently switched sides and entered the black power movement, put matters starkly. "When white America killed Dr. King," he announced, "she declared war on us. . . . Black people have to survive, and the only way they will survive is by getting a gun."[28]

Throughout the United States, race riots erupted in the days following Martin Luther King's assassination. One hundred sixty cities were convulsed in the violence. One hundred million dollars of damage was inflicted. Twenty thousand arrests were made. Forty-six people were murdered.

America was ceasing to look like a liberal utopia.

---

28   John A. Kirk, *Martin Luther King, Jr.* (London: Routledge, 2013), 182.

Edvard Munch, *Portrait of Nietzsche*

Vasily Perov, *Portrait of Dostoevsky*

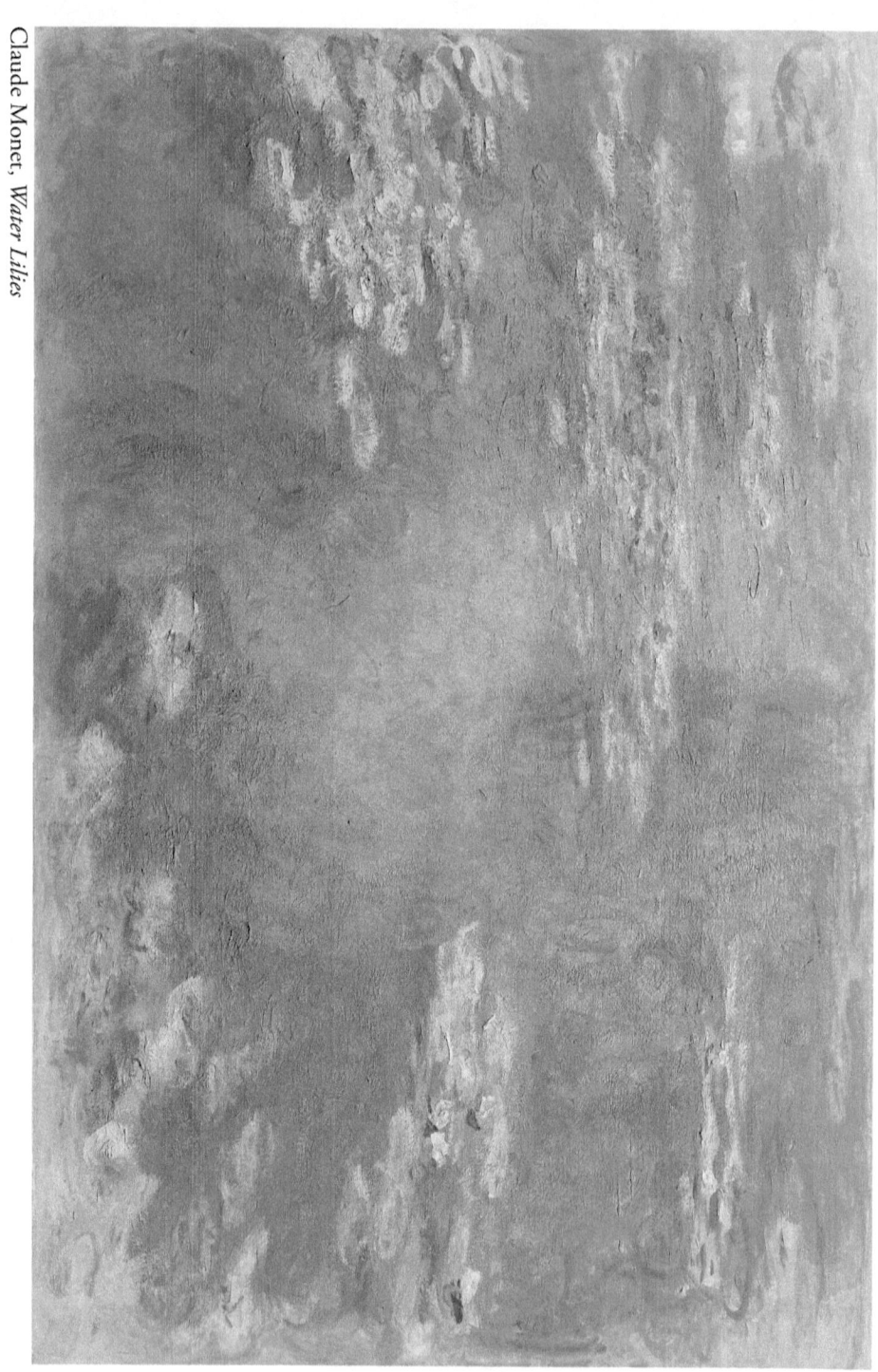

Auguste Renoir, *Luncheon of the Boating Party*

Vincent Van Gogh, *Starry Night*

Edvard Munch, *The Scream*

Pablo Picasso, *Portrait of Gertrude Stein*

Pablo Picasso, *Les Demoiselles d'Avignon*

Lenin's Tomb, Moscow
Jorge Láscar from Melbourne, Australia, CC BY 2.0 <https://creativecommons.org/licenses/by/2.0>, via Wikimedia Commons

Hubert Lanzinger, *The Standard Bearer*

Statue of Nazi Blockade Victims, Leningrad
VekaSpb, CC BY-SA 4.0 <https://creativecommons.org/licenses/by-sa/4.0>, via Wikimedia Commons

John Gast, *American Progress*

The Holy New Martyrs of Russia
Denis Kudlay/Shutterstock.com

PART III

Calling Off the Search

CHAPTER SEVEN

Dystopia

THE VICTORY OF THE SOVIET Union and her Western allies in 1945 seemed to vindicate the ideological worlds each had built in the face of nihilism. Yet only a generation later, both Communism and liberalism began to show signs that, propaganda notwithstanding, neither would last forever. Communism would fall first. Liberal democracy would suffer setbacks but manage to limp into the twenty-first century intact.

The "new world order" that attended the collapse of Communism (the phrase was that of President George H. W. Bush) would change the United States forever. Soon after the second millennium, it was clear that secular ideology was not the solution to the new Christendom's crisis of transcendence. Utopia in all its forms was a failure.

Few might have eyes to see, but the long-forgotten old Christendom, barely visible after so many centuries, would come to offer an alternative. As the search for meaning in secular ideologies was called off, paradise once again came to offer the West a point of transcendent orientation.

A Cry in the Wilderness

DESPITE CLAIMS TO THE CONTRARY, liberalism did not satisfy Christendom's transformational imperative. In America, the Eisenhower decade produced an unprecedented confidence in democracy and capitalism. But even as propagandists were declaiming the superiority of the American Way, some were beginning to perceive in it totalitarian tendencies. Utopia was beginning to look like dystopia.

Not surprisingly, traditional Christians were among the first to see the problem. They were distinct, however, from the many Christians with a utopian disposition. The latter continued to claim—and sometimes with greater and greater insistence—that despite its secular tendencies, humanism was the fulfillment of Christianity's world-transforming imperative. A good example was the Jesuit polymath Teilhard de Chardin. His book *The Phenomenon of Man* (1955) embraced Darwinism and effectively replaced the Incarnation with a future "omega point" in which humanity will reach its perfection through the biological and psychic process of evolution. The Anglican bishop John A. T. Robinson, for his part, published an influential book entitled *Honest to God* (1963), in which divine transcendence was largely rejected and man's communion with God reduced to a cultural and even secular level. Nevertheless, those Christians who had by now taken Karl Barth's lead and become acutely suspicious of efforts to blend the ancient faith with modern humanism were not impressed. Robinson was censored by the archbishop of Canterbury, and Teilhard's own Roman Catholic Church largely condemned his fanciful reorientation of salvation history.

There was hope that despite the continued fancies of modernists, Roman Catholic and even Protestant theologians were finally turning back to the solid foundations of first-millennium Christianity. The Orthodox Church offered a particularly strong patristic witness. After the First World War, numerous Orthodox theologians and philosophers had fled Communism and emigrated to western centers of learning such as Berlin, Paris, and New York. These Christians were largely free of modernist controversy. A partial exception was Sergey Bulgakov, whose doctrine of "sophiology" earned the rebuke of several bishops. However, fellow émigré Vladimir Lossky, through books like *The Mystical Theology of the Eastern Church* (1957), helped to reintroduce the West to the doctrine—largely forgotten since the Great Division—of deification. Even more influential was the work of Russian émigré Georges Florovsky (d. 1979). Teaching at a series of influential institutions, including Saint Vladimir's Seminary in New York, Harvard University, and Princeton University, he advanced what came to be known as the "neopatristic synthesis" of Orthodox theology at a time when modernism was disorienting so much of Western scholarship. His sober conviction that the West needed desperately to return to its Eastern foundations was expressed in a life of scholarship and ecumenical witness. Many Protestants and Roman Catholics were beginning to appreciate such a point of view, for the effects of secular humanism were now clearly exacting a negative, even apocalyptic price on the civilization and culture of the West.

In the face of the ideological world building that followed the First World War, for instance, the Anglican convert T. S. Eliot published an essay entitled *The Idea of a Christian Society* (1939). In it he warned against modern Christianity's failure to provide a total way of life for what had become only a nominal religious identity for most in the West. As concerned about values of liberal democracy as he was about Communism and the looming menace of National Socialism, he insisted that

> *we must abandon the notion that the Christian should be content with freedom of cultus, and with suffering no worldly disabilities on account of his faith. However bigoted the announcement may sound, the Christian can be satisfied with nothing less than a Christian organization of society—which is not the same thing as a society consisting exclusively of devout Christians. It would be a society in which the natural end of man—virtue and well-being in community—is acknowledged for all, and the supernatural end—beatitude—for those who have the eyes to see it.[1]*

The Russian Orthodox émigré Nicolas Berdyaev also used the rise of ideological world building as the backdrop for a prophetic warning to Western Christendom. In *The Fate of Man in the Modern World* (1935), he declared that

> *what is taking place in the world to-day is not a crisis of humanism (that is a topic of secondary importance), but a crisis of humanity. . . . We are*

---

1   T. S. Eliot, *Christianity and Culture: The Idea of a Christian Society and Notes toward the Definition of Culture* (New York: Harcourt Brace, 1976), 27.

witnessing the process of dehumanization in all phases of culture and of social life. Above all, moral consciousness is being dehumanized. Man has ceased to be the supreme value: he has ceased to have any value at all. . . . Humanism has become powerless and must be replaced.[2]

Nicolas Berdyaev

A return to traditional Christianity, then, was the only way out of the dehumanized world unintentionally created by humanism.

More culturally far-reaching than Eliot, Berdyaev also stressed the need for a return to traditional Christianity's metamorphocentric or transformational values. "The creative gift of transfiguration," he noted in reviewing the record of modernism, "is disappearing from art."[3] In fact all of modern culture has inevitably fallen since the Renaissance, when a transcendent vision of man as the image of God gave way to one in which man is determined by an untransfigured world. Berdyaev alludes repeatedly to Dostoevsky and Nietzsche as the first to see this nihilistic tendency. For instance, he applies the former's concept of "everything is permissible" and the latter's concept of the "will to power." As these intellectual prophets foresaw, the Western vision of man has since the First World War become defined by an "ontology of nihilism."[4]

Interestingly, the Orthodox philosopher saw reformational Christianity, with its emphasis on man's depravity and the world's distance from heaven, as a cause of rather than a solution to the modern crisis of Christendom. This applied especially to the neo-Calvinism of Barth.

---

2   Nicholas Berdyaev, *The Fate of Man in the Modern World* (Ann Arbor: University of Michigan Press, 1935), 25–26.

3   Ibid., 35.

4   Ibid., 38.

Even in modern European religious and theological thought this process of dehumanization is evident. . . . Karl Barth with his dialectic theology is the dehumanization of Christianity. This mode of thought discovers in the creative world only sin and powerlessness. There remains a fervent faith in God, but in a God absolutely transcendent, separated by an abyss from the world and from man. The image of God in man is shattered. . . . Karl Barth's world and his humanity are godless, but God remains.

Berdyaev sees in Barth "a passionate reaction against humanism in Christianity which has resulted in a degradation or even denial of man."[5] Against the utopian Christianity of theological liberals, Barth's view reestablishes transcendence. But in doing so it also abolishes heavenly immanence.

Berdyaev sees in the reformational Christianity of the Roman Catholic Church a similar tendency, though one less prone toward nihilism. The rise of neo-Thomist scholasticism in the twentieth century is a case in point.

Thomism . . . remains optimistic, and we discover in it elements of that old humanism which date back to the medieval renaissance. In Thomism man is not denied, he is merely diminished: man is regarded as an insignificant being, possessing neither real freedom, nor creative capacities; he is a second-rate being.[6]

Having reviewed Western theological developments from an Eastern point of view, Berdyaev nevertheless emphasized that neither form of reformational Christianity—Barthian or Thomistic—is nearly as dangerous to the survival of Christendom as secular ideology.

This is the theme taken up by C. S. Lewis, himself a convert from atheism after the First World War. Describing what he called a "mere Christianity"—by which he meant a form of the faith grounded in tradition but appealing to all sincere Christians—he brought attention to the manifold shortcomings of modernity. One of the greatest and most threatening was

---

5   Ibid., 38–39.
6   Ibid., 39.

the trend toward dehumanization of which Berdyaev had written. For Lewis, the decline of Western anthropology was to be found especially in efforts by modern educators, those custodians of culture. In his view they were following the tendencies of atheistic philosophy in seeking to eradicate strong convictions about morality and beauty.

To confront this development, the Oxford literary scholar and accidental theologian wrote a book with the dystopian title *The Abolition of Man* (1943). In it he laid out one of the greatest problems of modernity. He brought attention to discrete human faculties and their place within the body, specifying the stomach, chest, and head. By reducing man to the status of an animal driven solely by instinct (signified by the stomach) and transforming the world through the use of rationalism alone (signified by the head), the West is becoming a civilization of "men without chests." Here Lewis was alluding to traditional Christian anthropology's attention to the centrality of the nous, or "heart" (sometimes translated as "mind" in a non-rationalistic sense). Man's rational and instinctive faculties are secondary to his noetic ones, and it is the latter that link him to the transcendent divine reality.

Nevertheless, however fervently Protestant, Roman Catholic, and Orthodox writers called nihilistic Christendom back from the abyss, theirs remained little more than a cry in the wilderness.

Totalitarianism, Hard and Soft

IT WAS NOT ONLY CHRISTIANS who had lost confidence in utopia. During the generation that followed the Second World War, many believers and unbelievers alike were in agreement that the outcome of secular ideology was some degree of totalitarianism. The ultimate example was of course the Soviet Union with its overwhelmingly totalitarian state. But many could not help but observe that while such "hard" totalitarianism was absent in the liberal West, a gentler form was beginning to show itself.

Novelists had already begun to depict fictionally the Communist way of life as not utopia but dystopia. In 1940 Arthur Koestler, himself a former Communist, published a story set within the Stalinist show trials and called *Darkness at Noon*. Other exposés were penned by the democratic socialist

George Orwell. He produced a depiction of Stalinism entitled *Animal Farm.* Then, in 1949, he published the most influential dystopian novel of all, *1984.* It introduced into the vocabulary of nihilistic Christendom such phrases as *big brother, thoughtcrime,* and *newspeak.*

Nevertheless, when Stalin died in 1953, many intellectuals hoped that a new, freer stage in the history of Communist utopia would ensue. They were largely disappointed. Nikita Khrushchev now assumed leadership (1953–64). He was a true believer in Communism. Some of his policies, to be sure, were decidedly beneficial. The new general secretary launched a destalinization campaign with the conviction that ridding the Soviet Union of terror and the personality cult would free her to do what Lenin had promised—transform the world into a socialist utopia. In 1956, Khrushchev issued a notorious "Secret Speech" to the party congress meeting in Moscow. The stunned audience listened to him catalog the crimes of a leader who for decades had been hailed as the mystical embodiment of transcendent Leninism. Instead of bringing unbounded progress, Stalin had instead arrested Communism in its march toward progress. Under his brutal and conceited rule, the new leader complained, the Soviet Union had become as much a dystopia as a model of freedom and happiness.

Few could argue against the first half of this assertion. But establishing freedom and happiness was another matter. In order to cultivate support for destalinization in the Soviet leadership, Khrushchev decided to loosen totalitarian controls on the press. Suddenly, a group of writers appeared who called Communism's record into question. Their most remarkable publication was a short novel entitled *One Day in the Life of Ivan Denisovich* (1962) by Alexander Solzhenitsyn. The author had been a victim of Stalinism and spent years in Siberia for no crime at all. His autobiographical novel depicts that experience and in so doing places the Soviet Union in a dystopian light. Significantly, Solzhenitsyn was an Orthodox Christian, and his exposé draws subtly on traditional Christianity in making its case against totalitarianism. Other believers—especially those living out the Orthodox Christian way of life in the few parish churches and monasteries that survived the cultural revolution—were not given the same freedoms of expression. In fact, the short-lived ideological "thaw" under Khrushchev unfolded against the backdrop of a new wave of anti-Christian persecution.

Economic life also failed to bring substantial improvements under Khrushchev. The command economy, over which Gosplan (the state planning agency) kept totalitarian watch, proved impervious to the needs of society. Several ill-conceived reform policies were introduced and were derisively labeled "hare-brained schemes" by Khrushchev's neo-Stalinist enemies on the Politburo. These policies produced few benefits. In the meantime, Russia's humiliation during the Cuban Missile Crisis of 1962 destroyed what little credibility Khrushchev still had. Two years later a Politburo putsch forced him into retirement and reimposed a stable but moribund bureaucracy. Soviet dystopia was again secure.

In the end, the only momentous reform bequeathed by the impetuous reformer was the reorganization of the dreaded secret police. Though still dreadful, the new KGB would never again commit mass violence against the population as had the Cheka and NKVD before it.

But on the American side of the Iron Curtain, where freedom of the press remained a legally protected institution, novels and other works made the case that the hard totalitarianism of Communism was echoed in a less blatant, more flexible, and softer totalitarianism of liberal democracy.

An early example had been the work of Aldous Huxley. In 1932, he published a novel entitled *Brave New World*. It tells the story of a fictional society of the future in which citizens, enjoying the benefits of modern science, live exclusively for pleasure. Their happiness is assured by a mass-produced drug called "soma." It is issued as a ration and consumed on a regular schedule—except when trauma or unrelieved doubts about utopia require a special "soma holiday." Huxley was apparently using the drug as a metaphor for the pleasures of consumerism that may have been absent during the Great Depression but became a basis for liberal democracy after World War II. Soma makes striving for transcendence unnecessary. It possesses, one character explains, "all the advantages of Christianity and alcohol; none of their defects."

Yet such a civilization is not the utopia that had been envisioned by the secular humanists since the Renaissance. To attain perfect happiness, it has become necessary to surrender individual autonomy. Citizens of Huxley's

Aldous Huxley

dystopia are expected to live by a soft totalitarianism that, while permeating every belief and value of their culture, is not imposed on them involuntarily. They are active participants in a "World State" that provides them with the means of happiness. Religion has been abandoned, along with art and philosophy. A new secular mythology orients the culture. For instance, to honor their civilization they celebrate the memory of industrialists like Henry Ford. The famous Model T, produced for a kind of consumerist Everyman, features prominently in the new mythology. The linear calendar refers to Ford and not the Incarnation. When crosses are displayed, the upper section is removed to form a "T" after the automobile. Transcendence has been erased, and a drugged but happy humanity is the better for it.

After the Second World War, Huxley watched in dismay as his fictional depiction of dystopia became increasingly nonfictional. In 1958, when anticommunist feeling was at its height (in England as well as America), he published a sequel to his famous novel. It was entitled *Brave New World Revisited*. A generation on, Huxley pointed to ways in which liberal democracy was beginning to be overwhelmed by a soft totalitarianism.

Numerous signs were visible to those with eyes to see them. For instance, just two years before Eisenhower's warning against a "military-industrial complex," *Brave New World Revisited* brought attention to the alliance of big business and big government in what Huxley called a new "Power Elite." He listed the many ways in which the liberal order was subverting itself, often in ways envisioned by the original novel. For instance, he reviewed his earlier fictional depiction of "hypnopaedia," a practice in which children are indoctrinated during sleep by whispered recordings of social ideals. He compared this to the nonfictional rise of subliminal and music-based advertising, by which nonrational means are used to create willing consumers. "Orpheus," he noted cynically, "has entered into an alliance with Pavlov." Huxley also reviewed the novel's fictional depiction of soma and compared it to the nonfictional use of sedatives—mass produced and prescribed on a grand scale—to relieve the stress of modern society. The sexual revolution was yet to come, but the nonfictional decline of marriage and rise of a culture of hookups it would soon bring matched the fictional elimination of family and the widespread sex entertainment provided in the novel.

Perhaps most profoundly, Huxley noted the recent tendency of liberal democracy to subvert from within the very principles of liberalism. Granted, as dystopia displaces utopia—or rather grows organically from it—the outward forms of liberal democracy, such as constitutions and rule by law, will remain intact.

But these liberal forms will merely serve to mask and adorn a profoundly illiberal substance. . . . The quaint old forms—elections, parliaments, Supreme Courts and all the rest—will remain. The underlying substance will be a new kind of non-violent totalitarianism.[7]

Totalitarianism was therefore the inescapable destiny of the West, Huxley suggested, whether Communist or liberal. The only distinction in its latter form was that it would most likely be of a "non-violent" or soft variety.

Another critique of utopia's unexpected and therefore absurd outcomes was the collective work of scholars affiliated with the Frankfurt School. Founded in Weimar Germany, it drew together a wide range of talented social scientists and philosophers. Their common denominator was Marxism. They were dismayed that the November Revolution had not produced a socialist political order and that many workers even went on to vote for conservative parties. Convinced that capitalism must be abolished before the promises of humanism could be realized, they considered liberal democracy a functional dystopia. Contrary to the promises of Marx, the proletariat did not choose to overthrow the bourgeoisie when given the opportunity. In fact, it came to embrace the values of the oppressors. This was astonishing to Marxist intellectuals. The Frankfurt School developed an entirely new method of understanding the calamity, something they called "critical theory."

Its insights brought even more attention to the dystopian condition in which twentieth-century Christendom lived. For with the horrors of Stalinism visible to all in the wake of the Great Terror, Western Marxists invested in the ideals of humanism could not advocate the Communist approach to world building. In fact, critical theorists called the whole ideological project of utopia into question. Forced by their humanist values to call off the search for meaning not only in Nazism but in Communism and liberalism as well, they adopted a subversive relationship to any culture based on ideology. As atheists, they also opposed traditional Christianity. Rejecting the paradisiacal culture of the old Christendom (about which they knew almost nothing), they likewise rejected the ideological

---

7   Aldous Huxley, *Brave New World Revisited* (New York: Perennial, 1965), 110.

projects that had come to replace it. Instead, they advocated a policy of principled cultural deconstruction. As had happened recurringly since the thirteenth-century Pope Innocent III, the West was once again confronted by a cosmo-anthropological pessimism.

Critical theory pursued its line of negation along two axes. First, it considered nearly every expression of contemporary culture inherently oppressive by its failure to point to truly liberating patterns of behavior. It accepted Marx's claim that modernity is trapped in a web of alienation. This caused the dehumanization of humanity. To confront dystopian reality, critical theorists applied a negative method of what they called "cultural criticism" (*Kulturkritik*). It rested on a conviction that the condition of advanced capitalism, when the material needs of man are largely met, distorts reality. Culture becomes illusionary as it is determined by the values of a once struggling but now triumphant middle class.

An example is the modern hero, whose promethean autonomy was designed during the Renaissance to advance bourgeois individualism. As a cultural trope, the self-determined hero has been depicted in artworks ever since. Raphael's *Sistine Madonna* depicted emasculated angels and thus served to free the individual from a sense of heavenly dependence; Jane Austen's *Pride and Prejudice* encouraged individuals to imagine their lives transformed by great romances; Tchaikovsky's *Symphony Pathétique*, while intensely pessimistic, modeled an heroic individual struggle with adversity. But the "liberal notion" of individualism, one sympathetic historian of the Frankfurt School has observed, "had been fully undermined by the gradual liquidation of the autonomous subject in modern society."[8] Human autonomy has been swallowed up by a capitalistic "culture industry" that produces only a sensation of authentic individuality. Artistic representations of the heroic individual such as might be found in a John Wayne western no longer have an historically liberating effect. They are mere commodities. They lack authenticity and are culturally powerless.

---

8   Martin Jay, *The Dialectical Imagination: A History of the Frankfurt School and the Institute of Social Research, 1923–1950* (Boston: Little, Brown, 1973), 178.

A second line of negation was more comprehensive. It claimed that science and rationality are fundamentally oppressive. Both originated in the seventeenth-century reaction against reformational Christianity but quickly assumed equally malevolent tendencies. Francis Bacon—the father of modern science—thought that empiricism would liberate man from irrationality. But in fact the history of "enlightenment" since his time has been the history of enslavement. In a book entitled *Dialectic of Enlightenment* (1944), critical theorists Max Horkheimer and Theodor Adorno presented a negative assessment of utopia by attributing modern oppression to the rise of eighteenth-century rationalism. Their central argument was expressed in a double aphorism: "Myth is already enlightenment, and enlightenment reverts to mythology." What they meant by this was that secular modernity is not necessarily superior to religious antiquity. They were particularly interested in the desecration of the modern world, or what Weber called "disenchantment." They claimed that religious myth was in some ways already enlightened before this process began during the Renaissance. What is more, they claimed that the so-called Enlightenment that followed Bacon was itself not fundamentally rational but mythological. In other words, the entire culture of utopia is actually dystopian in that it misrepresents modernity as a liberating process. In their words, it has become an "absurdity." For "the power of the system over human beings increases with every step they take away from the power of nature."[9]

Dating from the period more accurately termed "the benightenment," the West was in the process of disintegration. Modern man with his promethean autonomy was being swallowed up by a totalitarian culture expanding the scope of a rationalized and desecrated world.

The Triumph of Absurdity

AS THE FRANKFURT SCHOOL PRODUCED volume after volume of negative cultural criticism, another group of intellectuals was contributing to

---

9   Max Horkheimer and Theodor W. Adorno, *Dialectic of Enlightenment*, trans. Edmund Jephcott (Stanford, CA: Stanford University Press, 2002), 30–31.

postwar nihilism. The existentialists were mainly French philosophers whose experience of Nazi occupation stirred strong commitments to a life of action. They were for the most part atheists and took as a starting point the moral conundrum of Nietzsche that "God is dead." They were also impressed by Dostoevsky's question, issued through Alyosha Karamazov, of how an atheist could live a good life if "all is permitted." These nihilistic moral problems were never resolved and colored existentialism throughout the postwar decades. In a condition they called "absurdity," human life and the world itself were fundamentally meaningless. But even without an objective framework, man must find a way to liberate himself from the despair of absurdity.

The movement's most important representative was Jean-Paul Sartre (d. 1980). The child of a loveless marriage and the grandchild of one in which the husband refused for forty years to speak to his wife, the future philosopher learned as a boy to be deeply critical of human relationships. Nevertheless, in college he met a woman with whom he would share a relationship for the rest of his life—though only under the strictest conditions. Simone de Beauvoir (d. 1986) became Sartre's mistress and lifelong soulmate. However, by force of personality he reduced her to a kind of courtesan within the circle of intellectuals that surrounded him. He adamantly refused to marry her, though he gave her a ring to wear as consolation. He insisted on the freedom to conduct affairs with others, giving her the right to do likewise. He encouraged her to seek a career in letters like himself, though he also assigned her the duty of advocating for his intellectual preeminence. All the while, he required her to cook, clean, sew, and even manage his affairs with innumerable other lovers—all much younger and prettier than she. As Paul Johnson had noted, "this brilliant and strong-minded woman became Sartre's slave from almost their first meeting and remained such for all her adult life until he died."[10] Ironically, during all of this, de Beauvoir also became a founder of the feminist movement.

Sartre's relationship with de Beauvoir brought attention to his preoccupation with interpersonal domination and alienation. It was fortuitous, perhaps, that one of his earliest experiences with her was attending a performance of

---

10   Paul Johnson, *Intellectuals* (London: Phoenix, 1988), 235.

Brecht's *Threepenny Opera* in Berlin, before the Nazi introduction of cultural coordination. Fascinated by the work's use of "alienation-effect," the two lovers amused themselves on the way home that evening by repeatedly singing "Mack the Knife" to one another. If not romantic, it was at least a taste of liberating absurdity.

Alienation became an important theme in Sartre's philosophy. His first major work was a novel entitled *Nausea* (1938). In it a cerebral loner named Roquentin discovers that everything in the world around him is meaningless. This causes a sensation of nausea. Unable to share his inner experiences with others, he finds himself gazing one day on a chestnut tree in a park. Suddenly, he discovers the "clue to existence": everything that exists is superfluous and trapped in a state of "absurdity." Existence has no grounding in anything beyond itself. Every person is irreversibly divided from every other person by a radical condition of subjectivity.

Subjectivity became a key element in existentialism, and Sartre's subsequent works elaborated it. The most substantial work was a treatise entitled *Being and Nothingness* (1944), the very title of which documents the interpersonal specter of nihilism under which the West now lived. In it Sartre distinguishes two different approaches to existence, being "in-itself" and being "for-itself." Significantly, both reduce human existence to an isolated

Jean-Paul Sartre with Simone de Beauvoir

condition of egoism rather than relating humanity to a transcendent experience of divine participation. Being in-itself applies to passive, unconscious things like material objects. These have no subjectivity whatsoever. Being for-itself is by contrast dynamic. However, it exposes the individual to the reality of other individuals, and this represents a threat to selfhood. Sartre calls this assault on subjectivity the "Gaze." When others who possess being for-itself objectify the individual, as they must inevitably do, the individual's authentic selfhood easily dissolves into passive being in-itself. "The Other" (as Sartre negatively conceptualizes the human community) thus becomes the enemy of selfhood. It imposes exogenous categories of meaning on the individual. Only a principled division from other human beings can assure that the individual maintains his authentic subjectivity.

This led Sartre to the conclusion that love, especially the sacrificial love commanded by the gospel, subverts human authenticity. It is a conclusion similar to Nietzsche's. As we saw in the previous chapter, Zarathustra offered liberalism an extreme example of total freedom from the social will to power. The old Christendom had looked for transcendence in sacramental communion with both the divine and the human other. For the new Christendom being transformed by the existentialists, however, uniting oneself to the Other denies the only meaningful purpose of life, radical subjectivity. As Sartre starkly put it in a play entitled *No Exit*, "hell is other people."

Existentialists, following Nietzsche, subverted both Christianity and humanism when they denied an essential human nature that stabilizes morality and meaning. Of course, the rejection of Christianity was by this time commonplace. But an attack on humanism was more controversial. It opened the door to the nihilistic claim that human life is totally meaningless. Therefore, the existentialists felt it necessary to retain at least a vestige of Christianity's secular counterfeit. They located it in the promethean anthropology that dated to the Renaissance. But to be truly autonomous, they argued, man must abandon the illusion of possessing not only a God-given but also a nature-given essence.

Sartre tried to lay out the case for this in *Existentialism and Humanism* (1945). There he claimed that "existence comes before essence." This aphorism means that

*man first of all exists, encounters himself, surges up in the world—and
defines himself afterwards. If man as the existentialist sees him is not
definable, it is because to begin with he is nothing. He will not be anything
until later, and then he will be what he makes of himself. Thus, there is no
human nature, because there is no God to have a conception of it.*[11]

By denying any essence to man and embracing a nihilistic anthropology,
Sartre was extending what Nietzsche had already claimed with less precision
a half century earlier.

Sartre was also elaborating what he believed Dostoevsky had discovered,
albeit to the end of recovering his faith rather than losing it. "The existentialist," Sartre claimed to the contrary,

*finds it extremely embarrassing that God does not exist, for there disap-
pears with Him all possibility of finding values in an intelligible heaven.
There can no longer be any good a priori, since there is no infinite and
perfect consciousness to think it. . . . Dostoevsky once wrote "If God did
not exist, everything would be permitted": and that, for existentialism, is
the starting point. . . . Thus we have neither behind us, nor before us in a
luminous realm of values, any means of justification or excuse. We are left
alone, without excuse. . . . Man is condemned to be free.*[12]

A radical autonomy to act without any reference to moral absolutes thus
constitutes whatever vestiges of humanism the darkly subjectivistic anthropology of existentialism retained. Self-consciously more secular than anything before it, such a humanism was also severing its ties to the values that
inspired utopia during the Renaissance. Prometheus was becoming a demon.

The existentialist movement can be understood only in the uniquely
politicized context of postwar France. Once the land of revolution that
had bestowed on utopia the seeds of its ideology—"liberty, equality, and

---

11 Jean-Paul Sartre, *Existentialism and Humanism*, trans. Philip Mairet (London:
Methuen, 1948), 28.
12 Ibid., 33–34.

brotherhood"—France under the Third Republic had surrendered ingloriously to the Third Reich after only six weeks of fighting. What is more, resistance to the Germans under the puppet Vichy Régime was rare and ineffective. When liberated by American and British soldiers in 1944, the French were therefore suffering from national disgrace.

Postwar intellectuals were eager to reverse this and adopted an antagonistic mentality to everything that did not frame the transformational imperative in the most revolutionary way possible. As one historian noted, Sartre and his philosophy of alienation set the tone.

> *Hell being other people, one found one's identity through one's enemy, through the opposition of others; thus, it was better to choose that identity than have it imposed from the outside. . . . The imaginative exercise of empathy, the wish to understand the reasoning of those with whom one disagreed, was not widespread among French intellectuals in the aftermath of liberation. The point, after all, was not to understand the world, but to change it, and for that one did not need to know what the Other felt or thought but only who it was.[13]*

Furious hostility to everything conservative led Sartre to endorse Communism, even after the Great Terror had been exposed. He and de Beauvoir traveled to China, to Cuba, and even to the Soviet Union to see Marxist revolution in action. And on their return they praised what they had seen.

For Sartre's collaborator Maurice Merleau-Ponty (d. 1961), there were no limits to the existentialists' commitment to radical politics. An example was the latter's attack on Arthur Koestler, whose dystopian novel *Darkness at Noon* exposed the departure of Communism from humanism. In a book entitled *Humanism and Terror*, Merleau-Ponty rushed to Communism's defense. Merleau-Ponty defended the moral legitimacy of the Moscow Show Trials (something Koestler, resorting to humanism, had denied) by

---

13 Tony Judt, *Past Imperfect: French Intellectuals, 1944–1956* (New York: New York University Press, 2011), 54.

distinguishing between "subjective honesty and objective treason."[14] By this he meant that innocent victims of political terror nevertheless share in the guilt of real traitors when the judicial process is aligned with an objectively progressive movement. Because it is based in Marxism, the only effective science of historical progress, this applied to the Soviet Union. Marxism, he asserted, "is not a philosophy of history; it is *the* philosophy of history and to renounce it is to dig the grave of Reason in history."[15] Violent or not, unjust or not, revolutionary politics were the only legitimate commitment an existentialist intellectual could make.

Nevertheless, one atheistic Frenchman came to reject political violence even when enacted in the name of progress. Albert Camus (d. 1960) moved in the same existentialist circles as Sartre, de Beauvoir, and Merleau-Ponty.[16] Unlike Sartre, he actually fought in the Resistance. More importantly, unlike Sartre, he spent his life searching for the truth rather than merely asserting it. In the end, he parted company with Sartre's circle because, unlike them, he came to renounce the legitimacy of violence.

Camus started his writing career affirming the same nihilistic convictions as Sartre: God is dead, the world is meaningless, and man is condemned to live in absurdity. This was the message of his first successful novel, *The Stranger* (1942). It was even more explicit in a companion piece of philosophy published the same year, entitled *The Myth of Sisyphus*. The latter work used the ancient image of a hopeless man condemned to push a stone up a hill, knowing that at the top it will only roll back down and his labor will resume—and will do so for all eternity. It was a metaphor for the modern predicament as Camus understood it. Man lives now, in the wake of thinkers like Nietzsche, knowing that there is no underlying meaning to existence. His reflection explores the question of why, then,

Albert Camus

---

14 Maurice Merleau-Ponty, *Humanism and Terror: An Essay on the Communist Problem*, trans. John O'Neill (Boston: Beacon, 1969), 44.

15 Ibid., 153.

16 Camus explicitly rejected the existentialist label for one he termed "absurdist," but historians have for the most part dismissed any real distinction.

man does not simply commit suicide. This was a favorite theme of Dostoevsky, and Camus spent his life under the novelist's spell as much as under Nietzsche's. As with Sartre, the answer is found in man's will to resist absurdity, even if he knows he will never overcome it. And like Sartre, at this point in his life Camus looked to political engagement in the form of resistance to the Nazis as the highest form of existential living. Nevertheless, in the end life remains meaningless. Camus thus considered Sisyphus "the hero of the absurd."

However, within the extremist political atmosphere of postwar Paris, he came to renounce violence. His novel *The Plague* (1947) featured in metaphorical form the situation that Frenchmen (and all Westerners) had faced under the Third Reich. A merciless pestilence similar to the Black Death has caused a French Algerian city to quarantine. Scene after scene depicts the agonizing and apparently meaningless deaths of its citizens. All the time, a physician named Rieux patiently cares for every victim he comes across. In one memorable scene a child slowly dies in agony. This had been for Dostoevsky the most convincing argument against the existence of God. It was for Camus as well. Significantly, after the boy's death a priest suggests that Rieux accept the boy's death on the basis that "we should love what we cannot understand."[17] This of course is not something Rieux, or Camus (or Dostoevsky) can do. Theodicy had been one of the benightenment's greatest dead ends, as Voltaire's famous novel *Candide* had shown.[18] Rejecting the rationalistic justification of evil that originated in the new Christendom after the Great Division, Rieux also rejects its opposite: violent rebellion. He may be unable to stop evil, but he can fight it with sacrificial love. Here a former revolutionary named Tarrou serves as Camus's own voice. What is remarkable, though, is that he recognizes something more than moral meaninglessness. There is evil, as the plague demonstrates. And if there is evil, it must be detectable. The atheistic author could not accept a supernatural origin, but he does, through the revolutionary, declare that it abides in

---

17 Albert Camus, *The Plague*, trans. Stuart Gilbert (New York: Vintage, 1975), 218.

18 For the rise of theodicy within its deistic context, see *Age of Utopia*, 159–69.

every man. "We all have plague," Tarrou grimly reflects toward the end.[19]

Camus had studied Augustine in his early years and even wrote a dissertation on traditional Christianity's greatest Latin father. Though an atheist, he remained fascinated with Christian anthropology throughout his life and even, a year after publishing *The Plague,* visited a Dominican monastery to exchange views with its Roman Catholic inhabitants. That he reached the conclusion that all men suffer from what Christians call original or primordial sin ("we all have plague") represents a turning point in his life's work. For now, that evil had no particular source. It spread throughout society as randomly as rats, and there was nothing the Dr. Rieuxes of nihilistic Christendom could do to stop it. There was certainly nothing revolutionaries like Tarrou could do to eradicate it, despite counterarguments by Sartre. But if evil could be traced into the recesses of the human heart, there it might be challenged through a weapon Christians had long held in their arsenal: repentance.

And this brings us to Camus's last novel, *The Fall* (1957). It too is deeply influenced by Nietzsche and Dostoevsky. The story is simple. It centers on a protagonist named Jean-Baptiste Clamence. He is an atheistic judge used to exercising total control over his life and the world around him—in other words, he is "something of a superman."[20] Yet he appears in a bar one day and compulsively begins to tell a nameless bartender about a past action that has come to oppress him. Years earlier, his silent interlocutor learns, he had been walking along the Seine embankment when he noticed a young woman pass by with a dark expression on her face. He somehow had known what would come next and smiled when he heard over his shoulder the telltale splash. The woman had thrown herself to her death.

This, obviously, is a retelling of the scene from *Demons* in which Stavrogin coldly observes the suicide of Matryosha. At this very time, it might be noted, Camus was in fact working on a project to dramatize Dostoevsky's novel. In *The Fall,* the memory of the observed suicide also haunts the Zarathustrian protagonist. There is something that confronts his nihilistic

---

19 Camus, *Plague,* 252.
20 Albert Camus, *The Fall,* trans. Justin O'Brien (New York: Vintage, 1984), 28.

values and will not allow his conscience to forget. He longs to confess but can do so only to a stranger without a name in an environment without transcendence. In other words, he seeks a kind of nihilistic counterfeit of sacramental confession. "I have a very old and very faithful attachment to dogs," he observes vaguely, "because they always forgive."[21] The man's name also makes an oblique allusion to the penitential renewal of traditional Christianity. His namesake, Jean-Baptiste (John the Baptist), had preached a "baptism of repentance." Even the surname is significant. "Clamence" is similar to the French word for "clemency," which in both languages means "forgiveness."

The atheist Sisyphus had pushed the stone of absurdity up the mountain without any alternative but futile rebellion. The atheist Rieux had realized that the meaningless absurdity of evil can be opposed only with sacrificial love. Now the atheist Clamence realizes, almost against his will, that the source of evil is himself. Contrary to the nihilism by which he has lived, there is a way of confronting this evil. But like his final protagonist, Camus himself would never attain victory over it. He would not turn to traditional Christianity and its call to repentance. He remained an atheist until his dying day.

As often happens, that day came unexpectedly. As he was returning home from a holiday in Provence, his car veered off the road and crashed into a tree. His death, cutting short a life spent sincerely exploring ways to escape the specter of nihilism, was, like the existentialist movement as a whole, a triumph of absurdity.

Inescapable Alienation

IN THE YEAR CAMUS DIED, France's ally and new patron the United States was entering one of the most dystopian decades in her history. Very few would have seen it coming. The year 1960 was marked by Kennedy's election victory against Richard Nixon and the beginning of eight years of legislative idealism. The Massachusetts Democrat managed to invigorate

---

21 Ibid., 120.

the White House with highly educated advisors who supported progressive causes like the civil rights movement. Johnson broadened this priority after Kennedy's assassination and his own election to the presidency in 1964. As we noted in the previous chapter, it was Johnson who brought the Civil Rights Act and the Voting Rights Act to fulfillment. He also launched a policy called the Great Society aimed at reducing and even eliminating poverty. Like the Eisenhower years that preceded them, the Democratic administrations of the 1960s were nothing if not optimistic. Yet first Kennedy and then Johnson opened a door into a war that exposed utopia's most complacent nation to the specter of nihilism.

America's new enemy was Vietnam, which like many third world nations had been delivered from colonialism in the years following the Second World War. The liberal democracies of Western Europe no longer had the strength to manage oversees empires. Happily, their liberal ideology made them amenable, unlike any previous empire in history, to relinquishing power voluntarily and encouraging home rule. There were exceptions, of course. Vietnam was one of them, and the French fought until 1954 to retain influence there. Another exception was the French colony of Algeria, where revolution and terrorism resulted in hundreds of thousands of deaths (and earned endorsements from radical intellectuals like Sartre). But in many cases Middle Eastern, African, and Asian colonies were granted freedom and were encouraged to form democratic nation-states. That many of these soon degenerated into authoritarian dictatorships (such as that in Nigeria) and ferocious civil wars (such as that between India and Pakistan) does not change the fact that at their inception they were in many ways a projection of liberal world building.

When Communism loomed, however, fledgling states proved illiberal and undemocratic. Such was the case in Vietnam. There, an insurgency led by Ho Chi Minh had embraced Communism in an effort to unite the nation, north and south. He created a North Vietnam dependent on the Soviet Union and China. In the south, he organized a Communist insurgency called the Viet Cong to overthrow the nominally democratic government of Ngo Dinh Diem.

However, as we have seen, the American Way was inextricably bound to anticommunism, and the Truman Doctrine had promised military support wherever Communism threatened a state with at least aspirations toward liberalism. When Communist forces seemed poised to swallow up South Vietnam, Kennedy sent thousands of "military advisors" to organize resistance. When the Diem regime proved incapable of resisting, these advisors supported a violent coup in which Diem was assassinated. Taking advantage of political chaos, the Viet Cong became even bolder and began to press on South Vietnam and its American advisors. In 1964, an altercation between a United States naval vessel and North Vietnamese torpedo boats in the Gulf of Tonkin gave Johnson what he had been waiting for: justification for militarized world building. Misrepresenting the facts of the altercation, the White House obtained from Congress a resolution to go to war against North Vietnam.

In the nine years that followed, America's first "forever war" resulted in the deaths of more than a million Vietnamese and nearly sixty thousand American soldiers. American warplanes dropped more bombs on their enemy than they had dropped on Germany during the Second World War. Viet Cong tactics prevented the superior American forces and their South Vietnamese allies from ending the conflict swiftly. Instead, Communist insurgents attacked small units and disappeared into the jungle before counterattacks could be ordered.

Amid this guerrilla warfare, American commanders and their soldiers became embittered and cruel. In the Mekong River delta, General Major Julian Ewell killed thousands of Vietnamese civilians in an effort to wipe out the Viet Cong. In the village of My Lai in 1968, hundreds of unarmed men, women, and children were massacred by frenzied American soldiers. Such carnage was not limited to momentary derangement. For instance, the CIA created something called the Phoenix Program to abduct, torture, or murder more than eighty thousand South Vietnamese civilians suspected of having Viet Cong sympathies. In 1972 the contradictions of liberal world building were captured graphically in an image of a nine-year-old girl named Kim Phuc running naked in terror from an American napalm strike on her village. Dehumanization caused demoralization, and as more and more young soldiers were conscripted into the war machine, drug use and a practice of murdering commanding officers (called "fragging") became more and more commonplace. None of this was consistent with the liberal values of the American Way.

Back in the safety of the United States, the civilian population soon became disgusted with the war. Many were already agitated by the civil rights movement and used Martin Luther King's strategy of peaceful mass protest as a model of antiwar activity. In 1960 an organization called Students for a Democratic Society (SDS) was formed that combined socialism and civil rights. In 1962 Tom Hayden helped author its Port Huron Statement declaring a commitment to fundamental political and social changes. The United States, though the "wealthiest and strongest country in the world," had devolved into an "apathetic and manipulative" system of oppression. What the postwar Baby Boomer generation "had originally seen as the American Golden Age was actually the decline of an era." In the face of this dystopia, truly enlightened youth had come to realize that "there simply are no alternatives, that our times have witnessed the exhaustion not only of Utopias, but of any new departures as well."[22] With these convictions in place, the SDS naturally turned to the organization of antiwar protests when the Gulf of Tonkin Resolution was passed and America found herself fighting a futile war in Vietnam.

College campuses became the flashpoints for something like militant passivism. In Berkeley, California's flagship public university served as a barometer. For years its entrance at Telegraph Avenue and Bancroft Way was clogged by battles between protesters and policemen. At Columbia University in New York City, antiwar activists actually took an administrator hostage during a week-long siege of the campus in 1968. At Kent State University in Ohio, four people were shot to death during an antiwar protest in 1970.

But resistance to the failing liberal utopia of America was not limited to antiwar protests. The Port Huron manifesto had coined the term "New Left" to distinguish young radicals from those implicated in the dystopian

---

22 "The Port Huron Statement," in *The Port Huron Statement: Sources and Legacies in the New Left's Founding Manifesto*, ed. Richard Flacks and Nelson Lichtenstein (Philadelphia: University of Pennsylvania Press, 2015), 239–84.

ideologies of American liberalism and Soviet Communism. Members of this New Left were inspired by Marxism but turned off by its post-Stalinist bureaucratic outcome. The failure of reform Communism during the Khrushchev years disinclined them from looking to Moscow for inspiration. Even Sartre lost confidence in the Soviet Union. When she led the armies of the Warsaw Pact into Hungary in 1956 to suppress reforms there, she forever lost the sympathy of fellow travelers on the road to utopia. Some western radicals looked to alternative voices of Communist extremism such as Trotsky, Mao, or Che Guevara. But figures like these were appealing only to the New Left's violent fringe.

Less utopian radicals were influenced by Marxist philosophers like Hebert Marcuse (d. 1979), a critical theorist of the Frankfurt School who immigrated to the United States and taught at several universities there. He went further even than Horkheimer and Adorno in criticizing the dystopian "enlightenment project." In a book entitled *One-Dimensional Man* (1964), he dismissed liberal democracy as a failed utopia as "totalitarian" as the Soviet Union. As he put it in the opening sentence, "a comfortable, smooth, reasonable, democratic unfreedom prevails in advanced industrial civilization."[23] This "unfreedom" is the result of a cunning tolerance for dissent that coopts transcendent aspirations and reintegrates them back into the liberal order. Liberal democracy has thus created a "one-dimensional" society by suppressing potentially negative reflection about itself.

Supremely conscious of the role of a deadening consumerism in bringing about "democratic unfreedom," Marcuse offers a meditation on buying a new car to illustrate the demise of the transformational imperative. As the imaginary mental process unfolds, the attenuated voice of transcendence is repeatedly suppressed by the dominant voice of passive conformity.

I ride in a new automobile. I experience its beauty, shininess, power, convenience—but then I become aware of the fact that in a relatively short time it will deteriorate and need repair; that its beauty and surface are

---

23 Herbert Marcuse, *One-Dimensional Man: Studies in the Ideology of Advanced Industrial Society* (Boston: Beacon, 1964), 1.

cheap, its power unnecessary, its size idiotic; and that I will not find a parking place. I come to think of my car as a product of one of the Big Three automobile corporations. The latter determine the appearance of my car and make its beauty as well as its cheapness, its power as well as its shakiness, its working as well as its obsolescence. In a way, I feel cheated. I believe that the car is not what it could be, that better cars could be made for less money. But the other guy has to live, too. Wages and taxes are too high; turnover is necessary; we have it much better than before. The tension between appearance and reality melts away and both merge in one rather pleasant feeling.[24]

The possibility of transcendence dissolves as the liberal values of consensus and consumption become total. Modern man becomes alienated without even knowing it.

Such nihilism was the impetus for what Marcuse called, with an ironic allusion to Dante, the "great refusal." Many historians sympathetic to the New Left have found in Marcuse elements of optimism. But for those holding either traditional Christian or secular humanistic values, the final words of *One-Dimensional Man* are decidedly pessimistic:

The critical theory of society possesses no concepts which could bridge the gap between the present and its future; holding no promise and showing no success, it remains negative. Thus it wants to remain loyal to those who, without hope, have given and give their life to the Great Refusal.[25]

To be authentic, modern man—especially in the form of idealistic youth—should opt out of the alienated society that has grown out of utopia. Since there is really no longer anything meaningful that can be done to transform the world, principled nonparticipation in the civilization and culture of the West is the only ethical way of life.

In 1967, such pessimism was expressed in a film entitled *The Graduate.*

---

24 Ibid., 226.
25 Ibid., 257.

Nowhere in its narrative is explicit reference made to the New Left or the emerging counterculture (to be discussed in the next chapter). However, the film's excruciating depiction of the American Way makes those radical alternatives conspicuous by their absence. It presents an unrelenting image of the dystopian outcome of utopia.

The opening scene shows the face of Ben Braddock (played by Dustin Hoffman). The eponymous graduate has returned to Los Angeles from a college on the East Coast, where he has auspiciously completed the first stage of a middle-class way of life. But rather than radiating confidence and hope—rather than beaming with joy at returning to his childhood home—his expression is full of alienation. It is nearly catatonic. And it will remain this way with only rare exceptions until the film's final memorable scene.

Like a factory product, Ben is carried down the airport's people conveyor toward a destination he seems to have no desire to reach. He lacks any autonomy. The music that plays is appropriate. "The Sounds of Silence" by Simon and Garfunkel is a pessimistic ballad about the alienation of modern society. Its paradoxical theme, silence's sound, brings attention to a civilization overshadowed by nothingness. A nihilistic silence haunts human relationships. People talk without speaking, and they hear without listening. Communion has been lost, and in its absence people bow and pray to a neon god of their own making. Though this idol is not named, it can be interpreted as the consumeristic materialism that depends on flashy advertising (neon or otherwise) to function. The song suggests that society is a dystopia wherein man is alienated from God and from himself. And in such a society there only remains an empty darkness.

This is the world to which Ben returns in the opening scene. It is a failed utopia rather like that described by Marcuse. Mother and father welcome their only child back to an upper-middle-class, air-conditioned, pool-endowed home in sunny California. They are smiling. Everyone is smiling. Guests appear and join in the party, all of them laughing and all of them smoking and drinking. One pulls Benjamin aside and imposingly asks him to consider one great word that could be the key to a successful future: "plastics." A symbol of technological innovation following the Second World War, the industrial product of polymer science also brings to mind the replacement of traditional materials with cheap imitations. It is the symbol of a counterfeit culture. Accordingly, everything that liberal democracy in its advanced capitalistic stage has come to offer is available to the young man. He has landed a coveted scholarship for graduate school, and the world is his oyster. But most symbolic of his ensured prosperity is his parents' graduation gift: a brand new, shiny red Alfa Romeo.

Yet this marvel of the consumer economy means nothing to the sullen Ben. Neither his cheerful parents nor his privileged surroundings nor his leisurely swims alter the dread expressed in his passive stare. He looks around in vain for transcendence. To escape his dystopian circumstances, he resorts to an affair with the middle-aged friend of his parents, the notorious Mrs. Robinson (about whom Simon and Garfunkel wrote another song). It is a lurid and ridiculous affair and exposes the emptiness of a society with nothing to pursue but the American Dream. In one scene he visits the woman and her husband to find them watching television—a postwar invention that, according to Marcuse, tranquilizes society with unending entertainment. In this case, *The Newlywed Game* is being shown in all its slapstick idiocy. It is another of the film's clever symbols. Adultery and divorce are looming, and Mrs. Robinson's clueless husband laughs cynically over a program's mindless content while pouring his wife's lover a glass of whiskey.

Toward the end of the film, Ben desperately turns to Mrs. Robinson's daughter Elaine for love. He even chases her to Berkeley, where she is a student. None of the counterculture is shown in the scenes there, a remarkable detail considering the campus's notoriety at the time. Since viewers would naturally have associated Berkeley with the New Left's alternative to Ben's world, it is possible the film was trying to make this alternative conspicuous by its absence—suggesting it was the only solution to the unremitting alienation that has dominated the story. In any case, the girl decides to marry another young man—a frat boy "make-out king"—and Benjamin drives frantically to the wedding to intervene. In a metaphor for the failure of the American Dream, his sports car—which by now looks like a wreck due to neglect—runs out of gas on the way there.

He has to run the final stretch, only to find that he is too late. But upon entering the church—built in a nonliturgical modernist style—he is able through force of will to lure the girl away from her new husband. As the crowd—headed by a vengeful Mrs. Robinson—pursues the couple, Benjamin bars the door behind them by ramming a cross through its handles. He and his now adulterous girlfriend settle into a passing bus as the film reaches its unforgettable conclusion.

As the bus pulls away and the two sit side by side, a victorious smile briefly animates the graduate's face. For a moment, communion with another person seems to have been achieved. Elaine (played exquisitely in this scene by Katharine Ross) is also smiling, silently. But then she glances at Ben and her smile fades. She turns pensively away, for Ben's expression has reverted to its catatonic stare. Alienation has become inescapable.

As "The Sounds of Silence" begins to play again, the camera's perspective changes to that of another vehicle following the bus down the road and then coming to an abrupt stop. As the bus continues into the distance, the viewer is left with a realization that there is nothing on the road ahead—the American Way—that promises an escape from dystopia.

CHAPTER EIGHT

Spiritual Freefall

I**N THE DECADES FOLLOWING THE** Second World War, utopia had begun to look dystopian. Many had reached the conclusion that, like Nazism, Communism and liberalism had their own totalitarian tendencies and that these originated in the utopian project itself. The problem brought attention to the failing promises of secular humanism. Ever since the Renaissance, Christianity's great counterfeit had offered the West a means of escaping anthropological pessimism and cosmological contempt. It seemed to rescue the transformational imperative. But it did so by desecrating the world and man's place within it. As a result, utopia proved to be a spiritual prison house to which Christianity, even in its modern forms, had often been consigned.

Yet even now, as secularism revealed its shortcomings, Christendom's intellectual leadership could not bring itself to look for solutions in the deep past of the first millennium. As we have seen, Huxley sought mystery to escape an overly rationalized society, but instead of learning about hesychasm, he buried himself in Hinduism. Horkheimer and Adorno lamented the effects of disenchantment but had no interest in the mystical worship of the Franks or Byzantines. The tragic Camus longed for an explanation of the evil he saw in Nazism, but despite an exposure to Augustine could never submit himself to the liberating grace of repentance. Marcuse's "great refusal" was an echo of the ascetic impulse of the old Christendom. However, he too was an atheist and, as leader of the New Left, chose to communicate mainly with atheists. A paradisiacal culture shaped by the authenticity of repentance was for such intellectuals simply not attractive—or even comprehensible.

On the other hand, even when "spirituality" was used as a solution for dystopia it usually proved vague and ungrounded. Such was not always the case. We have noted how a small number of Western intellectuals began to turn—or rather return—to traditional Christianity in the face of meaninglessness. However, most did not, and experiments in religion—often indulgent and always tenuous—created an entirely new problem for nihilistic Christendom. In fact, the latest quest for transcendence would lead the West into a spiritual freefall.

Hippiedom

THE PLUNGE BEGAN IN A corner of Christendom called hippiedom. During the 1960s, middle-class Baby Boomers known as hippies (named for being "hip") found themselves alienated from a society that, for all its prosperity and opportunity, appeared steeped in racism, militarism, and materialism. Hippies hoped to create a culture radically at odds with an "establishment" rooted in the liberal order. Their counterculture would possess an expressly transcendent character, spiritual to the core. But by rejecting the broader legacy of secular humanism as well as traditional Christianity, hippiedom quickly descended into its own version of nihilism.

Hippiedom was amorphous and defies simple classification. As a cultural movement, it attracted millions of people but was never given explicit ideological definition. It did exhibit certain discernible traits. One of the most interesting was an earnest religiosity. Hippies were renegades from secular humanism. They longed for transcendence. Irreligious by conventional Christian standards, they nevertheless framed their cultural protest with spiritual ideals. They even elaborated their own kind of sacramentality.

This can be seen by taking up the most ubiquitous expression of hippiedom, the nihilistic triad of "sex, drugs, and rock-and-roll." A variant of this now-familiar phrase was first used in *Life* magazine in 1969. In an article on the difference between political revolutions and cultural revolutions, Edward Kern noted that while protected from the former, liberal democracy is undoubtedly experiencing an instance of the latter. The counterculture's "clean break with tradition . . . points to profound changes to come in the structure of American society." Among these changes is the emergence of a sort of ersatz religiosity. "The counter culture," he notes, "has its sacraments in sex, drugs, and rock."[1]

The countercultural triad was a response not only to the unbearable secularity of humanism but to the pessimistic legacy of reformational Christianity. A desecrated cosmos had been engineered by the benightenment but found its blessing even earlier in the reforms of John Calvin and other sixteenth-century theologians. Indeed, its lineage stretched back to the rationalistic and legalistic tendencies of eleventh-century Roman Catholicism. The old Christendom of the first millennium, which had largely been spared such tendencies, had continued in the Orthodox East until the westernization of Russia under Peter the Great. By now, however, it was virtually unknown in the West. The hippies and their countercultural allies in the New Left knew only of the Christianity of the Western reformations (papal and Protestant) and the secularized humanistic reaction to them. But the West to which these reformations belonged had been formed within the first millennium, and the hippies could not escape a transformational imperative that had once oriented culture toward heavenly immanence. Reinventing Western religiosity, the hippies looked to sex, drugs, and rock-and-roll to transcend the dystopia of the secular establishment.

Drugs were the starting point. While each element of the pseudo-trinitarian counterculture was closely integrated into a total way of life, new forms of psychedelic intoxication offered the most powerful counterfeit of divine participation. Already by the 1950s, pharmaceutical corporations were advancing the science of inebriation to an all-time high. During the Second World War, a firm called Sandoz Laboratories in Switzerland developed a new synthetic chemical called lysergic acid diethylamide, or LSD for short. After the war, the firm brought the drug to market despite the fact that the chemist who invented it reported experiencing an assault by demonic beings after sampling it.

---

1   Edward Kern, "Can It Happen Here?" *Life* 67:16 (October 17, 1969), 68–78.

The Cold War was heating up, and the American CIA was looking for substances it could use for counterespionage and interrogation. One of the subjects recruited for tests near Stanford University in California was Ken Kesey (d. 2001). He was so enthralled by the hallucinations LSD caused that he organized large-scale "acid parties" (after the nickname of the drug) in his home for years to come. His countercultural way of life became a model for many hippies after the successful publication of his psychological novel *One Flew over the Cuckoo's Nest* (1962).

But already by this time a more reputable advocate for psychedelic drugs appeared in the person of Aldous Huxley. The author of *Brave New World*, in which the fictional drug soma provides the pharmaceutical infrastructure for dystopia, he proved by the end of his life very prone toward the drug's nonfictional realization. In 1953 he began to take the hallucinogenic mescaline and soon published an account of the experience in *The Doors of Perception*. Huxley was by now fully engrossed in Hinduism and believed such drugs opened the way to higher states of spiritual enlightenment. Then he graduated to LSD. He spent the remainder of his days dropping acid and writing about its mystical effects. In fact, he actually ended his life on an acid trip. Confronted by terminal cancer, he instructed his wife to administer a lethal dose of the drug so that death might find him, not in communion with God, but in a state of drug-induced pseudo-transcendence.

But by far the most notorious advocate of psychedelic sacramentality was Timothy Leary (d. 1996). He was a sort of Dionysus in academic robes. A doctor of psychology lacking any respect for his profession's canons of research, Leary was an early example of the rebelliousness that would soon characterize American campuses. He moved from university to university until finally settling into a lectureship at Harvard, studying the use of hallucinogens for mental illness. In 1960, he decided to visit Mexico and experiment with the drugs himself. He later declared the resulting five-hour hallucination taught him more about the mind than all previous scholarly studies. Back at Harvard, Leary eagerly read and reread Huxley's *Doors of Perception* and was delighted when the famous novelist agreed to visit him. He in turn visited Huxley just days before the latter's death and later dedicated to him a book cowritten with an associate named Richard Alpert.

The book, entitled *The Psychedelic Experience,* became a drug-use manual for hippies in the years ahead.

By this time Leary's position at Harvard had become untenable due to his unethical practice of getting high with students. On one occasion, he plied guests at his twelve-year-old daughter's birthday party with so many hallucinogenic pills that one of them actually tried to break into the girl's bedroom to rape her. Interestingly, the episode actually caused the dissolute Leary to wrestle with the question of why such an action could be considered morally wrong. He found the solution in Mill's harm principle. Unphased by the incident, he turned to his daughter's would-be assailant and calmly reflected, "You have the right to do anything you want so long as you don't lay your trip on anyone else."[2]

Dismissed by Harvard, Leary was happy to be freed of the constraints of the academy. He immediately found patrons willing to finance an alternative psychological institute in Millbrook, New York. He recruited a wide range of young people to attend his classes there and introduced many of them to LSD. In 1964 Leary was visited by his West Coast counterpart in counterculture, Ken Kesey, who had traveled across the country hosting acid parties in a psychedelically painted school bus. The entourage called themselves the Merry Pranksters.

During his Millbrook years, Leary continued working with his former Harvard colleague Richard Alpert, a popularizer of Asian religions. Like Huxley, the latter ultimately converted to Hinduism after visiting India and became a leading advocate for New Age spirituality back in America. Alpert collaborated with Leary at Millbrook in forming a new religion called the League of Spiritual Discovery. It claimed hallucinogens were its sacraments. In a manifesto reading like something from Dada, Leary declared that through a "divine process" drugs were "making this planet a Garden of Eden." Though appropriating the paradisiacal language of Christianity, the new psychedelic religion had of course nothing to do with the kingdom of heaven. It was almost entirely nihilistic. Every human being, the manifesto declared, "is God." And because of this, one must renounce affiliations

---

2   Quoted in Robert Greenfield, *Timothy Leary* (New York: Harcourt, 2006), 122.

with traditional forms of belief, especially Christianity. The goal of life is to escape the dystopian materialism of the West by coming alive to spiritual experience.

Drugs were the league's sacramental centerpiece. "To turn on," Leary insisted,

> *you need a sacrament. A sacrament is a visible external thing which turns the key to the inner doors. A sacrament must bring about bodily changes. A sacrament flips you out . . . A sacrament which works is dangerous to the establishment . . . Today the sacrament is LSD. . . . Treasure LSD while it still works. In fifteen years it will be tame, socialized, and routine.*[3]

As the counterculture's most influential authority on and advocate for the use of hallucinogens, Leary reached, directly or indirectly, an enormous number of young Americans alienated from secular humanism and Christianity as they had come to know it.

Sexual promiscuity was the second main element in the countercultural way of life. It was frequently linked to drug use. If psychedelics were the pseudo-sacramental means of transcending oneself, uninhibited sexuality was the means of linking transcendence to others. This was the spiritual context for what became known as the "sexual revolution."

The revolution had a broader context in the culture of modernism. The need for sexual "liberation" was premised on a conviction that modern man was alienated by centuries of Christian and later humanist repression of the libido. Freud had studied this extensively, yet as we noted in chapter 3, he did not encourage free love. That task fell to his demoralized followers. Both before and after the Second World War, for instance, Surrealist painters had made wide use of Freudian theory. As with other forms of modernism, their compositions were a contradictory mix of nihilism and the hope that runaway dehumanization could still be averted. Surrealism had in fact been born of the Dada movement as artists like Max Ernst moved away from purely negative creativity. In *Oedipus Rex,* for instance, he produced a work

---

3   Timothy Leary, *Turn On, Tune In, Drop Out* (Oakland, CA: Ronin, 1999), 3–4.

that tried to communicate the consequences of sexual repression as Freud conceived them.

More openly libidinous was the Spaniard Salvador Dali. He looked to dreams for inspiration, following Freud's teaching about erotic symbolism. One result was *Giraffe Aflame* (1937), showing the African animal engulfed by a fire symbolizing either violence or lust or both. In the foreground, two female figures are propped up with scaffolding—a dreamlike visualization suggesting how the autonomous individual of humanism is really just an illusion. A work called *Dream Caused by the Flight of a Bee around a Pomegranate a Second before Awakening* (1944) is another reflection on the erotic dissolution of the rational subject. It mixes desire for sex, in the form of a naked woman lying prone, with desire for violence, in the form of a pair of ferocious tigers bearing down on her. With *Young Virgin Autosodomized by the Horns of Her Own Chastity* (1954), the modernist made his opinions about psychosexual repression even more intentionally Freudian. It is noteworthy that like Picasso, Dali was a womanizer throughout his life and even took elaborate notes on both his actual and imaginary exploits. When he provocatively chose to publish a sexualized autobiography based on these notes, the comparatively modest George Orwell observed that "Dali is a good draughtsman and a disgusting human being."

Nevertheless, for leaders of the counterculture, the boundaries of sexuality were dissolving like the dreamworld of a Surrealist painter—or the senses of an hallucinating druggie. As Ernst and Dali had looked to sexual fantasy and dreams for an escape from nihilism, so hippies looked to sexual experimentation in their flight from dystopia. For them, sexuality would reconsecrate a desecrated cosmos.

On the one hand, experimentation required a greatly expanded knowledge about the sexual functions of the human organism. One pioneer of the liberation movement was the researcher Alfred Kinsey, who produced reports on male and female sexuality respectively entitled *Sexual Behavior in the Human Male* (1948) and *Sexual Behavior in the Human Female* (1953). More than anything Freud had ever published, these books described the full range of their topics in exhaustive detail. They also assumed an objective, scientific tone, treating any sexual act as legitimate. As one colleague observed, Kinsey "liked to feel that he was absolutely unconstrained by moralistic forms."[4] His work therefore represented a kind of transvaluation of sexual values. He based his findings on controlled laboratory studies, but like Leary he was a Dionysian enthusiast and not inclined to maintain professional boundaries. Many of his experiments were conducted in his own home, often with him participating in the acts under investigation. He insisted especially on recording the research on film and spent much time reviewing it later. Though radical, his books proved wildly popular with young people, and he toured the country giving talks to wide-eyed undergraduates about the new world of pleasure that was opening up to a post-Christian Christendom.

Another prerequisite for the sexual revolution was motivation to abandon restraints that had been in place for centuries. Within the counterculture, activists and writers assumed an almost prophetic role in advocating a sexual utopia. They spoke the language of Christendom's transformational imperative but with a decidedly nihilistic accent. One of the most influential theorists was Marcuse, author of *One-Dimensional Man,* who even before the rise of the New Left had published a book entitled *Eros and Civilization* (1955). It claimed that sexual liberation ranks higher than economic liberation as a priority for advanced liberal democracies. For him, sexual freedom is a goal that should become the new front in radical politics. As one historian has put it, Marcuse "introduced the notion of a utopian world in which the entire body would become 'eroticized' and all physical activity would turn into sexual 'play.'"[5]

But scholars and theorists were not going to change the culture by themselves. More popular agents of revolution were needed. One was pornography. The fifties had seen the appearance of *Playboy* magazine, and other periodicals such as *Penthouse* and *Hustler* followed. Sexually explicit themes began to appear in mainstream movies, often accompanied by nudity. Sometimes films were little more than vehicles for nudity. Andy Warhol, notorious

---

4   Quoted in James H. Jones, *Alfred Kinsey* (New York: Norton, 1997), 608.
5   David Allyn, *Make Love, Not War: The Sexual Revolution* (New York: Routledge, 2001), 197.

for nihilistic pop-art representations of Marilyn Monroe, turned to film-making and produced a series of sexually explicit spectacles that would have been unimaginable only a decade earlier. At the broadest level, public nudity became fashionable among the hippies. Nudist beaches became a fad, and at rock festivals enamored female fans introduced the Dionysian practice of flashing male musicians performing on stage. The American counterculture was becoming a veritable pornotopia.

In this environment, sexuality ceased to be a bond limited to husband and wife. Adultery and fornication became normalized in films ranging from the adventures of James Bond to the romances of Woody Allen. Premarital sex became normative among teenagers and young adults. Dating replaced courtship, with the result that young men and women acted like marriage partners without committing themselves to a life of publicly accountable, unconditional love. And without Christianity and other traditional religions to shape their values, they easily moved on to new partners in what came to be known, at best, as "serial monogamy." In fact, monogamy itself was called into question. In some cases married couples shared each other's spouses, a practice called "wife swapping" or "swinging." In 1970 a swingers convention in Chicago was attended by 184 couples.[6] The practice was also depicted in the movie *Bob & Carol & Ted & Alice* (1969), which rather than being an obscure expression of the cultural underground was a box office hit starring major Hollywood celebrities (including Natalie Wood and Elliot Gould) and earning nominations for four Academy Awards.

The third element of the countercultural triad was rock-and-roll. The great tradition of orchestral and operatic music inherited from the nineteenth century was largely dead by the time hippiedom came into being. Based on the elite culture of Europe's modern aristocracy, classical music had, in the hands of the romantics, begun to appeal to a growing but still imitative middle class. Nevertheless, composers like Wagner despised their audiences, and modernists who came later were even more contemptuous. As we observed in chapter 3, classically trained composers such as Stravinsky moved on to

---

6   Ibid., 208.

increasingly unmelodious forms of composition.[7] When the Great War shattered the social basis for classical music, composers lost the incentive to produce pleasing popular works. Arnold Schoenberg (d. 1951) went even further. He simply annihilated the classical tradition of tonality altogether. For him the future belonged to "atonality," a hypercerebral method of composition that appealed to almost no one but like-minded modernists. His later invention of something called twelve-tone music did little to reverse classical music's descent into irrelevance. One of utopian Christendom's most glorious achievements therefore became a thing for antiquarians. In the future, opera houses became more museums of a lost form of art than places where new monuments of Western culture were premiered.

All that was left for a civilization of music lovers were the vital experiments in melody that came from popular culture. Among the most influential were styles known as rhythm-and-blues and gospel. Both had substantially African American origins. For America's commercialized white majority, the great example of a popular synthesis of these and other styles (such as country-and-western) was the music of Elvis Presley. In the mid-fifties he performed songs on television programs that reached tens of millions of Americans. His lyrics were often coarse and sentimental, but the catchy melodies of songs like "Hound Dog" (1956) and "Jailhouse Rock" (1957) appealed to many who were losing confidence in the culture of the liberal establishment. Presley's signature practice of thrusting his hips back and forth during performances (often a scandal to television producers) was a sign of how the new form of music—increasingly labeled "rock-and-roll"—would assimilate the values of the sexual revolution.

The transition from early rock to the music of the counterculture is exemplified by the career of the Beatles. The group started with relative modesty, wearing suits and ties while singing innocuous love songs like "Love Me Do" (1962), a combination of rhythmic melody and inane but cheerful lyrics. Then John Lennon and Paul McCartney discovered acid. This changed everything. For the latter, in retrospect, taking the drug "was a

---

7   By the end of his career, Stravinsky returned to composing more conventional and melodic works, but the damage had by then been done.

truly religious experience. . . . It started to find its way into everything we did, really. It colored our perceptions."[8]

Lennon was even more enthralled. He later casually estimated—though probably with gross exaggeration—that by the time of the group's dissolution he had been using LSD on average every other day. George Harrison and Ringo Starr were also users. Already phenomenally creative songwriters, the Beatles used their experience with drugs to take rock music in a new direction.

The most important signpost was an album entitled *Sgt. Pepper's Lonely Hearts Club Band* (1967). The album made use of a full range of technical innovations, from synthesizers to echo machines to simulated applause. It also depended on the might of the capitalistic record industry, with the ability to mass-produce records and market them to millions of Baby Boomers. But the art itself was thoroughly influenced by the counterculture's drug sacramentality. "Lucy in the Sky with Diamonds," with its hallucinatory imagery, drew on the experiences of Lennon's acid trips (enthusiastic fans brought attention to the coincidental fact that the acronym of the title was L-S-D). The final track, "A Day in the Life," is also an effort at hallucinatory transcendence. Interestingly, it mimics the classical sonata form. The first part, sung by Lennon, narrates the escape from everyday news reports (and uses synthesizers and electronic echoes to suggest an altered mental state induced by psychedelics). After a racing second part about modern society's frantic work schedule, sung by McCartney, the piece returns to its first theme with another dreamy meditation by Lennon. The song is one of the most stirring and beautiful expressions of what was coming to be known as "psychedelic rock."

As an experiment in countercultural music, *Sgt. Pepper* made such a strong impression on fans and critics that one reviewer in the mainstream London *Times* declared the album's release "a decisive moment in the history of Western civilization."[9] This was an exaggeration. But the album was one

---

8   Quoted in Jerry Zolten, "Sgt. Pepper—with a Little Outside Help—Taught the Band to Play," in *The Beatles, Sgt. Pepper, and the Summer of Love*, ed. Kenneth Womack and Kathryn B. Cox (New York: Lexington, 2017), 17–42.

9   Quoted in Kenneth Womack, "Introduction: It Was Fifty Years Ago Today!," in

of many indicators—and more convincing than most—that the counterculture was beginning to enter the mainstream culture. The hippies, it turned out, had something to say to the West's so-called establishment.

A hint of this is to be found in the 1967 Summer of Love, an event that combined all three pseudo-sacraments into a unified approach to life. It occurred the very year *Sgt. Pepper* and *The Graduate* were released. The phenomenon was centered on the Haight-Ashbury district of San Francisco but had many satellite manifestations, such as Sunset Strip in Hollywood and Greenwich Village in Manhattan. From England, the Beatles even got involved. In a live performance broadcast throughout the world to an audience measured in the hundreds of millions, they premiered a song that could be taken as an anthem for the event: "All You Need Is Love." During the year, first McCartney, then George Harrison made pilgrimages to Haight-Ashbury to see what was happening. There and in other parts of Northern California, numerous events brought the countercultural movement to its fulfillment.

The Summer of Love was more than an event. Many claimed it modeled a new way of life. It included a run-up in nearby Monterey that represented the first rock festival. This three-day Monterey Pop Festival drew tens of thousands of hippies into a nonstop experience of transcendence mediated by sex, drugs, and rock music. The festival featured the first significant American appearances of famed musicians such as Jimi Hendrix, the Who, and Janis Joplin. From these bands, leading personalities Hendrix, Joplin, and Who drummer Keith Moon would all later die of drug overdoses. During its appearance, Jefferson Airplane set the tone for these and thousands of other unnecessary deaths with the transcendence-through-intoxication hit "White Rabbit." Its haunting lyrics, alluding to hallucinatory images from *Alice in Wonderland,* speak explicitly of taking pills.

The nihilism of the counterculture was becoming more and more emphatic. The Grateful Dead, which played at the festival, seemed to flaunt self-destruction with its very name. But the most explicit indication that transcendence was becoming transgression occurred when musicians began

Womack and Cox, *Beatles,* 1–14.

to destroy their equipment on stage. Jimi Hendrix ended his set by dousing his guitar with lighter fluid and setting it on fire. But this paled when the Who, in what was becoming their signature gesture of contempt, smashed their instruments to pieces in a sort of *Götterdämmerung* finale.

To be sure, the Monterey Pop Festival was a post-Wagnerian effort at creating a total work of art. Like the *Ring of the Nibelung*, it consisted not only of successive days of music but of a transcendent way of life. Nietzsche might have approved, had he somehow lived long enough and been able to shake his attachments to classical refinement. The experience was nothing if not Dionysian. As overamplified ecstatic music drowned the fairgrounds, hippies were totally liberated from moral constraints, spacing out on acid or disappearing into their Volkswagen buses to enjoy free love with partners they would never see again. It was as close to a bacchanalia as any member of Christendom had gotten since the days of pagandom. No ritual murders were performed, of course. But one hippie resident of Haight-Ashbury that summer, Charles Manson, would later do exactly that.

The Monterey Music Festival set a precedent for subsequent countercultural events in the years ahead. The most famous occurred at Woodstock

Woodstock Festival, 1969
James M Shelley, CC BY-SA 4.0 <https://creativecommons.org/licenses/by-sa/4.0>, via Wikimedia Commons

in 1969. There, on a farm in upstate New York, some half million hippies gathered over the course of four days to experience, if only briefly, a total way of life completely set against that of mainstream America. It would be remembered ever after as the crowning event of hippiedom.

But the most sustained effort at creating a countercultural counterutopia was the Summer of Love in 1967. By the time it concluded in October, more than a hundred thousand people had come from around America to see the great experiment of Haight-Ashbury. Millions more had been exposed to it through mainstream newspapers, magazines, and television. There was an intense interest in the values of the counterculture, as if liberal democracy needed more than a secular ideology to inspire it. Significantly, the event occurred against the backdrop of a wave of race riots known as the Long Hot Summer, as well as against the continuously mounting deaths in Vietnam. This made the effort to remake the world through the transcendent values of love attractive.

In July, as Haight-Ashbury swelled with visitors and journalists, *Time* magazine published a front-page article about the hippies. The author encouraged his large readership to learn from the counterculture. "It could be argued," he wrote,

> *that in their independence of material possessions and their emphasis on peacefulness and honesty, hippies live considerably more virtuous lives than the great majority of their fellow citizens. . . . In the end it may be that hippies have not so much dropped out of American society as given it something to think about.*[10]

In a year in which the dystopian outcome of the American Way was being exposed by *The Graduate,* mainstream society was indeed prepared to think about a new cosmology.

What the hippies offered was a vision of man and the world grounded in a new way of thinking, one no longer strictly secular. It was, in fact,

---

10 Quoted in Danny Goldberg, *In Search of the Lost Chord: 1967 and the Hippie Idea* (New York: Akashic, 2018), 134.

neopagan. And though it would never win more than a minority of true believers, its cultural influence would be tremendous.

Modern Christianity Disintegrates

BUT TO UNDERSTAND THE APPEAL of neopaganism, it is first necessary to trace the decline of Christianity in its various modern forms. Since the time of the Great Schism, these forms had been dedicated to the goals of first reformation and then utopia. However, under the specter of nihilism a third form began to appear in which these goals simply disintegrated. And since traditional Christianity remained largely despised or unknown, it played little role in holding the faith together. This third modern form can therefore be called "disintegrative Christianity." It was an outgrowth to some extent of its utopian predecessor, being concerned primarily with secular matters. And as utopia began to disintegrate, so did a form of Christianity based on it.

During the first millennium, the West had drawn its strength from the springs of traditional Christianity. After the Great Division, this source was partially cut off, and the paradisiacal culture that depended on it became desiccated. First reformational and then utopian variants of Christianity provided some compensation. Yet as we have seen, by the postwar period the soft totalitarianism of liberal democracy—though still nascent—produced a civic religiosity that both drew on the Christian heritage and subverted it. This religiosity flourished within liberal democracy because of an accidental (and therefore temporary) opposition to Communism. It was predominantly Christian, thanks to Christendom's religious inheritance. But it was in no way concerned with the doctrinal integrity that had long oriented the West toward the kingdom of heaven. This religiosity was fundamentally compromised by its incapacity for transcendence, a product of, rather than alternative to, what Weber had called "disenchantment" and the Frankfurt School the "enlightenment project." It served to trap man within the saeculum.

An example was the all-American theology of Norman Vincent Peale. In 1952, the Protestant pastor had written a best-selling book entitled *The Power of Positive Thinking*. The book made him a "minister of millions," contributing to what one biographer has called postwar America's "process

Norman Vincent Peale

of religious and cultural restructuring."[11] The book had little to do with salvation, though its utopian message was couched in biblical quotes. Rather, it was designed to bring out the infinite potential of Everyman in living his life within this world. In this sense it was a Christian handbook about the American Dream. Occupying the most advanced civilization in history, it argued, modern Americans have nearly limitless potential to achieve individual self-realization. Interestingly, the book placed great stock in the use of mantras to realize personal success. Such methods, drawn from recent studies in psychology, promised the reader personal happiness and material improvement.

However, such views were by the end of the 1960s beginning to seem like the cause rather than the remedy of dystopian alienation. It is possible to imagine the graduate Ben Braddock's parents among the three million

---

11   Quoted in Carol V. R. George, *God's Salesman: Norman Vincent Peale and the Power of Positive Thinking* (Oxford: Oxford University Press, 2019), 126.

Americans who listened to Peale's weekly radio program or the ten million who read his syndicated newspaper column. For Peale, God became little more than a means toward the individual's self-actualization. And that left scant place for authentic communion with Him or one's community. There was nothing really transcendent about the cosmology Peale fostered. It was simply another piece (however large) of America's doctrinally denuded civic religion.

Needless to say, not all forms of American Christianity were so completely owned by liberal ideology. Mainline Protestantism may have proven the most susceptible to the lure of civic religiosity, but many of its leaders took a principled stand against the decline of doctrine. In a book entitled *The Kingdom of God in America,* Richard Niebuhr famously expressed dismay at the liberal theological claim that "a God without wrath brought men without sin into a kingdom without judgment through the ministrations of a Christ without a cross."[12]

Other Protestants—especially those who were heirs to Barthian "neo-orthodoxy"—followed suit. One was the American evangelist Billy Graham, a pastor to presidents since his meeting with Eisenhower at the inaugural National Prayer Breakfast in 1952.[13] He was nothing if not fervently convinced by reformational Christianity's emphasis on the perilous human condition resulting from original sin. His massive rallies—which he dubbed "crusades"—featured the same altar calls that had energized America's earlier great awakenings. And while he spoke effusively of God's love, he matched it with threats about God's burning wrath. Karl Barth once met with Graham and lamented the practice of assembling massive crowds to preach to them "the Gospel at gunpoint." Nevertheless, both men were advocates of reformational Christianity and joined many other Protestant leaders in defending its doctrines about man and God.

But many Christian pastors did not defend them. One of the most

---

12 H. Richard Niebuhr, *The Kingdom of God in America* (Middletown, CT: Wesleyan University Press, 1988), 193.

13 Graham earlier met with President Harry Truman but made such an overbearing impression on that occasion that he was not invited back to the White House until after the next election. He learned from the mistake.

remarkable exceptions concerned the issue of abortion. In a rush to accommodate postwar modernity, leaders within several mainline Protestant bodies began to advocate for abortion rights. The killing of a fetus had been universally and consistently opposed within Christendom since Pentecost. In fact, the practice was considered so abominable that it was regularly cited by early apologists as the ultimate sign of pagandom's ruin. However, in the atmosphere of the countercultural movement, nineteen hundred years of moral conviction suddenly collapsed. Arguments for a woman's right to obtain an abortion—usually grounded in the Millian individualism of mainstream feminism—gained traction in Protestant bodies that no longer had significant roots in doctrinal tradition.

In 1967, as the Summer of Love transformed the atmosphere of Greenwich Village, a local Baptist pastor named Howard Moody formed a nationwide Clergy Consultation Service on Abortion. As the *New York Times* reported in a front-page article, its goal was to help women bypass state laws that prevented them from terminating unwanted pregnancies.[14] The influence of the sexual revolution was evident in this and other of Moody's "ministries" (such as one in which he drove a richly furnished van stocked with cookies baked by his parishioners from street to street, offering prostitutes a comfortable break between tricks). Then in 1973 the Supreme Court issued its decision in *Roe v. Wade*, making abortion a constitutional right. As pro-life forces began to mobilize against the decision, Moody's abortion service provided inspiration for the creation of the Religious Coalition for Abortion Rights. Significantly, the coalition counted in its official membership numerous mainline Protestant bodies, such as the Episcopal Church, the Presbyterian Church, and the United Church of Christ. The United Methodist Church provided the office space for its headquarters in Washington, DC.[15]

Another example of Protestant Christianity's disintegration is the case of James Pike (d. 1969). Elected Episcopalian bishop of California in 1958, he

---

14 Edward B. Fiske, "Clergymen Offer Abortion Advice," *New York Times*, May 22, 1967.

15 Michael J. Gorman and Ann Loar Brooks, *Holy Abortion? A Theological Critique of the Religious Coalition of Reproductive Choice* (Eugene, OR: Wipf and Stock, 2003), 6.

ministered to America's oldest Protestant body in San Francisco, the heart of the countercultural movement. He completed the construction of Grace Cathedral in the city, insisting that its stained glass windows depict not only Christian saints but non-Christian secular heroes such as Einstein. This was all very utopian.

But a creeping nihilism was also visible in the bishop's beliefs and actions. Soon after his election, he began to call the doctrine of the Trinity into question, dismissing it as "excess baggage" for Christians to carry in modern times.[16] He also abandoned the doctrine of the Virgin Birth, suggesting Jesus was the natural offspring of Joseph. Though an attenuated court of bishops objected to his openly publicized doubts about these doctrines of traditional Christianity, no significant

James Pike
CC BY-SA 2.5 <https://en.wikipedia.org/wiki/File:James_a_pike.jpg> via Wikipedia

disciplinary action was taken by the Episcopalian leadership. In fact, one outcome of the controversy was the decision to retire not Pike but the body's formal use of the term "heretic" when addressing doctrinal matters.

In the meantime, Pike divorced his second wife and began living with a mistress, until she committed suicide. In 1966, the year he decided to retire from the episcopate to pursue more satisfying interests, he began exploring sorcery in an effort to commune with his deceased son. The following year he actually conducted a televised séance in which he made contact with the "other side" (as he described it in a book by the same title). In an equally bizarre twist, he perished of exposure in the Palestinian desert after making a trip there with a third wife to research the Dead Sea Scrolls.

---

16 William Stringfellow and Anthony Towne, *The Bishop Pike Affair: Scandals of Conscience and Heresy, Relevance and Solemnity in the Contemporary Church* (New York: Harper and Row, 1967), 22.

Roman Catholicism was historically better equipped to resist the drift toward disintegrative Christianity. But between 1962 and 1965, the Second Vatican Council fundamentally changed the way adherents lived and experienced the Christian faith. The overall tendency was to encourage modernization, and this, taking place beneath the specter of nihilism, resulted in reform with a sledgehammer.

A good example of this was the case of Mary Daly (d. 2010), who not only theologized with a hammer but embraced what in certain ways was an expressly Nietzschean application of the will to power in sexual relations. An early impression in her academic career was created by the Second Vatican Council, which she attended with unrestrained enthusiasm. She was the product of two leading Roman Catholic universities, Notre Dame (where she earned her doctorate) and Boston College (where she was a full professor). In the wake of the council she began to distinguish herself as a radical feminist, going so far as to promote the arguments of Simone de Beauvoir. The latter, as we saw in chapter 7, was an advocate of the atheistic existentialism of Sartre and embraced his theory of the "Gaze," by which individuals are deprived of their authentic humanity insofar as they enter a relationship of unconditional love with the "Other." This nihilistic vision of community, of course, is traced back to the philosophy of Nietzsche.

Daly was not unconditionally supportive of de Beauvoir (or Nietzsche), but she did use the radical feminist argument to demolish systematically the Roman Catholic Church's anthropological heritage. Daly's first book, in fact, signaled the desire to join Christianity and feminist existentialism: it was entitled *The Church and the Second Sex*. After that, she went on to publish *Beyond God the Father* (echoing Nietzsche's famous work on nihilistic ethics), in which she dismantled the doctrine of the Trinity. By one recent (and affirmative) assessment, Daly promised to liberate Christian women by "deconstructing patriarchal religion, myth, and imagery, and reclaiming/ making women's lost or suppressed religious heritage in a gynocentric context."[17] As Daly wielded her theological hammer in the name of women's lib-

---

17 Marilyn Frye and Sarah Lucia Hoagland, "Introduction," in *Feminist Interpretations of Mary Daly*, ed. Sarah Lucia Hoagland and Marilyn Frye (University

eration, she continued to teach with impunity, since she was tenured and the Jesuit leadership of Boston College considered her work a valuable contribution to modern Christianity. They were also, apparently, afraid to stand up to the counterculture. But when her dean insisted she lift her ban on admitting men to her classes, she decided to retire and move on to other feminist projects. Eventually, she moved on from Roman Catholicism as well.

Another area of radical change in the Roman Catholic Church was the near annihilation of fasting. Traditional Christianity had always been a way of life, imposing ascetical demands on life in the world to bring transfiguration to it. Regular fasting had long been a part of the sanctification of time. In Eastern Christendom, Wednesdays and Fridays, the weekly commemoration of Christ's betrayal and Crucifixion respectively, had since ancient times been marked by abstention from meat and dairy products. This transformational practice was reduced by the Franks prior to the Great Division, resulting in the loss of the Wednesday fast. But at the time of Vatican II, the Roman Catholic Church still called on her members to avoid meat on Fridays. An allowance for fish (as well as dairy, though the latter was not included in the ancient practice) had resulted in a regular way of life defined by moderate fasting on what were called "Fish Fridays." In the wake of the council, however, even this attenuated standard of asceticism was abandoned. In 1966 the American conference of bishops followed a cue from Pope Paul VI and nullified the expectation that the faithful would abstain from meat on all Fridays (only those during Lent remained fasting days). National councils of bishops in other Western lands did the same. Now, with the exception of a very easy and brief abstention from meat on the six Fridays of Lent, a believer "in good standing" could on virtually all other days of the year abstain, as it were, from abstinence.[18] The transcendent effects of regular fasting simply disintegrated.

Another secularizing effect of Vatican II was the alteration of the liturgy. Partly in response to directives from the council and partly in an effort to act on its "spirit," national churches and individual parishes initiated

---

Park: University of Pennsylvania Press, 2000), 1–26.

18 Ash Wednesday and Good Friday were the two other exceptions.

revolutionary changes in the approach to worship. Saints who, by modern scientific standards, were deemed insufficiently historical were dumped from a calendar once determined by the burning faith of the fathers. The result— what some called "Paul's Purge," after the reigning pope—was the silencing of prayers to beloved saints like George, Christopher, and Katherine of Alexandria.[19]

Another debilitating change affected liturgical orientation, or the practice of facing eastward during worship. The context of this practice was the ancient tradition of facing paradise, located symbolically in the east (Gen. 2:8). With early exceptions in Rome, churches were generally built with "orientation," that is, an eastward disposition (the Latin for "east" is *oriens*). The symbolism meant that a world transformed by liturgy looked beyond itself to the kingdom of heaven. But now, in an effort to combat endemic clericalism, the celebrant of the Mass was directed to face westward, toward the congregation. The result was an experience in which clergy and laity shared an ongoing face-to-face exchange. As one approving historian has put it, "the personal encounter of facing the people of God . . . proclaimed louder than words that the action now belonged to the whole community and was not something the priest did *for* the community."[20] The pernicious legacy of centuries of clericalism seemed to be broken. However, as the priestly celebrant turned his back on paradise in order to "affirm" the presence of the laity, worship became an exchange between laity and priest rather than between God's people (laity with priest at their head) and God. The symbolic linkage between heaven and earth was weakened.

The disorientation of Roman Catholic worship was closely linked to a new approach to temple architecture. As with the struggle against clericalism, so in this case innovations sprang from a desire to overcome the deleterious Baroque inheritance. Since the sixteenth century, Western forms of church construction had been influenced by the gold-saturated, naturalistically decorated, and statue-filled interiors of Rome's famous Jesuit churches. The

---

19   Stephen Bullivant, *Mass Exodus: Catholic Disaffiliation in Britain and America since Vatican II* (Oxford: Oxford University Press, 2019), 161.

20   James F. White, *Roman Catholic Worship: Trent to Today* (Collegeville, MN: Pueblo, 2003), 117.

effect of this Baroque inheritance was a piety centered on the self, a devotion mediated by richly decorated objects that reduced the believer's experience of community. The Council of Trent, struggling against Protestant individualism, reinforced the tendency. Now, Vatican II sought to eliminate it. But as with other outcomes, the new temple architecture started with a heavenly vision of liturgy and ended with a largely secular one.

An example was the reorientation of space. As the priest was now required to face the laity, so the altar and accompanying holy objects were rearranged to create an experience of lay ownership. In some cases, churches were built that placed the altar in the middle of the nave. In others, the altars were pulled away from the eastern wall (in contrast to Orthodox architecture, altars did not accommodate a full circuit of censing). In both cases, the altar was stripped of any Baroque decoration to the point of being a plain table built in a style rather like that of midcentury furniture.

An example was set by Saint John's Abbey Church in Collegeville, Minnesota. Designed by the modernist architect Marcel Breuer, it was completed in 1961 on the eve of Vatican II and provided a model for the church

Vatican II Assembly

construction and remodeling that followed. Shaped as a trapezoid, the church abandons basilica-like linear orientation and centers its vast interior space around the altar. Stark, unadorned sheets of poured concrete make up the walls and ceiling. Gone is iconography and with it the visual confirmation of the heavenly presence of saints. Instead, a reserved use of stained glass is dedicated entirely to representing abstract geometrical shapes. Most striking is the building's exterior facade. Its trapezoidal hulk stands behind a looming concrete bell tower resembling a highway road sign.

The road that issued from Vatican II began with a constructive vision of Christianity but ended in its disintegration. The popes who, along with innumerable cardinals, scholars, and artists, presided over the greatest reform of Roman Catholicism since the eleventh century had little idea what they had started. As if to spite the relatively modest directives toward change issued from the conciliar leadership and its supporting institutions, a groundswell of radical innovations followed almost immediately.

Launched at the beginning of the sexual revolution, these reforms inevitably turned toward the questions of clerical celibacy, divorce, and birth control. No major changes to traditional Roman Catholic teaching about any of these issues were endorsed by the papacy, but major changes happened all the same. After all, the signal had been given that the church belonged to the laity as much or more than to the clergy—and the laity of the West was eager to embrace modernity. As a result, priests abandoned their ministry and took wives. Nuns abandoned the cloister and began dressing like laypeople. Pastors blessed parishioners to practice birth control. Marriages were dissolved at a breathtaking pace, with the United States claiming no less than 90 percent of the church's worldwide total of divorces.[21] A malicious joke arose that there was no marriage a well-educated canon lawyer could not "annul." Parish priests, sensing the restlessness of their flock or being so inclined themselves, grossly exceeded the official limits of liturgical experimentation. In 1970, the Vatican was compelled to issue an official chastisement of priests introducing "individualism and idiosyncrasies" into the Mass.

---

21 Ross Douthat, *Bad Religion: How We Became a Nation of Heretics* (New York: Free Press, 2012), 102.

But by then it was too late. Reformational Christianity was becoming disintegrative Christianity. Decades of turmoil lay ahead, as did the formation of a traditionalist insurgency. As the future pope Cardinal Joseph Ratzinger ruefully noted in 1984, because of the reform process launched by Vatican II the Roman Catholic Church had gone "from self-criticism to self-destruction."[22]

To many in the West, the transcendent source of civilization and culture—traditional Christianity—was long forgotten.

Neopaganism

WHICH BRINGS US BACK TO the hippies. At a time when mainstream society was growing weary of secular humanism but found less and less inspiration in disintegrative Christianity, the counterculture promised a solution in neopaganism. Paganism itself, of course, had been the main counterforce to the rise of Christendom nineteen centuries earlier. Now, as secular ideologies began to fail and authentic witness to traditional Christianity remained obscured in the background, pagandom's counterfaith exploded in a dizzying variety of beliefs and practices.

One of the most influential was based on Hinduism. Though passing interest in it had been shown by transcendentalists such as Ralph Waldo Emerson, the permanent establishment of Asia's greatest religion in the United States had only begun in 1893 at the Chicago World Parliament of Religions. There an itinerant Indian guru named Swami Vivekananda announced a mission to the West, and the following year he founded the first Vedanta Society. This is what drew Aldous Huxley to the faith. But it was not until the rise of the postwar counterculture that its influence really started.

Three important countercultural figures served to popularize Hinduism and related forms of New Age spirituality. They did so in 1967, the year of the Summer of Love. One was Richard Alpert, Leary's collaborator in

---

22 Elio Guerriero, *Benedict XVI: His Life and Thought*, trans. William J. Melcher (San Francisco: Ignatius, 2016), 310.

psychedelic religiosity. He traveled to India and converted to Hinduism, returning soon after under the convert name of Ram Dass to rescue America's disaffected society from secular alienation. Another countercultural figure was the poet Allen Ginsberg, who helped organize a hippie event early in the year at San Francisco's Golden Gate Park. It was called the "Human Be-In." Later seen as the prelude to the Summer of Love, this event featured a speech by Leary extolling the pseudo-sacraments of rock music, LSD, and free love. Leary for the first time unveiled his famous slogan "turn on, tune in, and drop out." America's mainstream culture was totally bankrupt, he declared, and the only authentic thing a human being could do was to abandon it for something transcendent. The event was attended by Richard Alpert and a former teacher at the local New Age American Academy of Asian Studies, Allan Watts. Ginsberg himself, a convert to Hinduism, repeatedly led the crowd in chanting the Hindu mantra "Om." A week later he organized a public talk in San Francisco attended by thousands, featuring the founder of the American Hare Krishna movement.

In addition to Alpert and Ginsburg, a third advocate for Hindu-inspired neopaganism in 1967—and by far the most influential—was George Harrison, the bass guitarist of the Beatles. Before visiting Haight-Ashbury that year, he made contact with the founder of Transcendental Meditation and eventually organized a pilgrimage to India, where all four members of the band entered an ashram for intensive study in the spiritual discipline. The Beatles' *White Album* was mostly composed during this trip and under the influence of Hindu-inspired methods of spiritual transcendence.

Within years, Hinduism, Buddhism, Taoism, and derivative forms of neopaganism such as Transcendental Meditation and Krishna Consciousness—along with practices like yoga and Asian martial arts—were becoming a part of mainstream Western culture. Each claimed to offer healing to a secular-sick society unable to find transcendence anywhere else.

The disintegration of modern Christianity had assured this. As Ross Douthat has argued in a book entitled *Bad Religion,* church "reformers had overestimated the potential for sustaining religious practices by marrying them to secular causes." He quotes a contemporary who observed that

progressive [Christian] clergy shed their vestments on the sacristy floor,
threw their incense in the trash, and sold their golden vessels to antique
dealers, only to discover that somehow the puritanical young men and
women who had marched with them on the picket line had got hold of
all these discards and more besides—tarot cards, Ouija boards, Tibetan
prayer wheels, and temple gongs. The Latin had been eliminated from the
Mass so that the young could comprehend it, but they preferred instead to
chant in Sanskrit. Campus chaplains had ceased trying to sell prayer and
were selling social action instead, but their former constituents were hunt-
ing up Hindu gurus and undertaking systematic regimens of meditation
and fasting.

Douthat concludes that "transcendence, it turns out, was still what people wanted from religion."[23]

During this time, the Orthodox Church—protected from the counterculture by the fact that her membership consisted largely of recent immigrants—maintained traditional Christianity's transcendent character. But because she was concealed behind the walls of self-segregated ethnic parishes, few had any idea that this "best-kept secret of American religion" even existed.

To be sure, mass neopaganism had no future in any institutional or formal sense. Ideological liberalism, as Archbishop Benjamin Petersen has observed, "has the power to suck the life out of any spiritual conviction." However, in the period following the countercultural movement, its influence on popular culture was vital indeed. Neopaganism appealed to a growing demographic in the West that defined itself as "spiritual but not religious." Accordingly, more and more celebrities espoused it; more and more cultural media such as movies depicted it; and, paradoxically, more and more forms of disintegrative Christianity tried to assimilate it.

Within the first group, Shirley MacLaine was a pioneer. In 1983 the actress published a best-selling book entitled *Out on a Limb*, detailing her wide range of esoteric spiritual beliefs. Showing the nondoctrinal character

---

23 Douthat, *Bad Religion*, 106–7.

of New Age religiosity, she reviewed beliefs in Transcendental Meditation, reincarnation, and unidentified flying objects (UFOs). In 1986 the book was turned into a successful television miniseries. That same year, Oprah Winfrey began to host the most successful daytime talk show in history. In it, the former actress featured regular conversations with New Age advocates. She herself took the lead, declaring her television "ministry" to be more than mere information and entertainment. Her show, she declared, promised "to transform people's lives." Unlike any religion in history—Christianity, Hinduism, or otherwise—hers was one grounded in individualism. It was a strange, even bizarre inversion of Christianity's divine "I Am."

> *I am talking about each individual coming to the awareness that, "I am Creation's son. I am Creation's daughter. I am more than my physical self. I am more than this job I do. I am more than the external definitions I have given myself. . . . Those roles are all extensions of who I define myself to be, but ultimately I am Spirit come from the greatest Spirit. I am Spirit."*[24]

What was remarkable about the *Oprah Winfrey Show* was that, as it used its popularity to build a multifaceted media empire encompassing such platforms as the Oprah Book Club and *O: The Oprah Magazine,* it grounded itself in—and contributed to the formation of—a spiritual marketplace. And it used a derivative neopaganism to provide the superficially transcendent resources to do so.

A second medium for the dissemination of New Age spirituality was film. Hollywood proved itself fertile missionary territory for neopaganism. An example was the success there of the Church of Scientology, which after its formation in the 1950s made great efforts to recruit into its membership celebrities such as John Travolta and Tom Cruise. Los Angeles soon began to rival the Bay Area as a center for neopagan houses of worship and New Age bookstores.

---

24   Kathryn Lofton, *Oprah: The Gospel of an Icon* (Berkeley: University of California Press, 2011), 4.

One of the earliest and most successful film projects to propagate neopagan spirituality was the *Star Wars* series. Its creator, George Lucas, was raised in the mainline Methodist Church but lost his faith in Christianity and, through the influence of the pagan mythologist Joseph Campbell, turned to Buddhism and other forms of Asian spirituality. Buddhism represents the single most identifiable influence in the series' efforts at world building. The elite Jedi order with its dedication to meditative "mindfulness" is derived directly from the Zen tradition. Taoism is also mined for its concept of *chi*, an energy that permeates the cosmos (and is featured in derivative Asian practices such as martial arts and feng shui). It is this energy that the series famously dubs "the Force," and with its impersonal nature it assimilates itself to the traditional liturgical expression of Christianity, "the Lord be with you." As for Christianity, the series makes only subversive allusions to it. The evil Darth Vader, for instance, is revealed to have been born of a virgin with a messianic calling to save the cosmos. But he, like the protagonist of the blasphemous yet popular novel-made-movie *The Last Temptation of Christ*, utterly fails in the face of temptation.

Many other Hollywood films took up the mission to propagate New Age spirituality. In 1985 *Cocoon* told the tale of old people temporarily rescued from mortality by benevolent space aliens. In 1993 *Little Buddha* told the tale of a boy born in a spiritually alienated Seattle (filmed in black and white), who, after being invited to visit Bhutan (filmed in color), discovers he is the reincarnation of a great Buddhist monk. In 2009 *Avatar* told the tale of a physically disabled human (a metaphor for modern society's spiritual condition) sent to a distant planet by rapacious colonizers, only to convert to the alien society's benevolent animistic religion. In 2010 *I Am* told the tale—this time factual—of a religiously seeking film producer (Tom Shadyac) who tires of American materialism and finds relief in speaking to New Age spiritual masters around the globe. Interestingly, in this case an implicit nod of approval was offered to traditional Christianity, for the movie's title is an allusion to the alleged reply made by G. K. Chesterton to a question posed by an early twentieth-century progressive newspaper: "In your opinion, what is wrong with the world today?" Chesterton, a convert to Anglicanism (and later Roman Catholicism) before the onset of its disintegration, declared, with the penitential simplicity of a first-millennium desert father, "I am."

The third principal way in which New Age piety spread was through muddled and often inane efforts by Christian leaders to appropriate non-Christian forms of "spiritual wisdom." Lost on them was the fact that the apostolic tradition of the first millennium contained all that was needed to sustain a civilization with a supporting culture that directed its members toward the heavenly rather than secular transformation of the world. In the wake of the countercultural movement, many Protestants and Roman Catholics lost confidence in the traditional elements of their faith and tried to supplement it with exogenous religious beliefs and practices. This, after all, had been the tendency of a civic religiosity that spoke of a "Judeo-Christian tradition" in which patently exclusive faiths were mingled together. The recently formed ecumenical movement—with its World Council of Churches and National Council of Churches—gained the sympathy of mainline Protestantism and, after Vatican II, some elements within Roman Catholicism. Even more, the interfaith movement sponsored by generous and well-meaning Christian bodies opened the door to a level of syncretism never before seen in the history of Christendom. As it turned out, neopaganism was more than happy to open its religious storehouses to such seekers.

Now non-Christian elements began to appear in the churches that had once been the foundation of Western civilization. One source of "inspiration" was New Age ritual. The most jaded Christian pastors, often suffering from a stifled sacramental impulse dating to the Protestant Reformation, began scouring America's religious landscape for alternative forms of worship.

The Episcopal Church was a case in point. More than a century earlier, her Anglican cousins had rediscovered traditional Christian liturgy through the Oxford Movement. However, ideological liberalism and American civic religiosity occluded wide Episcopalian interest in the movement well into the postwar period. A midcentury "liturgical movement"—led by Roman Catholics such as Joseph Jungmann and particularly influential at the Second Vatican Council—helped create a new appreciation for the worship of the first millennium. But its effects were limited, especially when Episcopalians, along with post-conciliar Roman Catholics, fell into the trap of modernism and its impulse toward restless innovation. Departing radically from the traditional orientation of the liturgical movement (and, incoherently, sometimes working in tandem with it), parish church after parish church leapt into the abyss of liturgical nihilism.

The Episcopalian cathedral of Saint John the Divine in New York City set the standard. One of the largest churches in the world, it became a sort of flagship for New Age experimentation. In 1975, for instance, it hosted an interfaith festival that opened with a pagan Egyptian fire ritual. In 1981 it premiered (innovation being considered appealing rather than repelling) an avant-garde "Earth Mass" in which a group of women symbolizing "Mother Earth" performed modernist dances in front of the clergy at the altar. The cathedral also began to hold an annual animal procession near the time of the Roman Catholic feast of Francis of Assisi, during which camels, horses, bulls, and even elephants were marched through the nave to a centrally located altar, where they received a sacramental blessing. Every December the cathedral joined with neopagans throughout the Northern Hemisphere to celebrate the winter solstice. Every October it joined with Wiccans and other sorcerers to offer a service for Halloween that culminated in a "procession of the ghouls." And, in a bizarre twist that speaks to the spiritually unstable state of modern Christianity, alongside this slew of New Age services the cathedral introduced a largely forgotten element of first-millennium Christendom: the office of Compline (though it had long been known to traditional Orthodox and Roman Catholic parishes).

The Episcopal Church's bishop of New York was not alone in endorsing New Age liturgical experimentation. On the opposite side of the country was Grace Cathedral in San Francisco, over which James Pike once presided. It too showed great restlessness in the face of declining membership and the lure of New Age transcendence. In 1994, the cathedral therefore hosted its first "Rave Mass," the invention of a defrocked Roman Catholic friar named Matthew Fox who now considered himself a nondenominational priest. "We don't have a lot of time," he noted in an interview,

to fiddle around with whether we're in this denomination or that one. I challenge you to find any twenty-year-old who can tell the difference between a Presbyterian, a Lutheran, a Methodist, an Episcopalian and a Roman Catholic. And who cares?

Despite this, Pike's successor as Episcopalian bishop of San Francisco, William Swing, declared Fox's faith both "orthodox and biblical" when receiving him into his diocese as a priest.[25]

Fox's Rave Mass was intended to draw the attention of youth raised on and unable to appreciate alternatives to television and rock-and-roll. Accordingly, it featured deafening music, flashing lights, and wild dancing. It was a sort of indoor Woodstock, spiritualized and done in miniature. This was not the only liturgical experiment introduced at Grace Cathedral. In 2004 the cathedral was also the site of celebrating the "U2charist," a reconstruction of the Episcopalian communion service using the songs of U2 rather than hymnography. Then, in 2018, it premiered a "Beyoncé Mass," in which the popular black singer's songs provided theological content.[26]

New Age spirituality provided worn-out Christian leaders with a way to reimagine the deity they worshipped. Absorbing Daly's transvaluational theology, some were embarrassed by the fact that for traditional Christianity, the First Person of the Trinity was called Father and the Second Person had become incarnate with a specifically male humanity. Some began to search for pseudo-trinitarian alternatives such as "Creator, Redeemer, and Sanctifier." This was not enough for the most radical Christian feminists, however. One named Sallie McFague proposed renaming the Trinity "the Mother, the Lover, and the Friend." At the Beyoncé Mass, a "womanist" replacement for the Our Father was prayed. It opened with:

Our Mother
Who is in heaven and within us
We call upon your names.

---

25 "'Rave Masses' Seek to Appeal to Those Raised on Television," *Los Angeles Times*, April 30, 1994.

26 Deborah Sokolove, *Performing the Gospel: Exploring the Borderland of Worship, Entertainment, and the Arts* (Eugene, OR: Cascade, 2019), 67.

Whereas traditional Christianity offered absolutely no justification for this, pagan doctrines drawn from pantheistic religions did.

On Maundy Thursday in 1984, the cathedral of Saint John the Divine added to its growing notoriety by hanging at the high altar a crucifix representing the Savior as a woman. Entitled "Christa," its purpose was to manifest to parishioners the existence of a "feminine divine." Activists in other mainline bodies introduced similar changes. In 1993, a Presbyterian-sponsored conference in Minneapolis entitled "Re-Imagining God" brought more than two thousand Protestant women together to discuss "God language" and to participate in feminist acts of worship. One ritual invented for the occasion was the ceremonial consumption of milk mixed with honey as a substitute for the Eucharist. A prayer was introduced that directed worship toward "Sophia," a feminine representation of the divine. "Sophia," participants prayed, "we celebrate the nourishment of your milk and honey. . . . Our maker Sophia, we are women in your image."

Several presentations called on women to appropriate meaningful symbols from non-Christian sources such as Native American spirituality. The conference's radically disintegrative tendencies were revealed by one of the speakers when she declared, during commentary on her presentation, "I don't think we need a theory of atonement. . . . I don't think we need folks hanging on crosses and blood dripping and weird stuff."[27]

Weird rather were such forms of Christianity as those now held in the thrall of neopaganism. As we shall see in the conclusion, Protestant, Roman Catholic, and Orthodox Christians who hoped to arrest the fall of the West would turn to a very different counterculture for inspiration—one defined by traditional Christianity.

From Transcendence to Transgression

IN THE MEANTIME, THE WEST was continuing its freefall into the spiritual abyss of nihilism. By the early 1970s, hippiedom had largely run its

---

27 Philip Jenkins, *Hidden Gospels: How the Search for Jesus Lost Its Way* (Oxford: Oxford University Press, 2001), 175–76.

course. But the counterculture lived on. How could it not? The prevailing culture, shaped almost entirely by secular ideology, continued to desiccate Christendom in a way not seen since the fourteenth century. A new culture with sustaining values was needed. But in a post-hippie, spiritually disintegrative West, those values were no longer directed toward transcendence. They found fulfillment in the act of moral transgression.

A relatively superficial but indicative example of this is found in the course of rock music during the decades that followed hippiedom. Like all art descending from modernism, it acted as a solvent for established beliefs and values. It also tended to dissolve itself. Styles of composition evolved rapidly and often in competition with one another. One might use the Doors as a starting point. They released their first album in 1967, the year of the Summer of Love, and it featured a remarkably dark, profanity-laced song about patricide, incest, and hatred. The song is entitled "The End," and the experience of dissolution it speaks to is welcomed as "my only friend." The Doors' style is often called psychedelic rock (sometimes acid rock), but soon after their singer Jim Morrison's death by drug overdose in 1971, new styles of rock began proliferating. Many fell within the category of hard rock. But from it evolved at least two streams of even darker music, each built on a series of negations. Heavy metal negated hard rock and was in turn negated by something called thrash metal, which in turn was negated by black metal—and so on. From hard rock flowed a second stream of morbidity called punk rock. After negating its inspiration, it was in turn negated by something called death rock, which in turn was negated by gothic rock—and so on.

The names of the bands that made up the psychedelic rock successor movement in the decades that followed the Summer of Love give expression to the disintegrative character of Western culture. Some (like Iron Maiden, Dead Kennedys, and Megadeth) alluded to violence. Some (like Queen, the Sex Pistols, and the Circle Jerks) alluded to sexual perversity. Some (like Black Sabbath, Judas Priest, and Bad Religion) alluded to blasphemy. Nihilism was their brand, and to distinguish themselves many bands went beyond mere words to commit acts of vandalism and violence. The hard rocker Keith Moon (drummer of the Who) was in the habit of compulsively dropping explosives into the toilets of whatever hotel his band happened to be staying in while on tour. As we have noted, the Who as a group developed the routine of trashing their equipment at the end of performances. The death rock band T.S.O.L. periodically vandalized churches and desecrated graveyards in their native Orange County, California.

Ritual violence became especially prominent with punk rock. The most visible example was the slam dance, in which fans would stage a mock riot by fighting in a circle before performers, frequently jumping up to confront them on stage before hurling themselves back into the crowd in what came to be known as the "stage dive." Ozzy Osborne, the original lead singer of Black Sabbath, whose albums would sell more than a hundred million copies, gained notoriety for publicly biting the heads off small animals and being sued (unsuccessfully) by parents whose children committed murder or suicide under his influence. The outrageous gothic rocker Marilyn Manson (his assumed name alludes to pop culture icons and is intended to fuse eroticism with cult murder) did his best to obtain similar infamy, and indeed when the Columbine shooting of 1999 occurred, the press blamed him for contributing to the culture of violence that provided its context. Perhaps the most noteworthy acts of nihilism were committed by black metal bands, many of whom posed (or sincerely identified) as Satanists and used harrowing death imagery to enhance their stage presence. The Norwegian Varg Vikernes, lead singer of Burzum (whose name was taken from the word for "darkness" in one of the fictional languages of J.R.R. Tolkien), burned down a series of churches near Bergen, including one dating to the twelfth century. He later stabbed to death another black metal musician and fellow Satanist (inflicting no fewer than two dozen wounds in the process).[28]

The nihilistic direction of hard rock was paralleled in other areas of Western culture. At the most rarefied level, it was expressed in a new philosophy called postmodernism. The life and especially the death of one of its earliest proponents, Michel Foucault (d. 1984), provides a fascinating and disturbing look into the West's widening cultural abyss.

---

28 Dayal Patterson, *Black Metal: Evolution of the Cult* (Port Townsend, WA: Feral House, 2013), 171.

Michel Foucault

As a young Frenchman born in the wake of the First World War, Foucault fell under the influence of atheism, despite—or by his account, because of—years spent at a strict Jesuit secondary school. He found it impossible to believe in anything, whether religious or secular. In the avant-garde atmosphere of Paris, for instance, he studied great modernist philosophers such as Marx but could not accept their claims to scientific objectivity. Like Sartre, he was drawn to revolutionary violence but could not bring himself to identify with the finite economic goals of Communism. Foucault briefly joined the French Communist Party, but after reading Nietzsche's "Richard Wagner in Bayreuth" and other essays in *Thoughts out of Season,* he reconceived the purpose of radical philosophy. A nagging desire for transcendent infinitude had always consumed him, leading him to seek in life what he called the "limit-experience," a sensation of overstepping moral boundaries. Siegfried, who defines himself by "crossing through the fire" summoned by a divine Wotan, was Nietzsche's great example. In reading *Thoughts out of Season,* Foucault would have recognized himself both in Wagner's hero and in the philosopher with a hammer who learned from him.

Foucault's concept of the limit-experience was closely connected to his conclusion that the utopian project born of the Renaissance had been a mistake. Secular humanism in his judgment was a delusional system of beliefs and values. He was convinced by incessant readings and rereadings of Nietzsche that no objective moral laws exist and that man is simply the product of the will to power. Strikingly, he brought his predecessor's famous nihilistic dictum that "God is dead" to an anthropological conclusion: Foucault came to assert that with the irreversible death of God in Western culture there had come an equally irreversible "death of man." As he put it:

The Nietzschean undertaking might be understood as finally putting an end to the proliferation of questioning about mankind. Was not the death of God, in fact, revealed in a double murderous act that, at the same time that it put an end to the absolute, assassinated man himself? Because man, in his finitude, is inseparable from the infinite, which he both negates and heralds. The death of God is accomplished through the death of man.[29]

Humanism, in Foucault's judgment, was dead. Like Christianity, it had been nothing but an expression of the will to power. Since the death of God had "put an end to the absolute," all knowledge and truth claims about beliefs and values were nothing more than assertions of the will to power.

Foucault's lifelong research interest was sexuality, and his final, posthumous book was a study of its "history." He was a highly promiscuous homosexual and regarded traditional sexual morality with great suspicion. In fact, in his efforts to dismantle traditional values, he became an apologist for the Marquis de Sade, whose pornographic novels had shocked even the radical philosophes of the so-called Enlightenment. Applying a Nietzschean genealogical method to transvalue values about sexuality—that is, taking a sledgehammer to them—he concluded that sexuality is in fact not a function of nature but a function of will. It is a product of the oppressive culture of Christendom—especially under the influence of its secular "enlightenment project"—to discipline and control society by placing it within an inescapable moral labyrinth. The bald, grinning professor delighted in shocking his middle-class students with claims that, in the words of one biographer, "sexuality has existed only since the eighteenth century and sex only since the nineteenth century."[30] He would of course concede, as his audience raised its hands in confusion, that humans have been procreating since the origin of the species. But the very concept of normative *sexuality* and even *sex* itself, he asserted, are the inventions of a power-based knowledge system (something he called a cultural "discourse") that has taken over the West. The sooner it

---

29 Quoted in Didier Eribon, *Michel Foucault*, trans. Betsy Wing (Cambridge, MA: Harvard University Press, 1991), 157.

30 Allan Megill, *Prophets of Extremity: Nietzsche, Heidegger, Foucault, Derrida* (Berkeley: University of California Press, 1985), 253.

is destroyed, the sooner people can explore a plurality of "sexualities," knowing that no single one is objectively good.

This last point was for him of great importance. He lived through the sexual revolution and participated in its greatest excesses. However, he emphatically opposed a utopian approach to gay or other forms of sexual liberation. He once dismayed a homosexual activist by declaring that the gay liberation movement is yet a new form of moral hegemony. Even the word "gay" should be avoided when speaking about the identity of marginalized groups. "Our pursuit of pleasure," he insisted, "has been limited in large part by a vocabulary foisted upon us. People are neither this nor that, gay or straight. There is an infinite range of what we call sexual behavior."[31] Thus one of the most influential philosophers of what would become known as identity politics was himself convinced that there is no objective basis to sexual identity. Man is dead, and therefore any liberating or utopian project to bring progress to his earthly condition misdirects the will to power.

It is impossible to isolate Foucauldian philosophy from the transgressive personality that produced it. His life centered on the transformational "limit-experience." And the bolder the limits, the greater the experience of transcendence. The most exhilarating act of all was to defy one's very mortality. Often, Foucault was driven toward acts of partial self-destruction. He practiced self-harm throughout his life. And like Dostoevsky and Nietzsche, he was so fascinated by the experience that he wrote reflections on it. More than once he contemplated suicide. He abused narcotics and on one occasion in 1975 joined a pair of American philosophers in dropping acid in Death Valley, California. He also practiced perverse forms of sexuality with an endless stream of unknown male lovers. Applying the transgressive example of de Sade's characters, he frequently engaged in sadomasochism.

What is perhaps most striking is that he conducted these affairs in the early 1980s, after the onset of the deadly epidemic known as Acquired Immunodeficiency Syndrome (AIDS). By this time, he was a highly sought-after guest professor and once a year spent time teaching at Berkeley. During the

---

31   James Miller, *The Passion of Michel Foucault* (New York: Doubleday, 1993), 254.

days he lectured on how the moral "limit-experience" was the most transcendent act a person could perform, and during the evenings he acted on that teaching in San Francisco's gay bars and bathhouses. The Summer of Love had not only drawn the hippie counterculture to the city, but within a decade a sexual subculture had formed there as well. As a biographer notes, "group sex was in; promiscuity was hip; and so was an uninhibited openness to the polymorphously perverse."[32] Foucault consumed all that the new subculture had to offer. And he did so when knowledge of its risks were widely publicized—especially in the Bay Area.

Nevertheless, the philosopher who may have been the most authentic disciple yet of Zarathustra—bolder even than the migraine-enfeebled Nietzsche—continued to live out the transvaluation of values in San Francisco's bathhouses. And after contracting AIDS he continued with nihilistic abandon.

An insight into how he could have engaged in acts that were so dangerous and potentially lethal for others is found in a conversation with a fellow professor at Berkeley in 1983. Significantly, the conversation occurred after Foucault, appearing pale and weak, collapsed on one of the university's lawns from the effects of the disease. When asked later by his colleague if he feared AIDS, Foucault scoffed. The meaning of life was not to be found in such concerns as relationships, success, or longevity. It was certainly not found in communion with God. Rather, it was to be found in an unbroken but disjointed and ultimately meaningless series of Dionysian limit-experiences. "Are you afraid to die?" he asked his colleague with a smile. He then related his conviction that the truly beautiful death is one that resembles an hallucinogenic trip in which the mind simply departs from the body for good, no longer concerned with matters like the truth. "And besides," he added, "to die for the love of boys: What could be more beautiful?"[33]

When Foucault did die a year later from AIDS, he did so almost with a sense of delight. He seemed to fear nothing. Fading slowly on his hospital bed, he alternated between agonizing pain and nervous laughter. In the

---

32 Ibid., 252.
33 Ibid., 350.

words of his biographer James Miller, he did so "knowing that he would soon slip over to the other side of that threshold, just dust without words now, no longer speaking, no longer listening, no longer seeking, no longer caged, truly a 'wordless thing in an empty place'—free of the need for the truth at last."[34] In death Foucault entered on a very different kind of limit-experience—one in which the truth would no longer be subject to his or any man's will.

---

34 Ibid., 374.

CHAPTER NINE

A Good Place without God Is Nowhere

T HE "DEATH OF GOD" THUS brought the age of nihilism to a "death of man," and this, announced by Foucault but manifested more broadly in a popular counterculture, signaled the fall of utopia. Christendom, the civilization with a supporting culture that once directed its members toward the heavenly transformation of the world, fell into cosmo-anthropological despair when traditional Christianity no longer animated it. Though humanism had forestalled this outcome by reorienting the transformational imperative toward the saeculum, after a half millennium its vision of man proved a tragic counterfeit of the faith that once made the West what it was. Deprived of its paradisiacal culture, a disoriented Christendom wandered beyond utopia and fell into the abyss of nihilism.

Ideological world building had given utopia a new lease on life. For the better part of a century, the transformational promises of Communism, Nazism, and liberalism provided a shield against the grinning visage of nihilism. Each ideology in its own way reaffirmed the saeculum by weaving transcendent myths about it. But whether they looked for reassurance to Marx or Darwin or Mill, they could not evade Dostoevsky's or Nietzsche's observations that the death of God results in any moral action becoming permissible. Nihilism, it turned out, was the inescapable outcome of secular humanism.

Perhaps this had been dimly foreseen centuries earlier during the height of the Renaissance, when Thomas More coined the term that came to characterize Christendom's secular alternative to paradise. *Utopia* means literally "nowhere." And in his playful way, the English humanist coined a variant of it, *eutopia,* which he used in his book's subtitle. The second term means "good place." It is this, of course, that ultimately came to give *utopia* its meaning.

And so to extend More's play on words, it can be said that if there is anything the history of Christendom demonstrates during its age of nihilism, it is that a good place without God is nowhere.

When Transformation Became Stagnant

AT ABOUT THE TIME FOUCAULT was seeking alternatives to liberalism in the bathhouses of San Francisco, a young man named Georgy Shevkunov was exploring alternatives to Communism in the monasteries of Russia.

A recent graduate of the Soviet Institute of Cinematography, Shevkunov had been surrounded for years by the cultural achievements of utopia. The institute itself had been specially founded by the Bolsheviks to advance their world-building enterprise. It was designed as an organ of propaganda, like the newspaper *Pravda.* Among the many fine filmmakers affiliated with the institute was Sergey Eisenstein, whose classic *October* had been commissioned for the 1927 decennial celebration.

Another was Andrey Tarkovsky. He had taken the art of filmmaking in a direction less subserviently aligned with Communism. Without challenging ideological uniformity directly, he expressed criticism of the totalitarian culture. In the monumental *Andrey Rublev* (1966) he explored the piety and creativity behind some of traditional Christianity's greatest iconography. Because of his dissatisfaction with Communism he spent his final years in exile. His last film, *The Sacrifice* (1986), was a reflection on the horrors of nuclear destruction and the collective guilt shared by all who have participated in the building of dystopia. The opening scene features the protagonist, an old, highly sensitive and educated man, instructing his mute son to water a barren tree faithfully so that, like a tree in a story recounted from a saint's life, it might be renewed. If one were to perform the same prayerful ritual act every day without fail, he tells the boy, "the world would be changed."

The exchange is a typically obscure one (Tarkovsky's films are anything but simple), but it sets the tone for the final scene. There, after the nuclear apocalypse has occurred, the protagonist "goes crazy" by assuming responsibility for the suffering of the entire world. He repents, and as he does so the film enters its final sequence with the playing of Bach's stirring hymn of repentance, "Erbarme dich." The man burns his house down—a possible metaphor for abandoning utopia—and then we are returned to the tree, a symbol of forgotten paradise. There his mute son, once again, is faithfully pouring water into the desiccated roots. And with what water is he irrigating them? Looking up into the branches, the boy tells us by unexpectedly uttering his very first words (and the last of the film): "In the beginning was the Word—why is that, Papa?" The words were of course those of the Evangelist John, and they became Tarkovsky's final statement to the West. Soon after *Sacrifice* was released, he died.

In 1982, Georgy Shevkunov inherited the legacy of a film institute that inspired both one of Communism's most aggressive propagandists and one of its most sensitive critics. Yet in his case, neither secular ideology nor artistic ingenuity was what mattered. Shevkunov was concerned with living an authentic life of spiritual transcendence.

Everything around him, he later reported in a memoir entitled *Everyday Saints and Other Stories,* appeared sullied and deceitful. He recalls how as a child he was told—as were virtually all children of utopia—myths about the linkage of progress and godlessness. He recalls the way his elementary school teacher cheerfully imparted Marxism and Leninism. And he recalls how, as he and others of his generation looked around, Communism appeared as a deception. It was not the "truth," as its official newspaper claimed. It was a patent lie. He came to wonder if it was really true, as the totalitarian system insisted, that the great intellectuals of the past were idiots for their faith in God. "Or were we the idiots?"[1] He and his circle of friends initially dabbled in the New Age spirituality available to any youth of the Soviet or American counterculture. The consequences of contact with its demons set in, and

---

1   Archimandrite Tikhon (Shevkunov), *Everyday Saints and Other Stories,* trans. Julian Henry Lowenfeld (Dallas: Pokrov, 2012), 6.

Shevkunov drew back in horror. Then, after much hesitation (considering the anti-Christian mood of the times) he resolved to be baptized. One of the first things he did afterward was to act on his sponsor's recommendation to visit an out-of-the-way monastery near the ancient town of Pskov. Once there, he fell in love with the old Christendom that flourished within its sacramental and liturgical life.

So changed was Shevkunov after only ten days that when he returned to the saeculum he experienced a kind of spiritual culture shock. Alighting from his bus during the journey home, he caught sight of a man in the street munching aimlessly on a roll. There was nothing unusual in this. No one in the secular order consumed food that was anything other than an earthly form of nourishment. No one was particularly grateful for it. No one asked the Creator to bless it. But mystically, the sight appalled him. He had spent more than a week among holy men whose every bite of food—and whose every step taken and word spoken—was made with prayer and gratitude, with a conviction about God's abiding presence. He had lived in a place where heavenly immanence was a constant reality. He had beheld the paradisiacal transformation of the world.

Tikhon Shevkunov
Пресс-служба Общественной палаты РФ, CC BY 4.0 <https://creativecommons.org/licenses/by/4.0>, via Wikimedia Commons

All of this was a complete contrast to utopia: "I had never encountered such kindness in the secular world," he observed.[2] He soon returned to the monastery, and in his heart he never left again. Eventually tonsured a monk with the name Tikhon, he became an advocate for the West's return to its first-millennium Christian roots.

Shevkunov's reorientation from utopia to paradise occurred during the early 1980s, a portentous time in the history of the Communist West. The Soviet Union was just then veering away from the self-confidence of her early decades, when revolutionary commemorations had triumphantly proclaimed the victory of secular humanism. The cultural thaw of Khrushchev had been reversed under his successor, Leonid Brezhnev (1964–82), but ideological uniformity was still in trouble. Alexander Solzhenitsyn, whose short novel *One Day in the Life of Ivan Denisovich* exposed the reality of Soviet dystopia, had now been deported for publishing abroad a monumental account of dystopian repression entitled *The Gulag Archipelago*. In the very year of his deportation, he had joined with a group of Soviet dissidents in publishing a collection of essays entitled *From under the Rubble* (1974). It declared the bankruptcy of totalitarianism and, more directly than *Gulag,* called on Russians to return to the Orthodox faith.

Solzhenitsyn himself contributed several of the book's essays, and their insights represent, as it were, his parting observations about Communist dystopia in its state of ideological stagnation. Interestingly, their content echoed a collection of essays published prior to the Russian Revolution. In that book, entitled *Landmarks,* Nicolas Berdyaev and other Orthodox intellectuals, such as Sergey Bulgakov, had lamented the intelligentsia's effort to create a civilization that excluded traditional Christianity. Solzhenitsyn repeated the lament. On the one hand, he echoed Bulgakov's call to repentance. The rise of secular ideologies had disabled Christendom, preventing its members from seeking the heavenly rather than the merely secular transformation of the world. Modern man had become an ideological rather than a spiritual being, and this grossly distorted his true humanity. As the twentieth century came to an end, Solzhenitsyn

---

2   Ibid., 17.

Alexander Solzhenitsyn
Bert Verhoeff for Anefo, CC0, via Wikimedia Commons

warned, "we are even now . . . reluctant to recognize that the universal dividing line between good and evil is not between countries, not between nations, not between parties, not between classes . . . It divides the heart of every man." Given this anthropological reality—learned from traditional

Christianity—"there is no way out, except that of repentance."[3]

Repentance was not, of course, likely to arise in a culture whose ideology was shaped by indignation. Communist mythology continued to present history as a story of ever-increasing progress driven by the eradication of class enemies and religious faith. However, by the middle of the 1980s it was becoming increasingly difficult for the state to convince the Soviet population of these myths. People like Shevkunov were everywhere.

Leonid Brezhnev, who had replaced Khrushchev as the Soviet leader, spoke of "real-existing socialism." But in fact the totalitarian economy with its investments in cradle-to-grave social welfare—to say nothing of the military and space race—was chronically unsustainable. Khrushchev's "economic miracles" had turned into curses. Massive efforts to increase agricultural production mostly met with failures or shortcomings. This included the utopian Virgin Lands Campaign to irrigate the deserts of northern Central Asia. Such projects often contributed to what can be called a "fantasy economy" in which great achievements were recorded in the ledger books of Gosplan but in reality never existed. Buses were built without engines in order to meet production targets. Enormous crops were harvested only to rot in the field due to inadequate transportation.

The case of Ryazan in southern Russia is a poignant example.[4] In 1957 Khrushchev had publicly (and, it turned out, recklessly) promised to overtake the United States in agricultural production by 1960. After meager results in 1958, a Communist Party apparatchik in Ryazan named Alexey Larionov heroically pledged to double meat production in his province the following year. Almost immediately, fellow bureaucrats, caught up in the euphoria of building socialism, increased the pledge even further. Khrushchev was ecstatic, and when the conservative Politburo leadership warned against publishing the promises in *Pravda,* he overruled them. Soon,

---

3   Alexander Solzhenitsyn, "Repentance and Self-Limitation in the Life of Nations," in *From under the Rubble,* trans. under the direction of Michael Scammell (Glasgow: William Collins and Sons, 1975), 105–43.

4   A good summary of what follows is found in Roy A. Medvedev and Zhores A. Medvedev, *Khrushchev: The Years in Power,* trans. Andrew R. Durkin (New York: W. W. Norton, 1978), 94–101.

regional apparatchiks were revising their 1959 meat targets upward with dizzying optimism. Khrushchev flew to Ryazan to confer the prestigious Order of Lenin on Larionov personally.

Though Lenin had once claimed there were no fortresses which the Bolsheviks could not storm, the fact was that in the case of Ryazan (and other provinces), no amount of revolutionary zeal could alter the natural limitations of animal husbandry. As the year progressed and local bureaucrats began to realize this, orders were made to slaughter not only state-owned cattle but those belonging privately to collective farmers. When this failed to solve the problem, the order went out—unbelievably—to slaughter the province's dairy herds. Then all cattle reserved for breeding purposes were slaughtered. And still the quota was nowhere near being met. Soon Ryazan's increasingly desperate party leaders were traveling to neighboring provinces to purchase cattle there, often by squandering money budgeted for other economic necessities. There were even cases in which the local party bosses organized cattle heists, sending armed agents across the borders into surrounding provinces. None of these measures worked. And yet, in December 1959, the Ryazan party leadership published a declaration throughout the Soviet Union claiming to have fulfilled their pledge to the heroic building of socialism. Larionov was declared a Hero of Socialist Labor.

In fact, the economy of Ryazan had been ruined. Since the cattle farms had been completely emptied, the miserable province could contribute only a pittance of meat to the Soviet economy the following year. An investigation was ordered. And on the eve of the investigating committee's report to the local party gathering, the erstwhile hero of Communist world building Larionov committed suicide.

Brezhnev inherited this fantasy economy and proved incapable of reforming or improving it. Because of this, his tenure as general secretary came to be known as the "era of stagnation." The possibility of a substantive reallocation of resources to consumer goods was further diminished when he resolved to achieve nuclear parity with the United States through intercontinental ballistic missile (ICBM) production.

This is not to say that no one benefited from the command economy. A thin stratum at the top of society known informally as the *nomenklatura* had long enjoyed access to scarce resources such as apartments near metro stations, foreign goods stores, automobiles, and country dachas. This element, so similar to the oppressive elite about which Marx fulminated, was protected by the neo-Stalinists within the Politburo and other party agencies. It was this conservative element, in fact, that had ousted Khrushchev and replaced him with a compliant Brezhnev.

By the time Brezhnev died in office in 1982, having presided over a bureaucratic gerontocracy for eighteen years, Soviet citizens were challenging the stagnating utopia with cynical political humor. One slogan quipped, "They pretend to pay us, and we pretend to work." Another featured Stalin, Khrushchev, and Brezhnev sitting in a train representing the Communist state while it travels through a countryside representing historical progress. The train suddenly stops. Stalin tries to get it moving again by ordering the engineer to be shot. Nothing happens. Then Khrushchev orders the engineer's reputation to be rehabilitated posthumously. Still, nothing happens. Only then does Brezhnev come up with a solution that satisfies everyone: he reaches over and simply pulls down the window blinds. "There," he declares with satisfaction. "Now the train is moving."

Into the Dustbin of History

BUT THE SOVIET UNION WAS not moving, and both the leadership and the people knew it. So, in 1985 a young Communist who was a true believer in utopia was recruited to provide leadership in reform. President Mikhail Gorbachev (1985–91) was different from his predecessors, however—even from the well-meaning reformer Khrushchev. He was resolved to avoid any reversion to the cruelty and duplicity of Bolshevism. This was his redeeming virtue. But it also proved fatal to the totalitarian system he inherited.

Gorbachev started his reforms with a policy called *Perestroika* ("restructuring"). It gave primacy to the stagnating economy. However, he received little political support from the neo-Stalinists, who correctly perceived a threat to their economic privileges. Therefore, Gorbachev implemented a secondary policy called *Glasnost* ("openness"). Its purpose was to free Soviet society to discuss the problems of the system. It aimed to create what liberal democracy had long had: a civil society that is both educated about its state and critically invested in improving it. His hope was to create popular support for restructuring an economy that had been created through Stalin's Revolution from Above. What he provoked, however, was a revolution from below.

The turning point was April 26, 1986. On that night a nuclear reactor exploded at the Chernobyl power station about fifty miles north of Kiev. The reactor had been built without a containment structure, a design limitation imposed by scarce financial resources. The accident therefore became a symbol of Soviet economic backwardness. It was initially covered up by officials, making it a symbol also of Communist totalitarianism. As it turned out, the explosion caused a chain reaction—not within the station's other reactors, but in the simmering civil society that had briefly formed during Khrushchev's thaw and was now released by Glasnost.

Much earlier, when Lenin was declaring the creation of the totalitarian system in 1917, fellow Bolshevik Leon Trotsky had coined the phrase "dustbin of history" to characterize—and vilify—all social elements that were not aligned with and submissive to Communism. Now the Soviet population began to stir that dustbin to recover those elements of the old Christendom that had been discarded in it. To be sure, much of the "refuse" there was not particularly religious: millions who had perished through collectivization were finally recognized; political figures like Bukharin were rehabilitated; and responsibility for the Katyn Forest Massacre was acknowledged.

But much of what civil society found in the dustbin of history was religious. And the revival of Orthodoxy this inspired was spectacular. Priests long persecuted were now free to evangelize. Some did so by giving talks and writing books. These included Gleb Yakunin and Alexander Men (who was mysteriously murdered in 1990). Others, such as Georgy Kochetkov, did so by celebrating the Orthodox Church's transformational divine services, though with such experimental enthusiasm that he was eventually disciplined by his bishop. Many churches were reopened, and in 1988 the government allowed the Moscow Patriarchate to organize the millennial celebration of the founding of Russian Christianity. Held in Kiev, the capital of the Ukrainian Soviet Socialist Republic, it was a reminder that long before Communism existed, Eastern Slavs were united by a common Orthodox faith. At first thousands and then millions of converts flooded into Orthodox churches for baptisms and services throughout the Soviet Union. Bibles and saints' lives were published and widely distributed.

One of the most remarkable examples of this revival was a volume entitled *Father Arseny*. It was written and began to be distributed in *samizdat* ("self-published") form under Brezhnev and was finally published in book form only in 1993. It is the story of an obscure priestmonk who is victimized by the Communist terror but never ceases to radiate faith, hope, and charity to those suffering imprisonment alongside him. Many scenes depict him in the labor camp system facing all the horrors of totalitarianism. What is particularly interesting from an historical point of view is how his story provided a point of reference for innumerable believers who had themselves experienced repression or knew others who had.

In fact, *Father Arseny* makes a fascinating contrast to some examples of Jewish literature about the Holocaust wherein disbelief in the Incarnation and Resurrection served to preclude hope in redemptive suffering. In *Night*, for instance, Eli Wiesel guides his readers to a Nietzschean conclusion about the Holocaust's meaning. In the book's harrowing central scene, an innocent Jewish child is hung up as if on a crucifix to die. Wiesel, along with numerous reviewers, regarded the scene as a manifestation of how the age of nihilism resulted in "the death of God." What is more, the author extended this insight (as Foucault would later do within a different context) to imply that the scale of totalitarian terror resulted also in the death of man. "At Auschwitz," Wiesel wrote, "not only man died but the idea of man."[5]

In the case of *Father Arseny*, however, the suffering caused by Communist terror—no less horrifying than Nazi genocide—is never able to overcome hope in the resurrection. It does come close. In one scene Father Arseny finds himself alone in a field, staring at a mass grave of tens of thousands of innocent terror victims. "Suddenly the words of prayer drained out of me," the priestmonk admits,

---

5   Quoted in Ellen S. Fine, "Witness of the Night," in *Elie Wiesel's Night*, ed. Harold Bloom (New York: Chelsea House, 2001), 47–68.

and I found myself on this field lost, crushed by memories, doubts and an unfathomable emptiness. . . . A feeling of absolute hopelessness, heartsickness and a deep despair came over me; I felt overwhelmed. I was so utterly despondent that I felt lost and unhinged inside. An unbearable soul-rending pain tore out of me with a groan. "My Lord, why didst Thou allow this?"

His faith having reached a point of temptation as great as that experienced by the Jewish Wiesel, the Christian Arseny then makes the sign of the cross. Suddenly, his despair dissipates and the specter of nihilism withdraws from the field. A breeze begins to blow. A lark begins to sing in the branches overhead.

And I realized that life went on and would go on in just the same way as it had before the death of all of these people. Life will continue, and will always continue. This is the law of God, and the world created by Him follows His design.[6]

The scene ends with a sense of victory as Father Arseny bows in the direction of the dead—for after all, in the risen Christ all are in fact alive—and blesses the four corners of the cosmos in all directions.

Perhaps the single most profound expression of the reappearance of the old Christendom within the new Christendom of the Soviet Union was a film entitled *Repentance* (1987). The film was directed by the Georgian filmmaker Tengiz Abuladze and saw the light of day only through the influence of one of Gorbachev's strongest Georgian supporters, foreign minister Eduard Shevardnadze. The film embodied the main theme of Solzhenitsyn's call to cultural revival, repentance through a thoroughgoing repudiation of secular ideology.

The film's premise is that a woman has resolved to exhume the body of a recently buried town mayor named Varlaam. It turns out that the woman, named Keti, is the daughter of parents who were arrested and cruelly

---

6   *Father Arseny, 1893–1973: Priest, Prisoner, Spiritual Father*, translated by Vera Bouteneff (Crestwood, NY: St. Vladimir's Seminary Press, 1998), 90–91.

executed by the mayor many years earlier during the revolutionary transformation of the town. Varlaam is an obvious analogue to Stalin, and the film recounts in allegorical ways—stunning and frequently touching—the horror of the Great Terror. To emphasize what many Soviets now believed was the moral equivalence of Communism and Nazism, Varlaam wears a toothbrush moustache.

But the film's real import is not the retelling of the terror, but the telling of how it delegitimates the current generation of town leadership. The brutal mayor was succeeded by a son named Abel—played by the same actor to make the linkage obvious—who represents Brezhnev and the neo-Stalinists who retained totalitarianism in a more civilized form. Abel and his wife are seen relaxing in the luxury of their apartment among the town elite, an allusion to the privileged life of the nomenklatura. However, Abel has his own son, a stormy teenager named Tornike. Tornike is tormented by the fact that the woman exhuming his grandfather's body is ultimately revealed to be telling the truth. Once this happens, he can no longer accept his town the way it is or identify with his father. Clearly, Tornike is Gorbachev—or better yet, the post-Soviet Everyman that the reforming general secretary was freeing to call out lies for what they are and replace them with "the truth."

The number of times the Russian word *pravda* is used in the film—especially in light of the fact that the primary language is Georgian—would have caught the attention of Soviet citizens used to the dubious claims of the official Communist newspaper. As he cleverly opposes traditional Christianity to secular ideology, Abuladze leads his viewers to reconsider the very basis of their civilization and its supporting culture. One telling subplot is the fate of the ancient town church, where frescoes depicting the Garden of Eden have been damaged by the installation of "more progressive" laboratory equipment. Eventually Varlaam has the church blown up, like so many in the Soviet Union—most memorably Christ the Savior Cathedral in Moscow (photographs of which were then being retrieved from the dustbin of history). With great artistry, the film suggests that Russia (and with her all of the West) long ago deviated from the truth.

Which brings us to the film's powerful final scenes. After being placed on trial for refusing to let the body of the town mayor remain buried, Keti is consigned to a mental hospital (a not infrequent sentence under the KGB, which was reluctant after Khrushchev's reforms to conduct mass arrests and executions). This violation of the truth so estranges Tornike from everything around him that he decides to confront his father during the course of an otherwise charming soirée at their home. After Abel strikes the boy in a fit of rage (violence, Abuladze suggests, will always remain just below the surface for a society built on lies and terror), Tornike disappears into his room. A moment later a shot rings out. Abel goes to the door and peeks in. There he sees his son lying on the floor, dead by suicide.

What follows is breathtaking, though it occurs in but a moment. Abel closes the door, rather like the political joke (recounted above) that depicted Brezhnev closing the blinds to reality. But now, under Gorbachev, the Soviet people were demanding openness. And so after a moment, as the camera maintains a focus on the closed door, a crack appears, and then Abel's face returns to gaze openly on his dead son—the latest victim of Varlaam's legacy of violence and lies.

After this, the film's title is finally fulfilled. Abel repents. With harrowing intensity, he declares himself the cause of all the town's sorrows. He may not have ordered a single arrest or execution, but he realizes mystically that he is guilty of what his father did and what he has failed to renounce. He is then seen on the edge of a ravine from which he himself now heaves the evil corpse of Varlaam-Stalin into the public garbage dump—or dustbin—of the long-suffering and long-deluded utopian town.

The film's final scene follows immediately. It so impressed the increasingly emboldened Soviet Union's civil society that university students turned the final sentence into a much-used public slogan. An old woman is seen walking down a street past the storefront window of a bakery where Keti now makes her living baking cakes in the form of churches (religion itself having been eradicated). The passing woman resembles a peasant pilgrim. She asks, "Does this road lead to a church?"

Keti responds almost with embarrassment. "No," she sighs. "This is Varlaam Street. And it doesn't lead to a church."

The pilgrim looks back in disbelief, and then utters the film's famous final question: "What good is a road if it doesn't lead to a church?"

In the few years remaining to the Soviet Union, these words were repeated often by those who would dare build a society on the foundations of the old Christendom rather than the new.

But in any case, Communism had not long to live. The ideologically committed but heroically humane Gorbachev watched with helpless despair as the revolution from below gained strength in the years after Chernobyl. Economic discontent led to strikes by miners—never a good sign in the purportedly socialist state. Then demands for democracy appeared as Boris Yeltsin publicly tore up his Communist Party membership card. Most desta-bilizing were outbursts of nationalism. Lithuania went so far as to declare her intention to secede from the Soviet Union.

On the Politburo, the neo-Stalinists realized that the end was near but did everything they could to forestall it. On August 19, 1991, a group of them, including Minister of the Interior Boris Pugo (whose surname is related to the Russian verb "to frighten"), ordered the detention of Gorbachev and the creation of a dictatorial emergency committee. This August Putsch went nowhere, especially as millions of Soviet citizens had had enough of utopia's lies. Yeltsin was seen atop a tank in the streets of Moscow, and Gorbachev was soon released from house arrest. As for Pugo, he committed suicide.

All four elements of the totalitarian system now came crashing down. Gosplan was dissolved and a free-market economy promised. Ideological uniformity—never fully achieved—was relinquished, and symbols of the pre-Communist past, such as the name of Saint Petersburg, were restored. The KGB was liquidated, and its agents were filmed anxiously shredding documents at the once-dreaded Lyubyanka headquarters in Moscow. Finally and most astonishingly, the Communist Party itself was outlawed (though the action was later canceled on the principle of democratic pluralism).

By the end of 1991, the Union of Soviet Socialist Republics was no more. On December 25, Mikhail Gorbachev removed his personal items from the Kremlin office of the general secretary—an office occupied before him by Brezhnev, Khrushchev, and Stalin—as the president of a now independent Russian Federation, Boris Yeltsin (1991–99), moved in. The Soviet flag with its hammer and sickle was lowered from the Kremlin flagpole, and the Rus-sian national tricolor was raised in its place.

Toppling of Dzerzhinsky statue at the Lyubyanka after the August Putsch, 1991
Dmitry Borko, CC BY-SA 4.0 <https://creativecommons.org/licenses/by-sa/4.0>, via Wikimedia Commons

After only seventy-four years, utopia's most ambitious experiment in world building was cast into what one of its chief architects had called the dustbin of history.

The Progressive Disintegration of Liberalism

AND YET THE THREE DECADES that followed the collapse of Communism witnessed the progressive disintegration of its ideological rival, liberalism. This process was progressive in two senses. In the first, liberal disintegration grew progressively more noticeable as the memory of Communism faded. In the second sense, it followed the fortunes of *progressivism*—a variant of liberalism, but one that suffered from a self-destructive tendency toward limitless transformation. Like Brünhilde before Siegfried's funeral pyre, liberalism rode its fearless horse, progressivism, to a kind of heroic self-immolation.

Progressivism proved to be the destiny of liberalism and brought it to fulfillment. Since the Great War liberalism's most elaborate expression, the American Way, had been defined in opposition to first Nazism and then Communism. Only when those two great utopian alternatives had been defeated did liberalism really come of age. Until then, it was comparatively moderate and adapted itself to preexisting patterns of religion and culture. Its maturation began with the counterculture of the sixties, and it finally came of age when the Berlin Wall fell. With roots in Mill, liberalism in its progressive form may have continued to resist the temptation toward collective violence. But with help from Nietzsche, its obsession with individualistic liberty led its advocates to transgress the very boundaries within which it was once content to operate.

Patrick Deneen has attributed the shortcomings of liberalism to this transgressive tendency. It reached a point of failure, he asserts paradoxically, because it surpassed all the limits that were placed on it:

Liberalism has failed—not because it fell short, but because it was true to itself. It has failed because it has succeeded. As liberalism has "become more fully itself," as its inner logic has become more evident and its self-contradictions manifest, it has generated pathologies that are at once deformations of its claims yet realizations of liberal ideology. A political philosophy that was launched to foster greater equity, defend a pluralist tapestry of different cultures and beliefs, protect human dignity, and, of course, expand liberty, in practice generates titanic inequality, enforces uniformity and homogeneity, fosters material and spiritual degradation, and undermines freedom. Its success can be measured by its achievement of the opposite of what we have believed it would achieve.[7]

With the collapse of Communism, liberalism in its progressive form was free to become what it had always (imperfectly) been: a totalitarian movement that, like its defeated ideological rivals, builds utopia while subverting the humanistic values that define it.

Liberalism's distant historical model was, of course, traditional Christianity. Yet there was a sharp difference between ideological world building and the source of Christendom's original culture. During the first millennium, the transformational imperative had been regulated by asceticism. Humility had been the chief virtue and repentance its most perfect expression—a cultural dynamic ritualized inwardly in confession and outwardly in the annual Great Fast. Christendom's paradisiacal culture always looked to the kingdom of heaven beyond this world, providing a total vision of life that was not dependent for its fulfillment on the saeculum. As a secular ideology, by contrast, progressive liberalism had no transcendent anchor. It was fueled by indignation. It replaced the rituals of repentance with counterfeits of ritualized politics.

This is why, in the absence of a cold war, the United States and her allies—sometimes known as Atlanticists because of their geopolitical center—relentlessly continued liberal world building in lands recently rid of Communism. Anti-Russian policies simply assumed post-Soviet forms. Globalist expansion and military intervention both followed the old pattern. As the Yeltsin administration humiliatingly submitted itself to a new American unilateralism, NATO pushed its way first into central Europe and then to the very doorsteps of Russia. In 1999 Poland, Hungary, and Czechia were

---

7   Deneen, *Why Liberalism Failed*, 3–4.

enrolled in the anti-Russian alliance. In 2004 seven more nation-states were added, including Romania and the Baltics. In 2008, NATO commanders publicly voiced an interest in adding Georgia and Ukraine to the list of members. Needless to say, all these states became (or in the case of Georgia and Ukraine signaled interest in becoming) members of the European Union, cementing them in ideological liberalism. Along with free markets, their governments quickly embraced progressive policies such as open immigration and cultural diversity. All the while, the United States and her allies fought wars and supported insurgencies in Serbia, Afghanistan, Iraq, and Syria to strengthen liberal democracy in the West and to build it where it did not yet exist.

Back in the United States, liberalism entered a new phase in its transformation of the world. As we have noted, since the time of Mill it had been primarily concerned with the liberty of the individual in the face of the state. But strangely, as Deneen has noted, the expanding state now manifested itself as not a threat to individual liberty but rather a crutch for it. In the hands of progressives, government became the "agent of individualism."[8] The earlier Millian form of liberalism, to be sure, had advanced the Renaissance ideal of the autonomous individual by resisting encroachments by the state. And it was this not-yet-mature liberalism that appealed to conservative liberals in the face of incipient progressivism after the Great War. But as liberalism reached progressive maturity during the late twentieth century, individual autonomy came to depend more and more on separation from traditional communities such as church, family, and locality. This became especially pronounced during the countercultural movement, when traditional beliefs and values were thrown to the wind because they were associated with repression. In 1968 millions of Ben Braddocks awoke from their dystopian catatonia to seek radical alternatives to the West that once was. Cultural boundaries that had heretofore held liberals to a policy of moderation were now transgressed with abandon.

An early sign appeared in 1973 when a liberal Supreme Court created a constitutional right to abortion in *Roe v. Wade*. This was one of the

---

8   Ibid., 59.

government's most effective ways of wresting young people from the clutches of traditional communities and making them dependent on the state for their liberty. Not only were young women no longer bound by two millennia of moral conviction about the value of unborn human life, but they were encouraged to cast off the teachings of parents and pastors. The Democratic Party was at first reluctant to link its platform to the progressive ruling. Senators such as Joseph Biden called for limits on abortion access. Yet in less than thirty years, liberation through abortion rights was being offered to women without limits, and not by Democrats alone but by many Republicans as well. As Deneen notes, "one of the liberal state's main roles [became] the active liberation of individuals from any limiting conditions."[9] Eventually, unlimited liberty became the standard of liberalism. Biden himself set an example. First as vice president and then as president after 2020, he fully recanted his earlier support for limitations on an act that the old Christendom had considered the ultimate disgrace of pagandom.

The abortion issue marked a turning point in the trend toward liberal limitlessness. All sorts of new and largely fictitious "communities" were created in the closing decades of the twentieth century to enhance the autonomy of their individual members. This was the birth of "identity politics," when groups that otherwise had little inner coherence were declared monoliths and became self-consciously dependent on progressive ideology for their identity and even existence.

The largest group was the female half of the population. A "women's community" had never existed in monolithic form, since normal women (and men) do not define themselves primarily by their sex but by a wide range of traits including faith, ethnicity, social class, work, interests, and so on. Nevertheless, liberal feminism did its best to shape women into a politicized aggregate. When anti-abortion forces began to mobilize against *Roe*, for instance, feminists were quick to link "women's liberation" with political liberalism. The fact that anti-abortion forces were led in many cases by women was dismissed as a case of deficient group identity. Some women, it turned out, were less womanly than others.

---

9   Ibid., 49.

Other ideologically manufactured groups followed, ranging from "the black community" to "the gay community." Ethnically defined identity groups were particularly fictitious, not only in that members held a wide range of completely disparate beliefs but because the progressive values imposed on them were often incompatible with their authentic ethnic heritage. An example is "the Hispanic community." Grateful for liberal attention to the plight of immigrants from the south, Hispanics—who are predominantly Roman Catholic in faith—nevertheless had as a group very different views on social and moral issues than the secular elites who defined their interests at the Justice Department in Washington, DC.

Indirectly, then—and in contrast to the violent collectivistic demands of Nazism and Communism—the liberal state gained unprecedented influence in a society increasingly divided by ideological pluralism. According to Deneen,

> *This very liberation in turn generates liberalism's self-reinforcing circle, wherein the increasingly disembedded individual ends up strengthening the state that is its own author. From the perspective of liberalism, it is a virtuous circle, but from the standpoint of human flourishing, it is one of the deepest sources of liberal pathology.*[10]

Convinced of its role in defending and even creating individual liberty, the liberal state grew ever bolder in imposing a progressive model of the world on the societies it ruled.

But the state was only one player in the progressive totalitarian drift. Commercial media platforms from newspapers to cable programming became bastions of progressive uniformity into which thoughtful alternative voices were scarcely ever admitted. This lack of objectivity and broadmindedness was justified on the grounds that such exclusions advanced the unassailable cause of liberty. The effect, however, was ideological monophony. In the wake of the 2016 presidential election, for instance, nearly every major voice in the news media became openly hostile to the policies of Donald

---

10   Ibid., 59.

Trump (2017–21). Only the conservative Fox News Network offered a popular alternative, but it did so in an equally monophonic way. The maturation of liberalism was now dividing the ideology into its two core tendencies, progressivism and conservatism.

The news media also became a leading advocate for the new identity politics. In 2019 the *New York Times* began to sponsor what it called "The 1619 Project," a rewriting of the past to make black slavery and white supremacism the main theme of America's historical narrative. Criticized and in some cases even panned by historians for its ideological preoccupations and factual inaccuracies, the project nevertheless earned a Pulitzer Prize for its director. It provided support for progressive claims that even after the civil rights movement the United States remained in a dehumanizing state of "systemic racism."

When civil rights protests, race riots, and looting exploded after the police killing of George Floyd in 2020, this overwhelmingly racist narrative about the past was joined to sexual identity politics and New Age goddess spirituality in the activities of an organization called, innocuously, Black Lives Matter. The news media showed a strong bias toward this formerly unknown

Methodist church displaying Black Lives Matter banner, 2020
Glendale United Methodist Church - Nashville from Nashville, TN, United States, CC BY 2.0
<https://creativecommons.org/licenses/by/2.0>, via Wikimedia Commons

organization, avoiding serious consideration of positions it held that in other contexts would have been considered extremist and dehumanizing. As a result, the initials "BLM" became ubiquitous in mainstream neighborhoods, main-street storefronts, and mainline Protestant churchyards. Long forgotten was the stand against racism advocated only a generation earlier by Martin Luther King and centuries earlier by traditional Christianity.

Even the West's corporate leadership began to impose what restrictions it could on the liberal legacy of conservative politics. Social networking platforms Facebook and Twitter, for instance, distinguished themselves during the Trump years by censoring what their Silicon Valley executives judged ideologically unacceptable posts by right-wing users. Conservatives within the Republican Party often tried to roll back progressive gains in social policy only to be opposed by what they called the "woke corporate elite." An example occurred in 2016 when the chief executive officer of Paypal participated in a boycott of business in North Carolina after that state's democratically elected legislature passed a law banning the use of bathrooms designated for the opposite sex by transgender persons claiming to be that sex. As a result of such pressures, the legislature capitulated and repealed the law. The stable boundaries of human anatomy and democratic lawmaking disintegrated under the assaults of progressive definitions of liberation.

Hollywood became a major advocate of progressivism's emerging soft totalitarianism. Once the victims of McCarthyite persecution, its producers and agents repeatedly discriminated against conservative actors and screenwriters. The practice of blacklisting ideological nonconformists reached a high point during the Trump administration, despite the fact that entertainment moguls like Harvey Weinstein—a major donor to progressive causes—defied the feminist lobby by committing outrageous acts of sexual misconduct. In the end, the great majority in the entertainment industry continued to advance the progressive cause against traditional values, whatever they might be. In fact, representative gatherings like the annual Academy Awards projected a level of ideological uniformity matched only by the film establishment of the former Soviet Union.

Because it assumed the values of the counterculture, liberal totalitarianism was very different from its harder variants. Its default view of normative

America became consistently critical and disparaging. One of many examples was the Academy Award–winning film *American Beauty* (1999). Set in a suburb symbolizing (as did the very title) the American Way, it explores career ambition, marital conflict, materialism, disillusionment, and, in the case of the protagonist, sexual fantasies about the next-door neighbors' underage daughter. The only morally attractive residents in the neighborhood are a same-sex couple that keep their heads low to avoid all the ugliness. Interestingly, the film's titular subject of "beauty" was not defined by the protagonist's pedophilia but by a no less ironic and absurd subject. In one scene, a charismatically disturbed teenager delivers a kind of Dadaist monologue on transcendence by showing a home movie he has made of a piece of garbage—a discarded plastic shopping bag—caught in an alley's whirlwind. A denizen of dystopia, he declares the apparition "the most beautiful thing" he has ever seen. Accompanied by tender piano music, the scene is the film's final statement about beauty in a society that is anything but beautiful.

Hollywood had to make money on the films it produced and thus was never completely free to disdain the society that supported it. Less constrained was academia. It manifested the tendencies of soft totalitarianism more openly, especially when protected by the liberal institution of tenure.

The American university system had been greatly expanded by the postwar baby boom, and in many ways this changed it forever. Beginning in the 1950s, the student population surged and campus construction boomed. Nevertheless, for much of the student body the university became little more than a degree mill ensuring access to the American Dream. And for many students, there was no need to await the hedonistic rewards of a white-collar career. Subprime state colleges and quite a few private colleges provided the setting for what one author has called the "five-year party."[11] The legacy of hippie promiscuity, the ease of student indebtedness, and a much-lamented but never arrested creeping grade inflation all contributed to the degradation

---

11   College towns that hosted such campuses, he notes, came to "welcome the students the way a medieval village prepared for a raid by the Vikings." Craig Brandon, *The Five-Year Party: How Colleges Have Given Up on Educating Your Child and What You Can Do about It* (Dallas: Benbella, 2010), 77.

of campus life. Long considered a monument of Western civilization, the university became a metaphor for decadence. Even for serious students, the academy's role in preserving high culture and fostering delight in intellectual discovery was often secondary. What is more, as enrollments mushroomed, the professoriate drew increasingly on alienated existentialists, critical theorists, and New Left activists. By the time America no longer had a Communist competitor, her professorial establishment had been thoroughly transformed from a liberal bastion of anti-Communism to a progressive force for cultural revolution. Thus as parental authority and disintegrative Christianity ceded influence, college campuses became the new moral cradle for America.

At first, professors in the humanities and social sciences nursed their students on Marxism and other transformative social theories. Then, as the New Left began to flounder, postmodernism replaced political activism. As we have seen, Foucault was one of the earliest critics of ideological world building. His posthumous influence was tremendous. So was that of fellow French philosophers Jacques Derrida, Jean-Francois Lyotard, and Jean Baudrillard. These postmodernists and the American faculty that fell under their spell in the years following the toppling of the Berlin Wall abandoned hopes of building a perfect society. They replaced objective standards of knowledge and morality (even revolutionary ones) with epistemological uncertainty and a playful approach to moral transgression.

The postmodernist turn they navigated was nothing if not ironic. A new, antitransformational imperative was pursued, and often in the mode of dark humor. In the case of Baudrillard it became self-consciously nihilistic. For this Frenchman, nothing was solid and reliable. Not only is God dead, he declared (repeating Nietzsche), but "reality is dead." Nothing escaped his philosopher's hammer, even Foucault. One of his books is laughingly entitled *Forget Foucault*. And he continued laughing, titling a subsequent work "Forget Baudrillard." He found the great ideological world-building project of the twentieth century particularly amusing. He was fascinated by America, studying her popular culture and recording his conclusions in books with intentionally fatuous titles like *Cool Memories*. He conceded the greatest of liberal democracies to be utopian, but only in a nihilistic sense:

America lacks any cultural authenticity whatever. He presented southern California—an utterly artificial community irrigated by aqueducts and enlightened by movie stars—as a postmodernist utopia. This made America's cultural capital neither Washington, nor Boston, nor New York, but . . . Disneyland. There, in the Magic Kingdom, everything is an undisguised simulacrum, a self-conscious deception, grounded in realities no more real than commercial advertising, mass consumption, and a day's desire to be passively entertained.

Postmodernism's contempt for objectivity, also inherited from Nietzsche, was closely related to suspicion that all forms of knowledge and culture are inherently oppressive. The anti-utopian philosophy therefore rejected the historical civilization and culture of the West. It redirected Christendom's transformational imperative toward a nihilistic end. In 1987, for instance, Jesse Jackson—the self-proclaimed but contested successor to Martin Luther King—organized a march in Palo Alto, California, in which protestors chanted, "Hey, hey, ho, ho, Western Civ has got to go!" They were successful: Stanford University—founded by one of America's great capitalists and a training ground for the nation's elite—readily responded by abolishing its Western Culture program. Studies of the West, in other cases where they were retained, turned from authors like Dante, Milton, and Dostoevsky to those historically underrepresented or unrecognized. The aesthetics of urban graffiti was taught, for instance, and topics like *Hamlet,* if offered at all, were transformed by applying the device of "queer theory." Classics departments were displaced by ethnic studies. The latter were then augmented by women's studies, which were augmented by gender studies, which were augmented by gay studies, and so on. A pretentious vocabulary impenetrable to anyone but academic mandarins helped shape a new "cultural politics" to help distinguish enemies from comrades in the struggle to overthrow all received hierarchies—all with the effect of establishing new ones. As Roger Kimball observed early in the course of this development, "one of the great ironies that attends the triumph of political correctness is that in department after department of academic life, what began as a demand for emancipation recoiled, turned rancid, and developed into new forms of tyranny and control."[12]

In desperate resistance, a group of dissident academics led by Peter Boghossian in 2018 created an imaginary discipline called "grievance studies." Its goal was to expose the absurdity of the new academic establishment by infiltrating it with ideologically correct but absurdly fictitious scholarship. The effect was like the fabled emperor's new clothes. Jargonistic research papers framed around postmodern theory on topics like "feminist astronomy" and "canine rape culture" were submitted to, accepted by, and published in professional journals—all to the great embarrassment of editorial boards after the hoax was revealed. Nevertheless, such rebellions were ultimately powerless in lessening the iron grip of ideological correctness.

The Ideological Dead End

MORE DISRUPTIVE TO PROGRESSIVE TOTALITARIANISM was the reaction of conservative journalists, pastors, and politicians. Beginning in the 1980s, they launched a countermovement to what they considered the methodical annihilation of Western culture. However, their conservative values and historical ideals were largely those of pre-progressive liberalism and therefore also perpetuated the counterfeit values of secular humanism—even when framed by religious nostalgia. In other words, neoconservatives were also ideologues.

The resulting conflict came to be known as the "culture wars." In the year Communism collapsed in the Soviet Union, the term sprang into circulation through an eponymous book by James Davison Hunter. He defined a culture war as

a political and social hostility rooted in different systems of moral understanding. The end to which these hostilities tend is the domination of one cultural and moral ethos over all others. . . . The principles and ideals that mark these competing systems of moral understanding are by no means

---

12 Roger Kimball, *Tenured Radicals: How Politics Has Corrupted Our Higher Education* (Chicago: Ivan R. Dee, 2008), xxxvi–xxxvii.

trifling but always have a character of ultimacy to them. They are not merely attitudes that can change on a whim but basic commitments and beliefs that provide a source of identity, purpose, and togetherness for the people who live by them.[13]

This conflict—at once cultural and political—was waged incessantly as Republicans ousted Democrats from the presidency only to be ousted in turn. Perpetually unresolved, it revealed that by the end of the twentieth century the West had ceased to be a civilization with a supporting culture that directed its members toward a coherent vision of transforming the world.

The culture wars began in earnest in the United States during the presidency of Ronald Reagan (1981–89). Under his administration, some of the New Left's early gains were reversed by figures such as Secretary of Education William Bennett, whose later *Book of Virtues: A Treasury of Moral Stories* (1993) expressed his effort to restore what were considered to be traditional Western values. The Reagan administration was certainly known for conservatism, and it was fiercely anti-Communist. It also made a place for the civic religiosity that had accented the American Way during the 1950s.

However, devout Protestants were an important constituency, and this had the effect of redefining conservatism. Organizations like Jerry Falwell's Moral Majority and Pat Robertson's Christian Coalition began to pull Republican politics in a decidedly evangelical direction, sometimes to the dismay of conservatives from other Christian communities. One of these was Richard John Neuhaus. A Lutheran pastor with leftist leanings during the 1960s (who would eventually convert to Roman Catholicism), he abandoned the progressive counterculture after *Roe* and called for the restoration of a religiously transcendent anchor for American politics. Secularism, he warned in *The Naked Public Square: Religion and Democracy in America* (1984), "will lead—not next year, maybe not in twenty years, but all too soon—to totalitarianism."[14]

---

13 James Davison Hunter, *Culture Wars: The Struggle to Define America* (New York: Basic Books, 1991), 42.

14 Quoted in Damon Linker, *The Theocons: Secular America under Siege* (New York: Anchor, 2007), 49.

Nevertheless, Republicans and their allies within the religious right did not maintain the initiative in the culture wars. Many of their gains were rolled back by the Democratic administrations of Bill Clinton (1993–2001) and Barack Obama (2009–17). Indeed, the achievements of the Reagan years were greatly overshadowed by progressive wins such as the Supreme Court ruling in *Obergefell v. Hodges* (2015), in which same-sex marriage was declared a constitutional right. To mark this significant event, Obama ordered that the White House—one of America's most recognizable public symbols—be bathed in the rainbow colors of the Gay Pride flag.

Conservative ascendancy in the culture wars returned briefly under Donald Trump, whose personal record of libertinism made him an unlikely favorite of evangelicals. Against expectations that Hillary Clinton would win the 2016 presidential election, the real estate tycoon, television celebrity, and political outsider upended national politics when he won. Trump ran on a populist conservative base opposing open immigration and political correctness. Domestically he subverted the globalist ideal of free trade, and internationally he signaled respect for Russia and criticism of NATO—all of which reversed long-standing establishment policies. His brash, controversial statements defied the liberal consensus that had prevailed since the Second World War. Though losing a bid for reelection in 2020, he left behind a radicalized atmosphere that neither Republicans nor Democrats could ignore. This fact was highlighted in 2022 when the Supreme Court overturned *Roe v. Wade* with a conservative majority made possible by the appointment of three anti-abortion justices under Trump.

In Western Europe, similar postliberal populist movements appeared and were frequently embroiled in culture wars. In France the right-wing Marine le Pen, a critic of large-scale Muslim immigration, led unsuccessful but electorally significant campaigns for the presidency in 2017 and 2022. In Britain, a 2016 referendum resulted in withdrawal from the European Union, a decision driven largely by dissatisfaction with liberal hegemony in economic, political, and cultural affairs.

Even more can be said about the weakening of liberalism in lands once ruled by Communists. Overnight, liberalism had taken the place of Communism in democratic Russia. University lectures, television programs, and taxicab conversations all focused not so much on whether she could become like the United States, but how soon. The same was true throughout the rest of Eastern Europe. The new ideology was strongly supported by a new political establishment, expeditiously planted with massive financial support from the West, in Moscow, Kiev, Warsaw, Budapest, and Prague. Harvard economist Jeffrey Sachs traveled extensively to Poland and Russia to persuade their governments to undertake a policy called "shock therapy." It was believed that wholesale privatization of state assets and the immediate exposure of industry to foreign competition, while economically harrowing in the short term, would eventually lead to prosperous free markets. Encouraged by a flood of seemingly inexhaustible financial support (and with promises of more), the new capitalists proved more than willing to give the idea a try. In the meantime, a formerly homogeneous culture was transformed by the pluralistic values of the sexual revolution and neopaganism.

However, the course of democratization, free-market consumerism, and cultural pluralism did not bring unambiguous progress to these lands, and liberalism was the loser. Russia is a good example. During the three decades following the end of the Soviet Union, urban centers like Moscow and Saint Petersburg came to resemble London, Paris, and New York; but the great majority of Russians saw little to show for the depredations of shock therapy. As an ideology, liberalism largely failed to win the hearts of the population.

This would explain the resilience of Vladimir Putin, who came to power in 2000 as a result of Yeltsin's economic mismanagement and the need for a less abject form of national leadership. To secure ongoing electoral victories, Putin placed sharp restrictions on the free press and appealed to Russian patriotism—both of which weakened the prospects for liberal democracy. He also reformed the economy with popular measures to reduce post-socialist kleptocracy and corruption. He initially welcomed cooperation with the United States and the European Union, but with the expansion of NATO and continuous criticisms of his policies by the governments of Western liberal democracies, he eventually pulled back from such cooperation.

This was the political and diplomatic context in which Putin turned on Ukraine, Russia's neighbor and a fellow member (along with Belarus) of Eastern Slavdom. In 2014 the pro-Russian president of Ukraine, Victor

Euromaidan Protests in Kiev, 2014
Mstyslav Chernov/Unframe/http://www.unframe.com/, CC BY-SA 3.0 <https://creative-commons.org/licenses/by-sa/3.0>, via Wikimedia Commons

Yanukovich, was overthrown with American and EU support in what was called the Euromaidan Revolution—so named after the "public square" (*maidan*) in Kiev where it transpired and the fact that the revolutionaries mostly desired Ukraine's entrance into the progressive European Union. Putin responded by occupying Ukraine's Crimean Peninsula. Then, when civil war erupted in the eastern region of the Donbas, Putin further subverted political integrity by sending military support to Russian separatists.

But there was also a cultural context for Putin's turn against Russia's Eastern Slavic neighbor. This was the ongoing conflict over values between Eastern European progressives and their populist adversaries. The postliberal culture wars may have erupted first in Reagan's America, but since that time they had spread throughout a post-Communist West in which no ideological alternative to liberal world building seemed to exist.

In Hungary, for instance, Viktor Orbán won the presidential election in 2010 on a self-consciously "illiberal" platform. He expressed strong support for Hungarian patriotism and declared the intention of limiting immigration. His Fidesz Party oversaw a revision of the constitution the effect of which was to roll back the post-Communist gains of progressivism. Unborn children were given political protection, and marriage was explicitly defined as a relationship between a man and a woman. Christianity was even explicitly referenced as a source of Hungarian national identity. In Poland, similar developments accompanied the rise of the Law and Justice Party. In 2015, one of its former members and a strong advocate for restrictions on EU influence was elected president. Andrzej Duda supported laws that effectively banned abortion altogether (with some exceptions) and prevented the adoption of children by gay couples. Beginning in 2020, many Polish municipalities gained wide attention—and censure by EU progressives—when they declared themselves "gender ideology–free zones."

Putin himself introduced the same anti-progressive rhetoric and policies as Orbán and Duda. In 2013, the Russian State Duma passed a law against "propaganda for non-traditional sexual relationships" designed to shield children from the kind of same-sex activism perceived to be influencing schools in America and the European Union. At almost the same time, another law banned adoptions by partners in same-sex unions. Here Putin was signaling identification with many of the values advanced by the Christian right in

Vladimir Putin speaking at the Valdai Club, 2019
Kremlin.ru, CC BY 4.0 <https://creativecommons.org/licenses/by/4.0>, via Wikimedia Commons

Hungary and Poland, to say nothing of America. However, on the matter of restricting abortion he did much less than his anti-progressive counterparts in other lands. For more than a quarter century after the collapse of Communism, in fact, Russia retained one of the highest per capita rates of abortion in the West. Nevertheless, and despite the Orthodox Church's unambiguous opposition to abortion, Putin generally allotted greater influence to the Moscow Patriarchate in matters of social and educational policy.

In 2021, he even went so far to deliver a speech in Sochi to the Valdai Club (a Russian version of the World Economic Forum) that declared the need for a culture fundamentally different from that of the United States and the European Union. He claimed progressivism has led to nihilism, to a "destruction of age-old values, religion and relations between people." He cited with particular emphasis the rise of transgenderism. And indeed, it did not help that the Biden administration was then issuing orders for the Lesbian, Gay, Bisexual, and Transgender (LGBT) flag to be hung with the American flag at embassies around the world (including Moscow).

Ultimately, however, Putin's growing hostility toward Ukraine had little to do with traditional Christian values about sexuality and social policy. It certainly had little to do with Orthodox Christianity, in that the majority of Ukrainians held the same faith as their brothers and sisters in Russia. Putin's decision was the result, it seems, of nothing more than geopolitics under the influence of secular ideology.

This ideology is sometimes called "the Russian World" (*russky mir*), though no authoritative definition of it exists. Like the ideology of "Official Nationality" once formulated under the westernized regime of Tsar Nicholas I (r. 1825–55), it is a strange expression of ideological modernity cloaked in tradition. It combined Russian cultural identity, Russian statecraft, and Russian Orthodoxy, but did so with the intentionally geopolitical goal of making Russia more competitive with the Atlanticists.

The ideology was influenced in part by Alexander Dugin, once a neofascist dabbler in neopagan religions who with time became a critic of racism and an advocate of Russian Orthodox Old Belief. Though never formally acknowledged by Putin, Dugin put forward a "fourth political theory" to counter the failed ideologies of Communism, Nazism, and liberalism. He

Alexander Dugin
Fars Media Corporation, CC BY 4.0 <https://creative-commons.org/licenses/by/4.0>, via Wikimedia Commons

asserted that by embracing the Russian World as a fourth and final ideology, Russia and her Eastern Slavic partners would effectively depart from the West and establish an alternative civilization and culture. By discarding liberalism's cult of progress, these Eurasianists would rebuild the world on the lost experience of transcendence. Dugin applied the German philosopher Martin Heidegger's concept of *Dasein* ("being-there") to civilization and culture, claiming that meaning can be acquired in the present only by living existentially without concern for progress. This is, indeed, a reminder of what the West once was during the first millennium. But like the secular ideologies it was designed to replace, Dugin's "fourth political theory" was a counterfeit of heavenly immanence. It too was designed to create a good place without God.

And it was this secular ideology that led to the decision to invade Ukraine on February 24, 2022. The unconscionable act is best explained as the failure of an heir to utopia, Vladimir Putin, to find a truly transcendent alternative to ideological world building.

For this reason, the outbreak of the Russo-Ukrainian War makes a fitting if sorrowful end to the story of Christendom's tragic yet inescapable age of nihilism.

The Last Man and the Last Adam

W ITH THE COLLAPSE OF COMMUNISM, when Russia and other Eastern European lands initially saw in liberal democracy the only hope of keeping utopia alive, a best-selling book entitled *The End of History and the Last Man* (1992) appeared in America. The book did much to popularize the conviction that liberalism was the natural and inevitable successor to Communism. Its author, Francis Fukuyama, argued that with the passing of all viable alternatives to liberalism, a culture like that which developed in the United States after the Great War was the world's destiny. Only liberal democracy, he argued, possessed the properties that would ensure the continued expansion of reason and prosperity for the remainder of history. Because of this, history had effectively come to an end.

It was an audacious argument, even for a true believer in liberal world building. The argument was based in part on Hegel. The nineteenth-century philosopher had reacted with other idealists and romantics to the desecration of the world under the influence of secular humanism. During the eighteenth century, transcendence had largely been eradicated by the thought and culture of the so-called Enlightenment. Hegel invented a concept called the "world-spirit" (*Weltgeist*) that was intended to reconsecrate the world. It was in fact little more than a counterfeit of the old Christendom's principle of heavenly immanence.[1]

Hegel claimed civilization is guided by the world-spirit to obtain higher

---

1   For a discussion of philosophical idealism and its romantic outcome in light of traditional Christianity, see *Age of Utopia*, chapter 8.

levels of transcendence. As a key measure of progress, he spoke of the expansion of freedom through interpersonal "recognition." Fukuyama argues that liberal ideals of individualism and equality promote such freedom better than any other ideologies. In a truly utopian way, therefore, he presents liberal democracy as the highest form of progress.

In laying out his largely philosophical argument, Fukuyama recognizes that some critics consider liberal democracy a poor arena for man's pursuit of transcendence. Throughout his book he gives particular attention to the case of Nietzsche. In *Zarathustra* and elsewhere, the onetime disciple of Richard Wagner expressed dismay at the direction of liberalism under the influence of humanistic beliefs and values. Nietzsche was the first to lay the charge (which C. S. Lewis later expanded in a different direction) that liberalism produces a civilization of "men without chests," in which, as we noted in chapter 7, rational and sensual elements are satisfied at the expense of the heart. For Nietzsche the key issue was what the Greeks called *thymos,* the will to distinguish oneself from others. Under the influence of liberalism, he warned, the West would collapse in a state of *athymia* in which all would act alike, according to a "herd instinct." Nietzsche disparagingly called such a

Francis Fukuyama
Labraxa, CC BY 3.0 <https://creativecommons.org/licenses/by/3.0>, via Wikimedia Commons

state "the last man." As a result (to use Fukuyama's words), "the last man ceased to be human."[2]

However, Fukuyama argues that the sort of apocalyptic dehumanization prophesied by Nietzsche would in fact never come. It could not because liberal democracy contains an endless range of opportunities (such as political activism and economic enterprise) in which the heartfelt striving of thymos can be satisfied on terms of equal opportunity. Fukuyama coins the term *isothymia* ("equal-striving") to express this claim. He uses the pre-presidential Donald Trump as one example (however extraordinary) of an individual who strives within the boundaries of liberal values to achieve greatness.[3] Presumably he would accept Cesar Chavez and Greta Thunberg as others. And, in the end, he would also be forced to accept Jim Morrison and Michel Foucault.

As the last examples remind us, though, liberalism does not concern itself with the value of a particular form of isothymia. It affirms any expression of heartfelt striving provided it does not subvert the political order. This was not always the case. As we noted in chapter 6, at its inception during the postwar period, liberal democracy had possessed in anti-Communism a "strong god" (to appropriate Reno's vocabulary for transcendence). When Communism fell, however, so did this claim to transcendence. And when striving has no transcendent purpose, it has no ultimate meaning.

This explains the great despair that overshadowed the West's last man at the moment of his triumph. The claim—made by Fukuyama and others—that liberal democracy provides a better life for men than any previous form of Western civilization is not only highly contestable but in certain ways patently counterfactual. In those lands where it has advanced the furthest—North America and Western Europe—liberty has simply not brought general happiness. Libraries are filled with studies that confirm this. One such book is entitled *The Progress Paradox: How Life Gets Better While People Feel Worse*. Its author, Gregg Easterbrook, notes that in these lands, despite unprecedented prosperity and opportunity, clinical melancholy has

---

2   Francis Fukuyama, *The End of History and the Last Man* (New York: Free Press, 2006), xxii.

3   Ibid., 328.

increased tenfold since the Second World War.[4] Similar statistics apply to divorce and suicide.

In response, self-help authors, television hosts, and traveling gurus all came to crowd the public square, addressing the great despair of terminal utopia. We have already considered the *Oprah Winfrey Show*. For help in making their lives on earth happier, tens of millions of Americans also looked to people like Joel Osteen and Deepak Chopra—whose superficial wisdom looted, respectively, the spiritual treasuries of Christianity and Hinduism. And when one considers the case of newly democratic lands that underwent shock therapy to align them better with the American Way, happiness has been even more elusive. In the 1990s, Russian unemployment, inflation, and runaway corruption turned a large percentage of public opinion against liberal democracy. As the liberal social order dissolved, so did confidence that Fukuyama was correct.

A particularly interesting perspective on liberalism's happiness deficit has been offered by a Polish scholar and politician who experienced the transition from Communism to liberalism. Ryszard Legutko welcomed liberal democracy as the successor to Communist totalitarianism. However, in very little time the new order began to resemble the old. To document this, in 2012 he published a book translated as *The Demon in Democracy: Totalitarian Temptations in Free Societies*. Throughout, he brings attention to the uncanny similarities between hard totalitarianism and soft. While declaring the advantages of the new order over the old, he notes the common ideological premise of each: "Both communism and liberal democracy are regimes whose intent is to change reality for the better. . . . Both are nourished by the belief that the world cannot be tolerated as it is and that it should be changed."[5] In other words, both are outcomes of what I have called Christendom's indelible transformational imperative. And as expected, Legutko recognizes the hugely significant fact that change for either regime is measured exclusively in secular terms. This means that happiness—or

---

4   Gregg Easterbrook, *The Progress Paradox: How Life Gets Better While People Feel Worse* (New York: Random House, 2003), xvi.

5   Ryszard Legutko, *The Demon in Democracy: Totalitarian Temptations in Free Societies*, trans. Teresa Adelson (New York: Encounter, 2018), 5–6.

any other standard of well-being—is likewise limited to the saeculum.

But as we have noted throughout this history of the rise and fall of what the West once was, the old Christendom placed communion with God as the highest measure of human well-being. According to the teaching of the Church, man was the image of God initiated into a life of communion with God because of the Incarnation of God. In its most glorified expressions, well-being entailed divine participation, deification. And since every human being is the image of God, this also entailed participation in the human community—whether black or white, rich or poor, male or female.

The Great Division weakened the paradisiacal culture in which such expressions flourished, and with the rise of secular humanism they were completely reoriented toward the saeculum. This gave rise to the ideal of happiness as a counterfeit of divine communion. The pursuit of happiness became one of the three highest goals of ideological liberalism, as it was defined in nascent form in the preamble of the Declaration of Independence. But wounded by the drive toward autonomy, modern man could not find fulfillment even in this. Caught in the gaze of nihilism, he turned from a life in pursuit of happiness to one preoccupied with pleasure.

As Legutko notes, the turning point in this last development was the sexual revolution.

> Originally happiness was a quality that one could attribute to an entire life, not to its episodes or moments. . . . Pursuing happiness meant planning one's entire life so that it had its own moral consistency and internal harmony, both achieved through the inculcation of virtues. Bringing pleasure to the center of life engendered a different image of human nature. Human beings, in this view, no longer think of themselves in terms of the whole of their existence, but in terms of moments and episodes. . . . Hence the life dedicated to the accumulation of pleasures, but lacking an internal unity, will most likely not be a happy life because a human being cannot renounce his unity without negative consequences. The sexual revolution is arguably the most extreme manifestation of the episodic nature of man.[6]

---

6   Ibid., 108–9.

Such insights help explain why, during the second half of the twentieth century when liberal democracy seemed triumphant to observers like Fukuyama, its populations were so filled with despair.

But along with a decline in the happiness index, the very humanity of liberal democracy was simply beginning to disintegrate. This was demonstrated in a new condition called "gender dysphoria." The integrity of the human person had always been defined in traditional Christianity with reference to sex. God created human beings with bodies: "male and female created he them" (Gen. 1:27). Secular humanism in its original form also possessed a clear anthropology about sexual identity. However, by the end of the twentieth century, a conviction took hold—first in postmodernist academia, then in society as a whole—that the seat of human identity is not God's creation but man's will.

The obvious inspiration for this was Nietzsche, whose demolition of objective morality encouraged the atheistic individual to be the author of himself. As we saw in chapter 7, the existentialists used this anti-essentialist anthropology to create a model of the self. Simone de Beauvoir was the most radical, declaring in *The Second Sex* that "one is not born a woman; one becomes one." Her idea was that the self is surrounded by the social "other" seeking to destroy the self's self-determined authenticity. This, of course, was merely an extreme development in the progress of promethean autonomy. In a recent study of the rise of transgenderism, Carl Trueman has observed that in the case of de Beauvoir, "biology is ultimately regarded as a form of tyranny."[7] From this point it was only a matter of time until, in the wake of the sexual revolution, gender would no longer be a given. It would be "fluid"— subject entirely to the sexual orientation, the feelings, and especially the will of the individual.

Transgenderism, a recent study by Nancy Pearcey notes, has carried Western anthropology beyond the promethean ideal of secular humanism into a condition of "transreality." Postmodernist gender ideology declares

---

7   Carl R. Trueman, *The Rise and Triumph of the Modern Self: Cultural Amnesia, Expressive Individualism, and the Road to Sexual Revolution* (Wheaton, IL: Crossway, 2020), 259.

that rather than finding personal integrity in the union of body and soul, sexual identity has become an act of the will that defies the body. The body is no longer a given part of the human person. Sex is "assigned"—both at birth by a physician or a parent and then later during puberty and adulthood according to the preferences of the individual. In one of the greatest acts of transformation yet in the history of dystopia, the physical reality of the body is simply overthrown. And when sex is determined by the will rather than nature (or the Creator), the state again becomes the arbiter of freedom and even reality.

> *Your basic identity as male or female . . . no longer follows metaphysically from your biology but must be determined by an act of will. But whose will? Ultimately, it will come down to who has the most power—which means the state. . . . By rejecting the biological basis of gender identity, [sexual orientation and gender identity] laws empower the state to define everyone's identity.*[8]

Like the emperor's new clothes, gender identity—one of the key elements of personal integrity—no longer had a basis in reality.

Transgenderism became a precondition for liberation to such a degree that one's decision to be male or female determined preferences for things like public restrooms. The progressive state was quick to accommodate such historically unprecedented demands. In many cases laws were changed to allow high school boys claiming female identity to be admitted to girls' locker rooms. That this caused dismay in the latter (and their parents) was dismissed as irrelevant in the face of the boys' governmentally assured power to define their own reality. English grammar was likewise altered to accommodate the demand that pronouns like "he" and "she" no longer be used to privilege normal sexual identity. As we noted in the previous chapter, Foucault was one of the first to speak directly about a multiplicity of "sexualities," and transgenderism is only part of progressivism's ongoing

---

8   Nancy R. Pearcey, *Love Thy Body: Answering Hard Questions about Life and Sexuality* (Grand Rapids, MI: Baker, 2018), 214.

and unending drive toward anthropological nihility.

So it is not a surprise to discover, as we complete this account of the West's anthropological fall, that as gender began to disintegrate, so did humanity. We have observed how traditional Christianity defined the human being as the image of God. What is more, it claimed that the fullness of that image is found not in "the first man Adam," but in "the last Adam"—that is, Jesus Christ (1 Cor. 15:45). Paul declares that in Christ "dwells all the fullness of the Godhead bodily" (Col. 2:9). Because Jesus is both divine and human, He is the fulfillment of all human potential. Communion with Him raises humanity to the level of a divinity-bearing and divinity-participating creature. There is no human condition superior to union with Him—a condition known as sainthood.

For its part, secular humanism had likewise posited a stable definition of the human being. Much less exalted than that of traditional Christianity, this definition claimed ultimate human perfection lies in the attainment not of divine communion but of promethean autonomy.

Under the influence of Darwinist evolutionism and Nietzschean anti-essentialism, however, this all changed. Man ceased to be and began becoming. Thereafter, the dream of surpassing humanity inevitably entered the culture of the West. We noted in Part II that ideological world building in all three forms included claims that a new humanity of some sort would spring from utopia. The Communists spoke of a "new Soviet man." The Nazis, applying the Nietzschean concept of the superman, spoke of a master race categorically more evolved than "mongrel races." And, to quote James Burnham again, "liberalism believes man's nature to be not fixed but changing, with an unlimited or at any rate indefinitely large potential for positive (good, favorable, progressive) development."

So when encouraged by astonishing advances in twenty-first-century genetic, pharmacological, and computer technology, Western popular culture therefore began to embrace the dream of what is called transhumanism. It assumed all manner of expressions. For instance, in a 2014 movie entitled *Transcendence* (the title is significant), the dying protagonist's "consciousness" is somehow uploaded into a powerful computer, enabling him not only to extend his life indefinitely but to bring unprecedented progress to the world.

Nor did transhumanism remain merely a form of transformation-inspiring science fiction. Numerous ethicists and biologists began to take a serious interest in its possibilities. The inventor and publicist Ray Kurzweil gained wide attention by elaborating its possibilities for a West no longer seeking meaning in the present (or the past). In *The Singularity Is Near: When Humans Transcend Biology* (2005), he argues that an unimaginable acceleration of technological capacity will transform man from what he has been throughout recorded history into an almost unrecognizably superior being. Human cloning, nanotechnology (especially robotic devices released in the bloodstream), and artificial intelligence will all play a role. "The Singularity," he writes,

> *will allow us to transcend [the] limitations of our biological bodies and brains. We will gain power over our fates. Our mortality will be in our own hands. We will be able to live as long as we want (a subtly different statement from saying we will live forever).*[9]

Indeed, Zarathustra had declared that the coming superman will know when to die.

All of this led the once self-confident Fukuyama to admit in a second edition of his famous book that liberalism's last man might not be the last after all, and that history may not have reached its end.[10]

And Friedrich Nietzsche? Had the self-styled antichrist foreseen the transhumanist outcome of his superman—perhaps while sitting in Bayreuth watching a promethean Siegfried smash the eternal spear—his face might well have flashed with a malicious and spectral grin.

---

9   Ray Kurtzweil, *The Singularity Is Near: When Humans Transcend Biology* (New York: Penguin, 2005), 9.

10   In the second edition of his book, published in 2007, Fukuyama admits that emerging transhumanist technology may conceivably result in "new approaches to social engineering that will raise the possibility of new forms of politics." Fukuyama, *End of History*, 253–54.

Remembering Zion

H ISTORY, OF COURSE, HAS NOT reached its end and will not do so until the Second Coming of Christ. Until that time, the future of the West—and the Christendom that for two millennia has given life to it—is an open book whose final chapters remain unwritten.

An old Russian proverb states the end of time will not happen as long as somewhere on earth, Christians continue to serve the Divine Liturgy. As the cosmologically consummating act of the Church, sacramental worship ensures that the Incarnate God continues to fill the world with His presence. However, on the day on which the last Eucharist will be consumed at the last altar by the last priest, heavenly immanence will cease and Christ will appear in judgment. Prior to that Liturgy, the heavenly transformation of the world remains a continuous possibility. Afterward, the world will no longer have a transcendent purpose. There will be nothing to sustain it, only a kind of nihility. And then will come the end.

All of this is no more than a legend, of course, but it says a great deal about the rise and fall of what the West once was. It speaks to the mainspring of Christendom, the force that animated it in a perpetual and open-ended way since the Day of Pentecost. I have called this mainspring a "transformational imperative."

For a millennium, this imperative cultivated a paradisiacal culture in which the heavenly transformation of the world took place. The result was an age marked by the experience of paradise. It marked the West's "rise," and the result was a civilization unique among all those that ever were or ever will be. This is not to say that primordial Christendom was perfect and the first millennium a golden age. For traditional Christianity there can be no cosmic golden age, because the world will always be broken by sin. Not only did the evils that oppressed pagandom, such as hatred and deception, continue, but institutions like statecraft and marriage—though purportedly transformed by the gospel—were plagued with shortcomings and hypocrisy. Yet the gospel, as it had been proclaimed with doctrinal integrity since Pentecost, remained in place and served as the ultimate source of cultural influence and moral authority. Thus Christendom continued its orientation toward the kingdom of heaven.

During the second millennium, however, the same civilization experienced a "fall" that cut it off from its original, constituent culture. The cause of this tragedy was the Great Division. During the age of division, Western Christendom separated itself from the Orthodox Church, and for its part Eastern Christendom began to drift into cultural oblivion. Both the West and the East—both the new Christendom and the old—entered on paths of decline.

The effects were not so readily obvious in Eastern Christendom, where a civilization with a supporting culture that directs its members toward the heavenly transformation of the world remained intact. But in 1453, Byzantium finally disappeared under the Islamic tide of Turkish conquest. The old Christendom continued to flourish in Russia for centuries. There too, however, decline came in the form of nationalistic isolation from the wider Orthodox Church. The case of Maxim the Greek dramatically showed this.[1] What is more, oblivious disregard for Western Christendom contributed to a political culture in which the gospel's prophetic challenge to authority was muted—just when Roman Catholic popes were vigorously confronting unjust and impious statecraft in the West. Metropolitan Philip's sacrificial confrontation with Tsar Ivan the Terrible was an exception to what was otherwise a record of comparative political indifference. By the seventeenth century, a complacent national piety was so entrenched that the Old Believer Schism occurred. The division exhausted Russia's paradisiacal culture and

---

1   For the case of Maxim, see *Age of Division*, 313–14.

created the circumstances for an almost total suppression of the old Christendom through the process of westernization under Peter the Great.

But long before Russia became part of the West, the new Christendom had deviated significantly from the paradisiacal pattern of the first millennium. A series of genealogically related developments had followed on the Great Division. The papal reformation had been largely responsible for the schism from Orthodoxy, and true to its divisive character, it introduced a new way of envisioning Christian civilization. Most significant was probably a pronounced bifurcation of society into clergy and laity, the consequence of which was a clericalism that explains a great deal of what the new Christendom came to be. Not only papal supremacy—the bane of princes and prelates alike—but religious militarism, scholasticism, legalism, and above all the practice of indulgences all have their origin in the reformation launched by Leo IX and sustained by successors like Gregory VII, Urban II, and Innocent III. From this first phase of reformation issued a second under the name of Protestantism. The transformational imperative thus became externalized, and Western Christendom's shortcomings were subjected to institutionalized improvement. Indignation became a virtue. And as this occurred, a new pessimism arose around the human condition in the world.

An age of utopia followed on these developments, seeking ways in which the imperative could be salvaged. Francesco Petrarch, reeling from Western Christendom's accumulating anthropological pessimism, appropriated the concept of secularity from Augustine and used it to reorient his civilization from paradise to utopia. During the quattrocento that followed, secular humanism was put forward as a remedy for reformational Christianity. The transformational imperative was released from the stranglehold of purgatorial punishment and stavrocentric piety and directed toward the saeculum. In the wake of the wars of Western religion, benighted intellectuals like the philosophes went even further, abandoning Christianity and setting all hope in a systematically desecrated world. But Christendom's mainspring could not function in the absence of a transcendent purpose for very long. When romanticism failed to reenchant the cosmos, ideologies appeared that did so by projecting hope of transformation into the future. Secular humanism had always been a counterfeit of traditional Christianity. Now a kingdom of posterity replaced the kingdom of heaven.

Yet secular humanism was fundamentally untenable. Both Nietzsche and Dostoevsky realized this. And while very different in their responses, both were pioneers in pointing to this fact and to the looming specter of nihilism appearing above a desecrated Christendom. Confident in neither paradise nor utopia, the West began to pass beneath the shadow of a mounting despair. And though modernists might bask in its bleakness and social scientists acclimate man to its darkness, the Great War revealed there was no way to live in its gloom very long. Intellectuals such as G. K. Chesterton, T. S. Eliot, and Nicolas Berdyaev turned to traditional Christianity, but few in the West were ready for that. Most fled the gaze of meaninglessness through ideological world building. But by doing so, they either plunged into an abyss of moral transvaluation or surrendered to the fact that in the saeculum, transcendence must always be deferred. In either case, the outcome of cosmic desecration was not utopia but dystopia.

Not so Christendom in its original, first-millennium condition. Heavenly immanence ensured that through sacraments and the liturgy the transcendent fullness of human life is attainable now, in the world, in what so many traditional hymns declared was a transfigured "today."

This conviction is reflected in a characteristically Orthodox feature of temple architecture. By the end of the first millennium, a program for the presentation of icons was established in Byzantium and beyond. This program featured an iconostasis, or icon stand, joining (not dividing) the altar to the nave, in which worshippers assembled. This stand appeared long after the founding of Hagia Sophia and grew in height only gradually, but by the time of the Great Schism it was becoming a common feature of Eastern temple architecture. It featured a pair of doors called the Royal Gates at its center. These doors opened to expose worshippers to the sanctuary, located at the easternmost point of the temple. They symbolized the gates of paradise. Beyond them stood the altar as a symbol of the Tree of Life, which had been planted in the Garden of Eden but from which Adam had been banished. Now that Tree was again available to man because of the Incarnation. The altar table also symbolized the throne from which Christ rules the heavens and the earth. It was a projection, in other words, of His kingdom. A veil, which during the Divine Liturgy is opened or "torn in two," was installed on the iconostasis behind the Royal Gates to emphasize the mystery of this transformational reality.

The history of Christendom thus took place, as it were, before the gates of paradise. And on either side of them, the iconostasis featured (and today without exception throughout the world continues to feature) two icons of Christ. On the south side (to the right of the Gates) is one depicting the Second Coming. Here we may recall the Russian proverb telling of the continued life of the world through liturgical celebration. Christ Pantocrator sits in judgment with the Gospel book opened, demanding an account from the humanity that He has assumed of their desire to enter His kingdom. On the north side of the Gates is another icon of Christ, though it may appear as one of Mary the Birthgiver of God since she is the largest figure in it. This icon proclaims the Incarnation of Christ. The Lord is depicted as a Child resting in His Mother's lap, but He still possesses (if the iconography has not degenerated into the naturalism of the Renaissance) dignity, glory, and power. It is He who is clothed in brilliant raiment while His Mother is veiled in dark vesture. In most versions of this icon, the Virgin points toward Christ, as if to say, "Don't look at me, look at Him."

This very program of iconography has continued in the Orthodox Church to the present day. It is between these proclamations of the Incarnation and the Second Coming of Christ that life unfolds for members of the old Christendom—even those who live within the new Christendom of the West. As early Fathers of the Church such as Augustine noted, there is really only one division in world history, and its orientation is defined by the moment when God became man. This is what gives permanent meaning to the history of the world. The disoriented tripartite model of ancient-medieval-modern—introduced during the benightenment—is meaningless.

Standing in an Orthodox temple, therefore, one experiences iconographically the First and Second Comings of Christ on either side of the Royal Gates. And through these very Gates, paradise opens into the world as the clergy bear the Gospel and the Eucharist from the altar, the symbol of paradise.

IF THE ONGOING LITURGY OF Christians sustains the world, ideology will hasten its demise. This, certainly, is the story told by the age of nihilism. For in humanity's history of looking to the saeculum for fulfillment, ideology has proven to lead inevitably to estrangement, conflict, and despair.

Metropolitan Tikhon Mollard indicated this when communicating the Orthodox Church in America's "unconditional condemnation" of Russia's invasion of Ukraine in 2022. "Unjustified aggressive war is always a sin," he declared,

> *but it is particularly scandalous when the conflict involves two nations that are, historically, bulwarks of Orthodox Christianity. When a war involves not merely sister-peoples, but brethren in Christ, this should serve as a clarion-call to all Christians to reassess and reorder our priorities. We cannot put the world and the things of this world first; we must always begin with Jesus Christ.*

Since its origin during the age of utopia, ideology has produced many things, and some of them have been good. But none have been authentically transcendent. As we have seen, ideology, as the outcome of secular humanism, was a counterfeit of paradise. As Tikhon's observations about the motivating forces behind the Russo-Ukrainian War suggest, ideology looks to an irrevocably broken world—the saeculum—and demands of it a fraudulent means of transcendence.

Without a transcendent anchor, the saeculum inevitably degenerates into self-destruction. The holy father Augustine, who more than any other established the concept of secularity, would have frozen in horror had he foreseen the fruits of cosmological desecration. The secular disorientation of the West generated an indignation with no outlet but violence. This was especially true after the rise of Communism, Nazism, and liberalism. Within the space of a single half century, for instance, collectivization (10 million peasants killed), General Plan East (45 million Eastern Europeans killed), and *Roe v. Wade* (65 million unborn children killed) made this clear enough.

Only repentance can save the world. This, as we saw in chapter 2, was the insight of Dostoevsky. The tormented novelist was no church father, but he read church fathers and prophetically and insistently communicated their wisdom to the West in which he lived. Before the church fathers, of course, repentance was the teaching of Peter at Pentecost. And before that, Christ Himself declared, "Repent, for the kingdom of heaven has drawn near" (Matt. 4:17). Repentance before the face of Christ opens man to the kingdom of heaven. This is the path to transcendence that ideology can never attain. It is the path of humility, not that of indignation.

In the aftermath of the age of nihilism, many Orthodox, Roman Catholics, and Protestants have come to realize this. As utopia disintegrated, they turned to the deep past for a means toward the recovery of what the West in its proper condition once was. Though approaching it in distinct ways, theologians from each group are today looking for answers in what they consider traditional Christianity.

Protestant scholars such as Peter Leithart have gained respect for the cosmological vision that accompanied the conversion, rule, and legacy of Emperor Constantine. The Reformed theologian founded the Theopolis Institute, in which reflection on the role of traditional Christianity in modern society is advanced. At its core is a biblical cosmology in which the world becomes the "cosmic temple." Liturgy "isn't a marginal issue in Scripture," Leithart asserts.

> *It's the issue. God created the world as liturgical space, and He intends to fill it with joyous, eternal worship. Liturgy is the Alpha and Omega of the biblical story. It's the reason God created human beings and everything else. To talk about liturgy, we have to talk about everything. Liturgy stretches from the creation to the eschaton and to the ages of ages.*[2]

Another Protestant, Hans Boersma, has dedicated much of his scholarship to recovering the sacramental and liturgical context of traditional Christianity. In fact, he criticizes modern theologians for losing contact with Christianity's "Great Tradition" and falling prey to solvent forces of modernism

---

2   Peter J. Leithart, *Theopolitan Liturgy* (West Monroe, LA: Theopolis Books, 2019), 3.

and postmodernism. Until Christians learn to return to the deep past, he suggests, they will remain ineffectual in a world dominated by "the political and economic establishment of modern liberal democracies."[3]

The effects of disintegrative Christianity have led some Protestants to Roman Catholicism. Richard Neuhaus, a convert from Lutheranism, saw in his new faith a defense against the nihilistic tendencies of the counterculture. He promoted a resurgence of religiously based conservatism in America. The project was, to be sure, ideological. But it also sought sincerely a restoration of at least some elements of the old Christendom.

Labeled "theocons" by ideological adversaries, Neuhaus and other Roman Catholics such as R. R. Reno argued that the dead end of progressivism can be passed only by returning to a spiritual foundation for national culture. Critical of the evangelical position during the culture wars, they argued that a Roman Catholic vision of society grounded in natural law and traditional piety is best suited to save America. If politics is "downstream" from culture, they declared, it is the latter that needs to change first. Secular ideology by itself is worthless.

Neuhaus founded an influential journal called *First Things* dedicated to reinvigorating American culture with traditional Christianity. It was soon joined in its mission by *Touchstone*, an even more ecumenical platform featuring content from Roman Catholic, Protestant, and Orthodox scholars. Together, the two journals are a storehouse of Christian thinking about the fall of the West and the ways traditional Christianity might restore it.

The Roman Catholic defense of traditional Christianity was most effectively made by two successive popes, John Paul II (r. 1978–2005) and Benedict XVI (r. 2005–13). The first was of Polish origin and played an important role in inspiring the overthrow of Communism in his native land. John Paul spoke forcefully about what he labeled the West's "culture of death," pointing especially to the proliferation of legalized abortion. In an encyclical entitled *Evangelium vitae* (1995), he spoke of

---

3   Hans Boersma, *Heavenly Participation: The Weaving of a Sacramental Tapestry* (Grand Rapids, MI: Eerdman's, 2011), 19.

the heart of the tragedy being experienced by modern man: the eclipse of the sense of God and of man, typical of a social and cultural climate dominated by secularism, which, with its ubiquitous tentacles, succeeds at times in putting Christian communities themselves to the test. Those who allow themselves to be influenced by this climate easily fall into a sad vicious circle: when the sense of God is lost, there is also a tendency to lose the sense of man, of his dignity and his life; in turn, the systematic violation of the moral law, especially in the serious matter of respect for human life and its dignity, produces a kind of progressive darkening of the capacity to discern God's living and saving presence.

Pope John Paul was also a champion of the poor and earned for himself and the modern Roman Catholic Church the respect of many progressives. He was no ideologue.

Nor was his successor, Benedict, in whom (according to one writer) "all those schematic formulations *conservative/progressive, right/left* which stem from an altogether different sphere, namely, that of political ideologies, lose their meaning."[4] Pope Benedict linked his pontificate to that of John Paul by opposing resolutely any tendency toward theological modernism. He was particularly critical, as we saw in chapter 7, of the outcome of the Second Vatican Council. But in the face of the church's sexual abuse scandal and reports that the Vatican establishment was inhospitable to a traditional vision of church life, Benedict himself was soon compelled to abdicate. He was succeeded in turn by Pope Francis, who, by encouraging new approaches to marriage and worship, suspended the papal turn toward traditional Christianity.

Which brings us to the Orthodox Church. More than any other participant in the rise and fall of what the West once was, she has maintained traditional Christianity in its fullness. This is not to say the temptations of utopian Christianity have had no effect on some of her theologians. We have already commented on the case of Sergey Bulgakov, whose "sophiology" was

---

4   Joseph Pearce, *Benedict XVI: Defender of the Faith* (Gastonia, NC: Tan Books, 2021), 53.

rejected as problematic and possibly heretical by a twentieth-century synod of bishops. Also ambiguous were some writings of a theological consortium centered at Fordham University called Public Orthodoxy. It made a variety of provocative assertions about homosexuality and ecclesiology. Nevertheless, most Orthodox authorities advocate a vision of the world that is consistent with that of the fathers of the first millennium.

Building on the neopatristic synthesis of Florovsky and Lossky, for instance, Orthodox theologians such as Christos Yannaras in Greece have made sharp, even categorical distinctions between the culture of the modern West and that of first-millennium Christendom. The claim that "God is dead," Yannaras asserted, is unthinkable outside the history of Western Christendom. So is the false transcendence traced by ideologues (which would include Alexander Dugin) to secular philosophers such as Heidegger. Yannaras claimed first-millennium church fathers such as Dionysios the Areopagite are much more convincing in their cosmology. "The 'death of God,'" he concluded, "is but the end-result of the historical unfolding of [an] absolutized and double-edged rationalism, which took place in the nations of Western Europe over the span of approximately a millennium."[5]

In matters of morality, the Orthodox also bear witness within the West to a traditional Christian vision of the human condition. In 2000 a council of bishops was assembled in Russia to canonize the new martyrs who suffered under Communism. The place it did so was, significantly, the newly rebuilt Christ the Savior Cathedral in Moscow. On this occasion, the bishops issued a statement about social principles that encompassed most of the issues raised by the ideologies of socialism, nationalism, and individualism. These included abortion, contraception, genetic research, and marriage. In every case, the teaching of the first-millennium fathers was confirmed without change.

Orthodoxy has offered to the West an especially strong and consistent witness to traditional Christian worship. Modernized services (as found

---

5   Christos Yannaras, *On the Absence and Unknowability of God: Heidegger and the Areopagite*, ed. Andrew Louth, trans. Haralambos Ventis (London: T and T Clark, 2005), 22.

among evangelical Protestants) and interfaith experiments (as found among mainline Protestants) are unthinkable. So is the chaos experienced by the Roman Catholic Church in the aftermath of Vatican II. In America, where Roman Catholic traditionalists might occasionally serve the Mass in its pre-conciliar Latin form (something largely banned by Francis), Orthodox are used to a Divine Liturgy that has not changed significantly since the first millennium. And whereas the Mass itself is often the only service offered in a Roman Catholic parish, Orthodox parishes typically schedule Vespers, Matins, and other services that since antiquity have through their hymnography elaborated cyclical calendars (daily, weekly, and annual), thereby effecting the sanctification of the world. At the same time as Episcopalians might tentatively enhance the narrow range of their liturgical offerings with a traditional service like Compline and emergent evangelicals may rediscover the sacraments, the Orthodox continue without change an order of services followed by fathers, grandfathers, great-grandfathers, and an unbroken line of worshippers stretching back into the first millennium.

Consistency and continuity in traditional doctrine, moral practice, and worship have thus been maintained throughout the Orthodox Church in the West. This unified witness to post-Christian Christendom grew dramatically in volume by the end of the twentieth century. Saint Vladimir's Seminary in New York created a press dedicated to English-language publications for an anglophone audience and attracted a series of evangelization-minded theologians including Alexander Schmemann (d. 1983), John Meyendorff (d. 1992), and Thomas Hopko (d. 2015). Online platforms such as Ancient Faith Radio communicated Orthodoxy to an unprecedentedly large audience, not only of the Orthodox but of Roman Catholic, Protestant, and unchurched inquirers.

As Metropolitan Jonah Paffhausen of the Orthodox Church in America reminded the Orthodox of the West,

The Holy Spirit gives the Church her vision, which comes from our identity in Christ and His Body. This vision is identical with the vision of all those who have gone before us precisely because it is the same Body, with the same vocation, mission, and identity: to be the Body of Christ: the

One, Holy, Catholic, and Apostolic Church. Whenever we add elements to that vision, we distort it, no matter how noble our qualifications and agendas may be. Whenever we subtract from or diminish it, we do likewise. If we change the vision in any way, we exclude ourselves from it and from the Body which it constitutes.[6]

This reminder would readily be affirmed when placed not only in an Orthodox context, but in one belonging to traditional Roman Catholics and Protestants.

As the twenty-first century dawned, then, advocates of traditional Christianity increasingly brought to mind the memory of what the West once was.

BUT THE CURSE OF MEN is that they forget. Dismayed by the outcome of second-millennium Christendom, few in the West have had the resolve to look deeply into its past—into their past—to find answers. Few are resolved to remember.

This may have been the condition of the Jews during the sixth century before Christ. In 586 their capital city of Jerusalem was conquered by the Babylonians, and a grace-bearing civilization that had once flourished was all but destroyed. As with Christendom, the catastrophe took centuries to play out. At first the northern kingdom of Israel fell. The southern kingdom of Judah held out through a desperate policy of shifting alliances. But these entailed compromises with the faith. A religious syncretism eventually led to a disintegrative Judaism. When the end finally came, the Babylonians captured the last king, Zedekiah, massacring his sons before his eyes. They then blinded him so that he would suffer that vivid, horrendous memory for the rest of his life. As Solomon's Temple was razed and the Ark of the Covenant seized by the Gentiles, Zedekiah was marched with thousands of other Jews to captivity in Babylon. There, those who once directed worship of the one true God were cruelly forced to sing songs about Zion, the famous hill of

---

6   Jonah Paffhausen, "The Orthodox Church in America: Vision, Vocation, Mission, Identity," in *Reflections on a Spiritual Journey* (Yonkers, NY: St. Vladimir's Seminary Press, 2011), 139–44.

Jerusalem and symbol of Jewish cultural identity. The act of remembrance thus became an act of suffering.

Yet remember they did. It was during the Babylonian Exile that the scriptural reflection on the experience, Psalm 136 (137), was composed. Its text, which serves as the epigraph to this book, opens with unrestrained lamentation: "By the waters of Babylon, / there we sat down and wept, / when we remembered Zion."

The specter of nihilism overshadowed the displaced Jews as they gathered on the banks of the Euphrates. Like their post-Christian heirs, they were tempted to abandon their identity and embrace the beliefs and values of strange gods and false philosophies. After all, had not their own predecessors done the same, gradually embracing novel doctrines and practices?

But against this despair the psalmist raises hope in the form of sacred remembrance. "If I forget you, O Jerusalem," he declares on behalf of his people,

let my right hand wither!
Let my tongue cleave to the roof of my mouth,
if I do not remember you,
if I do not set Jerusalem
above my highest joy!

The only nihilism, then, would be oblivion about the sacred past. Civilization's vitality—"my right hand"—consists in the resolve to remember Zion and to rebuild what has been lost. Thus the final verses, which speak unflinchingly about the Jewish resolve to destroy the enemies of cultural authenticity: "Happy shall he be who takes your little ones / and dashes them against the rock!"

It is with such zeal that Christians have long applied Psalm 136 to their various acts of repentance. The memory of divine blessings lost because of the world's brokenness has always been stirred by these words. And whereas the psalmist spoke of blood vendettas against the Babylonians, the Christian knows that vengeance is no longer blessed for those transformed by the gospel of love and forgiveness. After all, only after the Incarnation is the full meaning of Old Testament Scripture revealed. Therefore the psalm's "little ones" become the demons, the passions, and the sins that oppose spiritual authenticity. Regrettably, the leaders of Vatican II were embarrassed by the psalm's final verses and defied tradition by ordering their omission when it was used in services. This cancellation of "offensive scripture" had the effect of ignoring another prophetic image of the verses: that of the "rock," Jesus Christ, against whom the demons are dashed to pieces and through whom victory over all spiritual enemies has been won.

The Orthodox Church continues to pray Psalm 136 in full at the divine services. And at one particularly significant point in the year, she does so in a way that is rich in meaning for a civilization with a supporting culture that has lost the key to a heavenly transformation of the world.

On each of the three Sundays preceding the Great Fast, the coming season of repentance is announced to Orthodox worshippers with the singing of Psalm 136 at Matins. Though penitential, the psalm is given a typically Eastern victoriousness by augmenting the Old Testament text with New Covenant refrains of "alleluia." Most significantly, it calls to the mind of those preparing for the Lenten journey the example of the Israelites longing for their homeland, longing to participate once again in the glory they have lost. What is more, the psalm is introduced on the Sunday when the parable of the Prodigal Son is read at the Liturgy. That important passage from the Gospel, and not the historical circumstances and resentments of the Jews, is the key to understanding the experience of exile. Worshippers realize that like the Prodigal Son's, their exile is self-imposed and not something to be blamed on others. Any tendency toward indignation, therefore, gives way to humility.

All that is needed for their return to Zion is *repentance* (literally, "a change of heart" in Greek). All that is needed is the heartfelt resolve to rise from the disoriented exile of the utopian pigpen and to return to the Father's house. All that is needed, in short, is a reorientation toward paradise.

And it is a heavenly orientation that Psalm 136 encourages when, on the day before the Great Fast begins (known as Forgiveness Sunday), the Orthodox Church also sings her most beautiful hymn to paradise.

O precious paradise, unsurpassed in beauty, tabernacle built by God, unending gladness and delight, glory of the righteous, joy of the prophets, and dwelling of the saints, with the sound of thy leaves pray to the Maker of all: may He open unto me the gates which I closed by my transgression, and may He count me worthy to partake of the Tree of Life and of the joy which was mine when I dwelt in thee before.

Series Acknowledgments

A HISTORY OF TWO MILLENNIA in four volumes is something that can be written only with enormous assistance from others. I would like to thank all the people who have helped educate, inspire, and encourage me since I first began teaching the long and fascinating history of the West more than a quarter century ago.

Among the first are the students who not only motivated my research by attending lectures but engaged course content in a way that substantially improved my understanding of the past. Many a conversation after class opened doors that could not be unlocked from my side of the lectern. Among the innumerable young people I have been blessed to teach, one— Allen Shiu of the University of California at Davis—will have to stand for the rest. During lingering conversations after class or on walks between classroom and office, he was an example of the dignity and intelligence of undergraduate education at its best.

My teaching responsibilities provided the context in which much of my vision of the past materialized over the years after earning first my doctorate and then a master of divinity (the reverse of the usual sequence). I would therefore like to thank those departmental chairpersons who entrusted me with the education of undergraduates at various institutions. These include Margaret Goodart and George Craft of California State University, Sacramento; Richard Gyug of Fordham University; the late John Squiller of Saint Basil Ukrainian Catholic Seminary; Jacquelyn Miller and Arthur Fisher of Seattle University; James Heugel and Darrell Hobson of Northwest University; Cara Anzilotti of Loyola Marymount University; Michael Hamilton and Rodney Stiling of Seattle Pacific University; and, finally, Adam Lockridge of Saint Raphael School.

I owe a special debt of gratitude to Eve Paraskeva Tibbs of Saint Katherine College (now the University of Saint Katherine) for her generosity and support when agreeing to take me on the faculty there. An inspiring administrator, a faithful theologian, and a great friend, she, along with Saint Katherine president Frank Papatheofanis, provided me with the opportunity to begin the research for this project.

I have learned so very much about Christendom from my professors and fellow scholars over the years. Whatever value is found in the history I have told simply echoes their zealous work, and whatever deficiency it suffers is of course exclusively my own.

My teachers at Saint Vladimir's Seminary endowed me with a way of relating the Orthodox faith to the world in which we live. This, as much as mere empirical research, provided the foundation for my account of Christendom. Thomas Hopko of blessed memory (whose final course, "The Vices and the Virtues," I was able to attend) profoundly influenced my seminary learning. Memory of his characteristically bold-yet-gentle presentation of Christianity's jaw-dropping realities continues many years later to remind me how "Orthodoxy is parodoxy." Paul Meyendorff and John Barnet also imparted insights and skills that continued to grow long after my ordination. Above all, I would like to thank Paul Lazor of blessed memory, whose love and piety were an inspiration to grow in a knowledge of the faith. If there is a pastoral teaching Father Paul imparted to me that most informs my story of the West, it is the proverb he often quoted: "Where there is no vision, the people perish" (Prov. 29:18).

Many others have contributed to my study of Christendom. I would like to thank, in particular, my old friend David Foote, a medievalist at the University of Saint Thomas, for his gentle and supportive critique of my arguments in *The Age of Division*. Daniel Lattier also reviewed the manuscript of *The Age of Division* (as well as *The Age of Paradise*). As an Orthodox priest with knowledge of Roman Catholic theology, he provided welcome insight into the scholastic consequences of the Great Schism. Anthony Kaldellis of Ohio State University provided both fascinating insights into the causes of the Great Schism and commentary on my account of it. I am indebted to the exuberant goodwill of Richard Emerson, whose wonderful podcast and blog on the poetry of Dante remind me of the paradisiacal beauty that, as I tried to communicate in *The Age of Utopia,* Western Christendom has always harbored in its heart of hearts. My vision of Christendom is grounded in a conviction that the gospel in its fullness reveals the kingdom of heaven as being manifestly present in this world. In this conviction I have been inspired by and benefited from correspondence with Stephen Freeman, author of *Everywhere Present* and of a blog and podcast by the name of *Glory to God.* Jonathan Jackson has provided generous encouragement and inspiration both in his writing and through numerous conversations. I am very grateful to him for this.

Not all historians who have commented on my intentionally provocative work have embraced all of it, of course, but even from those who have been critical, such as Gary Cyril Jenkins, I have obtained a better understanding of the complexities and challenges of writing a "grand narrative." I want in particular to thank Father Theodore Bobosh (whose writings are a spur to candor about the past) for his patient and critical commentary on various aspects of my work.

So many colleagues have provided encouragement over the years that it is impossible to name them all. During my time at Saint Katherine College, I was blessed to share an office hallway and (on alternating weekdays) an ambo with Father Andrew Cuneo, whose elegant presentation of Orthodox theology and knowledge of C. S. Lewis never ceased to fascinate. Gary Hartenberg was likewise a warm source of intellectual engagement, and I remember with gratitude his response to my ideas about Nietzsche in a sandwich shop one day in Encinitas. Kay Harkins, another treasure of Orthodox education, always reminded me that teaching and writing were, above all, spiritual pursuits. Finally, a vibrant atmosphere of Orthodox collegiality was crowned at Saint Katherine by the presence of Gaelan Anthony Gilbert, with whom I was blessed to team-teach a course on Dostoevsky, learning much in the process.

Among the others I would like to thank, mention must be made of Michael Matriotti and Andrew Tadie of the Matteo Ricci College of Seattle University, for whom the forces of institutional confusion failed to shake a love of Christian pedagogy. I remember dearly Professor Tadie's persistently optimistic manners, as well as a saying taped to his office door (attributed to Tolstoy) to the effect that everyone is trying to change the world today but no one is trying to change himself. I remember Professor Matriotti's faithful assurance to graduating students that, quoting the words of Saint Basil the Great, a great life awaits those who seek "everlasting rest where the sound of them that keep festival is unending, and the delight is endless of them that behold the beauty of [Christ's] countenance."

Many others have contributed to the story I have told about Christendom, often without knowing it. As long as I have known him, Dellas Oliver Herbel has not ceased to offer fascinating insights into Orthodoxy in the West, and I am grateful for all of them. James Magruder was the first to speak to me about the ninth-century schism between Constantinople and Rome as the "Nicolaitan Schism," a term I wholeheartedly appropriate in *The Age of Paradise* and beyond. Insights into the more recent past of Western film recounted in *The Age of Nihilism* include those of Father Andrew Gabriel Boyd, who introduced me to *I Am*, and Professor Andrew Nedd, who long ago was the first to share with me the beauty of Tarkovsky's *Sacrifice*. Within the parish I now serve as a priest (Saint Elizabeth in Poulsbo, Washington), I would like to thank the faithful people who have shared their thoughts about the history I have related. Among them are Jackson Fyodor Thompson, whose love of Orthodoxy in the Soviet Union introduced me to valuable sources, and Gregory Hendry, whose own family suffered in the New Martyrdom and whose interest in contemporary Orthodoxy in Russia has provided me with helpful insights.

Paradise and Utopia began as a podcast sponsored by Ancient Faith Radio. I would like to express my great appreciation for the visionary work of its chief executive officer, John Maddex. Bobby Maddex was also instrumental in producing the podcast, and I am grateful for his indefatigable energy and good spirits over the years. Among the many other dedicated people at Ancient Faith Publishing, Matthew Dorning provided excellent book cover designs, Melinda Johnson helped publicize each volume upon its release, and Timm Wenger oversaw the painstaking process of editing audio versions of the books. The first two volumes of the series were extensively edited by Nicholas Kotar, whose creativity and good spirits helped make the early stages of the project a delight. I would also like to thank sincerely the hard work and sharp eyes of my editor Katherine Hyde. She has walked with me throughout the course of this project. Her professionalism and strong faith have made the results much better than they could ever have been otherwise.

My family has provided unending support for this project. My parents have always given themselves sacrificially and lovingly in service of my historical studies. My father, Gordon, provided me with a childhood home in which literary and historical books were everywhere to be sampled (my ability to discuss Sherlock Holmes in *The Age of Utopia* is due to this), and my mother, Jananne, provided adamant support for my desire to add to their number. My sisters, Sarah and Rachel, engaged me in innumerable discussions about the present and the past, and though we may not always have been in agreement during the course of them, I can say with sincerity and gratitude that my vision of history would have been much the poorer had these discussions not occurred.

I cannot express strongly enough my gratitude to my wife, Yelena. For this project she has endured more than five years of incessant writing, preceded by another twenty years of research and teaching. More than this, she has endured disquisitions on historical topics ranging from Harold Hardrada to *Parsifal* to the Bolshevik Revolution—often without the opportunity to express alternative (and better) convictions. She has remained supportive throughout this process, and without her my work would have been inconceivable.

Finally, I would like to thank my beloved children, Elizabeth, Andrew, Katherine, Paul, and Gregory. Though life has not yet given them the opportunity to love history as I have come to love it, each reminds me every day that the journey leading from the present into the future must be navigated with a compass obtained from the past. It is to them that I dedicate this work.

Index

Illustrations indicated by page numbers in italics

About the Author

JOHN STRICKLAND IS AN ORTHODOX priest and former college professor. His first book, *The Making of Holy Russia*, is a study of the resilience of Christianity in the modern world. An active blogger and podcaster, he brings to the present work a lifetime of reflection on the religious background of the West. He lives in western Puget Sound with his wife and five children.

We hope you have enjoyed and benefited from this book. Your financial support makes it possible to continue our nonprofit ministry both in print and online. Because the proceeds from our book sales only partially cover the costs of operating **Ancient Faith Publishing** and **Ancient Faith Radio**, we greatly appreciate the generosity of our readers and listeners. Donations are tax deductible and can be made at **www.ancientfaith.com**.

To view our other publications,
please visit our website: **store.ancientfaith.com**

ANCIENT FAITH
RADIO

Bringing you Orthodox Christian music, readings,
prayers, teaching, and podcasts 24 hours a day since 2004 at
www.ancientfaith.com

www.ingramcontent.com/pod-product-compliance
Lightning Source LLC
Chambersburg PA
CBHW021659120626
46545CB00004B/1305